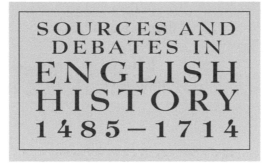

SOURCES AND DEBATES IN ENGLISH HISTORY 1485–1714

To
Jenny Renn
Katie
Jeffrey
with love

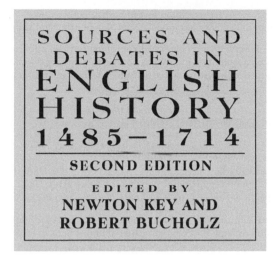

SOURCES AND DEBATES IN ENGLISH HISTORY 1485–1714

SECOND EDITION

EDITED BY
**NEWTON KEY AND
ROBERT BUCHOLZ**

WILEY-BLACKWELL

A John Wiley & Sons, Ltd., Publication

Library of Congress Cataloging-in-Publication Data

Sources and debates in English history, 1485–1714 / Newton Key and Robert Bucholz. – 2nd ed.

p. cm.

Includes bibliographical references and index.

ISBN 978-1-4051-6276-0 (pbk. : alk. paper) 1.   Great Britain–History–Tudors, 1485–1603–Sources. 2.   Great Britain–History–Stuarts, 1603–1714–Sources. 3.   Great Britain–History–Tudors, 1485–1603. 4.   Great Britain–History–Stuarts, 1603–1714.   I. Key, Newton. II. Bucholz, R. O., 1958–

DA310.S68 2009
942.05–dc22

2008040257

A catalogue record for this book is available from the British Library.

Set in 10/12.5pt Sabon by SPi Publisher Services, Pondicherry, India

Contents

List of Documents

List of Plates

Preface

In response to readers' suggestions, for this second edition we have completely reorganized the chapters and provided headnotes for each document (tinted sections in the text). We have also provided a detailed list of all documents. Each chapter includes: brief, overarching introductions with framing questions to help direct inquiry; documents grouped in themes and cross-linked to related documents; updated bibliographies of articles and essays (Historians' Debates) grouped according to key questions or fault lines; and Additional Source Collections.

This edition also features:

- new documents (for example, new selections illustrating gender relations, foreigners' views of England, and relations among England, Scotland, and Ireland)
- new themes and sections
- new translations of key sources
- additional explanations of archaic words and phrases
- revision of most selections based on comparison with original sources
- revised biographical information based on the new online *Oxford Dictionary of National Biography*

We have tried to select documents that can be read in more than one way, in order to promote discussion. As in the first edition, we have chosen those documents best open to multiple interpretations, because we consider thinking and arguing about the past to be the core of doing history. Also we have selected both "standard" sources, which have intrigued (or baffled) generations of students, and sources that have either never or not recently been published. Finally, as in the first edition, spelling and punctuation have been modernized and Americanized in most selections (except poems and published titles). Thus, "majestie" becomes "Majesty," and "Honoure" becomes "honor." The exceptions are words like "durst," "appeareth," and so on, where the meaning is quite clear (obscure meanings are explained in brackets). The rationale for this decision is easy enough in manuscripts, where, for example, "y" was used as a shorthand for "th," and, thus, writers meant "the" when they wrote "ye." But in print too, we decided it to be more useful for someone approaching the history of this age for the first time to spare them the "delights" of original orthography and black-letter print.

We would like to offer three ways to use this sourcebook based upon the various ways in which we and other professors have used the first edition of this work.

1. *As a companion to the early modern narrative.* The sourcebook helps to flesh out important subjects, documents, and intriguing events in the general narrative of the period. Chapters will add to discussion and debate when used in conjunction with any general textbook of early modern England or Britain, although we have, of course, specifically designed it for use with the new edition of Bucholz and Key, *Early Modern England.* While we present the documents in a roughly chronological fashion, the table below links the corresponding chapters of each book.

Sources and Debates	*Early Modern England: a Narrative History*
chapter 1	Introduction
chapter 2	chapter 1
chapter 3	chapters 2–4
chapter 4	chapters 4–5
chapter 5	chapter 6
chapter 6	chapter 7
chapter 7	chapters 7–8
chapter 8	chapter 9
chapter 9	chapters 9–10 and Conclusion

2. *To contextualize a larger work.* What was happening, what was being written, and what contemporary issues shaped great works such as More's *Utopia*, or Shakespeare's *Macbeth*, or Defoe's *Moll Flanders*? Placing such a longer work (often easily available in a modern edition) in the context provided by reading contemporary documents from the relevant chapter (in these cases, chapters 1, 6, and 9 respectively) will historicize and illuminate these works as well as the periods in which they were written. Alternately, you might seek out a rarer pamphlet or diary in its entirety from which we have usually only been able to select a portion to print here, and, again, contextualize it with material from the other documents in that chapter. Pamphlets can be found in their entirety if your institution subscribes to EEBO (see Bibliography of Online Document Archives). You might also use biographical information from ODNB (again, see Bibliography) to supplement the details about authors that we supply in the headnotes.

3. *Test claims made in historians' debates.* A major task of the historian is to look at vast quantities of documents and other evidence, and draw from it a generalization about the past. In your reading of *Early Modern England* or other

course texts you will have come across many such generalizations, as well as conflicting interpretations. Are these generalizations and interpretations borne out by the testimony of actual people who lived and died three and four hundred years ago? While the documents printed below are only a selection, they do contain the observations and thoughts of people who were there. Of course, historians can and do disagree *now* about what was said, done, or meant *then*. One of the pleasures of history is puzzling out which "side" is most compelling according to the evidence you have read; even better is to discover something of value in both views or arguments, or even to advance your own position, however tentatively. The articles and essays listed at the end of each chapter are selected based on brevity, succinctness, and clear positions taken to help you see clearly the historiographical divisions which your reading of the documents can "test."

In the end, this book asks you to play historian yourself. Using thoughts and images of the time, meeting, face to face (or, at least, eyeball to word) the people who lived in early modern England should not only give you deeper insight into their lives; it should enable you to construct your own interpretation of the past. That interpretation will have to be provisional, of course: this book can only provide a glimpse of the evidence that is "out there" for the period. And you will have to watch out for your own modern biases: the key is not to apply the condescension of the present to the past, but to listen to what the past, and above all the people in it, have to tell us. We believe that this enterprise will have the value of reminding you that what historians say about the past was not (or at least should not be) something they have made up. It is based on the careful parsing and weighing of what people in the past have left us and even then, another historian or another age may parse differently, or listen with different ears. The end result should give you a better understanding of what historians do, how we all construct our views of the past, and what weight we might legitimately place upon them in future. As we wrote in the preface to the first edition, we trust that encountering the "voices" of early modern English women and men (and some Irish, Scots, and Welsh voices too) will enliven and enrich your understanding of this crucial past. You might even find a space in your own personal philosophy or world-view for the words and thoughts of, say, Queen Elizabeth, or Mary Astell, or John Locke, or even the aggrieved mutterings of anonymous rioters. We welcome your comments and queries; contact us at earlymodernengland@yahoo.com.

Acknowledgments

We wish to thank our many students over the years, especially Jon W. Burkhardt, Kristan Crawford, Erin Crawley, Alex Dove, Andreas Dür, Jill Lauerman, Jennifer Lancaster, and Krystina Mendoza. We would especially like to thank the following historians and literary critics for terms, dating, sources, and interpretations: Barrett Beer, Nicholas Canny, Dagni Bredesen, Julie Campbell, Gary de Krey, Bill Gibson, Michael Graham, Martin Ingram, Erin R. Kidwell, Michael Landon, Pádraig Lenihan, Christina Lindeman, George Logan, Linda Levy Peck, Wilf Prest, Stephen Roberts, N. A. M. Rodger, Claire Schen, Anita Shelton, Johann Sommerville, Angus Stroud, Susan Wabuda, Joe Ward, Bailey Young, and Mike Young. Moreover, Mike Young and Jim Sack read a draft of the first-edition manuscript, and we are indebted to their perceptive comments. This book could not have been completed without the help of the librarians of Booth Library of Eastern Illinois and the Cudahy Library of Loyola University, as well as the librarians and archivists of the University of Illinois Library, the Newberry Library, the William Andrews Clark Library, the Huntingdon Library, the Lewis Walpole Library, the Beinecke Rare Book and Manuscript Library, the National Archives, the British Library, the Cambridge University Library, the Bodleian Library, and the Codrington Library of All Souls College for whose assistance we are quite grateful.

The author and publishers gratefully acknowledge the following for permission to reproduce copyright material: Cambridge University Press for T. Smith, *De Republica Anglorum*, ed. M. Dewar (Cambridge, 1982), 64–7, 70–2, 74, 76–7; W. W. Norton & Co. for original translation as used in T. More, *Utopia*, ed. G. M. Logan and R. M. Adams, rev. ed. (Cambridge, 1989, 2002), 15–20; Oxford University Press for A. G. Dickens, ed., "Robert Parkyn's Narrative of the Reformation," *EHR* 62, 242 (1947): 69–70, 72, 74, 78–80, 82; Royal Historical Society for T. Starkey, *A Dialogue between Pole and Lupset*, ed. T. F. Mayer (Camden Society, 4th ser., 37, 1989), 52–4; and *The Anglica Historia of Polydore Vergil, A.D. 1485–1537*, ed. Denys Hay (Camden Society, 74, 1950), 4, 5, 143, 145, 147. They also gratefully acknowledge the assistance of Jonathan Cape with permissions.

The publishers apologize for any errors or omissions in the above list and would be grateful to be notified of any corrections that should be incorporated in the next edition or reprint of this book.

Abbreviations

£, s., d.	One pound (£) = 20 shillings (sh.) = 240 pence (d.)
Bodl.	Bodleian Library, Oxford
BL	British Library
Bucholz and Key	Robert Bucholz and Newton Key, *Early Modern England, 1485–1714: A Narrative History*, 2nd ed. (Oxford, 2009)
CJ	*Journals of the House of Commons*
CSP(D)	*Calendar of State Papers (Domestic)*
EcHR	*Economic History Review*
EHR	*English Historical Review*
HC	*History Compass*
HJ	*Historical Journal*
HMC	Historical Manuscripts Commission
HR	*Historical Research*
HT	*History Today*
HWJ	*History Workshop Journal*
JBS	*Journal of British Studies*
JEcclH	*Journal of Ecclesiastical History*
JP	Justice of the Peace
LJ	*Journals of the House of Lords*
MP	Member of Parliament
n.s.	new style (Gregorian calendar, used on the continent); unless noted as such dates are old style (Julian calendar, used in England until 1752)
P & P	*Past & Present*
RO	Record Office
SixteenthCJ	*Sixteenth Century Journal*
SocH	*Social History*
SPD	State Papers, Domestic
SR	*Statutes of the Realm*, 11 vols. (1810–28)
TNA	The National Archives (Public Record Office), Kew
TRHS	*Transactions of the Royal Historical Society*

Abbreviations

CHAPTER ONE

Social Order and Tensions in Tudor England

To judge from the writings they left behind, the men and women of early modern England were obsessed with order – or frightened silly that it might break down. So what did they mean by order? How did sixteenth-century English people think families, villages, towns, the London metropolis, and the State should be ordered? How did these social groups function within themselves and with each other? The documents reproduced in the first section of this chapter portray contemporary social ideals of order, hierarchy, and stability. Those in the second section portray a messier world of disorder, tension, and change. What were English society and economy actually like ca. 1500? Perhaps only an outsider can say: the chapter concludes with two views of foreigners on the character of English society from about a century apart.

Of course all contemporaries who articulated an idealized order *thought* they were commenting on their reality. Sometimes, Tudor subjects even drew idealized portraits of disorder to show how the ideal is unattainable for sinful man in an inherently corrupt world. In recent years, historians have suggested that perhaps social hierarchy should not be conceived simply in terms of dominance from above or resistance from below, but in terms of shared obligations. Service and deference owed by the members of one rank to another were dominant values in late medieval England, and remained so well into the early modern period.

Below, we present the documents by theme. How might your vision of early Tudor society differ if you read them in chronological order? As you read the documents in this chapter, you might ask:

- Which images or models of society used by sixteenth-century contemporaries are most effective or convincing, and which least?
- How did the authors of these early modern sources think about continuity or tradition, and how did they think about change?
- What did they most like about their society? What did they dislike? What would they think of ours?

Great Chain of Being

1.1 *Sir Thomas Smith,* De Republica Anglorum *(written 1565, pub. 1583)*[1]

Early modern people embraced the socially conservative doctrine that every individual should know and keep his or her place in the divinely ordained social hierarchy. This ideal divided the English people by rank, age, and gender (see Bucholz and Key, introduction). It could be expressed metaphorically, as the Great Chain of Being (see the visual representation in Plate 1), or as a Body-Politic (see the verbal representation, document 1.2), but perhaps the most famous description of Tudor social structure is that by Sir Thomas Smith (1513–77), the first regius professor of civil law at Cambridge and – at the time of composition of *De Republica Anglorum* – a diplomat in France.

Note how Smith defines different social levels. Are his definitions and distinctions precise? Is it entirely clear who is and is not a knight, an esquire, or a gentleman? Are his distinctions closer to caste divisions (based on birth) or class divisions (based on income)? Assuming each chapter is of more or less equal length, does he spend time on these groups proportional to their numbers? Why might an agricultural laborer or cottager subscribe to such a hierarchical view?

Chapter 16. The Divisions of the Parts and Persons of the Common Wealth

We in England divide our men commonly into four sorts, gentlemen, citizens or burgesses, yeomen artificers, and laborers. Of gentlemen the first and chief are the king, the prince, dukes, marquises, earls, viscounts, and barons, and this is called … the nobility, … next to these be knights, esquires, and simple gentlemen.

Chapter 17. Of the First Part of Gentlemen of England Called Nobilitas Major

Dukes, marquises, earls, viscounts, and barons, either be created of [by] the prince or come to that honor by being the eldest sons, or highest in succession to their parents. For the eldest of duke's sons during his father's life is called an earl …, [etc.]

Chapter 18. Of the Second Sort of Gentlemen Which May Be Called Nobilitas Minor, *and First of Knights*

No man is a knight by succession…. Knights therefore be not born but made [by the king]…. Knights in England most commonly [are made] according to

[1] T. Smith, *De Republica Anglorum*, ed. M. Dewar (London, 1982), 64–7, 70–2, 74, 76–7.

Plate 1 *"The Great Chain of Being." (Source: Diego Valadés*, Rhetorica Christiana, *1579, © British Library.)*

Note the hierarchical levels of nature and society reaching to God at the top, while fallen angels plummet toward Hell on the right. What moral(s) might one draw from this image? How might this image or model have difficulty incorporating all social hierarchies within it? What other images or models, possibly drawn from nature, might also represent such a chain of being?

the yearly revenue of their lands being able to maintain that estate ... [but] not all [are] made knights in England that may spend a knight's lands but they only whom the prince will honor....

Chapter 19.   Of Esquires

Escuier or esquire ... be all those which bear arms (as we call them) ... which to bear is a testimony of the nobility or race from which they do come. These be taken for no distinct order of the commonwealth, but do go with the residue of the gentlemen....

Chapter 20.   Of Gentlemen

Gentlemen be those whom their blood and race doth make noble and known ..., for that their ancestor hath been notable in riches or for his virtues, or (in fewer words) [they represent] old riches or prowess remaining in one stock. Which if the successors do keep and follow, they be *vere nobiles*.... If they do not, the fame and riches of their ancestors serve to cover them so long as it can, as a thing once gilted though it be copper within, till the gilt be worn away.... The prince and commonwealth have the same power that their predecessors had, and as the husbandman hath to plant a new tree when the old faileth, to honor virtue where he doth find it, to make gentlemen, esquires, knights, barons, earls, marquises, and dukes, where he seeth virtue able to bear that honor or merits, to deserve it, and so it hath always been used among us. But ordinarily the king doth only make knights and create the barons and higher degrees: for as for gentlemen, they be made good cheap in England. For whosoever studieth the laws of the realm, who studieth in the universities, who professeth liberal sciences, and to be short who can live idly and without manual labor, and will bear the port, charge, and countenance of a gentleman, he shall be called master, for that is the title which men give to esquires and other gentlemen, and shall be taken for a gentleman.... (And if need be) a king [officer] of Heralds shall also give him for money, [a coat of] arms newly made and invented, which the title shall bear that the said Herald hath perused and seen old registers where his ancestors in times past had born the same....

Chapter 22.   Of Citizens and Burgesses

Next to a gentleman, be appointed citizens and burgesses, such as not only be free and received as officers within the cities, but also be of some substance to bear the charges.... Generally in the shire they be of no account, save only in ... Parliament....

Chapter 23.   Of Yeomen

Those whom we call yeomen next unto the nobility, the knights, and squires, have the greatest charges and doings in the commonwealth.... I call him a yeoman whom our laws call *Legalem hominem* ..., which is a freeman born English, who may spend of his own free land in yearly revenue to the sum of 40s. sterling [£2] by the year. ... This sort of people confess themselves to be no gentleman ..., and yet they have a certain preeminence and more estimation than laborers and artificers, and commonly live wealthily, keep good houses, do their business, and travail [work] to get riches: they be (for the most part) farmers to gentlemen, and with grazing, frequenting of markets, and keeping servants, not idle servants as the gentlemen doth, but such as get their own living and part of their masters: by these means do come to such wealth, that they are able and daily do buy the lands of unthrifty gentlemen, and after setting their sons to the schools, to the universities, to the law of the realm, or otherwise leaving them sufficient lands whereon they may labor, do make their said sons by these means gentlemen. ...

Chapter 24.   Of the Fourth Sort of Men Which Do Not Rule

The fourth sort or class amongst us is ... day laborers, poor husbandmen, yea merchants or retailers which have no free land, copyholders, all artificers, as tailors, shoemakers, carpenters, brickmakers, bricklayers, masons, etc. These have no voice nor authorities in our commonwealth, and no account is made of these but only to be ruled, not to rule other, and yet they be not altogether neglected. For in cities and corporate towns for default of yeomen, they are fain to make their inquests of such manner of people. And in villages they be commonly made churchwardens, aleconners [local brewing inspectors], and many times constables.

1.2   *Richard Morison,* A Remedy for Sedition *(1536)*[2]

Sixteenth-century authors worried that England was disordered, but disagreed as to the remedies. But all began with a fairly organic model of how society functioned. Sir Richard Morison (ca. 1510–56) was a humanist (he may have introduced the work of Niccolo Machiavelli [1469–1527] to England), who had lived in the household of the Catholic reformer Reginald Pole (1500–58) at Padua, but returned to England to write for Henry VIII's chief minister, Thomas Cromwell (ca. 1485–1540). He is often associated with that group of writers who sought to apply the new reformist ideas to social and economic problems, the Commonwealthmen. He published *A Remedy for Sedition* in the wake of the Pilgrimage of Grace of that year (see chapter 3), a dangerous rebellion against Henry's religious and governmental reforms. He sought, in part, to maintain the social *status quo* by restraining the commoners' lusts and appetites and by discouraging social mobility.

---

[2]   R. Morison, *A Remedy for Sedition* (n.p., 1536), sig. Aii–Aii(verso), Bii(verso).

How does he justify the current social order? What imagery (metaphors) does Morison use to explain English society? Which are most effective? Which least? What is he most afraid of? How does his view match that of Smith (document 1.1)?

When every man will rule, who shall obey? How can there be any commonwealth, where he that is wealthiest, is most like to come to woe? Who can there be rich, where he that is richest is in most danger of poverty? No, no, take wealth by the hand, and say farewell wealth, where lust is liked, and law refused, where up is set down, and down set up. An order, an order must be had, and a way found that they rule that best can, they be ruled, that most it becometh so to be.... For as there must be some men of policy and prudence, to discern what is metest [best] to be done in the government of states even so there must be others of strength and readiness, to do what the wiser shall think expedient, both for the maintenance of them that govern, and for the eschewing of the infinite jeopardies, that a multitude not governed falleth into: these must not go, arm in arm, but the one before, the other behind....

A commonwealth is like a body, and so like, that it can be resembled to nothing so convenient, as unto that. Now, were it not by your faith, a mad herring [joke], if the foot should say, I will wear a cap with an ouch [ornament], as the head doth? If the knees should say, we will carry the eyes, another while; if the shoulders should claim each of them an ear; if the heals would now go before, and the toes behind? This were undoubted a mad herring: every man would say, the feet, the knees, the shoulders, the heals make unlawful requests, and very mad petitions. But if it were so indeed, if the foot had a cap, the knees eyes, the shoulders ears, what a monstrous body should this be? God send them such a one, that shall at any time go about to make as evil a commonwealth, as this is a body. It is not mete, every man to do, that he thinketh best.

1.3   An Act Against Wearing Costly Apparel (1 Hen. VIII, c. 14, 1510)[3]

One indication of the contemporary obsession with order is the many sumptuary laws passed by parliament to prevent people from inferior social ranks wearing "sumptuous" or extravagant clothing reserved for their betters. Such laws from the fourteenth and fifteenth centuries reveal both the ideal of

---

[3]   *SR*, 3: 8–9.

the Great Chain of Being and fears that this ideal was being honored only in the breach. Such laws attempted to regulate dress quite rigidly and, although they might be used to encourage English manufacture, they mainly sought to preserve an ordered society of ranks, or at least a society in which people could be "placed" securely.

Can this 1510 Act be used to work out the status hierarchy in Tudor England? Is this an economic hierarchy? According to the preamble of the statute, why was this law passed? Is this the whole story? What might be the difficulties in enforcing such legislation? Further Acts – 6 Hen. VIII, c. 1; 7 Hen. VIII, c. 6; 24 Hen. VIII, c. 13; 1–2 Philip and Mary, c. 2 – followed. What does their proliferation suggest about their efficacy?

Forasmuch as the great and costly array and apparel used within this realm contrary to good statutes thereof made hath been the occasion of great impoverishing of diverse of the king's subjects and provoked many of them to rob and to do extortion and other unlawful deeds to maintain thereby their costly array: in eschewing whereof, be it ordained by the authority of this present Parliament that no person, of what estate, condition, or degree that he be, use in his apparel any cloth of gold of purple color or silk of purple color but only the king, the queen, the king's mother, the king's children, the king's brothers and sisters upon pain to forfeit the said apparel wherewith soever it be mixed, and for using the same to forfeit 20 pound. And that no man under the estate of a duke use in any apparel of his body or upon his horses any cloth of gold of tissue upon pain to forfeit the same apparel wherewith soever it be mixed and for using the same to forfeit 20 mark [£13 6s. 8d.]. ... And that no man under the degree of a baron use in his apparel of his body or of his horses any cloth of gold or cloth of silver or tinsel, satin, nor no other silk or cloth mixed or embroidered with gold or silver upon pain of forfeiture of the same apparel, albeit that it be mixed with any other silk or cloth, and for using of the same to forfeit 10 mark. And that no man under the degree of a lord or a knight of the Garter wear any woollen cloth made out of this realm of England, Ireland, Wales, Calais, or the Marches of the same, or Berwick, upon pain to forfeit the said cloth and for using of the same to forfeit 10 pound. And that no man under the degree of a knight of the Garter wear in his gown or coat or any other his apparel any velvet of the color of crimson or blue upon pain to forfeit the same gown or coat or other apparel and for using of the same to forfeit 40 shillings [£2]. ... And that no man under the degree of a knight, except esquires for the king's body, his cupbearers, carvers, and sewers having the ordinary fee for the same, and all other esquires for the body having possession of lands and tenements or other hereditaments in their hands or other to their use to the yearly value of 300 mark [£200] and lords' sons and heirs, justices of the one Bench or of the other, the master of the Rolls, and barons of the king's Exchequer, and all other of the king's Council and mayors of the city of London for the time being, use or wear any velvet in their gowns or riding coats or furs of marten in their apparel upon pain to forfeit the same fur and apparel wherewith soever it be mixed and for using of the same to forfeit 40 shillings. Nor no person other than the above named wear velvet in their doublets nor satin nor damask in their gowns nor coats, except he be a lord's son or a gentleman having in his possession or other to his use lands or tenements or annuities at the least for term of life to the yearly value of an hundred pound above all reprises, upon pain to forfeit the same apparel wherewith soever it be mixed and for using of the same to forfeit 40 shillings. Nor no person use or wear satin or damask in their doublets nor silk or camlet [silk and angora] in their gowns or coats not having lands or tenements in his possession or other to his use office or fee for term of life or lives to the yearly value of 20 pound, except he be a yeoman of the Crown or of the king's guard or grooms of the king's Chamber or the queen's having therefore the king's fee or the queen's upon pain to forfeit the same apparel wherewith so ever it be mixed and for using of the same to forfeit 40 shillings. And that no man under the degree of a gentleman except graduates of the universities and except yeomen, grooms, and pages of the king's Chamber and of our sovereign lady the queen's, and except such men as have … an hundred pound in goods, use or wear any furs, whereof there is no like kind growing in this land of England, Ireland, Wales, or in any land under the king's obeisance, upon pain to forfeit the same furs and for using of the same to forfeit 40 shillings. The value of their goods to be tried by their own oaths. And that no man under the degree of a knight except spiritual men and sergeants at the law or graduates of universities use any more cloth in any long gown than four broad yards, and in a riding gown or coat above three yards upon pain of forfeiture of the same. And that no serving man under the degree of a gentleman use or wear any gown or coat or such like apparel of more cloth than two broad yards and an half in a short gown and three broad yards in a long gown, and that in the said gown or coat they wear no manner [of] fur upon pain of forfeiture of the said apparel. … And that no serving man waiting upon his master under the degree of a gentleman use or wear any guarded hose or any cloth above the price of 20d. the yard in his hose except it be of his master's wearing hose upon pain of forfeiture of 3s. 4d. And that no man under the degree of a knight wear any guarded or pinched shirt or pinched partlet [neckerchief or collar] of linen cloth upon pain of forfeiture of the same shirt or partlet and for using of the same to forfeit 10 shillings. And that no servant of husbandry nor shepherd nor common laborer nor servant unto any artificer out of city or borough nor husbandman having no goods of his own above the value of 10 pound use or wear any cloth whereof the broad yard passeth in price two shillings nor that any of the said servants of husbandry, shepherds, nor laborers wear any hose above the price of 10d. the yard upon pain of imprisonment in the stocks by three days.

Social Order, Social Change, and the State

1.4   Act Against Pulling Down of Towns
(4 Hen. VII, c. 19, 1489)[4]

From the late Middle Ages on, many landowners found it profitable to abandon arable demesne farming, throw their peasant villagers off the land, and turn it to sheep-farming. This process, known as enclosure, was controversial and opposed by the Church and many in government. According to the preamble of the Act Against Pulling Down Towns why do the Church and the State fear depopulation? What happened when a town was pulled down? Does the statute mention other possible reasons for the State fearing depopulation? Why might a landlord want to destroy a town? *Qui bono* (who benefits)? (You might want to consider this question after reflecting on documents 1.5 and 1.6.)

The king our sovereign lord, having a singular pleasure above all things to avoid such enormities and mischiefs as be hurtful and prejudicial to the common wealth of this his land and his subjects, remembering that among all other things great inconveniences daily do increase by desolation and pulling down and wilful waste of houses and towns within this his realm, and laying to pasture lands which customarily have been tilled, whereby idleness ground and beginning of all mischiefs daily do increase, for where in some towns two hundred persons were occupied and lived by their lawful labors, now are there occupied two or three herdsmen and the residue fall in idleness, the husbandry which is one of the greatest commodities of this realm is greatly decayed, churches destroyed, the service of God withdrawn, the bodies there buried not prayed for, the patron and curates wronged, the defense of this land against our enemies outward feebled and impaired; to the great displeasure of God, to the subversion of the policy and good rule of this land, and remedy be not hastily therefore purveyed: Wherefore the king our sovereign lord by the assent and advice of the Lords spiritual and temporal and Commons in this present Parliament assembled and by authority of the same, ordains, enacts, and establishes that no person, what estate, degree, or condition that he be, that hath any house or houses, that any time within three years past has been or that now is or hereafter shall be let to farm with twenty acres of land at least or more lying in tillage or husbandry, that the owner or owners of every such house or houses and land be bound to keep, sustain, and maintain houses and buildings upon the said ground and land, convenient and necessary for maintaining and upholding of the said tillage and husbandry.

[4]   *SR*, 2: 542.

1.5 *Thomas More*, Utopia, Book I (1516)[5]

Laws and statutes like those above proliferated in response not only to perceived social ills but also to "waves" of prosecutions for very real assault and theft. Some humanists, in particular, found the legal punishments for those crimes harshly disproportionate. Thomas More (1478–1535) was a member of parliament, a lawyer and a humanist scholar who rose to be lord chancellor of England before dying a martyr's death in 1535 for not overtly embracing Henry VIII's break with Rome. His masterpiece, *Utopia*, was published in Latin in 1516, and translated into English and other languages soon thereafter. In *Utopia*, More himself is one of the characters. He meets a fictional traveler, Raphael Hythloday (remember that More wrote in the age of Columbus and Magellan), who describes an imaginary, perfect state (the word "utopia," coined by More, means "no place" in Greek) exactly opposite from the flawed kingdom of England geographically and temperamentally. The more that More learns about Utopia, the worse England's social and economic problems appear. Below, Hythloday's humanist analysis of why people stole, the danger of "men-eating sheep," and the irrational punishments for theft provide a justly famous indictment of Tudor England.

According to the discussion, what major problems does Tudor England face? How is the incidence of crime in England explained? How is enclosure explained? If Morison (document 1.2) had sat in on the discussion, how might he respond? How does the narrator – at this point the fictional Raphael – propose to solve these problems? Would his solution work? What, do you suppose, does the author think of the Great Chain of Being?

It happened one day when I [Raphael] was dining with him [Cardinal John Morton], there was present a layman, learned in the laws of your country [England], who for some reason took occasion to praise the rigid execution of justice then being practiced on thieves. They were being executed everywhere, he [the layman] said, with as many as twenty at a time being hanged on a single gallows. And then he declared he was amazed that so many thieves sprang up everywhere when so few of them escaped hanging. I ventured to speak freely before the Cardinal, and said, "There is no need to wonder: this way of punishing thieves goes beyond the call of justice, and is not in any case for the public good. The penalty is too harsh in itself, yet it isn't an effective

---

[5] T. More, *Utopia*, ed. G. M. Logan and R. M. Adams, rev. ed. (Cambridge, 2002), 15–20; reproduced by permission of W. W. Norton & Co., for original translation, T. More, *Utopia*, ed. R. M. Adams, 2nd ed. (New York, 1992), 9–10, 12–14.

deterrent. Simple theft is not so great a crime that it ought to cost a man his head, yet no punishment however severe can restrain those from robbery who have no other way to make a living. In this matter not only you in England but a good part of the world seem to imitate bad schoolmasters, who would rather whip their pupils than teach them. Severe and terrible punishments are enacted for theft, when it would be much better to enable every man to earn his own living, instead of being driven to the awful necessity of stealing and then dying for it. ....”

[Also, I said,] “There are a great many noblemen who live idly like drones off the labor of others, their tenants whom they bleed white by constantly raising their rents. (This is the only instance of their tightfistedness, because they are prodigal in everything else, ready to spend their way to the poorhouse.) What’s more, they drag around with them a great train of idle servants, who have never learned any trade by which they could make a living. As soon as their master dies, or they themselves fall ill, they are promptly turned out of doors, for lords would rather support idlers than invalids, and the heir is often unable to maintain as big a household as his father had, at least at first. ....”

“Yet this is not the only force driving men to thievery. There is another that, as I see it, applies more specially to you Englishmen.”

“What is that?,” said the Cardinal.

“Your sheep,” I said, “that commonly are so meek and eat so little; now, as I hear, they have become so greedy and fierce that they devour human beings themselves. They devastate and depopulate fields, houses and towns. For in whatever parts of the land sheep yield the finest and thus the most expensive wool, there the nobility and gentry, yes, and even a good many abbots – holy men – are not content with the old rents that the land yielded to their predecessors. Living in idleness and luxury without doing society any good no longer satisfies them; they have to do positive harm. For they leave no land free for the plough: they enclose every acre for pasture; they destroy houses and abolish towns, keeping the churches – but only for sheep-barns. And as if enough of your land were not already wasted on game-preserves and forests for hunting wild animals, these worthy men turn all human habitations and cultivated fields back to wilderness. Thus, so that one greedy, insatiable glutton, a frightful plague to his native country, may enclose thousands of acres within a single fence, the tenants are ejected; and some are stripped of their belongings by trickery or brute force, or, wearied by constant harassment, are driven to sell them. One way or another, these wretched people – men, women, husbands, wives, orphans, widows, parents with little children and entire families (poor but numerous, since farming requires many hands) – are forced to move out. They leave the only homes familiar to them, and can find no place to go. Since they must leave at once without waiting for a proper buyer, they sell for a pittance all their household goods, which would not bring much in any case. When that little money is gone (and it’s soon spent in wandering from place to place), what finally remains for them but to steal, and so be hanged – justly, no doubt – or to wander and beg? And yet if they go tramping, they are jailed as idle vagrants. They would be glad to work, but they can find no one who will hire them. There is no need for farm labor, in which they have been trained, when there is no land left to be planted. One herdsman or shepherd can look after a flock of beasts large enough to stock an area that used to require many hands to make it grow crops.

"This enclosing has led to sharply rising food prices in many districts. Also, the price of raw wool has risen so much that poor people among you who used to make cloth can no longer afford it, and so great numbers are forced from work to idleness. One reason is that after so much new pasture-land was enclosed, rot killed a countless number of the sheep – as though God were punishing greed by sending on the beasts a murrain that rightly should have fallen on the owners! But even if the number of sheep should increase greatly, the price will not fall a penny, because the wool trade, though it can't be called a monopoly because it isn't in the hands of a single person, is concentrated in so few hands (an oligopoly, you might say), and these so rich, that the owners are never pressed to sell until they have a mind to, and that is only when they can get their price. ...

"So your island, which seemed specially fortunate in this matter, will be ruined by the crass avarice of a few. For the high cost of living causes everyone to dismiss as many retainers as he can from his household; and what, I ask, can these men do but rob or beg? And a man of courage is more easily persuaded to steal than to beg.

"To make this miserable poverty and scarcity worse, they exist side by side with wanton luxury. The servants of noblemen, tradespeople, even some farmers – people of every social rank – are given to ostentatious dress and gourmandizing. Look at the cook-shops, the brothels, the bawdy houses, and those other places just as bad, the wine-bars and ale-houses. Look at all the crooked games of chance like dice, cards, backgammon, tennis, bowling and quoits, in which money slips away so fast. Don't all these pastimes lead their devotees straight to robbery? Banish these blights, make those who have ruined farmhouses and villages restore them or hand them over to someone who will restore and rebuild. Restrict the right of the rich to buy up anything and everything, and then to exercise a kind of monopoly. Let fewer people be brought up in idleness. Let agriculture be restored, and the wool-manufacture revived as an honest trade, so there will be useful work for the idle throng, whether those whom poverty has already made thieves or those who are only vagabonds or idle servants now, but are bound to become thieves in the future.

"Certainly, unless you cure these evils it is futile to boast of your justice in punishing theft. Your policy may look superficially like justice, but in reality it is neither just nor expedient. If you allow young folk to be abominably brought up and their characters corrupted, little by little, from childhood; and if then you punish them as grown-ups for committing the crimes to which their training has consistently inclined them, what else is this, I ask, but first making them thieves and then punishing them for it."

1.6   Complaint of the Norwich shoemakers against their journeymen (September 21, 1490)[6]

> While early modern England was overwhelmingly agrarian, towns played a role disproportionate to their puny size. As you read this "Complaint," ask yourself what sorts of problems city-dwellers worried about? Was there more order (or disorder) in towns or in the countryside? Norwich was the second-largest city in England at the time (in the 1520s, London had 50–70,000 inhabitants; Norwich about 10,000). (You might compare Norwich's problems with the situation in London, by examining document 1.8.) How does the Great Chain of Being help to explain the views expressed in the Complaint (consider a guild hierarchy of master, journeyman, apprentice)?

To our right honorable masters, the mayor, and his brethren alderman and to our good masters and weelwillers [well-wishers] of the Common Council of the city: Showeth to your great discretions the poor artificers and craftsmen of shoemakers of the said city, that where diverse journeymen and servants of the said craft greatly disposed to riot and idleness, whereby *[reacting to riots]* may succeed great poverty, so that diverse days weekly when them lust to leave their bodily labor till a great part of the week be almost so expended and wasted, against the advantage and profit werely [not only] of themselves and of their masters also. And also contrary to the law [of] God and good guiding temporal [temperance], they labor quickly toward the Sunday and festival days on the Saturdays and vigils [evenings before festival days] from four of the clock at afternoon to the deepness and darkness of the night following. And not only that sinful disposition but much worse so offending in the mornings of such fests, and omitting the hearing of their divine service. Wherefore prayeth the said artificers heartily, that the rather for good cause and also that virtuous and true labor might help to the sustentation of the said craft, that by your general assent may be ordained and enacted for a laudable custom, that none such servant or journeyman from henceforth presume to occupy nor work after the said hour in vigils and Saturdays aforesaid, upon pain by your discretions to be set for punishment alsweel of [as much against] the said artificers for their favoring and supporting, as for the said journeymen so working and offending. *[want no work on Saturdays and prayer hours]* *[overworked + poorly treated by journeymen]*

---

[6]   *Records of the City of Norwich*, ed. W. Hudson and J. C. Tingey (London, 1910), 2: 104.

1.7   Thomas Starkey, *Dialogue between Pole and Lupset (ca. 1529–32)*[7]

Starkey (ca. 1498–1538), another humanist writer associated with Cromwell, also often identified as a Commonwealthman, wrote a fanciful dialog between two real contemporaries Thomas Lupset (ca. 1495–1530) and Reginald Pole in order to ponder how one might improve the lot of all in the commonwealth. Which social groups do the speakers blame for England's ills? Is this diagnosis different from Morison's or More's (document 1.2 or 1.5)? Compare and contrast these sources by asking their respective views on the ideal society. Starkey thought government could initiate change that would help the poor. How might the Great Chain of Being be used to press for social change as well as the *status quo*?

Pole: There is also, in this politic body, another disease and sickness more grievous …, and that is this, shortly to say: A great part of these people which we have here in our country, is either idle or ill-occupied, and a small number of them exerciseth themself in doing their office and duty pertaining to the maintenance of the common weal, by the reason whereof this body is replenished and over-fulfilled with many ill-humors, which I call idle and unprofitable persons, of whom you shall find a great number, if you will a little consider all estates, orders, and degrees here in our country. First, look what an idle rout our noblemen keep and nourish in their houses, which do nothing else but carry dishes to the table and eat them when they have down [done]; and after, giving themselves to hunting, hawking, dicing, carding, and all other idle pastimes and vain [vanities], as though they were born to nothing else at all. Look to our bishops and prelates of the realm, whether they follow not the same trade in nourishing such an idle sort, spending their possessions and goods, which were to them given to be distributed among them which were oppressed with poverty and necessity. Look, furthermore to priests, monks, friars, and canons with all their adherents and idle train, and you shall find also among them no small number idle and unprofitable, which be nothing but burdens to the earth; insomuch that if you, after this manner, examine the multitude in every order and degree, you shall find, as I think, the third part of our people living in idleness, as persons to the common weal utterly unprofitable; and to all good civility, much like unto the drone bees in a hive, which do nothing else but consume and devour all such thing as the busy and good bee, with diligence and labor, gathereth together.

Lupset: Master Pole, me seemeth you examine this matter somewhat too shortly, as though you would have all men to labor, to go to the plough, and

[7]   T. Starkey, *A Dialogue between Pole and Lupset*, ed. T. F. Mayer (London, Camden Society, 4th ser., 37, 1989), 52–4, from TNA SP1/90; reproduced by permission of Royal Historical Society.

exercise some craft, which is not necessary, for our mother the ground is so plenteous and bountiful, by the goodness of God and of nature given to her, that with little labor and tillage she will sufficiently nourish mankind none otherwise than she doth all beasts, fishes, and fowls which are bred and brought up upon her, to whom we see she ministereth food with little labor or none, but of her own fertile benignity. Wherefore if a few of our people busy themselves and labor therein, it is sufficient; the rest may live in triumph, at liberty and ease free from all bodily labor and pain.

Pole: This is spoken, Master Lupset, even as though you judged man to be born for to live in idleness and pleasure, all thing referring and applying thereto. But, Sir, it is nothing so; but, contrary, he is born to labor and travail (after the opinion of the wise and ancient antiquity) none otherwise than a bird to fly, and not to live (as Homer saith some do) as an unprofitable weight and burden of the Earth. For man is born to be as a governor, ruler, and diligent tiller and inhabitant of this earth, as some, by labor of body, to procure things necessary for the maintenance of man's life; some by wisdom and policy to keep the rest of the multitude in good order and civility. So that none be born to this idleness and vanity, to the which the most part of our people is much given and bent, but all to exercise themselves in some fashion of life convenient to the dignity and nature of man. Wherefore, though it be so that it is nothing necessary all to be laborers and tillers of the ground, but some to be priests and ministers of God's Word, some to be gentlemen to the governance of the rest, and some [to be] servants to the same. Yet this is certain, that over-great number of them, without due proportion to the other parts of the body, is superfluous in any commonalty. It is not to be doubted but that here in our country of those sorts be over-many, and specially of them which we call servingmen, which live in service to gentlemen, lords, and others of the nobility. If you look throughout the world, as I think, you shall not find in any one country proportionable to ours like number of that sort.

Lupset: Marry, sir, that is truth. Wherein, me seemeth, you praise our country very much, for in them standeth the royalty of the realm. If the yeomanry of England were not, in time of war we should be in shrewd case; for in them standeth the chief defense of England.

Pole: O, Master Lupset, you take the matter amiss. In them standeth the beggary of England. By them is nourished the common theft therein, as hereafter at large I shall declare. Howbeit, if they were exercised in feats of arms, to the defense of the realm in time of war, they might yet be much better suffered. But you see how little they be exercised therein, insomuch that in time of war it is necessary for our ploughmen and laborers of the country to take weapon in hand, or else we were not like long to enjoy England, so little trust is to be put in their feats and deeds.

Wherefore doubt you no more but of them, like as of other that I have spoken of before (as of priests, friars, monks, and other called religious), we have over-many, which altogether make our politic body unwieldy and heavy, and, as it were, to be grieved with gross humors, insomuch that this disease therein may well be compared to a dropsy in man's body.

Foreigners View English Society

1.8 Andrea Trevisan's Report on England (ca. 1500)[8]

Historians particularly value commentary by foreigners. Why? On what subjects might the following report by a Venetian nobleman (most probably Andrea Trevisan, 1458–1534) to his Senate be most valuable? On what subjects might it be weakest or most unreliable? Can you reconcile the following foreign views of England with what Smith or More or Starkey wrote? How are English family relations most different from those on the continent according to this visitor from Venice? Is there an English national identity ca. 1500? Of what might it consist?

The English are, for the most part, both men and women of all ages, handsome and well-proportioned; though not quite so much so, in my opinion, as it had been asserted to me, before your Magnificence went to that kingdom [perhaps 1496]; and I have understood from persons acquainted with these countries, that the Scotch are much handsomer; and that the English are great lovers of themselves, and of everything belonging to them; they think that there are no other men than themselves, and no other world but England; and whenever they see a handsome foreigner, they say that "he looks like an Englishman," and that "it is a great pity that he should not be an Englishman"; and when they partake of any delicacy with a foreigner, they ask him, "whether such a thing is made in *their* country?"… [T]hey think that no greater honor can be conferred, or received, than to invite others to eat with them, or to be invited themselves; and they would sooner give five or six ducats [Venetian ducats varied from 3s. 6d. to 4s.; thus, about £2] to provide an entertainment for a person, than a groat [4d.] to assist him in any distress.…

The want [lack] of affection in the English is strongly manifested towards their children; for after having kept them at home till they arrive at the age of 7 or 9 years at the utmost, they put them out, both males and females, to hard service in the houses of other people, binding them generally for another 7 or 9 years. And these are called apprentices, and during that time they perform all the most menial offices; and few are born who are exempted from this fate, for every one, however rich he may be, sends away his children into the houses of others, whilst he, in return receives those of strangers into his own. And on inquiring their reason for this severity, they answered that they did it in order that their children might learn better manners. But I, for my part, believe that they do it because they like to enjoy all their comforts themselves, and that they are better served by strangers than they would be by their own children. Besides

[8] *A Relation, or Rather a True Account, of the Island of England …, about the Year 1500*, trans. C. A. Sneyd (London, Camden Society, 1847), 20–2, 24–9, 41–3.

which the English being great epicures, and very avaricious by nature, indulge in the most delicate fare themselves and give their household the coarsest bread, and beer, and cold meat baked on Sunday for the week, which, however, they allow them in great abundance. That if they had their own children at home, they would be obliged to give them the same food they make use of for themselves. That if the English sent their children away from home to learn virtue and good manners, and took them back again when their apprenticeship was over, they might, perhaps, be excused; but they never return, for the girls are settled by their patrons, and the boys make the best marriages they can, and, assisted by their patrons, not by their fathers, they also open a house and strive diligently by this means to make some fortune for themselves; whence it proceeds that, having no hope of their paternal inheritance, they all become so greedy of gain that they feel no shame in asking, almost "for the love of God," for the smallest sums of money; and to this it may be attributed, that there is no injury that can be committed against the lower orders of the English, that may not be atoned for by money.

Nevertheless, the apprentices for the most part make good fortunes, some by one means and some by another; but above all, those who happen to be in the good graces of the mistress of the house in which they are domiciliated at the time of the death of the master; because, by the ancient custom of the country, every inheritance is divided into three parts; for the Church and funeral expenses, for the wife, and for the children. But the lady takes care to secure a good portion for herself in secret, first, and then the residue being divided into three parts as aforesaid, she, being in possession of what she has robbed, of her own third, and that of her children besides (and if she have no children, the two thirds belong to her by right), usually bestows herself in marriage upon the one of those apprentices living in the house who is most pleasing to her, and who was probably not *displeasing* to her in the lifetime of her husband; and in his power she places all her own fortune, as well as that of her children, who are sent away as apprentices into other houses.… No Englishman can complain of this corrupt practice, it being universal throughout the kingdom; nor does any one, arrived at years of discretion, find fault with his mother for marrying again during his childhood, because, from very ancient custom, this license has become so sanctioned, that it is not considered any discredit to a woman to marry again every time that she is left a widow, however unsuitable the match may be as to age, rank, and fortune.

I saw, one day, that I was with your Magnificence at court, a very handsome young man of about 18 years of age [Richard de la Pole, d. 1525], the brother of the duke of Suffolk, who, as I understood, had been left very poor, the whole of the paternal inheritance amongst the nobility descending to the eldest son; this youth, I say, was boarded out to a widow of fifty, with a fortune as I was informed, of 50,000 crowns [Venetian crowns, or, about £10,000]. And this old woman knew how to play her cards so well, that he was content to become her husband, and patiently to waste the flower of his beauty with her, hoping soon to enjoy her great wealth with some handsome young lady: because when there are no children, the husband succeeds to the whole of the wife's property, and the wife in like manner to her husband's, as I said before; the part, however, belonging to the Church always remaining untouched. Nor must your Magnificence imagine that these successions may be of small value, for the riches of England are greater than those of any other country in Europe, as I have been told by the oldest and most experienced merchants, and also as I myself can vouch.... This is owing, in the first place, to the great fertility of the soil, which is such, that, with the exception of wine, they import nothing from abroad for their subsistence. Next, the sale of their valuable tin brings in a large sum of money to the kingdom; but still more do they derive from their extraordinary abundance of wool, which bears such a high price and reputation throughout Europe. And in order to keep the gold and silver in the country, when once it has entered, they have made a law, which has been in operation for a long time now, that no money, nor gold, nor silver plate should be carried out of England under a very heavy penalty. And everyone who makes a tour in the island will soon become aware of this great wealth ..., for there is no small innkeeper, however poor and humble he may be, who does not serve his table with silver dishes and drinking cups; and no one, who has not in his house silver plate at least £100...., is considered by the English to be a person of any consequence....

[A]t present, all the beauty of this island is confined to London; which, although sixty miles distant from the sea, possesses all the advantages to be desired in a maritime town; being situated on the river Thames, which is very much affected by the tide, for many miles ... above it; and London is so much benefitted by this ebb and flow of the river, that vessels of 100 tons burden can come up to the city, and ships of any size to within five miles of it; yet the water in this river is fresh for twenty miles below London. Although this city has no buildings in the Italian style, but of timber or brick like the French, the Londoners live comfortably, and, it appears to me, that there are not fewer inhabitants than at Florence or Rome. It abounds with every article of luxury, as well as with the necessaries of life but the most remarkable thing in London, is the wonderful quantity of wrought silver. I do not allude to that in private houses, though the landlord of the house in which the Milanese ambassador lived, had plate to the amount of 100 crowns [£25], but to the shops of London. In one single street, named the Strand, leading to St. Paul's, there are fifty-two goldsmith's shops, so rich and full of silver vessels, great and small, that in all the shops in Milan, Rome, Venice, and Florence put together, I do not think there would be found so many of the magnificence that are to be seen in London. And these vessels are all either salt cellars, or drinking cups, or basins to hold water for the hands; for they eat off that fine tin, which is little inferior to silver [pewter]. These great riches of London are not occasioned by its inhabitants being noblemen or gentlemen; being all, on the contrary, persons of low degree, and artificers who have congregated there from all parts of the island, and from Flanders, and from every other place. No one can be mayor or alderman of London, who has not been an apprentice in his youth; that is, who has not passed the seven or nine years in that hard service described before. Still, the citizens of London are thought quite as highly of there, as the Venetian gentlemen are at Venice, as I think your Magnificence may have perceived.

1.9   *"Journey Through England and Scotland Made by Lupold von Wedel" (1584–5)*[9]

The German knight von Wedel (1544–1615) had already traveled through Egypt and the Holy Land as well as Spain and Portugal by the time he visited the British Isles. We will return to his report when we consider Elizabethan London (see chapter 4). Here, note von Wedel's opinion of English society overall. Is there an English national identity according to his report? Has it changed since the beginning of the century?

Rare objects are not to be seen in England, but it is a very fertile country, producing all sorts of corn but no wine. There are plenty of sheep, cows, and various kinds of meat. The peasants and citizens are on the average rich people, not to speak of the gentlemen and noblemen. They are fond of pomp and splendor, both high and low. The value of the estates of the nobility cannot be reduced, for the eldest son inherits all; the others enter into some office or pursue highway robbery, as they also do in Scotland. The best tin of all Europe is found in the mines. The gentlemen and nobles keep more servants here than I saw in all my life elsewhere, a simple nobleman keeping perhaps twenty servants, but not so many horses as we do in Germany. When a gentleman goes out on horseback his servants follow on foot. The climate is temperate, similar to that in France, not too hot in summer, and the cold in winter is to be endured. Persons of noble birth enter into marriage with those of lower standing and vice versa, according to wealth and property. I have seen peasants presenting themselves statelier in manner, and keeping a more sumptuous table than some noblemen do in Germany. That is a poor peasant who has no silver-gilt salt-cellars, silver cups, and spoons.

HISTORIANS' DEBATES

Was early modern England a society of order and deference? Should we re-insert class and conflict into our explanation?

P. Burke, "The Language of Orders in Early Modern Europe," in *Social Orders and Social Classes in Europe since 1500: Studies in Social Stratification*, ed. M. L. Bush

---

[9]   "Journey Through England and Scotland Made by Lupold von Wedel in the Years 1584 and 1585," trans. G. von Bülow, *TRHS* n.s. 9 (1895): 268.

(London, 1992), as well as W. M. Reddy's essay on "class"; R. Britnell, "The Secular Social Order," *The Closing of the Middle Ages?: England, 1471–1529* (Oxford, 1997); P. R. Coss, "An Age of Deference," in *A Social History of England, 1200–1500*, ed. R. Horrox and W. M. Ormrod (Cambridge, 2006); C. W. Marsh, "Order and Place in England, 1580–1640: The View from the Pew," *JBS* 44, 1 (2005); A. Wood, "Custom, Identity and Resistance: English Free Miners and Their Law, c. 1550–1800," in *The Experience of Authority in Early Modern England*, ed. P. Griffiths, A. Fox, and S. Hindle (New York, 1996); J. Whittle, "Peasant Politics and Class Consciousness: The Norfolk Rebellions of 1381 and 1549 Compared," *P & P* Supplement 2 (2007).

Were contemporary views of social structure changing? Were their descriptions idealized?

D. Cressy, "Describing the Social Order of Elizabethan England," *Literature and History* 3 (1976); K. Wrightson, "Estates, Degrees and Sorts in Tudor and Stuart England," *HT* 37, 1 (1987); *idem*, "Estates, Degrees, and Sorts: Changing Perceptions of Society in Tudor and Stuart England," in *Language, History and Class*, ed. P. J. Corfield (Oxford, 1991); *idem*, " 'Sorts of People' in Tudor and Stuart England," in *The Middling Sort of People: Culture, Society and Politics in England, 1550–1800*, ed. J. Barry and C. Brooks (London, 1994); A. McLaren, "Reading Sir Thomas Smith's *De Republica Anglorum* as Protestant Apologetic," *HJ* 42 (1999); D. Postles, "The Politics of Address in Early-Modern England," *Journal of Historical Sociology* 18, 1–2 (2005); R. Tittler, "Seats of Honor, Seats of Power: the Symbolism of Public Seating in the English Urban Community, c. 1560–1620," *Albion* 24, 2 (1992); N. Wood, *Foundations of Political Economy: Some Early Tudor Views on State and Society* (Berkeley, 1994), esp. chs. on More, Starkey, Sir Thomas Smith.

Which groups were rising and falling in the early modern social order? Was it a mobile society?

A. Everitt, "Social Mobility in Early Modern England," *P & P* 33 (1966); L. Stone, "Social Mobility in England, 1500–1700," *P & P* 33 (1966); P. Clark and D. Souden, eds., *Migration and Society in Early Modern England* (1987), esp. the introduction; L. Stone, *Social Change and Revolution in England, 1540–1640* (1965), esp. extracts from R. H. Tawney, H. Trevor-Roper, J. H. Hexter, and Stone; F. Heal and C. Holmes, *The Gentry in England and Wales, 1500–1700* (Stanford, 1994), esp. chs. on lineage, family, and wealth; S. Hindle, *The State and Social Change in Early Modern England, 1550–1640* (Basingstoke, 2000), esp. ch. on social change and public policy; P. Fumerton, *Unsettled: The Culture of Mobility and the Working Poor in Early Modern England* (Chicago, 2006), esp. ch., "Mobilizing the Poor"; C. Brooks, "Apprenticeship, Social Mobility and the Middling Sort, 1550–1800," in Barry and Brooks, *Middling Sort of People*.

ADDITIONAL SOURCE COLLECTIONS

B. Coward, *Social Change and Continuity: England, 1550–1750*, rev. ed. (London, 1997).

A. Fletcher and D. MacCulloch, *Tudor Rebellions*, 5th ed. (London, 2004).

L. Manley, *London in the Age of Shakespeare: an Anthology* (London, 1986).

M. D. Palmer, *Henry VIII*, 2nd ed. (London, 1983).

R. H. Tawney and E. Power, eds., *Tudor Economic Documents* (London, 1924).

C. H. Williams, ed., *English Historical Documents, 1485–1558* (London, 1967).

CHAPTER TWO

Reviving the Crown, Empowering the State: the Tudor Challenge

The documents in this chapter show how the English monarchy emerged from the Middle Ages into the early modern period – and from the chaos and weakness of the Wars of the Roses (1453–1485) into an era of strong and successful rule under the Tudors. That, at least, was the story told by Tudor propagandists. Thus the *Chronicle* (pub. 1548) of Edward Hall (ca. 1496–1547), one of the sources upon which William Shakespeare (1564–1616) based his history plays, begins by lamenting the breakdown of order during the Wars of the Roses: "what misery, what murder, and what execrable plagues this famous region hath suffered by the division and dissension of the renowned houses of Lancaster and York."[1] According to Hall, these horrors ended when the first Tudor king, Henry VII, bearing Lancastrian blood, married Elizabeth of York, and their union brought forth the future Henry VIII (1491–1547). Hall, like Shakespeare, was anxious to praise the Tudor dynasty; one way to make Henry VII (reigned 1485–1509) and VIII (reigned 1509–47) look better was to make their immediate predecessors, the Yorkists Edward IV (reigned 1461–83) and Richard III (reigned 1483–85), look worse (see also Plate 2). But, in fact, the Yorkist kings had themselves sought to strengthen the Crown, stabilize the succession, and end the aristocratic gang-warfare of the 1450s and 1460s, later known as the Wars of the Roses.

As you read this chapter, ask:

- Were the first Tudors merely building on the achievements of their Yorkist predecessors or were they, in fact, "new princes," in Machiavelli's terms, taming an anarchic nobility?
- How important was the character of each individual monarch in the success of his government?
- How might these monarchs' thoughts and actions actually affect the lives of commoners?

[1] E. Hall, *Union of the Two Noble and Illustre Famelies of Lancastre & Yorke* (London, 1548), fol. i.

Plate 2 Edward Hall, *The Union of the Two Noble and Illustre Famelies of Lancastre &
Yorke*, title page (1550). (Source: © British Library.)

The image here is branches of a bush or tree intertwined with descendants of Edward III from about
1399 to 1547. How does this relate to the subject of Hall's book? How does it relate to its argument
(see section on "Claiming the Throne")?

Edward IV, Richard III, and the Reassertion of Royal Power

2.1   A Star Chamber Decree against "riots, excesses, and misgovernings" (November 13, 1471)[2]

The Wars of the Roses were such a bitter memory that contemporaries searched anxiously for their beginnings. Some dated the onset of pre-Tudor instability to Henry Bolingbroke's overthrow of Richard II (1377–99) and his accession as Henry IV (1399–1413), but this rather besmirched the Tudors' Lancastrian ancestry. A better case might be made for 1453, when the French inflicted a disastrous defeat in the Hundred Years' War leading to the loss of all English continental lands outside Calais, and coinciding with the first of the increasingly frequent mental breakdowns of the Lancastrian King Henry VI (1422–61). The resultant erosion of royal authority and prestige encouraged widespread disorder. By 1453, a more or less private war raged in the West Country. In response, the king, or rather his advisers, appointed Richard, duke of York (1411–60) "Protector of the Realm." (Who, normally, should be the realm's protector?) By 1461, the duke of York had rebelled against the Lancastrian monarchy he had sworn to protect, claimed the crown, and died in battle. His son, Edward, secured the throne in November 1461, but the Lancastrians continued to make rival claims based on descent and formal vows of allegiance. As a result, chaos sometimes reigned in the countryside. During the 1460s and 70s, Edward IV worked to end this disorder. In this example, he tried to thwart local bullying by his nobles' affinities, something for which Henry VII is often given credit. Using this decree can you identify who wields power in Nottingham? Does Edward's ultimate decision seem wise? Strong? Weak?

Edward, by the grace of God, king of England and France, and lord of Ireland, to all whom these present letters shall come, greeting. We have inspected the tenor of a certain act before us and our council ... in the office of the privy seal in our council chamber called the Star Chamber in our palace of Westminster made and issued on 24 October, in these words:

In the matter of the complaint of the mayor, aldermen, and commonalty of the town of Nottingham propounded before the king our sovereign lord and his council against Robert Hamson ..., and others, about great riots, excesses, and misgovernings, alleged to have been committed by the said Robert and others.... When the answer of the said Robert [etc.], being personally present, had been given to the said complaint, and the said mayor, aldermen, and commons had made their reply, and all that could be alleged by either party in that matter ..., had

---

[2]   W. H. Stevenson, ed., *Records of the Borough of Nottingham* (London, 1883), 2: 384–6.

been heard and understood, and when great deliberation had been taken thereon by our sovereign lord, then by the advice of his said council, the 24th day of October ... [1471], in the Star Chamber at Westminster, in full council, the king's highness being present, and before him both the parties abovesaid, it was, by the mouth of his chancellor of England, shown, opened, and declared [that Hamson and companions were not to be imprisoned as Nottingham officials had asked, because there was not sufficient proof; but they were each to find surety for good behavior, and to appear again in a year before the king and his council]. ...

And moreover, our said sovereign lord by his own mouth asked and questioned Henry, Lord Grey, then present, whether all the other persons named in the said complaint and articles of the same were his servants and followers, and whether he would bring them in or not to answer; the same Lord Grey then answering our sovereign lord that they were not his servants, and that he could not bring them in to answer. And thereupon our sovereign lord gave the same Lord Grey strict command and injunction that he should not support, favor, nor maintain them ... contrary to his laws henceforth, as he would answer to our said sovereign lord, and upon the pain that would fall thereon.

2.2   Ingulph's Chronicle *(ca. 1475)*[3]

State Papers (document 2.1, for example) are relatively lacking for the late fifteenth century; for many years the explosion of surviving paperwork for the Tudors gave historians the impression that they invented strong, centralized government. One type of source that is relatively plentiful for the Yorkist period but dies out during the Tudor period is the chronicle. *Ingulph's Chronicle* is one of two surviving at a Benedictine abbey in Lincolnshire. It relates the aftermath of an expensive and unpopular invasion of France in 1475, which did nevertheless benefit Edward because the French king agreed to pay him a subsidy to leave. While the humanist revolution in history writing (which sought to understand *why* historical events happened, rather than just recite them) exemplified by Polydore Vergil (see document 2.8) was just around the corner, it should be clear that this late medieval chronicle is no mere list of events, but includes both causes and consequences. Does the author appear to be biased in favor or against Edward IV's reign? According to the chronicle, is Edward IV working from a position of relative strength or weakness in the mid-1470s? Why were people upset about the French campaign? How did Edward maximize his revenue? Were his methods entirely legal?

[Following Edward IV's return from France in 1475], the king [himself] was compelled ..., together with his judges, to make a survey of the kingdom; and no

---

[3]   *Ingulph's Chronicle of the Abbey of Croyland*, trans. H. T. Riley (London, 1854), 473–5.

one, not even his own domestics [servants], did he spare, but instantly had him hanged, if he was found to be guilty of theft or murder. These rigorous sentences being universally carried into execution, public acts of robbery were soon put a stop to for a considerable time. For, if this prudent prince had not manfully put an end to this ... mischief, the number of people complaining of the unfair management of the resources of the kingdom – [after so much] treasure ... [had been seized] from the coffers ... and uselessly consumed [in the invasion] – would have increased to such a degree that no one could have said whose head, among the king's advisers, was in safety ..., especially those, who, induced by friendship for the French king or by his presents, had persuaded the king to make peace. ...

There is no doubt that the king felt his perplexed situation in this matter most deeply at heart, and was by no means ignorant of the condition of his people, and how readily they might be betrayed, in case they should find a leader, to enter into rebellious plans, and conceive a thirst for change. Accordingly, seeing that things had now come to such a pass that from thenceforth he could not dare in his emergencies to ask the assistance of the English people, and finding that ... it was through want of money that the French expedition had in such a short time come to nothing, he [therefore] turned all his thoughts to the question how he might in future collect an amount of treasure worthy of his royal station out of his own substance, and by the exercise of his own energies. Accordingly, having called Parliament together, he resumed possession of nearly all the royal estates, without regard to whom they had been granted, and applied the whole thereof to the support crown expenses. Throughout all the ports of the kingdom he appointed inspectors of the customs, men of remarkable shrewdness, but too hard, according to general report, upon the merchants. The king himself, also, having procured merchant ships, put on board of them the finest wools, cloths, tin, and other productions of the kingdom, and, like a private individual living by trade, exchanged merchandise for merchandise, by means of his factors, among both Italians and Greeks. The revenues of vacant prelacies [bishoprics], which, according to Magna Charta, cannot be sold, he would only part with out of his hands at a stated sum, and on no other terms whatever. He also examined the register and rolls of Chancery, and exacted heavy fines from those whom he found to have intruded and taken possession of estates without prosecuting their rights in form required by law. ... These, and more of a similar nature than can possibly be conceived by a man who is inexperienced in such matters, were his methods of making up a purse; added to which, there was the yearly tribute of £10,000 due from France, together with numerous tenths from the churches, from which the prelates and clergy had been unable to get themselves excused. All these particulars, in the course of a very few years, rendered him an extremely wealthy prince; so much so, that, for collecting vessels of gold and silver, tapestries, and decorations of the most precious nature, both for his palaces and for various churches, and for building castles, colleges, and other distinguished places, and making new acquisitions of lands and possessions, not one of his predecessors was at all able to equal his remarkable achievements.

2.3   *Philippe de Commines*, Memoirs, *on the 1470s (written 1489–96)*[4]

Still another insight into Edward IV's reign is provided by the Burgundian and French diplomat, Philippe de Commines (ca. 1447–ca. 1511). De Commines spent several years in England and met Edward IV. While he composed his *Memoirs* as a self-justification over a decade after he left England, what can we learn from his assessment of Edward's reign? How does his view compare with that provided by documents 2.1 or 2.2?

[The English] king cannot undertake such an exploit [as sending troops to the continent] without assembling his Parliament …, a very just and laudable institution, and on account of this the kings are stronger and better served when they consult Parliament in such matters. When these Estates are assembled, the king declares his intentions and asks for aid from his subjects, because he cannot raise any taxes in England, except for an expedition to France or Scotland or some other comparable cause. They will grant them very willingly and liberally, especially for crossing to France. There is a well-known trick which these kings of England practice when they want to amass money. They pretend they want to attack Scotland and to assemble armies. To raise a large sum of money they pay them for three months and then disband their army and return home, although they have received money for a year. King Edward understood this ruse perfectly, and he often did this.

[handwritten margin note: highlights the difference in how kings rule / highlights England as being low in money and needing to fund through the passion citizens have against enemies]

2.4   *Council of the North Regulations (July 1484)*[5]

In recent years, historians have pointed out that much of the English realm comprised borderlands. This was a problem for the Crown: the borderlands of Wales and the North (along the Scottish border) were farthest from Westminster and thus, not surprisingly, hardest for the English kings to control. One way to assert royal authority was to establish regional royal councils. The following are the articles established by Richard III for the Council in the North. Which group(s) does he seek to regulate? What problems does he seek to solve? As established here, is Yorkist rule in the North arbitrary? Is it personal? Is it bureaucratic?

These articles following be ordained and established by the king's grace to be used and executed by my Lord of Lincoln [John de la Pole, earl of Lincoln

---

[4] P. de Commines, *Memoirs: The Reign of Louis XI, 1461–83*, trans. M. Jones (Harmondsworth, 1972), 225.
[5] A. R. Myers, ed., *English Historical Documents, 1327–1485* (London, 1969, 1996), 558–9, from BL Harleian MS. 433, fol. 264b.

(ca. 1460–87), son of Richard III's sister and his heir apparent after Richard's own son, died in April] and the lords and others of his council in the North parts for his surety and the well-being of the inhabitants of the same.

First, the king wills that no lord nor other person appointed to be of his council, for favor, affection, hate, malice, or bribery, shall speak in the council otherwise than the king's laws and good conscience shall require, but be indifferent and in no way partial, as far as his wit and reason will allow him, in all manner of matters that shall be administered before them....

[The] council shall meet, wholly if it may be, once in the quarter of the year at least, at York, to hear, examine, and order all bills of complaints and others shown there before them, and oftener if the case require.

[The] council shall have authority and power to order and direct [in respect of] all riots, forcible entries, disputes, and other misbehaviors against our laws and peace ... in these parts....

[Our] council, for great riots ... committed in the great lordships or otherwise by any person, shall commit that person to ward in one of our castles near where the riot is committed....

[The] council, as soon as they have knowledge of any assemblies or gatherings made contrary to our laws and peace, [shall arrange] to resist, withstand and punish the same....

[We] will and straitly charge all and each of our officers, true liegemen, and subjects in these north parts to be at all times obedient to the commandments of our council in our name, and duly to execute the same, as they and each of them will eschew our great displeasure and indignation.

Claiming the Throne: Richard III, Henry VIII, and the Pretenders

2.5   *Act Settling the Crown on Richard III and his Descendants (1484)*[6]

What royal line would, in the end, establish its legitimacy? In April 1483 Edward IV undid much of his good work and threw the succession into doubt once more by dying and leaving a 12-year-old heir, Edward, prince of Wales, who briefly succeeded as Edward V. "Briefly," because the brother of the old king and uncle of the new, Richard, duke of Gloucester, soon after asserted his own right against that of his brother's descendants (Edward V and *his* younger brother, Richard, duke of York) to claim the crown as Richard III. What reasons does he give for usurping the throne from Edward V? Why does Richard trash his brother's achievements? How does this account jibe with that in documents 2.1 and 2.2? Is there a coherent argument about good government here, and, if so, what is it?

---

[6]   *Rotuli Parliamentorum ut et Petitiones, et Placita in Parliamento* (London, 1767–7), 6: 240–2.

We consider how that in the time of the reign of King Edward IV lately
deceased, the order of all politic rule was perverted, the laws of God and of
God's church and also the laws of nature and of England, [wherein] every
Englishman is inheritor, broken, subverted, and held in contempt, against all
reason and justice, so that this land was ruled by self-will and pleasure, fear and
dread, all manner of equity and laws laid aside and despised, whereof ensued
many inconveniences and mischiefs, as murders, extortions, and oppressions,
namely, of poor and impotent people, so that no man was sure of his life, land,
livelihood, nor of his wife, daughter, nor servant, every good maiden and
woman standing in dread to be ravished and defouled. …

[handwritten margin note: disgracing Edward as creating problems]

[When] such as [Edward IV] had the rule and governance of this land, delighting
in adulation and flattery and led by sensuality and concupiscence, followed the
counsel of persons insolent, vicious, and of inordinate avarice, despising the
counsel of good, virtuous, and prudent persons, the prosperity of this land daily
decreased, so that felicity was turned to misery, and prosperity into adversity,
and the order of policy, and of the law of God and man, confounded.

2.6 Richard III's Proclamation against Henry, earl of Richmond (June 23, 1485)[7]

Just two years after his somewhat dubious accession, Richard III faced a
challenge by Henry Tudor, earl of Richmond. King Richard issued this proclamation on the eve of battle, at Bosworth, Leicestershire. Who is his
intended audience? What are the charges against the opposing king? Why
should the English support Richard?

King Richard. Greetings. … For as much as the king our sovereign lord has certain
knowledge that Peter, bishop of Exeter; Jasper Tudor, son of Owen Tudor, calling
himself earl of Pembroke; John, late earl of Oxford; and Sir Edward Woodville, with
other diverse [men], his rebels and traitors, disabled and attainted by the authority of
the high court of Parliament, of whom many [have] been known for open murderers,
adulterers, and extortioners, contrary to the pleasure of God and against all truth,
honor, and nature, have forsaken their natural country …, [and] privily [secretly]
departed … into France, and there taking themselves to be under the obedience of the
king's ancient enemy, Charles [VIII, 1483–98], calling himself king of France; and to
abuse and blind the commons of this said realm, the said rebels and traitors have
chosen to be their captain one Henry Tudor, son of Edmund Tudor, son of Owen
Tudor, who of his ambition and insatiable covetousness encroaches and usurps
upon him the name and title of royal estate of this realm of England, whereunto he
has no manner of interest, right, title, or color, as every man well knows; for he is
descended of bastard blood both of the father's side and of the mother's side. For the

---

[7] H. Ellis, *Original Letters Illustrative of English History* (London, 1827), 2nd ser., 1: 162–6.

said Owen the grandfather was bastard born, and his mother was daughter to John, duke of Somerset, son to John, earl of Somerset, son to Dame Katherine Swynford, and of her in double adultery gotten [born]; whereby it evidently [clearly] appears that no title can or may be in him, who fully intends to enter this realm, purposing a conquest. And if he should achieve this false intent and purpose, everyman's life, livelihood, and goods would be in his hands, liberty, and disposition, whereby [w]ould ensue the disinheriting and destruction of all the noble and worshipful blood of this realm for ever, and to the resisting and withstanding of which every true and natural Englishman born must lay to his hands for our surety and welfare.

And to the intent that the said Henry Tudor might the rather achieve his false intent and purpose by the aid, support and assistance of the king's said ancient enemy of France, he has covenanted and bargained with him and all the council of France to give up and release in perpetuity all the right, title, and claim that the kings of England have, had, and ought to have, to the crown and realm of France, together with the duchies of Normandy, Anjou, and Maine, Gascony, and Guienne, the castles and towns of Calais, Guisnes, and Hammes, with the marches appertaining to the same, and sever and exclude the [heraldic] arms of France out of the arms of England for ever. ...

And besides this and the alienation of all these premises into the possession of the king's said ancient enemies, to the greatest destruction, shame, and rebuke that might ever fall to this said land, the said Henry Tudor and others, the king's rebels and traitors aforesaid, have intended at their coming, if they should have the power, to do the most cruel murders, slaughters, and robberies, and dis-inheritances, that ever were seen in any Christian realm.

For the avoidance of these and other incalculable dangers, and to the intent that the king's said rebels, traitors, and enemies may be utterly put from their said malicious and false purpose, and soon discomfited, if they succeeded in landing by force, the king our sovereign lord desires, wills, and commands all and everyone of the natural and true subjects of this his realm to call the foregoing to their minds, and like good and true Englishmen to fortify them-selves with all their powers for the defense of themselves, their wives, their children, and goods and inheritances, against the said malicious purposes and conspiracies which the said ancient enemies have made with the king's said rebels and traitors for the final destruction of this land.

2.7 Henry, earl of Richmond's speech to his army before the Battle of Bosworth Field (August 22, 1485?, pub. 1548)[8]

Compare and contrast Richard's proclamation with Henry's. What are the charges against the opposing king? Why should the English support either claimant? For Henry's speech we have only Hall's *Chronicle* (see above and Plate 2). How might Hall have tailored the speech to fit his overall argument?

[8]   Hall, *Union of the Two Noble and Illustre Famelies*, 3rd year of Richard III, fols. lv(verso)–lvi.

If ever God gave victory to men fighting in a just quarrel, or if He ever aided such as made war for the wealth and tuition [welfare] of their own natural and nutritive country, or if He ever succoured them which adventured their lives for the relief of innocents, suppressing of malefactors and apparent offenders – no doubt, my fellows and friends, but He of his bountiful goodness will this day send us triumphant victory and a lucky journey over our proud enemy and arrogant adversaries. For, if you remember and consider the very cause of our just quarrel, you shall apparently [by appearances, readily] perceive the same to be true, godly, and virtuous. In the which I doubt not but God will rather aid us (yea, and fight for us), than see us vanquished and profligated [put to flight], by such as neither fear Him nor His laws, nor yet regard justice or honesty. Our cause is so just that no enterprise can be of more virtue both by the laws divine and civil; for, what can be a more honest, goodly, or godly quarrel than to fight against a captain being an homicide and murderer of his own blood and progeny [that is, the rumored murders of his nephews, Edward V and Richard, duke of York, and even possibly of his brothers Edward IV and George, duke of Clarence]? – an extreme destroyer of his nobility, and to his and our country and the poor subjects of the same, a deadly mall [*malleus*, "hammer," thus, a destroyer], a fiery brand, and a burden untolerable? Besides him, consider who be of his band and company – such as by murder and untruth committed against their own kin and lineage, yea, against their prince and sovereign lord, have disherited [dispossessed] me and you, and wrongfully detain and usurp our lawful patrimony and lineal inheritance. For he that calleth himself king, keepeth from me the crown and regiment [regimen, government] of this noble realm and country, contrary to all justice and equity. Likewise, his mates and friends occupy your lands, cut down your woods, and destroy your manors, letting your wives and children range abroad for their living: which persons, for their penance and punishment, I doubt not but God, of His goodness, will either deliver into our hands as a great gain and booty, or cause them, being grieved and compuncted with the prick of their corrupt consciences, cowardly to fly and not abide the battle. Besides this, I assure you that there be yonder in that great battle men brought thither for fear and not for love, soldiers by force compelled and not with good-will assembled – persons which desire rather the destruction than the salvation of their master and captain; and finally, a multitude, whereof the most part will be our friends and the least part our enemies. For truly I doubt which is the greater, the malice of the soldiers toward their captain, or the fear of him conceived by his people. For surely this rule is infallible that as ill men daily covet to destroy the good, so God appointeth the good to confound the ill.... [Richard] hath not only murdered his nephew, being his king and sovereign lord, bastarded his noble brethren, and defamed his virtuous and womanly mother, but also compassed all the means and ways that he could invent how to stuprate [violate] his own niece under the pretence of a cloaked matrimony [Richard reportedly intended to marry Princess Elizabeth, his brother's daughter]: which lady I have sworn and promised to take to my mate and wife, as you all know and believe.

2.8   *Polydore Vergil,* Anglica Historia
(written ca. 1513; pub., Latin, 1534)[9]

In the end, it was Henry, duke of Richmond who won the battle of Bosworth Field and the crown on August 22, 1485. Now came the hard part: to establish his rule and line and so end the turmoil of the previous quarter century. The chief commentator on Henry VII's rule was a foreigner whom Henry himself hired as a professional historian, Polydore Vergil (1470?–1555). Although Vergil dedicated his manuscript English history to his patron, he was no apologist and dedicated himself to humanist source criticism and evenhandedness. According to Vergil, what hopes and fears appear to be driving Henry's actions immediately after Bosworth? For which parts of this narrative does Vergil not appear well informed? Might any group have considered Henry's avowed strengths to be weaknesses? Any of his weaknesses strengths?

After Henry had obtained power, from the very start of his reign he then set about quelling the insurrections. Accordingly, before he left Leicester, he despatched Robert Willoughby to Yorkshire with instructions to bring back Edward, the fifteen-year-old earl of Warwick, sole survivor of George duke of Clarence [and so, a Yorkist claimant to the throne] whom Richard had held hitherto in the castle called Sheriff Hutton. For indeed, Henry, not unaware of the mob's natural tendency always to seek changes, was fearful lest, if the boy should escape and given any alteration in circumstances, he might stir up civil discord. Having made for the castle without delay, Robert received the boy from the commander of the place and brought him to London, where the wretch, born to misery, remained in the Tower until his death, as will be recounted elsewhere. Detained in the same fortress was Elizabeth, elder daughter of King Edward, whom Richard had kept unharmed with a view to marriage. To such a marriage the girl had a singular aversion. … She would repeatedly exclaim, saying, "I will not thus be married … with a man who is the enemy of my family." This girl too, attended by noble ladies, was brought to her mother in London. Henry meanwhile made his way to London like a triumphing general, and in the places through which he passed was greeted with the greatest joy by all. Far and wide the people hastened to assemble by the roadside, saluting him as king and filling the length of his journey with laden tables and overflowing goblets. …

After this he summoned a Parliament, as was the custom, in which he might receive the crown by popular consent. His chief care was to regulate well affairs

---

[9]   P. Vergil, *Anglica Historia, A.D. 1485–1537*, ed. D. Hay (London, Camden Society, 74, 1950), 4–5, 143, 145, 147; reproduced by permission of Royal Historical Society.

of state and, in order that the people of England should not be further torn by rival factions, he publicly proclaimed that (as he had already promised) he would take for his wife Elizabeth daughter of King Edward and that he would give complete pardon and forgiveness to all those who swore obedience to his name. Then at length having won the good-will of all men and at the instigation of both nobles and people, he was made king at Westminster on 31 October and called Henry, seventh of that name. These events took place in the year[s 1485 and] 1486. ...

Henry reigned twenty-three years and seven months. He lived for fifty-two years. By his wife Elizabeth he was the father of eight children, four boys, and as many girls. He left three surviving children, an only son Henry prince of Wales, and two daughters, Margaret married to James king of Scotland, and Mary betrothed to Charles prince of Castile. ... His spirit was distinguished, wise, and prudent. ... He had a most pertinacious memory. Withal he was not devoid of scholarship. In government he was shrewd and prudent, so that no one dared to get the better of him through deceit or guile. ... He was most fortunate in war, although he was constitutionally more inclined to peace than to war. He cherished justice above all things; as a result he vigorously punished violence, manslaughter, and every other kind of wickedness whatsoever. Consequently he was greatly regretted on that account by all his subjects, who had been able to conduct their lives peaceably, far removed from the assaults and evil doing of scoundrels. ... But all these virtues were obscured latterly only by avarice, from which ... he suffered. This avarice is surely a bad enough vice in a private individual, whom it forever torments; in a monarch indeed it may be considered the worst vice, since it is harmful to everyone, and distorts those qualities of trustfulness, justice, and integrity by which the state must be governed.

2.9   *Francis Bacon on the character of Henry VII (1622)*[10]

⌐ written under guise of Edwards reign

Vergil's evaluation might be compared with that written a century later by the Jacobean scholar and politician Francis Bacon (1561–1626). Created Viscount St. Alban just before he began his *History of the Reign of King Henry VII*, Bacon was a prominent politician and government official, well versed in monarchical politics as well as the new natural philosophy. How might Henry be considered a new, Renaissance prince? Taking Bacon as your guide, does Henry VII sound like a good king? An effective one? To what degree did his experience and place in history shape his character and public persona? To what extent might his character have shaped that experience?

[10]   F. Bacon, *The Historie of the Raigne of King Henry the Seventh* (London, 1622), 243–6.

He was a prince, sad, serious, and full of thoughts, and secret observations, and full of notes and memorials of his own hand, especially touching persons, as whom to employ, whom to reward, whom to enquire of, whom to beware of, what were the dependencies, what were the factions, and the like; keeping (as it were) a journal of his thoughts. There is to this day a merry tale that his [pet] monkey (set on as it was thought by one of his chamber) tore his principal notebook all to pieces, when by chance it lay forth. Whereat the Court (which liked not those pensive accounts) was almost tickled with sport.

He was indeed full of apprehensions and suspicions. But as he did easily take them, so he did easily check them and master them: whereby they were not dangerous, but troubled himself more than others. It is true, his thoughts were so many, as they could not well always stand together; but that which did good one way, did hurt another. Neither did he at some times weigh them aright in their proportions. Certainly, that rumor which did him so much mischief (that the duke of York should [have] be[en] saved, and [was] alive) [see documents 2.10 and 2.11] was (at the first) of his own nourishing, because he would have more reason not to reign in the right of his wife. He was affable, and both well and fair spoken, and would use strange sweetness and blandishments of words where he desired to effect or persuade any thing that he took to heart. He was rather studious than learned, reading most books that were of any worth, in the French tongue. Yet he understood the Latin, as appeareth in that Cardinal Hadrian and others, who could very well have written French, did use to write to him in Latin.

For his pleasures, there is no news of them. … He did by pleasures, as great princes do by banquets, come and look a little upon them, and turn away. For never prince was more wholly given to his affairs, nor in them more of himself; insomuch as in triumphs of jousts, and tourneys, and balls, and masques (which they then called disguises) he was rather a princely and gentle spectator than seemed much to be delighted.

No doubt, in him as in all men (and most of all in kings) his fortune wrought upon his nature, and his nature upon his fortune. He attained to the crown, not only from a private fortune, which might endow him with moderation, but also from the fortune of an exiled man, which had quickened in him all seeds of observation and industry. And his times being rather prosperous than calm, had raised his confidence by success but almost marred his nature by troubles. His wisdom, by often evading from perils, was turned rather into a dexterity to deliver himself from dangers when they pressed him, than into a Providence to prevent and remove them afar off. …

Yet take him with all his defects, if a man should compare him with the kings his concurrents in France and Spain, he shall find him more *politique* [politically temporizing] than Louis XII of France [1498–1515], and more entire and sincere than Ferdinand of Spain. But if you shall change Louis XII for Louis XI [1461–83], who lived a little before, then the consort is more perfect. For that Louis XI, Ferdinand, and Henry, may be esteemed for the *tres magi* of kings of those ages. To conclude, if this king did no greater matters, it was long of himself; for what he minded, he compassed.

2.10 The Declaration of "Richard IV" (ca. 1497)[11]

> Like his Yorkist predecessors, Henry VII faced threats from pretenders to the throne, such as Perkin Warbeck (ca. 1474–99), a young man who claimed to be Richard, duke of York, Edward V's younger brother, escaped from the Tower of London to reclaim his usurped throne. Compare the argument of "Richard IV" (Perkin) for his legitimacy and the illegitimacy of Henry with similar arguments in Richard III's and Henry's declarations of 1485. What values are appealed to?

Whereas We ["Richard IV," that is Perkin] in our tender age, escaped by God's great might out of the Tower of London, and were secretly conveyed over the sea to divers other countries, there remaining certain years as unknown. The which season it happened one Henry son to Edmond Tydder [Tudor] – earl of Richmond created, son to Owen Tudor of low birth in the country of Wales – to come from France and entered into this our realm, and by subtle false means to obtain the crown of the same unto us of right appertaining: Which Henry is our extreme, and mortal enemy, as soon as he had knowledge of our being alive, imagined, compassed and wrought, all the subtle ways and means he could devise, to our final destruction, insomuch as he has not only falsely surmised us to be a feigned person, giving us nicknames, so abusing your minds; but also to deter and put us from our entry into this our realm.

2.11 Trial and Execution of Perkin Warbeck and Others (November 18–December 4, 1499)[12]

> Henry's response to pretenders – Lambert Simnel (1476/7, d. after 1534), Warbeck, and others – hardened over the course of his reign. Read carefully the trial and execution of Warbeck and other alleged rebels and consider the various actions and statements about their trial and execution. What is the significance of the different methods of executing each prisoner? Would all this be effective theater? If you were in the audience, what might have the most effect on you and why? Was the Tudor regime secure and the Wars of the Roses truly over?

And upon the Monday [November 18] ... sat at the Guildhall of London upon an *Oyer et Determiner* [law court] the mayor, with my lord chief judge, with

---

[11] A. F. Pollard, *The Reign of Henry VII from Contemporary Sources* (London, 1914), 1: 150–5, from BL, Birch MS. 4160.

[12] C. L. Kingsford, ed., *Chronicles of London* (Oxford, 1905), 227–8.

diverse other judges and knights; and there before them was indicted 8 prisoners of the Tower [of London], among the which was Thomas Mashborwth, sometime bowyer [archer] unto King Edward, 2 citizens of the city, that one named Finch, that other Proud, and 6 others, which were servants to M. Digby, marshal of the Tower, intending after the common fame to have slain their said M. [Digby], and to have set at liberty the earl of Warwick and Perkin.

And upon the Tuesday next ensuing was arraigned in the great hall at Westminster the said earl of Warwick, being of the age of 24 years or thereabout; upon whom sat for judge the earl of Oxinford [Oxford], under a cloth of State: where without any process of the law the said earl of Warwick, for treasons by him confessed and done, submitted himself to the king's grace and mercy; and so was there adjudged to be hanged, drawn, and quartered.

And upon the Saturday following next, being Saint Clements day [November 23], was drawn from the Tower unto Tyburn Perkin or Peter Warbeck, and one John a Water, sometime mayor of Cork, as before is said, at which place of execution was ordained a small scaffold, whereupon the said Perkin standing showed to the people there in great multitude being present, that he was a stranger born according unto his former confession; and took it upon his death that he was never the person that he was named for, that is to say the second son of King Edward IV. And that [claim] he was forced to take upon him[self], by the means of the said John a Water and other(s), whereof he asked God and the king of forgiveness; after which confession he took his death meekly, and was there upon the gallows hanged; and with him the said John a Water; And when they were dead, stricken down, and their heads stricken off; and after their bodies brought to the Friars Augustines, and there buried, and their heads set after upon London Bridge.

And upon the Thursday following [November 28], was the earl of Warwick beforesaid brought out of the Tower between two men, and so led unto the scaffold and there beheaded; and after the body with the head laid into a coffin and born again unto the Tower; which execution was done between 2 and 3 of the clock at afternoon. . . .

And at the next tide following the body was conveyed by water unto Byrsam [Bisham Abbey], a place of religion beside Windsor, and there by his ancestors entered and buried.

And upon the Friday next following, being Saint Andrews even [November 29], sat again at the Guildhall the mayor with the chief justice and other judges and knights; before whom was arraigned the forenamed 8 prisoners for life and death, being charged one Quest with 5 prisoners, and that other inquest with 3; of the which said 8 persons, 4 of them named Strangeways, Blewet, Astwood, and long Roger were adjudged to be hanged, drawn and quartered; which judgement was given upon Saint Andrews day [Saturday, November 30], the mayor and the foresaid judges there again sitting.

And upon Wednesday next ensuing was drawn from the Tower unto Tyburn the forenamed Blewet and Astwood, both upon one hurdle; and there hanged, and after beheaded, and their bodies brought unto the Friars Augustines, and there buried; which forenamed Astwood was, in the year [1494] that Richard Chawry was mayor drawn with other transgressors from Westminster unto the Tower Hill there to have been beheaded; whom the king at that season, of his most bounteous grace, pardoned.

Henry VIII and Cardinal Wolsey

2.12   Cardinal Wolsey's Report to Henry VIII on Proceedings in Star Chamber (ca. 1518)[13]

Early in his reign, Henry VIII tended to leave the hard work of government to his chief minister and archbishop of York, Thomas, Cardinal Wolsey (ca. 1473–1530). About 1518, Wolsey, anxious to please his master, wrote to the king on how he used the court of Star Chamber to keep order. Admittedly, the "new law of Star Chamber" was not completely new (compare with document 2.1); what is different about Wolsey's goals and exercise of power from, say, Edward IV's?

Your realm ... was never in such peace nor tranquility; for all this summer I have had neither of riot, felony, nor forcible entry, but that your laws be in every place indifferently ministered. ... Albeit, there hath lately ... been an affray between Piggot, your serjeant, and Sir Andrew Windsor's servants, for the seisin [freehold possession] of a ward whereto both they pretend titles; in the which fray one man was slain. I trust at the next term to learn them the law of the Star Chamber, that they shall ware [take heed] how from thenceforth they shall redress this matter with their hands.

2.13   Venetian Ambassador Sebastian Giustiniani's Report on Cardinal Wolsey (September 10, 1519)[14]

According to the ambassador, what are the bases of the cardinal's power? In what way was Wolsey a centralizing or decentralizing force for governmental power? What is the significance of the long walk to get to Wolsey's audience chamber? Does the ambassador approve or disapprove of the cardinal and his methods?

---

[13]   *Letters and Papers, Foreign and Domestic, of the Reign of Henry VIII* (London, 1864), 2, part 2: 1539, Aug. 1517 or 1518.
[14]   *CSP, Venice* (London, 1867), 2: 560.

The cardinal of York … is of low origin and has two brothers, one of whom holds an untitled benefice, and the other is pushing his fortune. He rules both the king and the entire kingdom. On my first arrival in England he used to say to me, "His majesty will do so and so." Subsequently, by degrees, he forgot himself, and commenced saying, "We shall do so and so." At this present he has reached such a pitch that he says, "I shall do so and so." He is about forty-six years old, very handsome, learned, extremely eloquent, of vast ability and indefatigable. He transacts alone the same business as that which occupies all the magistracies, offices, and councils of Venice, both civil and criminal, and all state affairs are managed by him.

He is pensive, and has the reputation of being extremely just. He favors the people exceedingly, and especially the poor, hearing their suits and seeking to despatch them instantly. He also makes the lawyers plead *gratis* for all poor men.

He is in very great repute, seven times more so than if he were pope. He has a very fine palace [in fact, two: York Place and Hampton Court, both later confiscated by Henry VIII], where one traverses eight rooms before reaching his audience chamber.

2.14   John Skelton, "Why Come Ye Not to Court?" (written 1522, pub. 1568)[15]

Here is another account of Wolsey's power. After circulating "Why Come Ye Not to Court?," Skelton (1460?–1529) attempted to ingratiate himself with Wolsey, and later attacked clergyman Thomas Bilney (see document 3.3 and Plate 3 below) in verse at the behest of Henry VIII. What does Skelton find most objectionable about Wolsey's power? Is his analysis here persuasive? Does no else benefit from it?

> In the Chancery, where he sits,
> But such as he admits,
> None so hardy to speak!
> He saith, "Thou hoddypeak [blockhead],
> Thy learning is too lewd,
> Thy tongue is not well thewd [well-mannered]
> To seek before our Grace!"
> And openly, in that place,
> He rages and he raves,
> And calls them "cankered knaves"!
> Thus royally he doth deal

[15] In *Pithy pleasaunt and profitable workes of maister Skelton, Poete Laureate* (London, 1568), sig. Mii–iv.

Under the King's broad seal;
And in the Chequer he them checks
In the Star Chamber he nods and becks,
And beareth him there so stout
That no man dare rowt!
Duke, earl, baron, nor lord,
But to his sentence must accord;
Whether he be knight or squire
All men must follow his desire. ...
    Why come ye not to court
To which court?
To the King's court,
Or to Hampton Court?
Nay, to the King's court!
The King's court
Should have the excellence
But Hampton Court
Hath the preeminence,
And York's Place,
With my Lord's Grace!
To whose magnificence
Is all the confluence,
Suits and supplications,
Embassades [embassies] of all nations.

2.15 Articles against Cardinal Wolsey, signed by the Lords (December 1, 1529)[16]

[handwritten: would approve / not approve annulment between / Henry VIII and Catherine of Aragon]

In 1529, Wolsey's power came crashing down, in large part because of his inability to solve the King's Great Matter (see Bucholz and Key, chapter 2, and below chapter 3). What other factors might have contributed to Wolsey's fall? How do the charges against him compare with earlier documents? Are they fair? How might he have defended himself? Are his failings political, religious, or personal failings?

*[handwritten right margin: *read reality w caution / kings were able to use their power against those who opposed them — historically known about Henry VIII especially in relation to Anne Boleyn]*

[handwritten: → representative of pope in England] *[handwritten: charged w treason]*

1. For obtaining [papal] legatine authority in England, to the injury of the king's prerogative and the immunity possessed by the crown for 200 years.
2. For making a treaty with the French king for the pope without the king's knowledge, the king not being named therein, and binding the said French king to abide his award if any controversy arose upon it. ...

[handwritten: relevant to rivalry between England and France / grounds for distrust]

[16] *Letters of Henry VIII, 1526–29: Extracts from the Calendar of State Papers of Henry VIII* (London, 2001), 218–23.

4. For having in diverse letters and instructions to foreign parts used the expression, "the king and I"; "I would ye should do thus," and "the king and I give unto you our hearty thanks," using himself more like a fellow to your highness than a subject.

5. For having caused his servants to be sworn only to himself, when it has been the custom for noblemen to swear their households first to be true to the king.

6. For having endangered the king's person in that he, when he knew himself to have the foul and contagious disease of the great pox broken out upon him in diverse places of his body, came daily to your grace [King Henry VIII], rouning [whispering] in your ear and blowing upon your most noble grace with his perilous and infective breath; and when he was healed, he made the king believe that it was only an impostume [swelling] in his head. . . .

8. For making ambassadors come first to him alone, so that it may be suspected he instructed them after his own pleasure, contrary to the king's command. . . .

12. For writing to ambassadors abroad, in his own name and without the king's knowledge, and causing them to write again to him, so as to conceal their information.

13. For discouraging the hospitality kept in religious houses, by taking impositions [bribes] of the heads of those houses for his favor in making abbots and priors and for visitation fees, which is a great cause that there be so many vagabonds, beggars, and thieves.

14. For surveying and relating at increased rents the lands of the [monastic] houses he had suppressed, putting out copyholders or compelling them to pay new fines.

15. For arrogant demeanor in the council chamber, letting no man speak but one or two great personages. . . .

19. For shamefully slandering many good religious houses, by which means he suppressed 30, exceeding even the powers given him in his bull, which enabled him only to suppress houses that had not more than six or seven in them. He then caused offices to be found by untrue verdicts that the religious persons had voluntarily abandoned their houses.

20. For examining matters in chancery after judgement had been given on them by the common law, and compelling parties to restore to the opposite party what they had recovered by execution in the common law. . . .

32. For promoting dissension amongst the nobles. . . .

37. For forbidding persons who had been before him in the Star Chamber to sue to the king for pardon. . . .

40. For stamping the cardinal's hat under the king's arms on the coin of groats made at York. . . .

43. For prohibiting two bishops from visiting the university of Cambridge to prevent the spread of Lutheran heresies.

44. They beg the king to make the cardinal an example.

40

Tudor Revolutions in England, Wales, and Ireland?

2.16   *Act in Restraint of Appeals (24 Hen. VIII, c. 12, 1533)*[17]

The fall of Wolsey and his death in 1530 did not end State centralization. Instead, many historians would argue that new ministers like Thomas Cromwell extended centralization – through the king's assumption of the headship of the Church (1534), through the assimilation of Wales into England (1536), through bureaucratic reform of the central administration, through the Act of Uses (1536), and, ideologically, through a new assertion of kingship. As early as 1515, Henry had declared "[b]y the ordinance and sufferance of God we are king of England, and the kings of England in time past have never had any superior but God alone."[18] The Act in Restraint of Appeals, often ascribed to Cromwell's influence, made the argument for the king's *imperium*, the idea that there is no claim to control over England above that of its monarch and government, more concretely. Who might object to this assertion most? Who is the "exterior person" targeted in the act? On the other hand, what governmental institutions stood to benefit from such a revolutionary change?

Where by diverse sundry old authentic histories and chronicles it is manifestly declared and expressed that this realm of England is an empire, and so hath been accepted in the world, governed by one supreme head and king having the dignity and royal estate of the imperial crown of the same, unto whom a body politic, compact [composed] of all sorts and degrees of people divided in terms and by names of spiritualty and temporalty, be bounden and owe to bear next to God a natural and humble obedience; he being also institute and furnished by the goodness and sufferance of Almighty God with plenary, whole, and entire power, preeminence, authority, prerogative, and jurisdiction to render and yield justice and final determination to all manner of folk resiants [residents] or subjects within this his realm, in all causes, matters, debates, and contentions happening to occur, insurge, or begin within the limits thereof, without restraint or provocation to any foreign princes or potentates of the world; the body spiritual whereof having power when any cause of the law divine happened to come in question or of spiritual learning, then it was declared, interpreted, and showed by that part of the said body politic called the spiritualty, now being usually called the English Church, which always hath been reputed and also found of that sort that both for knowledge, integrity, and sufficiency of number, it hath been always thought and is also at this hour sufficient and meet of itself, without the intermeddling of any

[17]   *SR*, 3: 427–8.
[18]   J. Guy, "Henry VIII and the Praemunire Manoeuvres of 1530–1531," *EHR* 97 (1982): 497, from Huntington Library, Ellesmere MS. 6109, vol. 34/C/49, Nov. 1515.

exterior person or persons, to declare and determine all such doubts and to administer all such offices and duties as to their rooms spiritual doth appertain. For the due administration whereof and to keep them from corruption and sinister affection the king's most noble progenitors, and the antecessors of the nobles of this realm, have sufficiently endowed the said Church both with honor and possessions. And the laws temporal for trial of propriety of lands and goods, and for the conservation of the people of this realm in unity and peace without ravin [robbery] or spoil, was and yet is administered, adjudged, and executed by sundry judges and administers of the other part of the said body politic called the temporalty, and both their authorities and jurisdictions do conjoin together in the due administration of justice the one to help the other. And whereas the king his most noble progenitors, and the Nobility and Commons of this said realm, at diverse and sundry Parliaments as well in the time of King Edward I, Edward III, Richard II, Henry IV, and other noble kings of this realm, made sundry ordinances, laws, statutes, and provisions [the Statutes of Provisors, 1351, and Praemunire, 1353, 1393] for the entire and sure conservation of the prerogatives, liberties, and preeminences of the said imperial crown of this realm, and of the jurisdictions spiritual and temporal of the same, to keep it from the annoyance as well of the see of Rome as from the authority of other foreign potentates attempting the diminution or violation thereof.... And notwithstanding the said good statutes and ordinances made in the time of the king's most noble progenitors in preservation of the authority and prerogative of the said imperial crown as is aforesaid, yet nevertheless since the making of the said good statutes and ordinances diverse and sundry inconveniences and dangers not provided for plainly by the said former acts, statutes, and ordinances have risen and sprung by reason of appeals sued out of this realm to the see of Rome, in causes testamentary, causes of matrimony and divorces, right of tithes, oblations, and obventions, not only to the great inquietation, vexation, trouble, costs, and charges of the king's highness and many of his subjects and resiants in this his realm, but also to the great delay and let to the true and speedy determination of the said causes, for so much as the parties appealing to the said court of Rome most commonly do the same for the delay of justice; and forasmuch as the great distance of way is so far out of this realm, so that the necessary proofs nor the true knowledge of the cause can neither there be so well known nor the witnesses there so well examined as within this realm, so that the parties grieved by means of the said appeals be most times without remedy.

2.17   Act for the Government of Wales
(27 Henry VIII, c. 26, 1536)[19]

Changes in government and religion would lead to a rising in the North in 1536, the Pilgrimage of Grace (see Bucholz and Key, chapter 2, and below

---

[19]   *SR*, 3: 563.

chapter 3). They also might well have provoked a rising in Wales, possibly only prevented by the king's own Welsh descent. In any case, Henry VIII and Cromwell were eager to suppress dissent and the 1536 statute can be read as an effort to squelch such a prospective rising. What problems was it intended to solve? What were the proposed solutions? What is left unanswered by this Act?

An act for laws and justice to be ministered in Wales in like form as it is in this realm. Albeit the dominion, principality, and country of Wales justly and righteously is and ever hath been incorporated, annexed, united, and subject to and under the imperial crown of this realm as a very member and joint of the same, wherefore the king's most royal majesty of … very right is very head, king, lord, and ruler; yet, notwithstanding, because that in the same country, principality, and dominion diverse rights, usages, laws, and customs be far discrepant from the laws and customs of this realm, and also because that the people of the same dominion have and do daily use a speech nothing like nor consonant to the natural mother tongue used within this realm, some rude and ignorant people have made distinction and diversity between the king's subjects of this realm and his subjects of the said dominion … of Wales, whereby great discord … and sedition hath grown between his said subjects. His highness, therefore, of a singular zeal, love, and favor that he beareth towards his subjects of his said dominion of Wales, minding and intending to reduce them to the perfect order, notice, and knowledge of his laws of this his realm, and utterly to extirp[ate] all and singular the sinister uses and customs differing from the same, and to bring his said subjects of this his realm and of his said dominion of Wales to an amicable concord and unity, hath by the deliberate advice, consent, and agreement of the lords spiritual and temporal and the commons in this present Parliament assembled, and by the authority of the same …, established that his said country or dominion of Wales shall be, stand, and continue forever from henceforth incorporated, united, and annexed to and with this his realm of England; and that all and singular person and persons born and to be born in the said … dominion of Wales shall have, enjoy, and inherit all and singular freedoms, liberties, rights, privileges, and laws within this realm and other the king's dominions, as other the king's subjects naturally born within the same have, enjoy, and inherit; and that all and singular person and persons inheritable to any manors, lands, tenements, rents, reversions, services, or other hereditaments which shall descend after the feast of All Saints next coming within the said … dominion of Wales, or within any particular lordship part or parcel of the said … dominion of Wales, shall forever … inherit and be inheritable to the same manors …, [etc.] after the English tenure, without division or partition, and after the form of the laws of this realm of England, and not after any tenure nor after the form of any Welsh laws or customs; and that the laws, ordinances, and statutes of this realm of England forever, and none other laws …, from and after the said feast of All Saints ..., shall be had, used, practiced, and executed in the said ... dominion of Wales and every part thereof in like manner, form, and order as they are and shall be ... executed in this realm.

2.18 *"State of Ireland and Plan for its Reformation"* (1515)[20]

> If there was a revolution in government that occurred between the mid-fifteenth and mid-sixteenth centuries in England or Wales, it might be contrasted with Tudor policy in Ireland. From the twelfth century, the kings of England had been lords of Ireland. But there is little sense of effective *imperium* in the report of 1515. How does Ireland appear to compare with England or Wales in the early sixteenth century?

There be more than 60 countries, called regions in Ireland, inhabited with the king's Irish enemies; some regions as big as a shire, some more, some less ... where reigneth more than 60 chief captains ... and every of the said captains maketh war and peace for himself, and holdeth by sword, and hath imperial jurisdiction within his room, and obeyeth to no other person, English or Irish except only to such persons as may subdue him by the sword.... Also, there is no folk daily subject to the king's laws, but half the county of Uriel (Louth), half the county of Meath, half the county of Dublin, half the county of Kildare.

2.19 *Act for the King of England to be King of Ireland* (33 Hen. VIII, c. 1, 1542)[21]

> Technically, the king of England was the overlord of Ireland, but mere lordship implied subservience to the papacy, as it was Pope Adrian IV (1154–59) who had bestowed the title on Henry II (1154–89). In 1542 Henry VIII and Cromwell changed that by proclaiming the former king of Ireland. To what degree does the 1542 Act echo the Act in Restraint of Appeals? Note that the Act claims that Henry assumed the kingship with the consent of the Irish Parliament. Why was it so important to say this?

Forasmuch as the king our most gracious dread sovereign lord, and his Grace's most noble progenitors, kings of England, have been lords of this land of Ireland, having all manner [of] kingly jurisdiction, power, pre-eminences, and

---

[20]   C. Maxwell, *The Foundations of Modern Ireland: Select Extracts from Sources Illustrating English Rule and Social and Economic Conditions in Ireland in the Sixteenth and Early Seventeenth Century*, part 1, *The Civil Policy of Henry VIII and the Reformation* (London, 1921), 16–7.
[21]   *The Statutes at Large, Passed in the Parliaments Held in Ireland* (Dublin, 1786), 1: 176.

authority royal, belonging or appertaining to the royal estate and majesty of a king, by the name of lords of Ireland. ... [And whereas there] hath been great occasion, that the Irish men and inhabitants within this realm of Ireland have not been so obedient to the king's highness and his most noble progenitors, and to their laws, as they of right and according to their allegiance and bounden duties ought to have been: wherefore at the humble pursuit, petition, and request of the Lords spiritual and temporal, and other the king's loving, faithful, and obedient subjects of this his land of Ireland, and by their full assents, be it enacted, ordained, and established by authority of this present Parliament, that the king's highness, his heirs and successors, kings of England, be always kings of this land of Ireland.

2.20 Submission of Two Ulster Chiefs (August 6 and October 1, 1541)[22]

In 1541, Henry's government sought to increase control in Ireland by the policy of surrender and regrant by which Gaelic clan heads gave up their quasi-independent status as Irish chiefs and accepted new positions as Anglo-Irish nobles. O'Donnell and O'Neill were the most powerful land-lords in the northern part of Ireland. Con O'Neill (1484–1559) was granted the title earl of Tyrone in October 1542. What were the grounds for independence and disobedience before 1541? Why would Gaelic clan chiefs accept these terms? What was in it for them? How are the Irish lords to be integrated into the English nation? Why were names and language such important issues? Could this be the basis of a Tudor Revolution in Ireland as has been argued for England?

Indenture made August 6, 1541, between Sir Anthony St. Leger, Deputy, and the Council and Manus O'Donnell. ...

(1) Manus O'Donnell will recognize and accept the king [Henry VIII] as his liege lord and king.
(2) He will not confederate with the rebels of the king, but persecute them to the utmost of his power.
(3) He will renounce the usurped primacy and authority of the Roman pontiff.
(4) Whenever he shall be called upon by letters of the Lord Deputy and Council, to come to any great hosting, he will come in his own person, with 70 horsemen, 120 kerne [Irish foot-soldier] and as many Scots, or send one of his most powerful men with the same number, for one month at his own expense.

---

[22] *Calendar of the Carew Manuscripts, Preserved in the Archepiscopal Library at Lambeth. 1515–1574*, ed. J. S. Brewer and W. Bullen (London, 1867), 183–4, 198–9.

(5) He will appear in the next great Parliament in Ireland, or send to the same some discreet and trusty person authorized by his writing, sealed with his seal.
(6) He will faithfully perform the articles contained in the king's letters sent to him at the time of his receiving pardon.
(7) He will receive and hold his lands from the king, and take such title as the King shall give him.
(8) He offers to send one of his sons into England, to the presence of his majesty, to be there reared and educated according to English manners.
(9) The lord deputy and Council promise to assist and defend O'Donnell and his heirs against all who injure him or invade his country.

Articles of the submission of Conn O'Neill.

(1) He utterly forsakes the name of O'Neill.
(2) He and his heirs shall use the English habits, "and to their knowledge the English language."
(3) He shall keep and put such of the lands granted to him as are meet for tillage "in manurance and tillage of husbandry," and cause houses to be builded for such persons as shall be necessary for the manurance thereof.
(4) He shall not take, put, or cess [collect] any imposition or charge upon the king's subjects inhabiters of the said lands other than their yearly rent or custom, but such as the deputy shall be content with; nor have any gal-lowglass [specialized soldiers, usually mercenary] or kerne but such as shall stand with the contentation of the deputy and Council.
(5) He shall be obedient to the king's laws, and answer to his writs, precepts and commandments in the Castle of Dublin, or in any other place where his courts shall be kept.
(6) He shall go with the king's deputy to all hostings, "rodes" [responses to hostile invasions], and journeys, with such a company as the Marchers of the county of Dublin do.
(7) He shall not maintain or succor any of the king's enemies, rebels, or traitors.
(8) He shall hold his lands by whole knight's fees.

HISTORIANS' DEBATES

How noteworthy were Edward IV and his achievements? Were the Wars of the Roses a period of innovation and centralization, or of status quo, or even decay?

Essay by C. Ross in *Fifteenth-Century England, 1399–1509: Studies in Politics and Society*, ed. S. B. Chrimes, C. D. Ross, and R. A. Griffiths (Manchester, 1972); K. Dockray, "Edward IV: Playboy or Politician?," *The Ricardian* 10 (1995); C. Carpenter, *The Wars of the Roses: Politics and the Constitution in England, c. 1437–1509* (Cambridge, 1997), chs. 8–9; D. R. Starkey, "From Feud to Faction:

English Politics *c.* 1450–1550," *HT* 32, 11 (1982); A. J. Pollard, "New Monarchy Renovated?: England, 1461–1509," *Medieval History* 2, 1 (1992); *idem,* "Fifteenth-Century Politics and the Wars of the Roses," *The Historian* [London] 57 (1998); G. Harriss, "Political Society and the Growth of Government in Late Medieval England," *P & P* 138 (1993).

Was Henry VII the first modern or the last medieval king?

S. Gunn, "Henry VII in Context: Problems and Possibilities," *History* 92, 307 (2007); M. Bush, "Tax Reform and Rebellion in Early Tudor England," *History* 76 (1991); J. P. Cooper, "Retainers in Tudor England," in *Land, Men and Beliefs: Studies in Early-Modern History*, ed. G. E. Aylmer and J. S. Morrill (Hambledon, 1983); S. Anglo, "Ill of the Dead: The Posthumous Reputation of Henry VII," *Renaissance Studies* 1, 1 (1987).

Was Tudor centralization innovative?; who was at the helm?

G. R. Elton, "King or Minister?: the Man behind the Henrician Reformation," *History* 39 (1954); P. Williams, Elton, and G. L. Harriss debate the Henrician Revolution in *P & P* 25 (1963), 29 (1964), and 31–2 (1965); D. Starkey, "After the Revolution," in *Revolution Reassessed: Revisions in the History of Tudor Government and Administration,* ed. C. Coleman and Starkey (Oxford, 1986); G. W. Bernard, "Elton's Cromwell," *History* 83 (1998); *idem,* "The Tyranny of Henry VIII," in *Authority and Consent in Tudor England: Essays Presented to C. S. L. Davies*, ed. Bernard and S. J. Gunn (Aldershot, 2002); S. Ellis, "A Crisis of the Aristocracy?: Frontiers and Noble Power in the Early Tudor State," in *The Tudor Monarchy*, ed. J. Guy (London, 1997); *idem,* "Crown, Community and Government in the English Territories, 1450–1575," *History* 71 (1986); J. A. Guy, "Thomas Wolsey, Thomas Cromwell and the Reform of Henrician Government," in *The Reign of Henry VIII*, ed. D. MacCulloch (1995); *idem,* essays in his *Tudor Monarchy* (London, 1997); "The Eltonian Legacy," *TRHS* 6th ser., 7 (1997), esp. articles by C. S. L. Davies and S. Adams.

How revolutionary was the Tudor court?

D. Starkey, "Which Age of Reform?," in *Revolution Reassessed*; *idem,* "Introduction: Court History in Perspective," in *The English Court: from the Wars of the Roses to the Civil War*, ed. Starkey, *et. al.* (London, 1987); Elton's essay on the Tudor court, *TRHS* 5th ser., 26 (1976); debate between Elton and Starkey, *HJ* 31 (1988); G. Walker, "Henry VIII and the Invention of the Royal Court," *HT* 47, 2 (1997); B. J. Harris, "Women and Politics in Early Tudor England," *HJ* 33, 2 (1990); R. Warnicke, "The Court," in *A Companion to Tudor Britain*, ed. R. Tittler and N. Jones (Oxford, 2004); E. Ives, "Henry VIII: the Political Perspectives," in MacCulloch, *Reign of Henry VIII*.

ADDITIONAL SOURCE COLLECTIONS

I. Arthurson, comp., *Documents of the reign of Henry VII* (Cambridge, 1984).

N. Davis, *Paston Letters and Papers of the Fifteenth Century* (Oxford, 1971–76), vols. 1–2.

K. Dockray, ed., *Edward IV: A Sourcebook* (Stroud, Glos., 1999).

K. Dockray, ed., *Richard III: A Source Book* (Stroud, Glos., 1997).

S. Doran, *England and Europe, 1485–1603*, 2nd ed. (London, 1996).

G. R. Elton, ed., *The Tudor Constitution: Documents and Commentary*, 2nd ed. (Cambridge, 1968, 1982).

M. Levine, *Tudor Dynastic Problems, 1460–1571* (London, 1973).

M. D. Palmer, *Henry VIII*, 2nd ed. (London, 1983).

A. F. Pollard, *The Reign of Henry VII from Contemporary Sources* (London, 1914), vol. 1.

J. R. Tanner, ed., *Tudor Constitutional Documents, A.D. 1485–1603, with a Historical Commentary* (Cambridge, 1922).

C. H. Williams, ed., *English Historical Documents, 1485–1558* (London, 1967).

CHAPTER THREE

Religious Reformations

Arguably, the most dramatic series of events of the English sixteenth century – and the most controversial among historians – was the Reformation. The drama should be apparent in the following selections as we see clergy, statesmen, reformers, martyrs, and simple parishioners wrestle with the challenge of Reformation and Counter-Reformation. The major points of contention among historians have been whether the English people were happy with their Church prior to the Reformation, and what proportion of the population committed either to Reformation or to maintenance of the Old Church once key changes began in the 1530s. Put another way, historians are divided as to whether they believe the major impetus for reform came from above or below, and whether the Reformation came quickly (implying that the people wanted it) or was long resisted. This much is certain: in 1533, Henry divorced Catherine of Aragon (1485–1536), prohibited her from appealing to Rome (see document 2.16 above), and married Anne Boleyn (ca. 1500–36). In 1534, the Act of Supremacy declared him "the supreme head of the Church of England." In 1536, another Act extinguished "the pretended power and usurped authority of the bishop of Rome, by some called the pope," in England.[1] But who really wanted these changes and who noticed (that is, did the changes affect parochial life)? The English Church and people experienced many further changes during Henry's reign and those of his children over the next three decades (to refresh your knowledge of these reformations and counter-reformations, see Bucholz and Key, chapters 2–5). What was their impact? For this chapter, ask:

- What aspect of the religion question is most important for each author?
- How do religious matters intersect with political, economic, and cultural ones, or even with the Great Chain of Being?
- For whom or what social group does each author speak?

---

[1] *SR*, 3: 492 (26 Hen. VIII, c. 1), 663 (28 Hen. VIII, c. 10).

The Old Church Remembered, Criticized, and Defended

3.1 *"The State of Melford Church ... as I, Roger Martyn, Did Know It" (ca. late sixteenth century)*[2]

What was the Church like on the eve of the Reformation? Historians often rely on recollections of late medieval parish life like that of Roger Martyn (ca. 1527–1615): after decades of religious turmoil, some 50 to 75 years after the practices he describes were abolished, he remembered fondly what religious life was like in the early-sixteenth-century Suffolk village of his boyhood. What was important to him about that life? What was the nature of his spirituality? Why might Church ritual and theatricality be especially appropriate in a farming community? Did such rituals promote community, hierarchy, or both? Does Martyn's account suggest that many villagers engaged in the religious rituals described?; that is, how active was the laity in the pre-Reformation Church?

At the back of the high altar in the said church there was a goodly mount, made of one great tree, and set up to the foot of the window there, carved very artificially with the story of Christ's passion, representing the horsemen with their swords and the footmen, etc., as they used Christ on the mount of Calvary, all being fair gilt, and lively and beautifully set forth. To cover and keep clean all the which, there were very fair and painted boards, made to shut to, which were opened upon high and solemn feast days, which then was a very beautiful show. Which painted boards were set up again in Queen Mary's time [1553–58]....

There was also ... at the back of the altar, a table with a crucifix on it, with the two thieves hanging, on every side one, which is in my house decayed; and the same I hope my heirs will repair and restore again one day....

Upon Palm Sunday the blessed sacrament was carried in procession about the churchyard under a fair canopy borne by four yeomen. The procession coming to the church gate went westward, and they with the blessed sacrament went eastward; and when the procession came against the door of Mr. Clopton's aisle, they with the blessed sacrament, and with a little bell and singing, approached at the east end of Our Lady's chapel, at which time a boy with a thing in his hand pointed to it, signifying a prophet as I think, sang standing on the turret ..., *Ecce Rex tuns venit* [Behold your king comes], etc., and then all did kneel down, and then rising up went and met the sacrament, and so then went singing together into the church. And coming near the porch, a boy or one of the clerks did cast over among the boys flowers and singing cakes, etc.

---

[2] W. Parker, *The History of Long Melford* (London, 1873), 70–3, from Norfolk RO, COL 8/3/1–10, T 129E.

On Corpus Christi day [Thursday after Sunday after Pentecost] they went likewise with the blessed sacrament in procession about the church green in copes [an outer vestment], and I think also they went in procession on St. Mark's day [April 25] about the said green, with hand-bells ringing before them, as they did about the bounds of the town in Rogation week [Monday through Wednesday after Ascension Day], on the Monday one way, on the Tuesday another way, on the Wednesday another way, praying for rain or fair weather as the time required; having a drinking and a dinner there upon Monday, being fast day; and Tuesday being a fish day [when Christians were required to abstain from meat] they had a breakfast with butter and cheese, etc., at the parsonage, and a drinking at Mr. Clopton's by Kentwell, at his manor of Lutons, near the ponds in the park, where there was a little chapel, I think of St. Anne, for that was their longest perambulation. Upon Wednesday being fasting day they had a drinking at Melford Hall. All the choir dined there, three times in the year at least: *viz.* St. Stephen's day [December 26], mid-Lent Sunday, and I think upon Easter Monday. On St. James's day [July 25?], mass being sung then by note, and the organs going in St. James's chapel (which were brought into my house with the clock and bell that stood there, and the organs that stood upon the rood loft) that was then a little from the road, which chapel had been maintained by my ancestors; and therefore I will that my heirs, when time serve, shall repair, place there, and maintain all these things again. ...

On St. James's eve there was a bonfire, and a tub of ale and bread then given to the poor, and before my door there was made three other bonfires, *viz.* on Midsummer eve [eve before June 24], on the eve of St. Peter and St. Paul [eve before June 29], when they had the like drinkings, and on St. Thomas's eve [eve before December 29], on which, if it fell not on the fish day, they had some long pies of mutton, and pease cods, set out upon boards, with the aforesaid quantity of bread and ale. And in all these bonfires, some of the friends and more civil poor neighbors were called in, and sat at the board with my grandfather, who had at the lighting of the bonfires wax tapers with balls of wax, yellow and green, set up all the breadth of the hall, lighted then and burning there before the image of St. John the Baptist. And after they were put out, a watch candle was lighted, and set in the midst of the said hall upon the pavement, burning all night.

3.2 Colet's Convocation Sermon, St. Paul's, London (Latin orig., pub. 1511; trans., 1531?)[3]

Martyn's warm memories notwithstanding, the pre-Reformation Church had its critics. On February 6, 1510 the humanist dean of St. Paul's, John Colet (1467–1519), preached at the Convocation of English clerics summoned to

---

[3] *The Sermon of Doctor Colete made to the Convocacion at Paulis* (English trans. of Colet's *Oratio habita*, n.p., n.d., 1531?), unpag.

discuss how to suppress heresy. Instead, he attacked his audience for their vena-
lity and worldliness. According to Colet, what are the problems of the Church?
(Compare with Starkey's diagnosis, document 1.7 above.) Who is to blame
for them? Can they be solved? Do Colet and other critics below really refute the
positive view of parochial religious life portrayed by Martyn (document 3.1)?
Alternately, did the "secular evils" he describes really affect everyday parochial life? Might both pictures of the pre-Reformation Church be accurate?

How much greediness and appetite of honor and dignity is nowadays in men of
the Church? How run they, yea, almost out of breath, from one benefice to
another; from the less to the more, from the lower to the higher? ... The second
secular evil is carnal concupiscence. Hath not this vice so grown and waxen in
the Church as a flood of their lust, so that there is nothing looked for more
diligently in this most busy time of the most part of priests than that that doth
delight and please the senses? They give themselves to feasts and banqueting;
they spend themselves in vain babbling; they give themselves to sports and plays;
they apply themselves to hunting and hawking; they drown themselves in the
delights of this world. ... Covetousness is the third secular evil, the which Saint
John the apostle calleth concupiscence of the eyes. ... This abominable pestilence
hath so entered in the mind almost of all priests, and so hath blinded the eyes of
the mind, that we are blind to all things but only unto those which seem to bring
unto us some gains. For what other thing seek we nowadays in the Church than
fat benefices and high promotions? Yea, and in the same promotions, of what
other thing do we pass upon than of our tithes and rents? ... Of thee, all the
suing for tithes, for offering, for mortuaries, for dilapidations, by the right and
title of the Church. ... The fourth secular evil that spotteth and maketh ill
favored the face of the Church, is the continual secular occupation, wherein
priests and bishops nowadays doth busy themselves, the servants rather of men
than of God; the warriors rather of this world than of Christ.

3.3   *Confession of John Pykas of Colchester (March 7, 1527)*[4]

The Church did not take critics lightly; instead, it often banished them from
the Church as heretics. Henry VII and Henry VIII either burnt or otherwise
persecuted Lollards and other late medieval heretics with enthusiasm. While
most Lollards pre-date the Lutheran Reformation, John Pykas, who confessed before a bishop's court in London, appears to have been a latter-day
Lollard. Why was the bishop's court so concerned about him? Were his

---

[4]   J. Strype, *Ecclesiastical Memorials: relating chiefly to Religion, and the Reformation of it, and the
Emergencies of the Church of England, under King Henry VIII, King Edward VI, and Queen Mary I*
(Oxford, 1822), 1.i: 121–3.

ideas "Protestant"? (Admittedly, the term would not become common in England until the 1550s.) How would Pykas react to Martyn's views on proper religious expression (document 3.1)? How might everyday life have changed if Pykas's ideas had been put into practice?

That about a five years last past, at a certain time, his mother, then dwelling in Bury, sent for him; and moved him that he should not believe in the sacraments of the Church, for that was not the right way. And then she delivered to this respondent one book of Paul's Epistles in English; and bid him live after the manner and way of the said Epistles and Gospels, and not after the way that the Church doth teach. Also, about a two years last past, he bought in Colchester, of [from] a Lombard [a North Italian, probably a banker] of London, a New Testament in English, and paid for it four shillings. Which New Testament he kept, and read it thoroughly many times. And afterward, when he heard that the said New Testaments were forbaden, that no man should keep them, he delivered it and the book of Paul's Epistles to his mother again. And so in continuance of time, by the instruction of his mother, and by reading of the said books, he fell into these errors and heresies against the sacrament of the altar; that he thought that in the sacrament of the altar, after the words of consecration, not the *very body* of Christ, but only *bread* and *wine*.

Which heresy he hath diverse time spoken and taught; not only in the house of Thomas Matthew, in the presence of the said Matthew's wife, William Pykas, and Marion Westden, daughter to Matthew's wife; but also in the houses and presences of John Thompson, fletcher [maker of bows and arrows]; Dorothy Lane, Robert Best, Mistress Swain, John Girling; John Bradley, blacksmith, and his wife; Thomas Parker, weaver; Margaret Bowgas, the wife of Thomas Bowgas; Mistress Cambridge, widow, of the town of Colchester: and also in the house and presence of John Hubbert, of East Donyland; Robert Bate, of the same; Richard Collins, alias Jonson, weaver of Boxstead; John Wiley, of Horkesley, weaver. Which all and singular persons, often and many times have had communication of the said articles with him ... and did affirm them to be of truth....

Also he saith, that he hath taught, rehearsed, and affirmed, before all the said persons, and in their houses at sundry times, against the sacrament of Baptism, saying that there should be no such things: for there is no baptism, but of the Holy Ghost.... Also he saith, that he hath in the places and presence aforesaid, spoken against the sacrament of confession, saying, that it was sufficient for a man that had offended to show his sins privily to God, without confession made to a priest. Yet notwithstanding this respondent hath yearly been confessed ..., but for no other cause, but that people should not wonder upon him.

Also he saith, that he hath heard diverse preachers preach, and especially Mr. Bylney [Thomas Bilney, censured in 1527 and executed as a relapsed heretic in 1531, see Plate 3] preach at Ipswich, that it was but folly for a man to go on pilgrimages to saints; for they be but stocks and stones; for they cannot speak to a man, nor do him any good. And also that men should pray only to God, and

Plate 3 Thomas Bilney ejected from the pulpit. (Source: J. Foxe, *Acts and Monuments of these Latter and Perilous Days, Touching Matters of the Church*, 1563, woodcut, © British Library.)

Depicted is Bilney's ejection in 1527; he was executed as a relapsed heretic in 1531 (see document 3.3). What does the pulpit represent in Protestant ideology? Compare Bilney's ejectors with his audience in this woodcut. Foxe's book is famous for portraying the Marian martyrs, although this clearly happened under Henry VIII, just before the Henrician Reformation. How are these the "latter and perilous days" for Foxe (relate to the Book of Revelation)?

to no saints. For saints can hear no man's prayer, for they are but servants. Which after this respondent heard preached, he did publish and declare it to diverse persons, and set it forward as much as in him was. Moreover he saith, that Mr. Bylney's sermon was most ghostly [spiritual], and made best for his purpose and opinions, as any that ever he heard in his life. ...

Also he confesses, that he hath spoken, rehearsed, and affirmed, in the presence and places aforesaid, and diverse other more; against pardons, saying and affirming, that pardons [indulgences] granted by the pope, or other men of the Church, are of no effect. For they have no authority to grant them. ...

Farther, he saith, that he hath now in his custody [several religious] books ..., which he had of a friar of Colchester: also a book ... which he had of old Father Hacker, alias Ebbe. Also he had the copy of a book ..., of his brother William Pykas. ... [Witnessed] by me John Pekas, of Colchester.

Henry VIII's Great Matter

3.4   Henry VIII to Anne Boleyn (n.d., ca. July 1528)[5]

The likes of Pykas alone could never have made a Reformation without the king. Early in his reign, Henry VIII was a staunchly orthodox Catholic, famously penning *Assertio Septem Sacramentorum* (*Defense of the Seven Sacraments*, 1522) against Martin Luther's *Babylonian Captivity of the Church*. As long as the king opposed Luther, there was little chance that English reformers would amount to anything more than a cabal of vocal but powerless intellectuals haunting Cambridge taverns. But by the late 1520s Henry was starting to question not only his marriage, but the Church that had sanctioned it, as will be obvious from the following love note to Anne Boleyn. The book Henry mentions was a treatise he was composing on the unlawfulness in Scripture of his marriage to his dead brother's wife, Catherine of Aragon, a marriage which had not produced the son and heir he desired. To judge from the letter, was Henry's interest in Anne more physical, emotional, and/or intellectual?

Mine own sweetheart, this shall be to advertise you of the great elengeness [loneliness] that I find here since your departing.... I am right well comforted in so much that my book maketh substantially for my matter; in looking whereof I have spent above four hours this day, which caused me to write the shorter letter to you at this time, because of some pain in my head; wishing myself (especially an evening) in my sweetheart's arms, whose pretty duckys [dugs, breasts] I trust shortly to cusse [kiss].

3.5–3.6   Cardinal Campeggio's letters on "the King's Great Matter"

Henry's decision to press forward with "the King's Great Matter" by pressuring the pope for an annulment, and intimidating his own clergy for support – ultimately, by employing his Parliament in an arguably revolutionary way – opened up religious debate and gave former heresies an airing in his kingdom (see Bucholz and Key, chapter 3). This, along with Henry's questioning of the papal power to grant the dispensation which made the marriage possible, alarmed the Church hierarchy. What do Lorenzo, Cardinal Campeggio's (1471/2–1539) letters of 1528 (document 3.5) and 1529 (document 3.6) reveal of those anxieties? What has changed between the dates of the two

---

[5]   *The Harleian Miscellany* (London, 1809), 3: 60.

letters? What are the bases for Henry's arguments? What are the bases for those of the papal envoy? How does Queen Catherine's position complicate matters? What threats to the Church does Campeggio relate in the later letter? Which are made by Henry? Does Campeggio offer counter-threats?

3.5 Cardinal Campeggio, Papal Legate in England, to Jacobo, Cardinal Salviati, secretary to Pope Clement VII (October 25, 1528)[6]

The king visited me privately, and we remained together alone for about four hours, discussing only two things. First, I exhorted him not to attempt this matter, in order to confirm and clear his conscience, to establish the succession of the kingdom and to avoid scandals; and that if he had any scruple, he could have a new dispensation.

In the second place, we disputed whether the prohibition [in Scripture, against marrying his brother's widow] existed in the Divine Law, or whether the pope could grant a dispensation; and if he could, whether the dispensation would be valid. His majesty has so diligently studied this matter that I believe in this case he is a great theologian and jurist. He said most plainly that he wanted nothing else than a declaration whether the marriage is valid or not; he himself always presupposing the invalidity; and I believe that an angel descending from Heaven would be unable to persuade him otherwise.

We then discussed a proposal for persuading the queen to enter some religious house. With this he was extremely pleased, and indeed there are good reasons for it. In all other matters the king is determined to allow her whatever she demands, and especially to settle the succession on her daughter in the event of his having no male heirs by another marriage. It was concluded that I and the cardinal [Wolsey] should speak to the queen about this on the day following.

Being conveyed in a boat by the cardinal we went on Saturday 24th to execute this mission. The cardinal and I conversed alone with the queen about two hours. Her majesty replied to us that she knew the sincerity of her own conscience; and that she wished to die in the Holy Faith and in accordance with the commands of God and the Holy Church and she wished to declare her conscience only to Our Lord, and that for the present she would give no other reply.

3.6 Campeggio at London to Cardinal Sanga, secretary to Pope Clement VII (April 3, 1529)[7]

During these holy days [Easter week] certain Lutheran books, in English, of an evil sort, have been circulated in the king's court. As yet I have been unable to obtain

---

[6] *Letters of Henry VIII, 1526–29: Extracts from the Calendar of State Papers of Henry VIII* (London, 2001), 62–3, from *Letters and Papers Foreign and Domestic, of the Reign of Henry VIII* (London, 1875), 4: ccccx–xi.
[7] *Letters of Henry VIII*, 107–8.

one, but I will endeavor to do so. I understand that by this book the Lutherans promise to abrogate all the heresies affecting the articles of the Faith, and to believe according to the divine law, provided that this king, with the most Christian king [of France], will undertake to reduce the ecclesiastical state to the condition of the primitive Church, taking from it all its temporalities [lands and goods]. I told the king that this was the devil dressed in angel's clothing, in order that he might the more easily deceive, and that their object was to seize the property of the Church; nor could any one promise the abrogation of so much heresy as now largely pervades the people. I represented that by councils and theologians it had been determined that the Church justly held her temporal goods. His majesty remarked that these Lutherans say that those decisions were arrived at by ecclesiastics, insinuating that now it is necessary for the laity to interpose. In reply I adduced various reasons, partly theological and partly temporal, telling him that this would be directly against his interests, for, as matters now stood, he obtained large sums of money; but if the laity had the goods of the Church this would no longer be the case, and they would probably grow rich and rebellious. The king also remarked that these men allege that the ecclesiastics, and especially the court of Rome, live very wickedly, and that we have erred in many things from the divine law. I replied that I would allow there were sins in Rome and in the court, because we are but men, but the Holy See had not deviated a jot from the true Faith. Finally, his majesty assured me of his good will, and that he had been and always would remain a good Christian, but that he had desired to communicate to me what had been told him by others; and if I wished to write to Rome, he was content, provided I did not state that I had heard it from his own mouth.

The Cardinal Wolsey was present, and after our departure thanked and commended me for my good offices.

The New Church Established

3.7   Edward Hall, "The Opening of the Reformation Parliament" (November 3–December 17, 1529, pub. 1548)[8]

Lollard-style anticlericalism, Lutheran theological reforms, and Henry's desire for a new, legitimate heir came together in the Reformation Parliament (1529–36). Edward Hall (see chapter 2 above) describes the beginning of that parliament. Is Hall, who sat in the Commons, a reliable reporter? Does he take a side? Were the members of the Commons Protestant? What was *their* agenda? What about Henry? Were his motives, as conveyed by Lord Chancellor More, stated honestly?

---

[8]   *Hall's Chronicle; Containing the History of England, During the Reign of Henry the Fourth … to the End of the Reign of Henry the Eighth…. Carefully Collated with the Editions of 1548 and 1550* (London, 1809), 764–8.

According to the summons the king of England began his high court of Parliament the third day of November. On which day he came by water to his p[a]lace of Bridewell, and there he and his nobles put on their robes of Parliament, and so came to the Blackfriars church, where a Mass of the Holy Ghost was solemnly sung by the King's Chapel, and after the Mass, the king with all the Lords of the Parliament and Commons which were summoned to appear at that day came into the parliament chamber, where the king sat in his throne or seat royal, and Sir Thomas More his chancellor standing on the right hand of the king behind the bar, made an eloquent oration, declaring that like as a good shepherd which not only keepeth and attendeth well his sheep, but also foreseeth and provideth for all things, which either may be hurtful or noisome to his flock, or may preserve and defend the same against all perils that may chance to come, so the king which was the shepherd, ruler, and governor of his realm vigilantly foreseeing things to come considered how diverse laws before this time were made now by long continuance of time and mutation of things, very insufficient and imperfect, and also by the frail condition of man, diverse new enormities were sprung amongst the people, for the which no law was yet made to reform the same, which was the very cause why at that time the king had summoned his high court of Parliament....

When the Commons were assembled in the nether [lower] house, they began to commune of their griefs wherewith the spiritualty [clergy] had before time grievously oppressed them ..., and in especial they were sore moved with six great causes.

The first for the excess fines, which the ordinaries [bishops, religious officials] took for probate of testaments [wills]....

The second cause was the great polling and extreme exaction [taxation], which the spiritual men used in taking of corpse presents or mortuaries; for the children of the defunct should all die for hunger and go a-begging rather than they would of charity give to them the sely [filly] cow which the dead man ought if he had but only one; such was the charity then.

The third cause was that priests being surveyors, stewards, and officers to bishops, abbots, and other spiritual heads, had and occupied farms, granges, and grazing in every country, so that the poor husbandman could have nothing but of them, and yet for that they should pay dearly....

The fourth cause was that ... spiritual men ... bought and sold wool, cloth, and all manner of merchandise....

The fifth cause was because that spiritual persons promoted to great benefices, and having there living of their flock, were living in the court in lords' houses ...; so that for lack of residence both the poor of the parish lacked refreshing, and universally all the parishioners lacked preaching and true instruction of God's word....

The sixth cause was to see one priest being little learned to have ten or twelve benefices and to be resident on none, and to know many well learned scholars in the university which were able to preach and teach, to have neither benefice nor exhibition.

These things before this time might in nowise be touched nor yet talked of by no man except he would be made an heretic, or lose all that he had, for the bishops were chancellors, and had all the rule about the king. ...

But now when God had illuminated the eyes of the king, and that their subtle doings was once espied: then men began charitably to desire a reformation, and so at this Parliament men began to shew their grudges.

Whereupon the burgesses of the Parliament appointed such as were learned in the law, being of the common house, to draw one bill of the probates of testaments [wills], another for mortuaries, and the third for non-residence, pluralities, and taking of farms by spiritual men. ...

The king ... caused two new bills to be made indifferently, both for the probate of testaments and mortuaries, which bills were so reasonable that the spiritual lords assented to them although they were sore against their minds, and in especial the probate of testaments sore displeased the bishops, and the mortuaries sore displeased the parsons and vicars.

3.8   Answer of the Ordinaries (1532)[9]

In 1532, the Commons petitioned the king, charging the ordinaries (bishops) with a wide array of offenses. These ranged from the usual money grubbing to too many Holy Days. The bishops submitted to the king a spirited reply to the Commons' charges beginning with the first. What was the charge? How was it related to the Protestant Reformation? To the Tudor revolution in government (see chapter 2)? What is the bishops' argument? Why did it infuriate Henry?

And where, after the general preface of the said supplication [of Parliament in 1532, to which the clerics were responding], your grace's Commons descend to special particular griefs, and first report [charge] that the clergy of this your realm, being your highness's subjects, in their convocations by them holden within this your realm, have made and daily make diverse factions of laws concerning temporal things, and some of them be repugnant to the laws and statutes of your realm, not having nor requiring your most royal assent to the same laws so by them made, neither any assent or knowledge of your lay subjects is had to the same, neither to them published and known in their mother tongue, albeit diverse and sundry of the said laws extend, in certain causes, to your excellent person, your liberty, and prerogative royal ..., [etc.]

To this article we say that ... we repute and take our authority of making of laws to be grounded upon the Scripture of God and the determination of Holy Church. ...

[9]   H. Gee and W. J. Hardy, eds., *Documents Illustrative of English Church History* (London, 1896), 154–8, from TNA, SP Henry VIII, v, 1016 (5).

And as concerning the requiring of your highness's royal assent to the authorizing of such laws as have been by our predecessors, or shall be made by us, in such points and articles as we have by good authority to rule and order by provisions and laws; we, knowing your highness's wisdom, virtue, and learning, nothing doubt but that the same perceiveth how the granting thereunto dependeth not upon our will and liberty, and that we, your most humble subjects, may not submit the execution of our charges and duty, certainly prescribed by God, to your highness's assent; although, of very deed, the same is most worthy for your most princely and excellent virtues, not only to give your royal assent, but also to devise and command what we should, for good order and manners, by statutes and laws, provide in the Church. ...

3.9   Submission of the Clergy (May 15, 1532)[10]

Henry reacted angrily to the Answer of the Ordinaries, saying that the bishops "be but half our subjects, yea, and scarce our subjects."[11] Why? Fearing worse, on May 15, 1532, they submitted. Compare this document with documents 3.8, and 2.16 above on the role of the monarch and royal prerogative. What has changed?

[We] offer and promise *in verbo sacerdotii* [on their sacred word] here unto your highness, submitting ourselves most humbly to the same, that we will never from henceforth presume to attempt, allege, claim ..., or to enact, promulge, or execute any canons, constitution or ordinances provincial, or by any other name whatsoever they may be called in our Convocation in time coming ..., unless your highness by your royal assent shall license us to make promulge, and execute the same, and thereto give your most royal assent and authority.

3.10   Pontefract Articles (December 2–4, 1536)[12]

Despite this high drama, it was only with the Dissolution of the Monasteries that the Reformation began to affect the world of most English men and women. In 1535, Thomas Cromwell, now Henry's vice-gerent of the Church, sent out a commission to investigate the practices and the wealth of the religious houses. The government dissolved the lesser monasteries in 1536, followed by the greater in 1539, and seized their properties. Because monasteries were traditionally supposed to provide charity and medical care, these actions were not well received. In the autumn of 1536, popular complaints

---

[10]   N. Pocock, *Records of the Reformation: The Divorce, 1527–33* (Oxford, 1870), 2: 257–8.
[11]   *Hall's Chronicle*, 788.
[12]   *Letters and Papers ... of the Reign of Henry VIII* (London, 1888), 11, no. 1246.

against the Dissolution, the changing religious regime, the changing Tudor constitution, and general economic malaise fueled a revolt in the North, known as the Pilgrimage of Grace. Led by Robert Aske (ca. 1500–37), some of the Pilgrims presented the Pontefract Articles to members of the king's council in Yorkshire. Why did the Northern rebels feel so aggrieved by the Dissolution? Were any of their grievances peculiar to the North (that is, far from London and Westminster)? Were their demands primarily religious, constitutional, or economic; or were they all interrelated?

1. The first touching our faith to have the heresies of Luther, Wycliff, Hus, Malan[g]ton, Ellecumpadus [Elicampadus], Bucerus, Confessio [Confessa] Gemaniae, Apologia Malanctionis [Malanctons], the works of Tyndale, of Barnys, of Marshall, of Rastall [Raskell], Saint Germaine, and such other heresies of Anabaptists thereby within this realm to be annulled and destroyed.

2. The 2nd to have the supreme head of the Church touching *cure animarum* [cure of souls] to be restored unto the see of Rome as before it was accustomed to be, and to have the consecrations of the bishops from him without any first fruits or pension to him to be paid out of this realm or else a pension reasonable for the outward defense of our faith.

3. Item we humbly beseech our most dread sovereign lord that the Lady Mary may be made legitimate and the former statute therein annulled for the danger of the title that might incur to the crown of Scotland, [and] that to be by Parliament.

4. Item to have the abbeys suppressed to be restored unto their houses, land, and goods.

6. Item to have the Friars Observants restored unto their houses again.

7. Item to have the heretics, bishops and temporal, and their sect to have condign punishment by fire or such other, or else to try their quarrel with us and our party takers in battle [that is, the ancient methods of trial by fire or trial by battle?].

8. Item to have the Lord Cromwell, the Lord Chancellor, and Sir Richard Riche knight to have condign punishment, as the subverters of the good laws of this realm and maintainers of the false sect of those heretics and the first inventors and bringing in of them. . . .

13. Item statute for enclosures and intacks [northern dialect for land enclosed from moorland] to be put in execution, and that all intacks [and] enclosures since *anno* 4 Henry VII [1488–9] to be pulled down except mountains, forest, and parks.

14. Item to be discharged of the quindene [quinzine] and taxes now granted by act of parliament.

15. Item to have the Parliament in a convenient place at Nottingham or York and the same shortly summoned.

16. Item the statute of the declaration of the [succession of the] crown by [the king's] will, that the same may be annulled and repealed.
17. Item that it be enacted by act of parliament that all recognisances, statutes, penalties new forfeit during the time of this commotion may be pardoned and discharged as well against the king as strangers....
20. Item to have the statute "that no man shall will his lands" [Statute of Uses, 27 Hen. VIII c. 10, 1535] to be repealed.
21. Item that the statutes of treasons for words and such like made since *anno* 21 [Henry VIII, 1529–30] be in likewise repealed....
23. Item that no man upon subpoena is from [River] Trent north to appear but at York or by attorney unless it be directed upon pain of allegiance and for like maters concerning the king.

Conservative Reaction

3.11   *Act Abolishing Diversity of Opinions (1539)*[13]

As should be obvious, by breaking the power of the Church, Henry VIII's reformation inadvertently encouraged and enabled ordinary people to make their religious beliefs known. This was the last thing the king wanted. Having eliminated papal power in England, he wanted to maintain a Church that was more-or-less traditional in theology and ritual. While he crushed the 1636 Pilgrimage and executed Aske and hundreds of other traditional Catholics, within a few years he had also executed Cromwell (d. 1540), and a number of outspoken Protestants as well. He also put the brakes on religious reform. "An Act Abolishing Diversity in Opinions," better known as the Act of Six Articles, codified the theology of the Henrician Church in order to stamp out the "great discord and variance ... amongst the clergy ... as amongst a great number of vulgar people." Are these articles more Catholic in doctrine and practice, or Protestant? Which of the authors of the various documents in this chapter would be most satisfied with these articles?

First, that in the most blessed sacrament of the altar, by the strength and efficacy of Christ's mighty word (it being spoken by the priest), is present really, under the form of bread and wine, the natural body and blood of our Savior Jesus Christ, conceived of the Virgin Mary; and that after the consecration there remaineth no substance of bread or wine, nor any other substance but the substance of Christ, God and man. *Secondly*, that communion in both kinds is

---

[13]   *SR*, 3: 739–40, 31 Hen. VIII, c. 14.

not necessary *ad salutem*, by the law of God, to all persons; and that it is to be believed, and not doubted of, but that in the flesh under form of bread is the very blood; and with the blood under form of wine is the very flesh, as well apart as though they were both together. *Thirdly*, that priests after the order of priesthood received, as afore, may not marry by the law of God. *Fourthly*, that vows of chastity or widowhood, by man or woman made to God advisedly, ought to be observed by the law of God, and that it exempteth them from other liberties of Christian people, which without that they might enjoy. *Fifthly*, that it is meet and necessary that private masses be continued and admitted in this the king's English Church and congregation, as whereby good Christian people, ordering themselves accordingly, do receive both godly and goodly consolations and benefits; and it is agreeable also to God's law. *Sixthly*, that auricular confession is expedient and necessary to be retained and continued, used and frequented in the Church of God.

3.12 Anne Askew's "Sum of My Examination Afore the King's Council at Greenwich" (1546, pub. 1547)[14]

Anne Askew (ca. 1521–46) had been married to a Lincolnshire gentleman, one Mr. Kyme, before the influence of the Reformed religion led her to London to seek both a divorce from her Catholic husband (she thenceforth referred to herself by her maiden name) and spiritual advice and polemics. Though she had connections with the female court of Henry's last queen, Catherine Parr (1512–48), Askew fell foul of the government's crackdown on reformers in the wake of the Act of Six Articles. She was imprisoned for heresy, questioned and tortured, and burnt to death in Smithfield just outside London's city walls on July 16, 1546. She evidently wrote two volumes of her examinations, which, smuggled out of prison, were published with commentary by John Bale (see document 3.14), and she later became one of the early martyrs in Foxe's *Acts and Monuments* (see document 3.17). How had the new, Reformed religion affected Askew? How did the ability to read Scripture empower people? What was her basic argument? What was that of her interrogators? How does she deploy expected social roles in her responses? How does she upset them?

I, being before the Council, was asked of [about] Master Kyme. I answered that my Lord Chancellor knew already my mind in that matter. They with that answer were not contented but said it was the king's pleasure that I should open the matter to them. I answered then plainly that I would not so do. But if

---

[14] *The lattre examinacyon of Anne Askewe latelye martyred in Smythfelde, by the wycked Synagoge of Antichrist, with the Elucydacyon of Iohan Bale* (Marpurg [i.e. Wesel], 1547), 14–24 (Bale's commentary omitted).

it were the king's pleasure to hear me, I would show him the truth. Then they said it was not meet for the king with me to be troubled. I answered that Solomon was reckoned the wisest king that ever lived, yet misliked not he to hear two poor common women, much more His Grace a simple woman and his faithful subject. So, in conclusion, I made them none other answer in that matter.

Then my lord chancellor asked me of my opinion in the sacrament. My answer was this, "I believe that so oft as I in a Christian congregation do receive the bread in remembrance of Christ's death and with thanksgiving according to his holy instruction, I receive therewith the fruits also of his most glorious passion." The bishop of Winchester bade me make a direct answer. I said, "I would not sing a new song to the Lord in a strange land."

Then the bishop said I spake in parables. I answered it was best for him. "For if I show the open truth," quoth I, "ye will not accept it." Then he said I was a parrot. I told him again I was ready to suffer all things at his hands, not only his rebukes, but all that should follow besides, yea, and that gladly. Then had I diverse rebukes of the Council because I would not express my mind in all things as they would have me. But they were not in the meantime unanswered for all that, which now to rehearse were too much, for I was with them there above five hours. . . .

The next day I was brought again before the Council. Then would they needs know of me what I said to [regarding] the sacrament. I answered that I already had said that [which] I could say. Then, after diverse words, they bade me, "Go by." Then came [privy councilors] my Lord Lisle, my lord of Essex, and the bishop of Winchester, requiring me earnestly that I should confess the sacrament to be flesh, blood, and bone. Then said I to my Lord Parr and my Lord Lisle that it was great shame for them to counsel contrary to their knowledge. Whereunto in few words they did say that they would gladly all things were well.

Then the bishop said he would speak with me familiarly. I said, "So did Judas when he unfriendly betrayed Christ." Then desired the bishop to speak with me alone. But that I refused. He asked me, "Why?" I said that in the mouth of two or three witnesses every matter should stand, after Christ's and Paul's doctrine, Matthew 18 and 2 Corinthians 13. . . .

Then the bishop said I should be burned. I answered that I had searched all the scriptures, yet could I never find there that either Christ or his Apostles put any creature to death. "Well, well;" said I. "God will laugh your threatenings to scorn," Psalm 2. Then was I commanded to stand aside.

Then came Master [William] Paget [(1505/6–63), at this time one of Henry's chief advisers] to me with many glorious words, and desired me to speak my mind to him. "I might," he said, "deny it again if need were." I said that I would not deny the truth. He asked me how I could avoid the very words of Christ: "Take, eat. This is my body, which shall be broken for you." I answered that Christ's meaning was there, as in these other places of the Scripture: "I am the door," John 10. "I am the vine," John 15. "Behold the lamb of God,"

John 1. "The rock stone was Christ," 1 Corinthians 10, and such other like. "Ye may not here," said I, "take Christ for the material thing that he is signified by, for then ye will make him a very door, a vine, a lamb, and a stone, clean contrary to the Holy Ghost's meaning. All these indeed do signify Christ, like as the bread doth his body in that place. And though he did say there, 'Take, eat this in remembrance of me,' yet did he not bid them hang up that bread in a box and make it a God or bow to it."

Then he compared it unto the king and said that the more His Majesty's honor is set forth, the more commendable it is. Then said I that it was an abominable shame unto him to make no better of the eternal Word of God, than of his slenderly conceived fantasy. A far other meaning requireth God therein than man's idle wit can devise, whose doctrine is but lies without his heavenly verity. Then he asked me if I would commune with some wiser man? That offer, I said, I would not refuse. Then he told the Council....

Then came to me Doctor Cox and Doctor Robinson. In conclusion we could not agree. Then they made me a bill [formal legal document] of the sacrament, willing me to set my hand thereunto, but I would not. Then on the Sunday I was sore sick, thinking no less than to die. Therefore I desired to speak with [Hugh] Latimer [see document 3.17]; it would not be. Then was I sent to Newgate in my extremity of sickness. For in all my life afore was I never in such pain. Thus the Lord strengthen you in the truth. Pray, pray, pray.

Protestant vs. Catholic under Edward VI, Mary I, and Elizabeth I

3.13 Cranmer's Answer to the Fifteen Articles of the Devon Rebels (1549)[15]

Edward VI (1547–53) succeeded his father, Henry VIII, as head of both State and Church. Under the Protectorate of his uncle, Edward Seymour, duke of Somerset (ca. 1500–52), the Edwardian Church moved in a more clearly Protestant direction both in theology and in liturgy, with a campaign against images and the dissolution of the chantries. In 1549, the Act of Uniformity established a single legal form of worship, with punishments reserved for those who did not comply. Further, a committee headed by Thomas Cranmer (1489–1556), archbishop of Canterbury "concluded, set forth, and delivered to his highness, to his great comfort and quietness of mind, [a new liturgy] in a book entitled, 'The Book of the Common Prayer and Administration of the Sacraments, and other Rites and Ceremonies of

---

[15] J. E. Cox, ed., *Miscellaneous Writings and Letters of Thomas Cranmer* (Cambridge, 1846), 163–5, 168, 172–3, 179–80.

the Church, after the Use of the Church of England.' "[16] But the new rites and ceremonies were not uniformly accepted. Somerset warned nobles in the countryside to expect disturbances. Indeed, Devon rose the day after the Prayer Book became the lawful liturgy for all parish churches. Soon the rebels of Cornwall and Devon issued a list of 15 demands from their camps outside Exeter. Archbishop Cranmer responded to their manifesto point by point. What did the rebels seek? Which of their demands draws Cranmer's fire most and why? How does he de-legitimize the rebels? How does he connect religious dissent with political disloyalty? You might compare and contrast the 1549 rebel demands with those from 1536 (document 3.10).

When I first read your request, O ignorant men of Devonshire and Cornwall, straightways came to my mind a request, which James and John made unto Christ; to whom Christ answered: "You ask you wot [know] not what." Even so thought I of you, as soon as ever I heard your articles, that you were deceived by some crafty papist, which devised those articles for you, to make you ask you wist [know] not what....

Your First Article Is This: "We will have all the general councils and holy decrees of our forefathers observed, kept, and performed: and whosoever shall gainsay them, we hold them as heretics."

First, to begin with the manner of your phrase. Is this the fashion of subjects to speak unto their prince, "We will have?" Was this manner of speech at any time used of the subjects to their prince since the beginning of the world? Have not all true subjects ever used to their sovereign lord this form of speaking, "Most humbly beseecheth your faithful and obedient subjects?" Although the papists have abused your ignorance in propounding such articles, which you understand not, yet you should not have suffered yourselves so much to be led by the nose and bridled by them, that you should clearly forget your duty of allegiance unto your sovereign lord saying unto him, "This we will have"; and that saying with armor upon your backs and swords in your hands. Would any of you that be householders be content that your servants should come upon you with harness unto their backs, and swords in their hands, and say unto you "This we will have?"...

But now, leaving your rude and unhandsome manner of speech to your most sovereign lord, I will come to the point.... You say, you will have all the holy decrees observed and kept. But do you know what they be? The holy decrees, as I told you before, be called the bishop of Rome's ordinances and laws: which how holy and godly soever they be called, they be indeed so wicked, so ungodly, so full of tyranny, and so partial, that since the beginning of the world were never devised or invented the like....

[16] *SR*, 4: 37–9, 3 Edw. VI, c. 1.

Your Second Article Is This: "We will have the law of our sovereign lord King Henry VIII concerning the Six Articles to be used again, as in his time they were."

Letting pass your rude style …, First, I examine you of the cause of your wilful will, wherefore you will have these six articles: which never were laws in no region but this; nor in this realm also, until … [1539]; and in some things so enforced by the evil counsel of certain papists, against the truth and common judgment both of divines and lawyers, that if the king's majesty himself had not come personally into the Parliament house, those laws had never passed. And yet within a year or little more the same most noble prince was fain to temper his said laws, and moderate them in diverse points: so that the statute of Six Articles continued in his force little above the space of one year. Is this then so great a matter to make these uproars, and to arise against the whole realm?…

Your Eighth Article Is This: "We will not receive the new service, because it is but like a Christmas game; but we will have our old service of matins, mass, evensong, and procession in Latin, as it was before. And so we the Cornish men, whereof certain of us understand no English, utterly refuse this new English."…

I would gladly know the reason why the Cornish men refuse utterly the new English, as you call it, because certain of you understand it not; and yet you will have the service in Latin, which almost none of you understand. If this be a sufficient cause for Cornwall to refuse the English service because some of you understand none English, a much greater cause have they, both of Cornwall and Devonshire to refuse utterly the late service; forasmuch as fewer of them know the Latin tongue than they of Cornwall the English tongue. But where you say that you will have the old service because the new is "like a Christmas game," you declare yourselves what spirit you be led withal, or rather what spirit leadeth them that persuaded you that the word of God is but like a Christmas game. It is more like a game and a fond play to be laughed at of all men to hear the priest speak aloud to the people in Latin, and the people listen with their ears to hear; and some walking up and down in the church, some saying other prayers in Latin, and none understandeth other. Neither the priest nor his parish wot [know] what they say. And many times the thing that the priest sayeth in Latin is so fond of itself, that it is more like a play than a godly prayer. …

Your Tenth Article Is This: "We will have the Bible and all books of scripture in English, to be called in again. For we be informed that otherwise the clergy shall not of long time confound the heretics."…

Although you savor so little of godliness that you list not to read his word yourselves, you ought not to be so malicious and envious to let them that be more godly and would gladly read it to their comfort and edification. And if there be an English heretic, how will you have him confuted but in English? And whereby else but by God's word? Then it followeth that to confute English heretics we must needs have God's word in English, as all other nations have it in their own native language.

3.14   Robert Parkyn's Narrative of the Reformation (ca. 1555)[17]

Robert Parkyn (d. 1569), a Yorkshire Catholic priest, chronicled England's changing religious situation first under Edward VI then, after his death in the summer of 1553, under his elder half-sister, Mary I (1516–58). After Somerset's failure to crush the Prayer Book and Kett's Rebellions in 1549–50, he was deposed as the king's chief adviser by John Dudley, earl of Warwick, later duke of Northumberland (1504–53). During the final years of Edward's reign, Northumberland promoted an even more Protestant settlement, including legislation allowing priests to marry, abolishing saint's days, and mandating a new, more Protestant *Book of Common Prayer* enforced by a second Act of Uniformity in 1552. To Fr. Parkyn's delight, this was all reversed under Mary. She began the process of returning England, Ireland, and Wales to Rome. The First Statute of Repeal rescinded her half-brother's Acts of Uniformity, as well as Acts concerning the marriage of priests, and ordered a return by December 1553 to the liturgy as practiced under her father. What changes did Parkyn find most objectionable between 1549 and 1553? Which affected the most people? Of which did he approve? Was Mary's Counter-Reformation popular?

Then was there a great Parliament held at Westminster at London the same winter, beginning the 4th day of November [actually, November 24, 1548] and there continued and kept to the 14th day of March [1549] ..., wherein the holy mass was subdued and deposed by Act of Parliament, and none to be used, but only a communion. ...

After the feast of the Annunciation of Our Lady *(anno domini* 1549), the king's majesty's acts was proclaimed, declaring how it was lawful by God's law priests to marry women, and so many was married indeed. ...

Consequently, followed straight monition, yea, and commandment (according to the king's majesty's acts) at visitations after Easter, that no priest should celebrate or say mass in Latin, or minister any sacrament in Latin words after the feast of Pentecost then next following, but only in English (as they would avoid the king's high displeasure and such penalties as was manifest in the said acts). And so the holy mass was utterly deposed throughout all this realm of England and other of the king's dominions at the said Pentecost, and in place

---

[17]   A. G. Dickens, ed., "Robert Parkyn's Narrative of the Reformation," *EHR* 62, 242 (1947): 69–70, 72, 74, 78–80, 82, from Bodl. MS. Lat.Th.d.15; reproduced by permission of Oxford University Press.

thereof a communion to be said in English without any elevation of Christ's body and blood under form of bread and wine, or adoration, or reservation in the pyx, for a certain English book was set forth in print, containing all such service as should be used in the church of God, and no other (entitled the *Book of Common Prayer* [1549])....

In the month of December [1550] all altars of stone was taken away ... of the churches and chapels from [River] Trent northwards and a table of wood set in the choir....

A great Parliament held at Westminster and begun the 23rd day of January and then continued and kept unto the 15th day of April ... 1552, wherein no goodness towards holy church proceeded, but all things contrary. For in the Parliament was deposed by act these three holy days [among others] before accustomed to have been kept holy, *viz.* Conversion of St. Paul [January 25], St. Barnabas [June 11], and Mary Magdalen [July 22]; and that a new communion book in English (called the *Book of Common Prayer* [1552]) should take effect at All Hallows day next ensuing date hereof (*viz.* first day of November), and so the Communion Book in English (which is above mentioned [1549]) to be of none effect. Oh, note the great instability and newfangledness of the heretic Warwick (alias duke of Northumberland) with his adherents, *viz.* carnal bishops of this realm and very traitors to God. For consequently after that Robert Holgate, archbishop of York, was come from the said Parliament, he sent straight commandment in beginning of June through all his diocese that the table in the choir whereupon the holy communion was ministered, it standing with the ends toward south and north, should be used contrary, *viz.* to be set in the choir beneath the lowest stair or grace, having the ends thereof towards the east and west, and the priest his face towards the north all the communion time, which was nothing seeming nor after any good order....

The virtuous lady Mary ... was proclaimed on the 19th of July [1553] ... at which proclamation all good people there being present highly rejoiced, giving thanks, honor, and praise unto Almighty God, and so went singing *Te Deum laudamus* into Paul's church....

In the meantime in many places of the realm, priests was commanded by lords and knights Catholic to say mass in Latin with consecration and elevation of the body and blood of Christ under form of bread and wine with a decent order as hath been used beforetime.... In August there was a proclamation set forth declaring how the gracious Queen Mary did license priests to say mass in Latin after the old ancient custom, as was used in her father's days....

Thus through grace of the Holy Ghost, the straight of holy church something began to amend and to arise from the old heresies before used in this realm ... [and] in many places of Yorkshire priests unmarried was very glad to celebrate and say mass in Latin with matins and evensong thereto.... And so in the beginning of September there was very few parish churches in Yorkshire but mass was sung or said in Latin on the first Sunday of the said month [August] or at furthest, on the feast day of the Nativity of Our Blessed Lady [September 8].

Holy bread and holy water was given, altars was reedified, pictures or images set up, the cross with the crucifix thereon ready to be borne in procession, and with the same went procession. And in conclusion, all the English service of laity used in the church of God was voluntarily laid away and the Latin taken up again (not only with matins, mass, and evensong, but also in ministration of sacraments), and yet all these came to pass without compulsion of any act, statute, proclamation, or law. ...

So to be brief, all old ceremonies laudably used beforetime in holy church was then revived, daily frequented, and used, after that the right reverend Father in God, the Lord Cardinal Pole, legate *a latere*, was entered this realm in the month of November [1554] bringing with him the Pope's power and authority.

3.15   The Vocacyon of Johan Bale *(1553)*[18]

Not everyone appreciated the return to Catholic practice under Mary. John Bale (1495–1563) was a prior before the Reformation who became an evangelical Protestant polemicist, editing Askew's *Examinations* (document 3.12). What does his report from Ireland suggest about Irish opinion on the Edwardian Reformation? Is Bale reliable? What aspects of Catholicism arouse his hostility most?

On the twentieth day of August [1553], was the Lady Mary with us at Kilkenny [in Ireland] proclaimed queen of England, France, and Ireland, with the greatest solemnity that there could be devised of processions, musters, and disguisings; all the noble captains and gentlemen thereabout being present. What-a-do I had that day with the prebendaries and priests about wearing the cope, crosier, and miter in procession.... [O]n ... the last day of August, I being absent, the clergy of Kilkenny ... blasphemously resumed again the whole papism, or heap of superstitions of the bishop of Rome; to the utter contempt of Christ and His holy word, of the king and Council of England, and of all ecclesiastical and politic order, without either statute or yet proclamation. They rung all the bells in that cathedral, minster, and parish churches; they flung up their caps to the battlement of the great temple, with smilings and laughings most dissolutely ...; they brought forth their copes, candle sticks, holy-water stock, cross, and censers; they mustered forth in general procession most gorgeously, all the town over, with *Sancta Maria, ora pro nobis,* and the rest of the Latin litany; they chattered it, they chanted it, with great noise and devotion; they banqueted all the day after, for that they were delivered from the grace of God into a warm sun.

---

[18]   *The Vocacyon of Johan Bale to the Bishoprick of Ossorie In Irelande his Persecucions in the same* (Rome [i.e. Wesel?], 1553), fols. 24, 27–27(verso).

3.16 Report on Marian Persecution to Philip of Spain from Simon Renard at London (February 5, 1555)[19]

While Parkyn (document 3.14) might have been correct to note that changes in the service "came to pass without compulsion," numerous clergy and a small, but significant portion of the laity refused to return to the old liturgy and faith. In response, Mary and her advisers began to persecute these Protestants as heretics. The fires celebrating the restoration of Catholicism in London in January 1555 soon had a darker significance, as reforming bishops and others were arrested, tried, and ordered to be burnt. Simon Renard (ca. 1513–73), the Imperial ambassador in London, questioned the efficacy of burning heretics. Is Renard an eyewitness? Is he convincing? How might his position sway what he reports?

The people of this town of London are murmuring about the cruel enforcement of the recent acts of parliament on heresy which has now begun, as shown publicly when a certain [John] Rogers [ca. 1500–55] was burnt yesterday. Some of the onlookers wept, others prayed to God to give them strength ..., others gathered the ashes and bones ..., yet others threatening the bishops. The haste with which the bishops have proceeded in this matter may well cause a revolt. ... I do not think it well that your Majesty [Philip] should allow further executions to take place unless the reasons are overwhelmingly strong. ... Tell the bishops that they are not to proceed to such lengths without having first consulted you and the queen. ... Your majesty will also consider that the Lady Elizabeth has her supporters and that there are Englishmen who do not love foreigners.

3.17 Foxe's Account of the Death of Bishops Latimer and Ridley (October 1555, pub. 1570)[20]

We know about the dying words and actions of those burnt under Mary from the *Actes and Monuments of These Latter and Perilous Days* which John Foxe (1516–87) published in four ever-lengthening editions (1563, 1570, 1576, 1583). Foxe, a fervent Protestant, did not become a Marian martyr, but instead fled to the continent as one of the Marian exiles. His book created a Protestant martyrology, although as we shall see (document 4.1 below), the return to Protestantism under Elizabeth would produce martyrs to the Catholic faith as well. Foxe immortalized one of the most

[19] *CSP Relating to ... England and Spain ...*, *July 1554–November 1558* (London, 1954), 13: 138–9.
[20] J. Foxe, *Actes and Monuments* (1570), 1937–9, from *Acts and Monuments* [...] *The Variorum Edition* (1570 ed., hriOnline, Sheffield) <http://www.hrionline.ac.uk/johnfoxe/>.

infamous burnings under Mary, that of Bishops Nicholas Ridley (1495–1555) and Hugh Latimer (ca. 1485–1555) at Oxford in October 1555. On what evidence does he seem to base his account? Is he a convincing historian? What do you suppose was the impact of the burnings on those who witnessed them? Next to the Bible, his *Book of Martyrs*, as it became known, became one of the most popular and influential books in the English language (see also Plate 3). How might Foxe's history influence the Elizabethan people's view of themselves?

Then the wicked sermon being ended, Dr. Ridley and Master Latimer kneeled down upon their knees to my lord Williams of Tame, the vice-chancellor of Oxford, and diverse other commissioners appointed for that purpose, who sat upon a form thereby. Unto whom Master Ridley said, "I beseech you, my lord, even for Christ's sake, that I may speak but two or three words."… The bailiffs and Dr. Marshal, the vice-chancellor, ran hastily unto him, and with their hands stopped his mouth, and said, "Master Ridley, if you will revoke your erroneous opinions, and recant the same, you shall not only have liberty so to do, but also the benefit of a subject, that is, have your life." "Not otherwise?" said Master Ridley. "No," quoth Dr. Marshal.… "Well," quoth Master Ridley, "so long as the breath is in my body I will never deny my Lord Christ, and his known truth: God's will be done in me." And with that he rose up, and said with a loud voice, "Well, then I commit our cause to Almighty God, who will indifferently judge all." To whose saying, Master Latimer added his old posy, "Well, there is nothing hid but it shall be opened."…

Then Master Ridley …, being in his shirt, he stood upon the foresaid stone, and held up his hand and said, "O heavenly Father, I give unto thee most hearty thanks, for that thou hast called me to be a professor of thee, even unto death; I beseech thee, Lord God, take mercy on this realm of England, and deliver the same from all her enemies."

Then the smith took a chain of iron, and brought the same about both Dr. Ridley's and Master Latimer's middle: and, as he was knocking in a staple, Dr. Ridley took the chain in his hand and shaked the same, for it did gird in his belly; and looking aside to the smith, said, "Good fellow, knock it in hard, for the flesh will have his course." Then his brother did bring him a bag of gunpowder, and would have tied it about his neck. Master Ridley asked him what it was; his brother said, "Gunpowder." "Then," said he, "I will take it to be sent of God, therefore I will receive it as sent from him. And have you any," said he, "for my brother?" (meaning Master Latimer). "Yea, sir, that I have," quoth his brother. "Then give it unto him," said he, "betime; lest ye come too late." So his brother went and carried off the same gunpowder to Mr. Latimer.…

Then they brought a faggot kindled with fire, and laid the same down at Dr. Ridley's feet. Thereupon Master Latimer said, "Be of good comfort, Master

Ridley, and play the man, we shall this day light such a candle, by God's grace, in England, as I trust shall never be put out." And so the fire being given unto them, when Dr. Ridley saw the fire flaming up towards him, he cried with a wonderful loud voice, "*In manus tuas, Domine, commendo spiritum meum: Domine recipe spiritum meum.*" And after, repeated this latter part often in English, "Lord, Lord, receive my spirit." Master Latimer crying as vehemently on the other side, "O Father of heaven, receive my soul!": who received the flame as it were embracing of it. After that he had stroked his face with his hands, and (as it were) bathed them a little in the fire, he soon died (as it appeared) with very little pain or none. And thus much concerning the end of this old and faithful servant of God, Master Latimer, for whose laborious travails, fruitful life, and constant death the whole realm hath cause to give thanks to Almighty God.

But Master Ridley, by reason of the evil making of the fire unto him, because the wooden faggots were laid about the gorse, and over-high built, the fire burnt first beneath, being kept down by the wood; which when he felt, he desired them for Christ's sake to let the fire come unto him. Which his brother-in-law heard, but not well understood, intending to rid him out of his pain (for which cause he gave attendance) as one in such sorrow, not well advised what he did, heaped faggots upon him, so that he clean covered him, which made the fire more vehement beneath, that it burned clean all his nether parts, before it touched the upper; and that made him leap up and down under the faggots, and often desire them to let the fire come unto him, saying, "I cannot burn." Which indeed appeared well; for, after his legs were consumed by reason of his struggling through the pain (whereof he had no release, but only his contentation in God) he showed that side toward us clean, shirt and all untouched with flame. Yet in all this torment he forgot not to call unto God still, having in his mouth, "Lord, have mercy upon me," intermingling his cry, "Let the fire come unto me, I cannot burn." In which pangs he labored till one of the standers-by with his bill pulled off the faggots above, and where he saw the fire flame up, he wrested himself unto that side. And when the flame touched the gunpowder, he was seen to stir no more, but burned on the other side, falling down at Master Latimer's feet. Which some said, happened by reason that the chain loosed; others said, that he fell over the chain by reason of the poise of his body, and the weakness of the nether limbs....

Signs there were of sorrow on every side. Some took it grievously to see their deaths, whose lives they held full dear; some pitied their persons, that thought their souls had no need thereof. His brother moved many men, seeing his miserable case.... But whoso considered their preferments in time past, the places of honor that they sometime occupied in this commonwealth, the favor they were in with their princes, and the opinion of learning they had, could not choose but sorrow with tears to see so great dignity, honor, and estimation, so necessary members sometime accounted, so many godly virtues, the study of so many years, such excellent learning, to be put into the fire, and consumed in one moment.

[handwritten margin notes: mixture between two — but leaned more Protestant in ideal]

[handwritten left margin: explaining difference between catholic practice (which continued) + catholic faith + belief]

3.18   *The Elizabethan Injunctions (1559)*[21]

The accession of Elizabeth on November 17, 1558 (d. 1603) signaled the end of the Marian restoration. Under Mary, Elizabeth may have played her cards close to her chest – but they were Protestant cards. Which Church, Henry's, Edward's, or Mary's, was being re-established by the Injunctions of 1559? If parochial practice followed these injunctions, how would ritual change, basically for the last time in the century? Roger Martyn (document 3.1) lived through Elizabeth's reign; what do you think he made of the 1559 changes?

All deans, archdeacons, parsons, vicars, and other ecclesiastical persons shall faithfully keep and observe ... all and singular laws and statutes made for the restoring to the Crown the ancient jurisdiction over the state ecclesiastical, and abolishing of all foreign power repugnant to the same....

The persons above rehearsed, shall preach in their churches, and every other cure they have, one sermon every month of the year at the least, wherein they shall purely and sincerely declare the Word of God, and in the same exhort their hearers to the works of faith, mercy, and charity specially prescribed and commanded in Scripture, and that works devised by men's fantasies, besides Scripture, as wandering on pilgrimages, setting up of candles, praying upon beads, or such like superstition, have not only no promise of reward in Scripture, for doing of them, but contrariwise, great threats and maledictions of God, for that they be things tending to idolatry and superstition....

Also that they shall provide within three months next after this visitation, at the charge of the parish, one book of the whole Bible, of the largest volume, in English. And within one twelve-months next after the said visitation, the Paraphrases of Erasmus also in English upon the Gospels, and the same set up in some convenient place within the said church that they have cure of, where their parishioners may most commodiously resort unto the same and read the same out of the time of common service.

HISTORIANS' DEBATES

Overviews of recent debate on the Reformation, whether it was an attempt to establish gospel-Christianity, or an attack on traditional religion, who was responsible, and whether it "took."

P. Marshall, ed., *The Impact of the English Reformation, 1500–1640* (London, 1997), see specific articles below; R. O'Day, *The Debate on the English*

---

[21]   *Iniunctions geven by the Quenes Maiestie* (London, 1559), sig. Aii–Aiii.

Reformation (London, 1986), esp. "The Reformation and the People"; E. J. Carlson, "Cassandra Banished?: New Research on Religion in Tudor and Early Stuart England," in *Religion and the English People 1500–1640*, ed. Carlson (*16th Century Essays & Studies* 45, 1998); P. Marshall's and A. Ryrie's introduction to *The Beginnings of English Protestantism* (Cambridge, 2002), as well as individual essays; M. Dowling, "New Perspectives on the English Reformation" (review essay), *JBS* 30, 1 (1991).

How should we characterize the Pre-Reformation Church?

P. Heath, "Between Reform and Reformation: the English Church in the Fourteenth and Fifteenth Centuries" (review essay), *JEcclH* 41 (1990); C. Harper-Bill, "Dean Colet's Coronation Sermon and the Pre-Reformation Church in England" (London, 1988, reprinted in Marshall, *Impact*); E. Duffy, *The Voices of Morebath: Reformation & Rebellion in an English Village* (New Haven, 2001), esp. "The Piety of Morebath" and "Banishing Saint Sidwell"; idem, "Morebath, 1520–1570: a Rural Parish in the Reformation," in *Religion and Rebellion*, ed. J. Devlin and R. Fanning (*Historical Studies* 20, 1997); idem, *The Stripping of the Altars: Traditional Religion in England c. 1400–c. 1580*, 2nd ed. (New Haven, 1992, 2005), esp. new introduction and section on the structures of traditional religion; M. Heale, "Training in Superstition?: Monasteries and Popular Religion in Late Medieval and Reformation England," *JEcclH* 58, 3 (2007).

What, if any, was the impact of Lollardy on the Reformation?

A. Hudson, *The Premature Reformation* (Oxford, 1988), esp. the final chapter; A. Hope, "Lollardy: The Stone the Builders Rejected?," in *Protestantism and the National Church in Sixteenth-century England*, ed. P. Lake and M. Dowling (London, 1987); J. F. Davis, "Lollardy and the Reformation in England" (1982, reprinted in Marshall, *Impact*); C. W. D'Alton, "Cuthbert Tunstal and Heresy in Essex and London, 1528," *Albion* 35, 2 (2003); R. Rex, *The Lollards* (Basingstoke, 2002), esp. chap. 5 "From Lollardy to Protestantism," and the conclusion.

Was the Reformation popular, shaped by grass-roots movements from below?

A. G. Dickens, *The English Reformation*, 2nd ed. (London, 1964, 1989), esp. the section on "The Complexities of the English Reformation"; idem, "The Early Expansion of Protestantism in England, 1520–1558," (1987, reprinted in Marshall, *Impact*); idem, review of J. J. Scarisbrick in *JEcclH* 36 (1985); D. M. Palliser, "Popular Reactions to the Reformation, 1530–70," in *Church and Society in England: Henry VIII to James I*, ed. F. Heal and R. O'Day (London, 1977); a special issue of *HR* 77, 195 (2004) on the work and influence of A. G. Dickens, including essays by A. Pettegree, C. Haigh, and E. Duffy; S. Brigden, "Youth and the English Reformation" (1982, reprinted in Marshall, *Impact*); idem, "Popular Disturbance and the Fall of Thomas Cromwell and the Reformers, 1539–1540,"

HJ 24, 2 (1981); G. Walker, "Saint or Schemer?: The 1527 Heresy Trial of Thomas Bilney Reconsidered," *JEcclH* 40, 2 (1989).

Was it unpopular and forced by a few powerful members of the elite from above?

J. J. Scarisbrick, *The Reformation and the English People* (Oxford, 1984), esp. the introductory comments and the study of wills as showing popular belief; C. Haigh, *English Reformations: Religion, Politics, and Society Under the Tudors* (Oxford, 1993), esp. the prologue and the conclusion, "The Reformations and the Division of England"; *idem*, "The English Reformation: a premature birth, a difficult labour and a sickly child" (review essay), *HJ* 33, 2 (1990); Haigh, ed., *The English Reformation Revised* (Cambridge, 1987), esp. Haigh's "The Henrician Reformation and the Parish Clergy," and R. Hutton's "The Local Impact of the Tudor Reformations" (reprinted in Marshall, *Impact*); M. Dowling, "Anne Boleyn and Reform," *JEcclH* 36 (1985); N. M. Sutherland, "The Marian Exiles and the Establishment of the Elizabethan Regime," *Archiv für Reformationsgeschichte* 78 (1987); C. S. L. Davies, "The Cromwellian Decade: Authority and Consent," *TRHS* 6th ser., 7 (1997).

Was there a post-Reformation religious culture? Was there a "confessionalization" of different regions/religions?

D. MacCulloch, *The Later Reformation in England, 1547–1603*, 2nd ed. (Basingstoke, 2001), esp. chs. on "The Reception of the Reformation" and "Principled Dissent"; *idem*, "Putting the English Reformation on the Map," *TRHS* 15 (2005); *idem*, "The Change of Religion," in *The Sixteenth Century, 1485–1603*, ed. P. Collinson (Oxford, 2002); E. H. Shagan, *Popular Politics and the English Reformation* (Cambridge, 2003), esp. the introduction and ch. 8 on the Edwardian people and the Reformation; H. A. Jefferies, "The Early Tudor Reformations in the Irish Pale," *JEcclH* 52, 1 (2001); C. Haigh, "The Reformation in England to 1603," in *A Companion to the Reformation World*, ed. R. Po-chia Hsia (Oxford, 2004); N. Jones, *The English Reformation: Religion and Cultural Adaptation* (Oxford, 2002), chs. on "Post-Reformation Culture" and "Choosing Reformations"; *idem*, "Religious Settlements," in *A Companion to Tudor Britain*, ed. R. Tittler and N. Jones (Oxford, 2004); Duffy on Mary's reign reprinted in Marshall, *Impact*.

Was the Pilgrimage of Grace essentially political? religious? constitutional? socio-economic? Did popular politics shape elite responses to the 1536 and 1540 rebellions?

G. R. Elton, "Politics and the Pilgrimage of Grace," in *Studies in Tudor and Stuart Politics and Government* (Cambridge, 1974, 1983), vol. 3; C. S. L. Davies, "Popular Religion and the Pilgrimage of Grace," in *Order and Disorder in Early*

Modern England, ed. A. Fletcher and J. Stevenson (Cambridge, 1985); Shagan, "Politics and the Pilgrimage of Grace Revisited," in his *Popular Politics*; M. L. Bush, "The Tudor Polity and the Pilgrimage of Grace," *HR* 80, 207 (2007); *idem*, "Review Article: A Progress Report on the Pilgrimage of Grace," *History* 90, 300 (2005); Shagan, "Protector Somerset and the 1549 Rebellions: New Sources and New Perspectives," *EHR* 114 (1999); Shagan debates Bush and G. W. Bernard on 1549, *EHR* 115 (2000); J. Youings, "The South-Western Rebellion of 1549," *Southern History* 1 (1979).

ADDITIONAL SOURCE COLLECTIONS

K. Aughterson, *The English Renaissance: An Anthology of Sources and Documents* (London, 1998).

G. Bray, ed., *Documents of the English Reformation* (Minneapolis, 1994).

D. Cressy and L. A. Ferrell, eds., *Religion and Society in Early Modern England: Voices, Sources and Texts*, 2nd ed. (London, 2005).

G. R. Elton, ed., *The Tudor Constitution: Documents and Commentary*, 2nd ed. (Cambridge, 1968, 1982).

A. Fletcher and D. MacCulloch, *Tudor Rebellions*, 4th ed. (London, 1997).

H. Haydn, ed., *The Portable Elizabethan Reader* (New York, 1955).

J. N. King, ed., *Voices of the English Reformation: a Sourcebook* (Philadelphia, 2004).

C. Lindberg, ed., *The European Reformations Sourcebook* (Oxford, 2000).

M. D. Palmer, *Henry VIII*, 2nd ed. (London, 1983).

C. H. Williams, ed., *English Historical Documents, 1485–1558* (London, 1967).

CHAPTER FOUR

Elizabethan Worlds

Queen Elizabeth and her subjects excelled in numerous arenas: exploration, trade and colonization, warfare and state-building, theology and religious polemic, theater and performance. Or, less sympathetically, they excelled in privateering and slaving, religious infighting and bigotry, plotting and dissimulation. What did the Elizabethans think they were achieving and how did this compare with what they actually achieved? In many religious and political disputes in this chapter – what to do about Mary Queen of Scots, or Catholic priests, or prophesyings – Elizabethans assume the attitudes of actors consciously presenting themselves and rehearsing arguments to an audience. Self-presentation, artifice, and the cultivation of an appearance of both command and spontaneity were part of the training of a Renaissance gentleman. The Tudor court was the great theater of monarchy, staging coronations, marriages, funerals, and the like, while London was a great theater of all that Renaissance life could afford.

Elizabethan foreign policy, domestic politics, religion, and literature were all intertwined. Although we have tried to distinguish these arenas and their relevant sources, you should also consider how the documents placed at the beginning, middle, and end of this chapter relate to and inform one another. In the following sources:

- What achievements made Elizabethan authors most proud?
- What issues caused the same authors the most anxiety?

Imperial Ambitions; Geopolitical Realities

4.1 Sir Humphrey Gilbert, "What commodities would ensue, this passage once discovered," A New Passage to Cataia (1578)[1]

England's first empire began with Wales and Ireland; by the end of Gloriana's reign, her subjects had made tentative forays into North America at Virginia,

[1] H. Gilbert, *A Discourse Of a Discoverie for a Newe Passage to Cataia* (Menston, Yorks., facsimile, 1576, 1972), sig. Hi–Hii(verso).

named after the Virgin Queen. Sir Humphrey Gilbert (1537–83) was among those courtier-adventurers who promoted the idea of English exploration, the achievements of English explorers, traders, and privateers and sought to expand their countrymen's horizons. Gilbert made several transatlantic voyages and was lost on the last of them, but he is also known for his ruthless campaign in Ireland (see document 4.3). Were his proposals consistent with English strategy in Ireland? Which of Gilbert's arguments for exploration seems most convincing? Which least? Which domestic problems do they intend to solve for England? Is his rationale for exploration entirely economic?

1. First, it were the only way for our princes to possess the wealth of all the East parts (as they term them) of the world, which is infinite ..., which *[universal benefit]* would be a great advancement to our country, wonderful enriching to our prince, and unspeakable commodities to all the inhabitants of Europe.

2. For through the shortness of the voyage, we would be able to sell all manner of merchandise, brought from thence, far better cheap, than either the Portuguese or Spaniard doth, or may do: And further, share with the Portuguese in the East, and the Spaniard in the West, by trading to any part of America, through *Mare de Sur* [South Seas, Pacific Ocean], where they can no manner of way offend us.

3. Also we may sail to diverse marvelous rich countries, both civil and others, out of both their jurisdictions, trades, and trafficks, where there is ... merchandise of an inestimable price. ...

4. Also we might inhabit some part of those countries and settle there such needy people of our country which now trouble the commonwealth and, through want here at home, are enforced to commit outrageous offences, whereby they are daily consumed with the gallows. ...

6. Beside the offering of our country commodities, which the Indians, etc. much esteem ..., they would have the cloths of this our country, so that there would be found a far better vent [market] for them, by this means, than yet this realm ever had, and that without depending, either upon France, Spain, Flanders, Portugal, Hamburg, Emden, or any other part of Europe. *[make it so it seems they would help them — not what happens]*

7. Also, hereby we shall increase both our ships and mariners without burdening of the state.

8. And also have occasion to let poor men's children to learn handicrafts, and thereby to make trifles and such like, which the Indians and those people do much esteem: by reason whereof, there should be no occasion, to have our country encumbered with loiterers, vagabonds, and suchlike idle persons.

4.2   A Spanish newsletter about Hawkins and Drake (December 1569)[2]

Despite the claim by one contemporary that "there are countries yet remaining without masters and possessors," England's best chance for wealth lay in snatching it from others.[3] This handwritten newsletter from Seville reports on the privateering raids of Sir John Hawkins (1532–95) and Sir Francis Drake (1540–96) against Spanish shipping from the New World. Newsletters were precursors to printed newspapers and continued through the end of the seventeenth century. Why might the Fuggers, an international banking house, subscribe to such letters? What type of information is included? What is the writer's opinion of Hawkins and Drake? Of Elizabeth? What is yours? Were they pirates? Were they terrorists?

From Cadiz this morning came the following news and immediately after it Don Melendez. He relates how John Hawkins the Englishman ... recently passed Cape St. Vincent with twenty-five well-found ships.... There he intercepted a ship trying to make its way to the Netherlands and carried it off together with its entire cargo. The crew he put on land ... to inform Don Melendez ... that he was proceeding to India [West Indies] and would await them ... [there, to call] them to account for the damage ... they had inflicted upon him during the previous year. Everyone was utterly horrified at these tidings, than which nothing could be worse for the king and the Indian trade, seeing that with a favorable wind Drake must now be close to the Indian Islands. At this juncture the ships from New Spain would certainly be loaded up and on their way, so that the Englishman would have them at his mercy.... And the most annoying part of this affair is that this Hawkins could not have fitted out so numerous and so well equipped a fleet without the aid and secret consent of the queen ... of England. It is the nature and habit of this nation not to keep faith, so the queen pretends that all has been done without her knowledge and desire.

4.3   Sir Henry Sidney to Queen Elizabeth on Munster and Connaught (April 20, 1567)[4]

Though nominally under English control, Ireland was the despair of many imperial projectors. In 1567 Sir Henry Sidney (1529–86), Elizabeth's lord

---

[2]   V. Von Klarwill, *The Fugger News-letters 1568–1605*, 2nd ser. (London, 1926), 7–8, Dec. 7, 1569, n.s.
[3]   [G. Best], *A True Discourse of the Late Voyages of Discoverie* (London, 1578), *The Fyrst Booke of the First Voyage*, 13.
[4]   *Calendar of the Carew Manuscripts, Preserved in the Archiepiscopal Library at Lambeth*, ed. J. S. Brewer and W. Bullen (London, 1869), lviii–lvix, from TNA, SP 63/20/66.

deputy there, reported to her on the situation in southwestern Ireland. Why is Ireland in so miserable a state? Whose fault is it? How does Sidney differentiate the Irish from the English? Does his report justify English involvement in Ireland? Would Ireland be fit for Gilbert's own colonial policy (document 4.1)? Irish opposition to English colonization in Munster provoked harsh martial law by Gilbert, acting as Sidney's subordinate. Gilbert reportedly ordered "that the heads of all those ... which were killed in the day, should be cut off from their bodies and brought to the place where he encamped at night ..., so that none could come into his tent for any cause but commonly he must pass through a lane of heads which he used *ad terrorem*."[5] Perhaps unsurprisingly, such state terrorism did little to settle the island; nevertheless, Gilbert was rewarded with a knighthood in 1570.

As touching the estate of the whole country ..., like as I never was in a more pleasant country in all my life so never saw I a more wasted and desolate land, no not in the confines of other countries where actual war hath continually been kept by the greatest princes of Christendom; and there heard I such lamentable cries and doleful complaints made by that small remain of poor people which yet are left, who (hardly escaping the fury of the sword and fire of their outrageous neighbors, or the famine which the same, or their extortious lords, hath driven them unto ...) make demonstration of the miserable estate of that country. Besides this, such horrible and lamentable spectacles there are to behold as the burning of villages, the ruin of churches, the wasting of such as have been good towns and castles, yea, the view of the bones and sculls of your dead subjects, who, partly by murder, partly by famine, have died in the fields, as in truth hardly any Christian with dry eyes could behold. ... Surely there was never people that lived in more misery than they do, nor as it should seem of worse minds, for matrimony among them is no more regarded in effect than conjunction between unreasonable beasts. Perjury, robbery and murder counted allowable. Finally I cannot find that they make any conscience of sin and doubtless I doubt whether they christen their children or no, for neither find I place where it should be done, nor any person able to instruct them in the rules of a Christian; or if they were taught I see no grace in them to follow it.

4.4 Earl of Essex, "The State of Ireland, as it appeared ... during the Rebellion" (1599)[6]

The Irish situation remained complex to the end of the reign. In response to the O'Neill rebellion, Robert Devereux, earl of Essex (1565–1601) had been

---

[5] T. Churchyard, *A Generall Rehearsall of Warres* (London, 1579), sig. Q[iv].
[6] H. Harington, ed., *Nugae Antiquae: Being a Miscellaneous Collection of Original Papers in Prose and Verse; Written ... by Sir John Harington* (London, 1779), 2: 294–303.

sent across the Irish Sea to command an immense force in 1599. According to Essex, which Irish problems are to be found within the Pale (the "Englishry," some 30 miles around Dublin), and which problems are endemic outside the Pale? Is the English failure in Ireland one of government or one of cultural awareness? Do the English want assimilation? How do the English and Irish in Ireland interact? Do these selections suggest the situation had changed between 1567 and 1599?

The chief causes of want [lack] of reformation in Ireland arise,

1. From the [Protestant] Churches for the most part, in general, being decayed so as the laws of God are not in any good sort or order therein ministered.
2. The good instructions delivered to governors from England, not put into execution....
3. No shire halls, nor other places fit for the ordinary administration of justice there.
4. No circuits nor quarter sessions there kept, as becometh.
5. The disorders of soldiers not punished....
7. The joining in marriage, fostering, and allying of the [Gaelic] Irishry with the [Anglo-Irish] English subjects.
8. No English laws or orders put in execution, or administered in Irish countries, where the English do govern.
9. No restitution made to the subjects of the Pale for any spoils on them committed by the Irishry.
10. The selling of horse armor, weapons, munition and furniture by the English subjects to the Irishry, and paying of great customs and duties in the Irish markets by the English subjects.
11. The great want of English tenants throughout the Pale.
12. The want of armor, weapons, munition, and furniture by the subjects of the Pale, and want of skill for lack of exercise, how to use English weapons ...
13. The want of schools throughout the Pale, either to learn younglings the English tongue, or to instruct the elder sort in rules of humanity....
15. A number of idle people – horsemen, kern [poor Irish foot soldier], galloglass [Irish armed retainer], and such like, with their followers, and dependers – do live traveling the Pale, and consuming the poor inhabitants thereof in eating their meat and drink....
19. Item, The borderers of the Pale bringing up their children after the savage and Irish manner, setting them at liberty at the age of sixteen years, or thereabouts, with companies of kern, to live unbridled by the spoil.
20. The not using English apparel and English behavior by many great gentlemen on the borders, of English birth.

21. Item, The maintaining of Irish harpers, rhymers, bards, poets, and such other their likes, in the Pale together, proving that the Irish behavior is too perfectly learned. ...

25. Item, The using to parley by borderers with the Irish neighbors privately ..., and joining with them in great league of friendship; by means whereof the secret service, intended by governors on their appointments, have been ... made known to the rebels. ...

26. Item, Loose, idle, and naughty people of the Irish countries, by whom the subjects are most offended, are not answered for, nor brought in by the captains or chieftains of the Irish. ...

27. The relieving of the Irishry with *aqua vitae* [distilled alcohol], made plentifully in the Pale, and to them conveyed as well in time of peace, as during their rebellion. ...

28. Item, The want of good laborers, handicraftsmen, and artificers. ...

29. The black rents [blackmail] and tributes, paid by the English subjects to the Irish neighbors, doth weaken the subject, and strengthen the enemy very much.

30. Item, The hue and cry not followed in form of law, on any robbery or spoils committed by the rebels. ...

31. Item, The spiritualities and temporalities [bishops and nobles] do not maintain the number of men appointed them by the laws, for the defense of the realm, to the distrengthening thereof.

32. The sheriffs and under-sheriffs of the English counties do use to accompany themselves with kern and suchlike Irish helpers, in ... doing of their offices. ...

For all which abuses and defects there are many good laws; yet such hath been the negligent execution of them, that they are at this time little regarded; therefore no hope of reformation, until the said laws are executed, or such as shall be thought necessary, without respect of persons.

4.5   *Elizabeth's Reply to the House of Commons's Demand for Mary's Execution (November 24, 1586)*[7]

During the last Tudor reign, the longer Elizabeth stayed unmarried, the clearer it became that the line of her cousin, Mary Queen of Scots (b. 1542, reigned 1542–67, d. 1587), would succeed her. But first Mary had to survive her own troubles in Scotland, borne not only of a realm torn between Protestant and Catholic, but of her own turbulent personal life. That turbulence culminated in the murder of her first husband, Lord Henry Darnley (1545/6–67) by the man she married as her second, James, earl of Bothwell (1534/5–78). In 1567, the dynastic problem posed by Mary Queen of Scots

[7]   [R. C.], *The Copie of a Letter to the Right Honourable the Earle of Leycester* (London, 1586), 23–8, 32.

became more acute, as her increasingly exasperated Protestant Scottish subjects forced the staunchly Catholic queen first to abdicate and then to flee to England. Although Mary was kept under virtual house arrest in the North, she became the focus for Catholic conspiracies against Elizabeth's rule. Rebellions and conspiracies led by the earls of Northumberland (1528–72) and Westmorland (1542/3–1601), the duke of Norfolk (1538–72), Robert Ridolfi (1531–1612), Francis Throckmorton (1554–84), and Anthony Babington (1561–86) dominated dynastic politics from 1569 to 1586. They were fueled by religious zeal, geopolitical ambitions, and even aristocratic resentment at the Tudors' centralizing policies. Though the Northern Rising of 1569 was crushed, the potential for plots and risings by English Catholics increased when the pope issued a bull excommunicating and deposing the heretical queen the next year (1570). By the 1580s, the English government could demonstrate clear links between domestic conspiracies, Mary Queen of Scots, and projected armed invasion by Spain, all encouraged by Rome. In October 1586, following evidence that Mary had given her consent to assassinate Elizabeth in what came to be known as the Babington Plot, a special commission of privy councilors and others tried and convicted the Queen of Scots at Fotheringhay Castle. Immediately the House of Commons urged Elizabeth to put her cousin to death. Elizabeth responded with the following "answer answerless." Do you find her answer clear? Why did Elizabeth hesitate to act? What principles would be threatened if she acted? If she failed to act?

The second answer made by the queen's majesty, delivered by her own mouth, to the second speech, uttered in the names of the Lords and Commons of the Parliament....

"I have strived more this day than ever in my life, whether I should speak, or use silence. If I speak and not complain, I shall dissemble; if I hold my peace, your labor taken were full vain....

"And since now it is resolved that my surety can not be established without a princess' end, I have just cause to complain, that I, who have in my time pardoned so many rebels, winked at so many treasons, and either not produced them, or altogether slipt them over with silence, should now be forced to this proceeding, against such a person....

"And now for your petition, I shall pray you for this present, to content yourselves with an answer without answer. Your judgement I condemn not, neither do I mistake your reasons, but pray you to accept my thankfulness, excuse my doubtfulness, and take in good part my answer answerless.... Therefore if I should say, I would not do what you request, it might peradventure be more than I thought: and to say I would do it, might perhaps breed peril of that you labor to preserve, being more than in your own wisdoms and discretions would seem convenient."

4.6 *Elizabeth to James VI of Scotland (February 14, 1587)*[8]

Mary was eventually executed on February 8, 1587 at Fotheringhay (see Bucholz and Key, chapter 5). Elizabeth's letter to James VI (b. 1566, reigned in Scotland, 1567–1625, in England from 1603) a few days later focused more on future relations between Scotland and England than on his mother's past. Compare this with her response to the Commons. What does Elizabeth claim, and is she believable?

My dear brother ..., I have now sent this kinsman of mine ..., to instruct you truly of that which is too irksome for my pen to tell you. I beseech you that – as God and many more know – how innocent I am in this case, so you will believe me that if I had bid aught I would have bid [abide] by it.... But as not to disguise fits most a king, so will I never dissemble my actions but cause them show even as I meant them. Thus assuring yourself of me that, as I know this was deserved, yet if I had meant it I would never lay it on others' shoulders, no more will I not damnify myself that thought it not.... And for your part, think you have not in the world a more loving kinswoman nor a more dear friend than myself, nor any that will watch more carefully to preserve you and your estate.

4.7 *William Camden,* Annals *(Latin, 1615; English, 1625)*[9]

The trial and execution of the Queen of Scots led to Elizabeth's greatest test: war with Spain. The Anglo-Spanish War had been building since the raids of Hawkins and Drake (see Plate 4, and document 4.2). It would be fought on three continents, and last until 1604. Thus, it was just as much a test for the seemingly invincible Spanish empire as it was for England. Both nations hoped God would tilt the balance in their favor. But, as one senior Spanish officer warned a papal diplomat just before the Armada sailed in 1588, "unless God helps us by a miracle the English, who have faster and handier ships than ours, and many more long-range guns, and who know their advantage just as well as we do, will never close with us at all, but stand aloof and knock us to pieces with their culverins [long barrel, small bore cannon]."[10] The next three sources discuss England's preparations for the Armada. As you read them, ask yourself "Why did England win"? Why did contemporaries think England won? According to William Camden (1551–1623), what is the source of England's strength?

[8]   *Elizabeth I: Collected Works*, ed. Leah S. Marcus, Janel Mueller, and Mary Beth Rose (Chicago, 2000), 296, from BL, MS. Cotton Caligula C.IX, fol. 212(recto).
[9]   W. Camden, *The History of the Most Renowned and Victorious Princess Elizabeth, Late Queen of England*, 4th ed., "compared with the original" (London, 1688), 405–6, 411.
[10]   G. Mattingly, *The Armada* (Boston, 1959), 216–7.

Plate 4 *A True Description of the Naval Expedition of Francis Drake, who with Five Ships Departed from the Western Part of England on 31th December 1577, Circumnavigated the Globe and Returned on 26th September 1580 with One Ship Remaining* (ca. 1587). (Source: Yale Center for British Art. Paul Mellon Collection, USA / Bridgeman Art Library.)

This map (pen, ink, and wash on vellum, supposedly by Drake himself) was repeatedly reproduced in the sixteenth and seventeenth centuries. What might contemporaries have learned or had confirmed by this map, which plots Drake's privateering circumnavigation? How might this map have been read differently by an English or a Spanish audience? (It may help if you superimpose the Spanish colonial empire in the Americas, Atlantic islands, and Philippines onto this map.) How does this map portray the regions where most sixteenth-century English explorations occurred?

Queen Elizabeth ... prepared with all diligence imaginable as strong a fleet as she could, and all things necessary for war. ... The command of the whole fleet she gave to Charles Lord Howard of Effingham [1536–1624], lord admiral of England ..., whom she knew, by his moderate and noble carriage, to be skillful in sea-matters ..., and of great authority and esteem amongst the sea-men of her navy. Him she sent early to the western parts of England, where Drake, whom she appointed vice-admiral joined with him. The Lord Henry Seymour, second son to the duke of Somerset, she commanded to lie upon the coast of the Low-Countries with 40 ships, English and Netherlandish [Protestant rebels], and to take care that the prince [duke] of Parma [Spanish regent of the Netherlands] came not out to sea with his forces. Though some there were who earnestly persuaded her to expect the enemy's coming, and to welcome him with a land battle. ...

[handwritten margin note: well-prepared thought of all possible plans of attack]

For land-service there were disposed along the southern coasts 20,000 men. Besides which two armies were raised of choice well-disciplined and experienced men: the one under the command of [Robert Dudley] the earl of Leicester [1532/3–88], consisting of 1,000 horse and 22,000 foot; which encamped at Tilbury, not far from the Thames mouth (for the enemy was fully resolved to set first upon London), the other under the leading of [Henry Carey] the Lord Hunsdon, consisting of 34,000 foot and 2,000 horse, to guard the queen's person. ...

In this troublesome season, some beat it many times into the queen's head, that the Spaniards abroad were not so much to be feared as the Papists at home; for the Spaniards would not attempt any hostility against England but upon confidence of help from them: and that therefore, for better security, the heads of that party were upon some pretense or other to be taken off [killed]. ... But the queen, disliking this as cruel counsel, thought it sufficient to commit some of the Papists, and those not of the chief, to custody at Wisbech in the Fens. And having her eyes and mind every way, she by frequent letters excited and quickened the Estates [of France], who were not asleep the while. Sir William Fitz-Williams, lord deputy of Ireland, she directed what he should do. The king of Scots she put in mind by her friends in Scotland, and by messengers, to be very wary of the Papists and the Spanish faction. But he, not ignorant how great a tempest and destruction hung overhead, was of his own accord forward and careful, and, according to his continual good affection to the true religion and the queen ..., had procured a confederacy to be entered into by the Protestants of Scotland for resisting the Spaniards. ...

The next day [July 20, 1588] the English discovered the Spanish fleet with lofty turrets like castles, in front like a half-moon, the wings thereof spreading out about the length of seven miles, sailing very slowly, though with full sails, the winds being as it were tired with carrying them, and the ocean groaning under the weight of them; which they willingly suffered to pass by, that they might chase them in the rear with a fore right wind.

4.8 The Miraculous Victory Achieved by the English Fleete *(Latin, 1598; English, 1599)*[11]

The Miraculous Victory, written in Latin by Emanuel van Meteren (1535–1612, the Flemish consul for Dutch merchants in London, and a fervent Protestant) and translated by Richard Hakluyt (1552?–1616, a compiler of geographical literature and a proponent of English strength and empire), was both description and propaganda. According to this reporter, why did England win? What values does his account embrace? How does the Armada story relate to those of imperial expansion, privateering, the succession, and the Counter-Reformation in England?

It seemeth that the duke of Parma and the Spaniards grounded upon a vain and presumptuous expectation, that all the ships of England and of the Low countries [the Protestants of the Spanish Netherlands, now in revolt] would at the first sight of the Spanish and Dunkirk Navy have betaken themselves to flight, yielding them sea room, and endeavoring only to defend themselves, their havens, and sea coasts from invasion. … They were in good hope also to have met with some rebels against her majesty, and such as were discontented with the present state, as Papists, and others. Likewise they looked for aid from the favorers of the Scottish queen, who was not long before put to death; all which they thought would have stirred up seditions and factions.

Whenas therefore the Spanish fleet rode at anchor before Calais …, the lord admiral of England being admonished by her majesty's letters from the court, thought it most expedient either to drive the Spanish fleet from that place …: and for that cause (according to her majesty's prescription) he took forthwith eight of his worst and basest ships which came next to hand, and disburdening them of all things which seemed to be of any value, filled them with gun-powder, pitch, brimstone, and with other combustible and fiery matter; and charging all their ordinance with powder, bullets, and stones, he sent the said ships upon the 28 of July being Sunday, about two of the clock after midnight, with the wind and tide against the Spanish fleet; which when they had proceeded a good space, being forsaken of the pilots, and set on fire, were directly carried upon the king of Spain's navy; which fire in the dead of the night put the Spaniards into such a perplexity and horror … that cutting their cables whereon their anchors were fastened, and hoisting up their sails, they betook themselves very confusedly unto the main sea.

In this sudden confusion, the principal and greatest of the four galliases [heavy, low-built vessel with both oars and sails] falling foul of another ship, lost her rudder: for which cause when she could not be guided any longer, she was by the force of the tide cast into a certain shoal upon the shore of Calais,

[11] R. Hakluyt, *The Principal Navigations, Voyages, Traffiques and Discoveries of the English Nation* … (London, 1599), 1: 601, 604–5, trans. from E. van Meteren, "The Miraculous Victory Atchieved (sic) by the English Fleete."

where she was immediately assaulted by diverse English pinnaces, hoys, and drumblers [small, fast vessels]. ...

Likewise upon the Scottish Western Isles of Lewis and Islay, and about Cape Cantyre [Mull of Kintyre] upon the mainland, there were cast away certain Spanish ships, out of which were saved diverse captains and gentlemen, and almost four hundred soldiers, who for the most part, after their shipwreck, were brought unto Edinburgh in Scotland, and being miserably needy and naked, were there clothed at the liberality of the King [James VI] and the merchants, and afterward were secretly shipped for Spain. ...

Upon the Irish coast many of their noblemen and gentlemen were drowned; and diverse slain by the barbarous and wild Irish. ... To conclude, there was no famous nor worthy family in all Spain, which in this expedition lost not a son, a brother, or a kinsman.

For the perpetual memory of this matter, the Zealanders [Dutch] caused new coin of silver and brass to be stamped: which on the one side contained the arms of Zealand, with this inscription: "Glory to God Only"; and on the other side, the pictures of certain great ships, with these words: "The Spanish Fleet"; and in the circumference about the ships: "It Came, Went, and Was. Anno 1588." That is to say, the Spanish fleet came, went, and was vanquished this year; for which, glory be given to God only.

Likewise they coined another kind of money; upon the one side whereof was represented a ship fleeing, and a ship sinking: on the other side four men making prayers and giving thanks unto God upon their knees; with this sentence: "Man purposeth; God disposeth, 1588."

4.9   *Queen Elizabeth's Tilbury Speech (August 9, 1588, recorded ca. 1623, pub. 1654)*[12]

Though the picture of Elizabeth giving this speech on horseback, clad in armor, is enshrined in British patriotic myth, historians have long debated whether it was actually given, and in the form portrayed here. In fact, the Armada had already been defeated by the time the speech was made. (Also, this text differs somewhat from that quoted in Bucholz and Key, chapter 5. Consider why different versions might exist; the difficulties in recording such a speech accurately; and the reasons the government might have had to "improve" on eyewitness accounts.) According to the queen, why would England win? Consider Elizabeth's use of gender tropes and theater: how does war limit her type of queenship and *vice versa*? (What can't she do?) Does this speech overcome the obstacles? (You may wish to compare this speech with her response to the Commons about Mary Queen of Scots [document 4.5] or about monopolies [document 4.17].)

My loving people, I have been persuaded by some that are careful of my safety to take heed how I committed myself to armed multitudes, for fear of treachery.

---

[12]   *Elizabeth I: Collected Works*, 325–6, from BL, Harleian MS. 6798, art. 18, fol. 87.

But I tell you that I would not desire to live to distrust my faithful and loving people. Let tyrants fear: I have so behaved myself that under God I have placed my chiefest strength and safeguard in the loyal hearts and goodwill of my subjects. And therefore I am come amongst you, as you see at this time, not for my recreation and disport, but being resolved, in the midst and heat of the battle, to live or die amongst you all; to lay down for my God and for my kingdom and for my people, my honor and my blood even in the dust. I know I have the body but of a weak and feeble woman, but I have the heart and stomach of a king and of a king of England too – and take foul scorn that Parma or any prince of Europe should dare to invade the borders of my realm. To the which rather than any dishonor shall grow by me, I myself will venture my royal blood; I myself will be your general, judge, and rewarder of your virtue in the field. I know that already for your forwardness you have deserved rewards and crowns, and I assure you in the word of a prince you shall not fail of them. In the meantime, my lieutenant general [Leicester] shall be in my stead, than whom never prince commanded a more noble or worthy subject. Not doubting but by your concord in the camp and valor in the field and your obedience to myself and my general, we shall shortly have a famous victory over these enemies of my God and of my kingdom.

Between Jesuits and Puritans

4.10   *William Allen on the martyrdom of Fr. William Filby of Oxford (1582)*[13]

The Royal Navy and the wind, if not God, disposed of the Spanish at sea, while at home Elizabeth's government sent would-be Catholic conspirators to the unhealthy fenland prison of Wisbech. Nevertheless, as we have seen, Philip II's plans were all the more alarming because Catholicism had revived from the 1570s. By the 1580s, the Jesuits were sending missionary priests into England, trained at colleges at Douai and Rome; many of those priests became involved in the plots against Elizabeth noted previously. The government, which had already prohibited asserting papal authority in England (1563) and importing papal bulls and other instruments from Rome (1571), now outlawed Catholic missionary work (1581), and made all Jesuits in England felonious (1585). The number of Catholic priests executed during Elizabeth's last decades approached that of the Protestants burned under Mary. The account of priestly martyrdom given by William, Cardinal Allen (1532–94) prompted several responses, including one by Lord Treasurer William (Cecil), Lord Burghley (1520/1–98) himself. Why might the English

---

[13] [W. Allen], *A Briefe Historie of the Glorious Martyrdom of XII Reverend Priests, executed within these twelvemonethes for confession and defence of the Catholike faith* (n.p. [Rheims?], 1582), 58–9.

government be so concerned about Allen's publication of the dying words of Fr. Filby? Protestants thought foreign-trained priests especially untrustworthy because they had been instructed to use any means, including slippery logic and dissimulation, to advance the Catholic cause. To judge from the exchange below, was the charge fair? What do you suppose was the impact of these executions on those who witnessed them?

On Wednesday being the 30 May these 4 venerable priests [M. William Filby, M. Lucas Kirby, M. Laurence Richardson whose right name was Johnson, and M. Thomas Cottam] were trailed from the Tower of London along the streets to Tyburn, about 7 in the morning, when they were come to the place of execution, William Filby (being the youngest, not above 27 years of age) was first taken from the hurdle, and being lifted into the cart, he blessed himself with the sign of the Cross ..., and so proceeded with these words: Let me see my brethren, looking to the other which lay on the hurdle and there withal holding forth his hands to them, said, Pray for me. Then speaking to the company, said: I am a Catholic, and I protest before almighty God that I am innocent of all these matters, whereof I am condemned, and I hope to be saved by the merits and death of our Savior Jesus Christ, beseeching him to have mercy on me and to forgive me my offences. And therewithal a proclamation was read for keeping the peace, and at the end thereof was said, God save the queen, to which he said, Amen.

The people asking him for what queen he prayed for, he answered, for Queen Elizabeth, beseeching God to send her a long and quiet reign, to his good will, and make her his servant, and preserve her from her enemies. With that M. Topcliff and others willed him to say, God save her from the pope. To whom he answered he is not her enemy, therewith the minister of S. Andrews in Holborn said, Note, that he saith the pope is not the queen's enemy. And then a preacher called Charke [spoke]. Yes, said he, you are a traitor, for you are sworn to the queen's sworn enemy. M. Filby looking aside, said, what do you mean, I never took oath in all my life. What, said Charke, then are you not a priest. You are deceived, said M. Filby, it is a vow and not an oath. After that one of the sheriff's men standing in the cart with M. Filby said unto him, what hast thou there in thy handkerchief, and therewithal taking the handkerchief from him found a little cross of wood with in it, which he holding up in his hands said, O what a villainous traitor is this, that hath a cross, diverse times repeating it, and diverse of the people saying the same. Whereunto M. Filby answered nothing, only smiling at them.

Then the articles, with the preface of the book printed by authority, was read, and his answers unto them. It was replied against him by some urging him further upon the same answer: if you hold this, then you can not be but a traitor to the queen's majesty, for that the pope hath deposed her by his bull. M. Filby said, that that bull was perchance called in again by this Pope Gregory XIII.... Then sheriff Martine called upon the hangman to dispatch, and the rope being about his neck, the sheriff said, Filby, the queen is merciful unto you, and we have authority from her to carry you back, if you will ask her mercy, and confess your fault do not refuse mercy offered, ask the Q. forgiveness, to whom M. Filby answered, I never offended her, well then said the sheriff make an end, and thus desiring all Catholics to pray for him he prayed, saying his *Pater noster*, and his *Ave*, and *In manus tuas*, etc., and when the cart was trailing away, he said, Lord, receive my soul, and so hanged knocking his breast several times, till some pulled down his hands, and so finished his life.

talked to parliment although had little influence over Elizabeth

4.11 *John Field and Thomas Wilcox,* First Admonition to the Parliament *(1572)*[14]

considere of puritans?

Strong Protestants had far more reason to be pleased with Elizabeth. Early in her reign, John Foxe and others championed her as the English Deborah (see document 3.17 above), leading the English Church out of papist superstition and persecution. But the honeymoon ended by the 1570s. Some Protestants saw the Elizabethan Settlement and the Thirty-Nine Articles as just the first step towards further reform, whereas the queen and some of her bishops viewed further reform as the first step towards anarchy. The clergymen John Field (1544/5?–88) and Thomas Wilcox (ca. 1549–1608) were two such critics. They laid out the Church of England's flaws in a pamphlet, asked Parliament "to reform God's Church," and were promptly incarcerated. What type of Church did they want, specifically with regard to Church government (how clergy were chosen), liturgy (how Church services were to be conducted), and Scripture study? Why did they appeal to Parliament instead of the Queen?

speaking against continued adoption of catholic tradition in church

Seeing that nothing in this mortal life is more diligently to be sought for and carefully to be looked unto than the restitution of true religion and reformation of God's Church, it shall be your parts (dearly beloved), in this present Parliament assembled, as much as in you lieth to promote the same, and to employ your whole labor and study, not only in abandoning all popish remnants both in ceremonies and regiment, but also in bringing in and placing in God's Church those things only which the Lord himself in his word commandeth....

Your wisdoms have to remove advowsons, patronages, impropriations, and bishops' authority, claiming to themselves thereby right to ordain ministers, and to bring in that old and true election which was accustomed to be made by the congregation.... Appoint to every congregation a learned and diligent preacher. Remove homilies, articles, injunctions, a prescript [prescribed] order of service made out of the mass-book. Take away the lordship, the loitering, the pomp, the idleness and livings of bishops....

removal of bishops from parliment

[14] *An Admonition to the Parliament* (n.p., n.d., Hemel Hempstead?, 1572)], sig. A[ii], [Aiii(verso)]–[Aiv], Biii–[Biii(verso)], [Dii(verso)–Diii].

state and church are separate

Whereas immediately after the last Parliament [1570–1] ..., the ministers of God's holy word and sacraments were called before her majesty's high commissioners, and enforced to subscribe unto the [Thirty-Nine] articles, if they would keep their places and livings, and some for refusing to subscribe were ... removed: May it please therefore this honorable and high court of Parliament ... to take a view of such causes as then did withhold and now doth [prevent] the foresaid ministers from subscribing and consenting unto those foresaid articles, by way of purgation to discharge themselves of all disobedience towards the Church of God and their sovereign, and by way of most humble entreaty for the removing away ... of all such corruptions and abuses as withheld them. ...

Albeit ... we have at all times borne with that which we could not amend in this book [of Common Prayer] and have used the same in our ministry, so far forth as we might ..., yet now being compelled by subscription to allow the same and to confess it not to be against the word of God in any point, but tolerable, we must needs say as followeth, that this book is an unperfect book, culled and picked out of that popish dunghill, the mass-book full of all abominations. ...

And as for the apparel, though we have been long [been] ... for order and decency commanded, yet we know and have proved that there is neither order nor comeliness nor obedience in using it. ... We marvel that ... copes, caps, surplices, tippets, and such like baggage, the preaching signs of popish priesthood, the pope's creatures, kept in the same form to this end, to bring dignity and reverence to the ministers and Sacraments, should be retained still, and not abolished.

4.12   Puritans described by Archbishop Whitgift (1574)[15]

By the 1590s, a German traveling through England noted at the University of Cambridge "that there is a certain sect in England, called Puritans. These according to the doctrine of the Church of Geneva, reject all ceremonies anciently held, and admit of neither organs nor tombs in their places of worship, and entirely abhor all difference in rank among churchmen, such as bishops, deans, etc."[16] Archbishop of Canterbury John Whitgift (1530/1?– 1604) responded to the reformers by identifying them, negatively, as Puritans and, less accurately, as Separatists. If they were not Separatists (that is, if they continued to attend parochial religious service according to the Church of England liturgy), then how were Puritans to be identified? Can you differentiate Field and Wilcox (document 4.11) from Whitgift?

This name Puritan is very aptly given to these men; not because they be pure, no more than were the heretics called Cathari [*katharos*, pure; medieval heretics];

[15]   J. Whitgift, *The Defense of the Aunswere to the Admonition, Against the Replie of T[homas]. C[artwright].* (London, 1574), 73–4.
[16]   *A Journey into England by Paul Hentzner, In the Year M.D.XC.VIII,* trans. H. Walpole (London, 1757), 58–9.

[handwritten: given sarcasm in an insult]

but because they think themselves to be *mundiores ceteris*, "more pure than others," as Cathari did, and separate themselves from all other churches and congregations as spotted and defiled. Because also they suppose the Church which they have devised to be without all impurity.... For why will they not come to our sermons or to our churches? Why will they not communicate with us in our sacraments, not salute us in the streets, nay, spit in our faces, and openly revile us? Why have they their secret conventicles? ... I know not why they should do so, except they think themselves to be contaminated by hearing us preach.... Which if they do, it argueth that they persuade themselves not only of such an outward perfection, but of such an inward purity also, that they may as justly for the same be called Puritans, as the Novatians [third-century schism which rejected concessions to the then reigning paganism] were.

[handwritten: Think of about delivering orders]

[handwritten: where is that behaviour in the faith?]

4.13   *Archbishop Grindal to Elizabeth on prophesyings (December 20, 1576)*[17]

The division between reformer and conservative in Elizabeth's Church was never clear. Take the issues of preaching and Bible study – both very dear to the Puritan heart. Yet several bishops, including Edmund Grindal (1519–83), archbishop of Canterbury, supported "prophesyings," gatherings of clergy and laity to discuss Scripture, as a way to ensure both more effective preaching and evangelizing in the provinces. Grindal defended the prophesyings in a letter to Elizabeth, against charges of "Papistry or Puritanism." Is Grindal's tone appropriate to his audience? What empowered him to take it? How do you suppose the queen reacted to this letter? Does the archbishop say anything that Elizabeth might want to hear? Would you label Grindal a reforming Protestant? A Puritan?

With most humble remembrance of my bounden duty to your majesty.... The speeches which it hath pleased you to deliver unto me, when I last attended on your highness, concerning abridging the number of preachers, and the utter suppression of all learned exercises and conferences among the ministers of the church, allowed by their bishops and ordinaries, have exceedingly dismayed and discomforted me.... I thought it therefore my duty by writing to declare some part of my mind unto your highness....

By preaching of God's word the glory of God is enlarged, faith is nourished, and charity increased. By it the ignorant is instructed, the negligent exhorted and incited, the stubborn rebuked, the weak conscience comforted, and to all those that sin of malicious wickedness the wrath of God is threatened. By preaching also due obedience to Christian princes and magistrates is planted in the hearts of subjects.... So as generally, where preaching wanteth, obedience faileth.

[17] *The Remains of Archbishop Grindal*, ed. W. Nicholson (Cambridge, Parker Society, 1843), 376–80, 382–4, 389.

No prince ever had more lively experience hereof than your majesty hath had in your time, and may have daily. If your majesty come to the city of London ..., what acclamations and prayers to God for your long life, and other manifest significations of inward and unfeigned love, joined with most humble and hearty obedience, are there to be heard! Whereof cometh this, madam, but of the continual preaching of God's word in that city, whereby that people hath been plentifully instructed in their duty towards God and your majesty? On the contrary, what bred the rebellion in the north [1569]? Was it not papistry, and ignorance of God's word, through want of often preaching? And in the time of that rebellion, were not all men, of all states, that made profession of the Gospel, most ready to offer their lives for your defense? Insomuch that one poor parish in Yorkshire, which by continual preaching had been better instructed than the rest (Halifax I mean) was ready to bring three or four thousand able men into the field to serve you against the said rebels. How can your majesty have a more lively trial and experience of the contrary effects of much preaching, and of little or no preaching? ...

But it is thought of some, that many are admitted to preach, and few be able to do it well. That unable preachers be removed is very requisite, if ability and sufficiency may be rightly weighed and judged. ... I, for mine own part ..., am very careful in allowing such preachers only, as be able and sufficient to be preachers, both for their knowledge in the scriptures, and also for testimony of their good life and conversation. And besides that, I have given very great charge to the rest of my brethren, the bishops of this province, to do the like. We admit no man to the office, that either professeth papistry or puritanism. Generally, the graduates of the university are only admitted to be preachers. ...

Now for the second point, which is concerning the learned exercise and conference amongst the ministers of the church: I have consulted with diverse of my brethren, the bishops, by letters; who think the same as I do, *viz.* a thing profitable to the Church, and therefore expedient to be continued. And I trust your majesty will think the like, when your highness shall have been informed of the manner and order thereof – what authority it hath of the scriptures. ...

The times appointed for the assembly is once a month, or once in twelve or fifteen days, at the discretion of the ordinary. The time of the exercise is two hours: the place, the church. ... The matter entreated of is ... some text of scripture ... is interpreted. ...

These orders following are also observed in the said exercise. ... No man may speak, unless he first be allowed by the bishop, with this proviso, that no layman be suffered to speak at any time. No controversy of this present time and state shall be moved or dealt withal. If any attempt the contrary, he is put to silence by the moderator. None is suffered ... to confute another. If any man utter a wrong sense of the scripture, he is privately admonished thereof, and better instructed by the moderators, and other his fellow-ministers. ...

Remember, madam, that you are a mortal creature. ...

And although ye are a mighty prince, yet remember that He which dwelleth in heaven is mightier.

4.14   Elizabeth to the Bishops on the "unlawful assemblies of a great number of our people out of their ordinary parishes ... called prophesyings" (May 7, 1577)[18]

Elizabeth did not respond directly to Grindal's missive until she issued a general letter of her own in May 1577, but her message was direct. What threats underlie both Grindal's and Elizabeth's statements? Why did she take such a hard line on this issue? (Elizabeth suspended Grindal from his functions as archbishop for five years, forgiving him just before his death.)

Considering it should be the duty of the bishops ... to see these dishonors against the honor of God and the quietness of the Church [prophesyings] reformed ...; we therefore, according to authority we have, charge and command you ... to take order through your diocese ... that no manner of public and divine service ..., nor any other rites or ceremonies, be in any sort used in the Church but directly according to the orders established by our laws. Neither that any manner of person be suffered within your diocese to preach ... but such as shall be lawfully approved and licensed. ... And ... we will and straitly charge you that you also charge the same [prophesyings] forthwith to cease and not to be used; but if any shall attempt or continue or renew the same, we will you not only to commit them unto prison as maintainers of disorders, but also to advertise us or our Council of the names and qualities of them. ... And in these things we charge you to be so careful and vigilant, as by your negligence, if we shall hear of any person attempting to offend ... without your correction or information to us, we be not forced to make some example or reformation of you.

Elizabethan Performances

It is no coincidence that Archbishop Grindal referred to Elizabeth's popularity in the city; or that another contemporary thought that during her coronation pageant "a man ... could not better term the City of London that time than a stage."[19] But Elizabethan London also began to house more permanent stage sets – the first purpose-built theater in 1576; the Globe from 1599. At least 430 different plays were performed in London between 1560 and 1600, and demand was rising (266 of those were presented in the 1590s). Playwrights often echoed Shakespeare in calling the world "A stage where every man must play a part" (*Merchant of*

[18]   E. Cardwell, ed., *Documentary Annals of the Reformed Church of England* (Oxford, 1839), 1: 375–6.
[19]   L. Manley, ed., *London in the Age of Shakespeare: an Anthology* (University Park, Pa., 1986), 285.

Venice, 1596–7, Act I, Scene I), and asserting that monarchs and politicians were like so many actors with set parts. It is difficult for us now to think what "all the world's a stage" might mean, because it has become an overused cliché. But, as you read the documents below, consider how the rigid social system of Elizabethan England constrained people to play parts and act suitable to their ranks. Consider the relationship between true feelings and acting; or the meaning of the injunction to "act themselves" (Philip Massingham, *The Roman Actor*, 1626).

4.15   Thomas Platter on London, the Theater, and the Court (1599)[20]

Thomas Platter (1574–1628), a young Swiss physician spent the late 1590s traveling in France, Spain, the Netherlands, and England. How might you distinguish the three regions of the metropolis: the merchants' city, the theatrical city, and the courtly city (usually Whitehall in Westminster, but here Hampton Court Palace just west of the city)? How is Elizabethan London saturated with both theatrical and global influences? To what extent is London a cosmopolis (world city)? To what extent is it parochial?

London is the capital of England and so superior to other English towns that London is not said to be in England, but rather England to be in London, for England's most resplendent objects may be seen in and around London; so that he who sightsees London and the royal courts in its immediate vicinity may assert without impertinence that he is properly acquainted with England. The town ... is situated on the river *Tamesis* [Thames] sixty Italian miles or 60,000 paces from the sea, which ebbs and flows as far as London and yet further, as may be observed every six hours from the banks and from the bridge. For which reason occan-craft are accustomed to run in here in great numbers as into a safe harbor, and I myself beheld one large galley next the other the whole city's length from St. Catherine's suburb to the bridge, some hundred vessels in all, nor did I ever behold so many large ships in one port in all my life....

And while a very fine long bridge is built across this stream, it is more customary to cross the water or travel up and down the town as at Lyons and elsewhere by attractive pleasure craft, for a number of tiny streets lead to the Thames from both ends of the town; the boatmen wait there in great crowds, each one eager to be first to catch one....

The wherries are charmingly upholstered and embroidered cushions laid across the seats, very comfortable to sit on or lean against, and generally speaking the benches only seat two people next to one another; many of them are covered in, particularly in rainy weather or fierce sunshine. They are

[20]   *Thomas Platter's Travels in England, 1599*, trans. and ed. C. Williams (London, 1937), 153–9, 166–7, 199, 201.

extremely pleasant to travel in and carry one or a couple of boatmen. I took a ferry across the river to a boathouse where the Thames runs in, and there I saw the queen's barge, quite closed up and very prettily designed with gangways....

At the top of one tower almost in the center of the [London] bridge, were stuck on tall stakes more than thirty skulls of noble men who had been executed and beheaded for treason and for other reasons. And their descendants are accustomed to boast of this, themselves even pointing out to one their ancestors' heads on this same bridge, believing that they will be esteemed the more because their antecedents were of such high descent that they could even covet the crown, but being too weak to attain it were executed for rebels; thus they make an honor for themselves of what was set up to be a disgrace and an example....

This city of London is so large and splendidly built, so populous and excellent in crafts and merchant citizens, and so prosperous, that it is not only the first in the whole realm of England, but is esteemed one of the most famous in all Christendom; especially since the wars in the Netherlands and France it has increased by many thousands of families who have settled in this city for religion's sake, and these have been very kindly received, and special places of worship allotted them in which to hear sermons in their own tongue – I myself went to the French church the day after my arrival on September 19th, and heard a French service there.

Most of the inhabitants are employed in commerce; they buy, sell and trade in all the corners of the globe, for which purpose the water serves them well, since ships from France, the Netherlands, Germany and other countries land in this city, bringing goods with them and loading others in exchange for exportation. For which reason they allow some ten per cent interest, because through shipping much may be effected and attained with money.

There are also many wealthy merchants and *banquiers* [moneychangers] in this city, some of whom sell costly wares while others only deal in money or wholesale transactions. In one very long street called Cheapside dwell almost only goldsmiths and money changers on either hand, so that inexpressibly great treasures and vast amount of money may be seen here.

The [Royal] Exchange is a great square place like the one in Antwerp ..., where all kinds of fine goods are on show; and since the city is very large and extensive merchants having to deal with one another agree to meet together in this palace, where several hundred may be found assembled twice daily, before lunch at eleven, and again after their meal at six o'clock, buying, selling, bearing news, and doing business generally....

On September 21st after lunch, about two o'clock, I and my party crossed the water, and there in the house with the thatched roof witnessed an excellent performance of the tragedy of the first Emperor Julius Caesar with a cast of some fifteen people; when the play was over, they danced very marvelously and gracefully together as is their wont, two dressed as men and two as women....

Thus daily at two in the afternoon, London has two, sometimes three plays running in different places, competing with each other, and those which play best obtain most spectators. The playhouses are so constructed that they play on a raised platform, so that everyone has a good view. There are different galleries and places, however, where the seating is better and more comfortable and therefore more expensive. For whoever cares to stand below only pays one English penny, but if he wishes to sit he enters by another door, and pays another penny, while if he desires to sit in the most comfortable seats which are cushioned, where he not only sees everything well, but can also be seen, then he pays yet another English penny at another door. And during the performance food and drink are carried round the audience, so that for what one cares to pay one may also have refreshment. The actors are most expensively and elaborately costumed; for it is the English usage for eminent lords or knights at their decease to bequeath and leave almost the best of their clothes to their serving men, which it is unseemly for the latter to wear, so that they offer them then for sale for a small sum to the actors. ...

Hampton Court is the finest and most magnificent royal edifice to be found in England, or for that matter in other countries, and comprises without the park (which has a wall round of one and a half miles in length, is full of game and has a lodge in its midst from which the queen can watch the chase) ten different large courts, and the same number of separate royal or princely dwellings, all adjoining one another however. And the entire construction is built of brick. ...

After leaving this extensive and pleasant garden, and presenting our gratuity to the gardener, the governor of the royal palace, one of the nobility, to whom we had previously sent in our letter of introduction, received us, and after he had returned our letter he presented us to his wife and daughters, who were to take us over all the inner royal apartments and cabinets, and show us all the treasures then in the place, and whatever the woman and daughters pointed out was all told us in French by an interpreter who was with us. The first room they showed us into contained the lively and lifelike portrait of the wild man and woman captured by Martin Frobisher, the English captain, on his voyage to the new world, and brought back to England alive. The man's face was much waled [marked with ridges], and both looked like savages, wore skins, and the woman carried a child in Indian dress in a linen cloth upon her shoulder. Above the woman were the words: *Ginoct Nutioc* [three Inuits seized and brought back to Bristol in late 1577 were named Kalicho, Arnaq, and Nutaaq; all died by the end of the year].

4.16 *"Journey Through England and Scotland Made by Lupold von Wedel" (1584–5)*[21]

We have met the traveler von Wedel before (see document 1.9 above). In this selection, the German focuses on ritual surrounding the queen. Consider the degree of artifice in Elizabeth's own words and actions. In the queen's

[21] "Journey Through England and Scotland Made by Lupold von Wedel in the Years 1584 and 1585," trans. Gottfried von Bülow, *TRHS* n.s. 9 (1895): 250–1, 258–65.

routine are there some activities or spaces that are more for ritual and others that are more for practical politics? How would you distinguish the ritual and the political? Why does von Wedel place so much emphasis on describing the clothing of participants? Again, how is Elizabeth's London saturated with both theatrical and global influences?

I believe the opening of Parliament took place on November 25 [1584]. All the streets and lanes in Westminster were well cleaned and strewn with sand when the queen made her entrance into the house, for it is a custom that on the first and last day of the session the king or queen shall be present in the assembly. At the head of the procession rode, two-by-two, eighteen lords and gentlemen of the court, after them fifteen trumpets, two gentlemen, each with 100 soldiers uniformly clad; now came fifteen members of Parliament in long red cloth coats, lined with white rabbit and reverses of the same almost down to the girdle. Next followed two gentlemen, the first with the queen's mantle, the other with her hat, their horses were led by servants. Now came two heralds, each in a blue mantle with two wings on it of beaten gold bearing the queen's arms, then three pairs of gentlemen of the Parliament in their usual robes, two heralds like those before followed by thirteen gentlemen of the Parliament, counts [earls] and barons, like the former, two heralds, seven pairs of bishops in long red robes with broad reverses of white linen and square caps of black stuff on their heads, then came five pairs of gentlemen of the Parliament in long red coats set with four stripes of rabbit fur. Now followed the Chancellor of the realm, behind him the Treasurer and then Secretary in their usual robes, with broad golden collars hanging down in the front and back to the saddle. Followed four men with scepters, each ornamented with a crown, followed some gentlemen of the Parliament clad like the others. All these, I have mentioned, had gold and silver trappings on their horses, the least valuable being velvet. Followed the huntsmen, about fifty in number, all of noble birth, with small gilt spears. These marched on foot. Now followed a horse, led by a gentleman, the trappings, saddle, and bridle all of gold covered with pearls, the latter being set with precious stones. On the forehead an ornament was fixed with one large diamond, and on the ears hung large pearls. Now followed the queen in a half-covered sedan chair, which looked like a half-covered bed. The chair and the cushions on which the queen was seated were covered with gold and silver cloth. The queen had a long red velvet parliamentary mantle, down to the waist, lined with ermine, white with little black dots, and a crown on her head. The sedan chair was carried by two cream-colored horses with yellow manes and tails, on the heads and tails yellow and white plumes were fastened, and they had saddles and trappings of golden stuff. Behind the queen another horse was led, having trappings of red velvet fringed with gold and ornamented with plumes. This horse was followed by twenty-four ladies and maidens, riding one after the other, and one in finer dress and her horse better caparisoned than the others.... The procession took its way to Westminster Church, where all the kings are buried. Here the queen dismounted, knelt down at the entrance and said her prayers, entered the church, where prayers were offered and chants performed. Then the queen went to the house of Parliament close by, and was led into a separate chamber, on the platform of which was a splendid canopy of golden stuff and velvet, embroidered with gold, silver, and pearls, and below it a throne, arranged with all royal splendors, on which the queen seated herself. The benches in this chamber had their seats as well as the backs covered with red sills, in the midst four woolsacks of red cloth were laid square.... On the woolsack nearest to the queen's throne sits the Chancellor, turning his back to the queen, on that to the right hand sit three judges, on that to the left three secretaries. Close to the bar, but outside of it, sit two clerks, on the benches around to the right side twenty bishops, two viscounts or peers, one marquis, to the left twenty counts and twenty barons. Thus the sitting of this Parliament begun, they had sittings every day until Christmas, but the queen, as I said before, was present only the first and last day.

4.17 Elizabeth's Golden Speech (November 30, 1601)[22]

Perhaps the queen's most commanding performance was her "Golden Speech" given to members of the House of Commons. It followed angry debates in the Commons about monopolies she had given out to her own courtiers, exacerbating a bad economy (see Bucholz and Key, chapter 5). So the plot is set in motion. The stage is the queen's own Presence Chamber at court, the audience her loyal Commons – but they are also cast extras. The stage directions are that the speaker of the Commons has just given thanks, and, along with 140 MPs, three low bows to the queen for her proclamation promising to reform the abuse of monopolies; and so the entire cast is kneeling at first. Are there other stage directions within her speech? What are her strengths and weaknesses as an actress? Was her audience charmed? Persuaded? Why or why not?

Mr. Speaker, We perceive your coming is to present thanks unto me; know it I accept with no less joy than your loves can desire to offer such a present, and more esteem it than any treasure or riches (for that we know how to prize), but loyalty, love, and thanks, I account them invaluable. And though God hath raised me high, yet this I count the glory of my crown – that I have reigned with your loves. This makes [that] I do not so much rejoice that God hath made me to be a queen, as to be a queen over so thankful a people, and to be the means under God to conserve you in safety, and preserve you from danger, yea to be

[22] S. D'Ewes, ed., *A Compleat Journal of the Votes, Speeches, and Debates* ... (London, 1693), 659–60.

101

the instrument to deliver you from dishonor, from shame, from infamy, from out of servitude and slavery under our enemies, to keep you from cruel tyranny and vile oppression intended against us. For better withstanding whereof we take very acceptably your intended helps. ... Of myself I must say this: I never was any greedy scraping grasper, nor a strait fast-holding prince, nor yet a waster. My heart was never set upon any worldly goods, but only for my subjects' goods [good]. What you do bestow on me, I will not hoard it up, but receive it to bestow on you again. Yea, mine own properties I account yours to be expended for your good. ...

Mr. Speaker, I would wish you and the rest to stand up, for I fear I shall yet trouble you with longer speech.

Mr. Speaker, you give me thanks, but I am more to thank you, and I charge you, thank them of the Lower House [Commons] from me. For had I not received a knowledge from you, I might have fallen into the lapse of an error, only for lack of true information. For since I was queen, yet did I never put pen to any grant but upon pretext and semblance made to me, that it was for the good and avail of my subjects generally, though a private profit to some of my ancient servants who had deserved well. But that my grants shall be made grievances to my people and oppressions to be privileged under color of our patents, our kingly dignity shall not suffer it. And when I heard it, I could give no rest unto my thoughts until I had reformed it. And those varlets, lewd persons, abusers of my bounty, shall know I will not suffer it. And Mr. Speaker, tell the House from me I take it exceeding gratefully that the knowledge of these things is come to me from them. ... For above all earthly treasure, I esteem my people's love, more than which I desire not to merit. ...

And in my governing this I have ever had the grace to use – to set the last judgement day before mine eyes, and so to rule as I shall be judged, and to answer before a higher judge, to whose judgement seat I do appeal [in] that never thought was cherished in my heart that tended not to my people's good. And if my kingly bounty have been abused and my grants turned to the hurt of my people, contrary to my will and meaning; or if any in authority under me have neglected or converted what I have committed unto them, I hope God they will not lay their culps [culpabilities] to my charge.

To be a king and wear a crown is a thing more glorious to them that see it than it is pleasant to them that bear it. For myself, I never was so much enticed with the glorious name of a king or royal authority of a queen as delighted that God hath made me His instrument to maintain His truth and glory, and to defend this kingdom from dishonor, damage, tyranny, and oppression. But should I ascribe any of this to myself, or my sexly weakness, I were not worthy to live, and of all, most unworthy of the mercies I have had from God. But to God only and wholly, all is to be given and ascribed. ... And though you have had and may have many mightier and wiser princes sitting in this seat, yet you never had nor shall have any that will love you better. Thus Mr. Speaker, I commend me to your loyal love, and you to my best care and your further counsels. And I pray you Mr. Comptroller and you of my Councils, that before these gentlemen depart into their countries [counties] you bring them all to kiss my hand.

4.18   John Clapham, "Certain Observations Concerning the Life and Reign of Queen Elizabeth" (ca. 1603)[23]

worked towards the end of her reign in court   *L after her death*

John Clapham (1566–1619) was clerk to Lord Treasurer Burghley in the 1590s. According to Clapham, what qualities made Elizabeth an effective ruler? How did she deal with courtiers' requests? Was there anything theatrical or artificial in her treatment of others?

Now … I will … proceed with the particular description of the queen's disposition and natural gifts of mind and body, wherein she either matched or excelled all the princes of her time; as being of a great spirit, yet tempered with moderation; in adversity never diverted; in prosperity not altogether serene; affable to her subjects, but always with due regard of the greatness of her estate, by reason whereof she was both loved and feared. In her latter time, when she showed herself in public, she was always magnificent in apparel, supposing haply thereby, that the eyes of her people, being dazzled with the glittering aspect of those accidental ornaments would not so easily discern the marks of age and decay of natural beauty. And she came abroad the more seldom, to make her presence the more grateful and applauded by the multitude, to whom things rarely seen are in manner as new.

stood strong against males before her – talked about similar to Henry VII

upheld look no matter age to reflect her power as equally influential as when she was young

She suffered not at any time any suitor to depart discontented from her; and, though ofttimes he obtained not that he desired, yet he held himself satisfied with her manner of speech, which gave hope of success in a second attempt. And it was noted in her that she seldom or never denied any suit that was moved unto her, how unfit so ever to be granted, but the suitor received the answer of denial by some other; a thankless office and commonly performed by persons of greatest place, who oft-times bear the blame of many things wherein themselves are not guilty, while no imputation must be laid upon the prince, and the vulgar sort for the most part discerning no more than what is personally apparent to their outward senses.

made suitors feel unworthy or wrong as an act of holding her strength – used virginity and beauty as strategy

In granting offices, she used many delays, but after long suit she gave them voluntarily. The one perhaps she did for that she loved to be sued unto and to be gratified with rewards, and the other that she might not seem to yield by importunity and so lose the thanks that a good turn freely bestowed deserveth. She was accounted in her latter time to be very near and oversparing of expense; and yet, if the rewards which she sometimes gave of mere motion and grace had been bestowed of merit with due respect, they had doubtless purchased her the name of a very liberal prince…. Certain it is, that some persons attending near about her would now and then abuse her favor and make sale of it, by taking bribes for such suits as she bestowed freely. Likewise purveyors and other officers of her household, under pretense of her service, would ofttimes for their own gain vex with many impositions the poorer sort of the inhabitants near the usual places of

[23]   E. P. Read and C. Read, eds., *Elizabeth of England: Certain Observations Concerning the Life and Reign of Queen Elizabeth by John Clapham* (Philadelphia, 1951), 85–6, from BL, Add. MS. 22,925.

her residence. And although it be accounted as great a fault for a prince to be ill himself as to have ill officers about him, yet the consideration of her sex (she being a woman and wanting convenient means to understand the grievances of her poor but by report of others) may seem to carry some color of excuse. She was very rich in jewels, which had been given her by her subjects; for in times of progress there was no person that entertained her in his house but, besides his extraordinary charge in feasting her and her train, he bestowed a jewel upon her; a custom in former times begun by some of her special favorites that, having in good measure tasted of her bounty, did give her only of her own; though otherwise that kind of giving was not so pleasing to gentlemen of meaner quality....

The selfsame day that the late earl of Essex entered the city with diverse noblemen and gentlemen of quality in a confused troop [February 8, 1600], when report was made unto her of the manner thereof, she being then at dinner seemed nothing moved therewith, but only said He that had placed her on that seat would preserve her in it; and so she continued at her dinner, not showing any sign of fear, or distraction of mind, nor omitting anything that day that she had been accustomed to do at other times....

She would often show herself abroad at public spectacles, even against her own liking, to no other end but that the people might the better perceive her ability of body and good disposition, which otherwise in respect of her years they might perhaps have doubted; so jealous was she to have her natural defects discovered for diminishing her reputation. As for flatterers, it is certain that she had many too near her, and was well contented to hear them.... She had in her time four principal favorites: namely, the earl of Leicester, Sir Christopher Hatton [ca. 1540–91], Sir Walter Ralegh, and the earl of Essex. All these successively enjoyed her grace in the highest measure, being men of very comely personage, and adorned with all outward gifts of nature, but much differing one from another in the disposition of their minds.

4.19   *Sir Robert Naunton,* Fragmenta Regalia *(written ca. 1634, pub. 1641)*[24]

Sir Robert Naunton (1563–1635) was in the last years of Elizabeth's reign a rising courtier patronized by Essex. He rose to become secretary of state under James I, and thus he brings insight of eminent political experience to his reminiscences of Elizabeth's rule. What are the costs – political and fiscal – to courtly display and empire? When in her reign did public performance and imperial reach threaten Elizabeth? How do Clapham's and Naunton's two summations of her (late) reign relate to earlier documents in this chapter?

The principal note of her reign will be, that she ruled much by faction and parties, which herself both made, upheld, and weakened, as her own great judgement advised....

[24] Sir R. Naunton, *Fragmenta Regalia, or, Observations on the late Queen Elizabeth, Her Times and Favourits* (n.p., [London], 1641), 6–8.

From whence, and in more instances, I conclude that she was absolute and sovereign mistress of her graces; and that all those to whom she distributed her favors were never more than tenants at will, and stood on no better ground than her princely pleasure and their own good behavior. And this also I present as a known observation, that she was (though very capable of counsel) absolute enough in her own resolutions, which was ever apparent even to her last, in that her aversation [aversion] to grant [Hugh O'Neill, second earl of] Tyrone [ca.1550–1616] the least drop of her mercy, though earnestly and frequently advised, yea, wrought only by the whole Council of State, with very many pressing reasons, and as the state of her kingdom then stood (I may speak it with assurance) necessitated arguments. . . .

We have not many precedents of her liberality, or of any large donatives to particular men; my lord of Essex's *Book of Parks* only excepted, which was a princely gift, and some few more of a lesser size to my lord of Leicester, Hatton, and others. Her rewards consisted chiefly in grants of leases, of offices, and places of judicature: but for ready money, and in any great sums, she was very sparing; which we partly conceive was a virtue rather drawn by necessity, than her nature, for she had many layings out, and to her last period. And I am of opinion with Sir Walter Ralegh, that those many brave men of our times, and of the militia, tasted little more of her bounty than in her grace and good word, with their due entertainment, for she ever paid the soldiers well, which was the honor of her times, and more than her great adversary of Spain could perform. So that when we come to the consideration of her frugality, the observation will be little more, than that her bounty and it were so interwoven together, that the one was suited by an honorable way of spending, the other limited by a necessitated way of sparing.

The Irish action we may call a malady, and a consumption of her times, for it accompanied her to her end; and it was of so profuse and vast an expense, that it drew near a distemperature of State, and of passion in herself. For toward her last she grew hard to please, her arms being accustomed to prosperity, and the Irish prosecution not answering her expectation and wanted success for a good while. It was an unthrifty and inauspicious war, which did much disturb and mislead her judgement, and the more, for that it was a precedent which was taken out of her own pattern: For as the queen (by way of diversion) had at the coming to the crown supported the revolted States of Holland, so did the king of Spain turn the trick on herself towards her going out, by cherishing the Irish rebellion.

HISTORIANS' DEBATES

Was the first British Empire Atlantic-wide and integrated, or localized, episodic, and unsuccessful?

N. Canny, ed., *The Oxford History of the British Empire*, 1, *The Origins of Empire: British Overseas Enterprise to the Close of the Seventeenth Century* (Oxford, 1998), esp. chs. by the editor and J. C. Appleby; B. Bradshaw and J. S. Morrill, eds., *The British Problem, 1534–1707* (London, 1996), esp. Morrill's introductory overview and H. Morgan on the Tudors; S. G. Ellis and S. Barber, eds., *Conquest and Union: Fashioning a British State, 1485–1725* (London, 1995), essays by Ellis, C. Brady, and J. Dawson on the Tudors; B. Bradshaw and P. Roberts, eds., *British Consciousness and Identity: The Making of Britain, 1533–1707* (Cambridge, 1998), esp. essays by the editors; E. Mancke, "Empire and State," in *The British Atlantic World*, ed. D. Armitage and M. Braddick (Basingstoke, 2002); N. Canny's and A. Pagden's introduction to their *Colonial Identity in the Atlantic World* (Princeton, 1987); "Elizabeth I and the Expansion of England" (conference proceedings), *TRHS* 6th ser., 14 (2004), esp. S. Adams's introduction and essays by R. A Mason, H. Morgan, and D. Armitage; D. Potter, "Britain and the Wider World," in *A Companion to Tudor Britain*, ed. R. Tittler and N. Jones (Oxford, 2004).

Was empire an imaginative construction more than a geographical entity?

D. Armitage, "The New World in British Historical Thought," in *America in European Consciousness, 1493–1750*, ed. K. O. Kupperman (Chapel Hill, 1995); D. B. Quinn, "Renaissance Influences in English Colonization," *TRHS* 5th ser., 26 (1976); N. P. Canny, "The Ideology of English Colonization: From Ireland to America" (1973, reprinted in *Theories of Empire, 1450–1800*, ed. D. Armitage, Aldershot, 1998); R. Helgerson, "The Voyages of a Nation," in *Forms of Nationhood: The Elizabethan Writing of England* (Chicago, 1992); L. Montrose, "The Work of Gender in the Discourse of Discovery," and M. C. Fuller, "Ralegh's Fugitive Gold: Reference and Deferral in *The Discoverie of Guiana*," in *Representations* 33 (1991), reprinted in *New World Encounters*, ed. S. Greenblatt (Berkeley, 1993).

Was the Armada a decisive turning point militarily? politically? or merely part of the construction of future myth?

I. A. A. Thompson's essay in M. J. Rodriguez-Salgado and S. Adams, eds., *England, Spain, and the Gran Armada, 1584–1604* (Edinburgh, 1991); F. Fernández-Armesto, "Armada Myths: the Formative Phase," in *God's Obvious Design: Papers for the Spanish Armada Symposium, Sligo, 1998*, ed. P. Gallagher and D. W. Cruickshank (London, 1990); S. Adams, in J. Morrill, ed., *The Oxford Illustrated History of Tudor & Stuart Britain* (Oxford, 1986); *idem* in P. Collinson, ed., *The Sixteenth Century, 1485–1603* (London, 2002); R. E. Scully, " 'In the Confident Hope of a Miracle': The Spanish Armada and Religious Mentalities in the Late Sixteenth Century," *Catholic Historical Review* 89, 4 (2003); S. Frye, "The Myth of Elizabeth at Tilbury," *SixteenthCJ* 23, 1 (1992); J. M. Green, " 'I my self': Queen Elizabeth I's Oration at Tilbury Camp," *SixteenthCJ* 28 (1997); articles by S. Adams and G. Parker in special issue on the Armada, *HT* 38, 5 (1988); M. J. Rodríguez-Salgado, "The Spanish Story of the 1588 Armada Reassessed" (review essay), *HJ* 33 (1990); W. MacCaffrey, "The Armada in its Context," *HJ* 32 (1989); J. E. A. Dawson, "William Cecil and the British Dimension of Early Elizabethan Foreign Policy," *History* 74, 241 (1989); articles by D. J. B. Trim, P. Croft, and P. E. J. Hammer in *Tudor England and its Neighbours*, ed. S. Doran and G. Richardson (Basingstoke, 2005).

Was Elizabethan government personal, court-centered, or de-centered and factionalized?

J. Guy, ed., *The Tudor Monarchy* (London, 1997), reprints essays by P. Collinson, S. Adams, and P. Williams on the ideology, the favorites, and the business of the Elizabethan Court; N. Jones, "Elizabeth's First Year: The Conception and Birth of the Elizabethan Political World," in *The Reign of Elizabeth I*, ed. C. Haigh (London, 1984); D. Dean, "Elizabethan Government and Politics," and R. Warnicke, "The Court," in Tittler and Jones, *Companion to Tudor Britain*; S. Adams, "Politics, Faction and Clientage in Late Tudor England," *HT* 32, 12 (1982); P. E. J. Hammer, " 'Absolute and sovereign mistress of her grace'?: Queen Elizabeth I and her Favourites, 1581–1592," in *The World of the Favourite*, ed. J. H. Elliott and L. W. B. Brockliss (New Haven, 1999); P. Lake, " 'The Monarchical Republic of Elizabeth I' Revisited (by its Victims) as a Conspiracy," in *Conspiracies and Conspiracy Theory in Early Modern Europe: from the Waldensians to the French Revolution*, ed. B. Coward and J. Swann (Aldershot, 2004).

Evaluating Elizabeth

P. Collinson, "Elizabeth I and the Verdicts of History," *HR* 76, 194 (2003); S. Bassnett, *Elizabeth I: A Feminist Perspective* (Oxford, 1988); F. Teague, "Queen Elizabeth in Her Speeches," in *Gloriana's Face: Women, Public and Private in the English Renaissance*, ed. S. P. Cerasano and M. Wynne-Davies (Detroit, 1992); T. M. Walker, ed., *Dissing Elizabeth: Negative Representations of Gloriana*, ed. (Durham, N. C., 1998), esp. the editor's introduction and essays by S. Doran, C. Levin, and P. E. McCullough; S. Doran and T. Freeman, eds., *The Myth of Elizabeth* (London, 2003), esp. essays by T. S. Freeman and A. Hadfield on contemporary criticisms of Elizabeth; C. Levin, "Elizabeth as Sacred Monarch," in *The Heart and Stomach of a King: Elizabeth I and the Politics of Sex and Power* (Pennsylvania, 1994); C. Haigh, *Elizabeth I* (London, 2000), esp. the conclusion.

Can we identify Catholics, Anglicans, and Puritans? (Post-Reformation struggles continued)

G. W. Bernard, "The Church of England, c. 1590–c. 1642," *History* 75 (1990); C. Durston and J. Eales, eds., *The Culture of English Puritanism 1560–1700* (Basingstoke, 1996), esp. P. Collinson, "Elizabethan and Jacobean Puritanism as Forms of Popular Culture"; N. Tyacke, ed., *England's Long Reformation, 1500–1800* (London, 1998), esp. the introduction, comment by Collinson on essay by E. Duffy, and long view of J. Gregory's concluding essay; C. Haigh, "Success and Failure in the English Reformation," *P & P* 173 (2001); N. Jones, "Religious Settlements," in Tittler and Jones, *Companion to Tudor Britain*; P. Collinson,

"Ecclesiastical Vitriol: Religious Satire in the 1590s and the Invention of Puritanism," in *The Reign of Elizabeth I: Court and Culture in the Last Decade*, ed. J. Guy (1995); P. Collinson, "Richard Hooker and the Construction of Christian Community," in *Richard Hooker and the Construction of Community*, ed. R. S. McGrade (London, 1997); D. MacCulloch, "Richard Hooker's Reputation," *EHR* 117 (2002); P. Lake, 'Business as Usual?: the Immediate Reception of Hooker's *Ecclesiastical Polity*' *JEcclH* 52, 3 (2001); N. Canny, "Why the Reformation Failed in Ireland, une Question Mal Posée," *JEcclH* 30 (1979); K. Bottigheimer, "The Failure of the Reformation in Ireland, a Question Bien Posée," *JEcclH* 36 (1985); C. Haigh, "Revisionism, the Reformation and the History of English Catholicism," *JEcclH* 36 (1985); P. McGrath in *JEcclH* 35 (1984) and 36 (1985); T. M. McCoog, "The English Jesuit Mission and the French Match, 1579–1581," *Catholic Historical Review* 87, 2 (2001); M. B. Rowlands, "Recusant Women, 1560–1640," in *Women in English Society*, ed. M. Prior (London, 1985); M. Questier, "Elizabeth and the Catholics," in *Catholics and the 'Protestant Nation': Religious Politics and Identity in Early Modern England*, ed. E. H. Shagan (Manchester, 2005).

ADDITIONAL SOURCE COLLECTIONS

K. Aughterson, *The English Renaissance: An Anthology of Sources and Documents* (London, 1998).

D. Cressy and L. A. Ferrell, eds., *Religion and Society in Early Modern England: Voices, Sources and Texts*, 2nd ed. (London, 2005).

S. Doran, *England and Europe, 1485–1603*, 2nd ed. (London, 1996).

G. R. Elton, ed., *The Tudor Constitution: Documents and Commentary*, 2nd ed. (Cambridge, 1968, 1982).

G. B. Harrison, ed., *The Elizabethan Journals* (Ann Arbor, 1938).

A. F. Kinney, *Elizabethan Backgrounds: Historical Documents of the Age of Elizabeth I* (Hamden, Conn., 1990).

J. M. Levine, ed., *Elizabeth I* (Englewood Cliffs, New Jersey, 1969).

J. I. McCollum, Jr., ed., *The Age of Elizabeth: Selected Source Materials in Elizabethan Social and Literary History* (Boston, 1960).

P. C. Mancall, ed., *Envisioning America: English Plans for the Colonization of North America, 1580–1640* (Boston, 1995).

G. W. Prothero, ed., *Select Statutes and other Constitutional Documents Illustrative of the Reigns of Elizabeth and James I*, 4th ed. (Oxford, 1913).

W. B. Rye, ed., *England as Seen by Foreigners in the Days of Elizabeth & James the First* (1865, reprinted, New York, 1967).

R. Salter, *Elizabeth I and her Reign* (Basingstoke, 1988).

D. Starkey, ed., *Rivals in Power: Lives and Letters of the Great Tudor Dynasties* (New York, 1990).

J. R. Tanner, ed., *Tudor Constitutional Documents, A.D. 1485–1603, with a Historical Commentary* (Cambridge, 1922).

CHAPTER FIVE

Masterless Men and the Monstrous Regiment of Women

As we have noted, the possible break down of order obsessed and terrified early modern society (see chapter 1). This chapter examines the "Babylonical confusion" that late Tudor and early Stuart homilies repeatedly warned against: from one-on-one scolding or brawling to violent, group actions. The reigns of Elizabeth and James were not necessarily *more* disorderly than other periods (see Bucholz and Key, chapter 6), but that did not prevent contemporaries from thinking so. Several questions should be asked about that perception and the evidence provided by the following documents:

- Why did contemporaries think their times more disordered than before? How accurate were they in this observation and in explaining it?
- Did violent events such as *charivari*s, food riots, enclosure riots, popular rebellions, or witchcraft persecutions tend more to break down or reinforce social order and values?
- How did the popular response to social ills and disorder compare and contrast with the elite response?

Rough Music, Food Riots, and Popular Rebellions

5.1 *Anonymous threatening note (1598)*[1]

Disorder usually began with "angry speeches" or "many outrageous words spoken" (1574), often inspired by drink.[2] Words were weapons with which

---

[1] J. P. Collier, ed., *Trevelyan Papers* (London, Camden Society, 1863), 2: 101.
[2] Late-sixteenth century contemporaries quoted in F. G. Emmison, *Elizabethan Life: Morals & the Church Courts* (Chelmsford, 1973), 128; and (below) *idem, Elizabethan Life: Disorder* (Chelmsford, 1970), 177.

to attack reputation. And reputation, in a face-to-face, largely oral culture, mattered. Constables, watchmen, and other minor officials met with regular verbal abuse. Thus, in 1588, one constable received "evil words" from two blacksmiths he had asked to shoe his horse. Other such officials were subject to "opprobrious and threatening words" when they put a vagrant in the stocks. Since we usually only know about verbal assaults between parishioners or neighbors when they ended up in civil or consistory (Church) court, we might well ask again the question we asked in chapter 1: are such cases evidence of a lawful or lawless society? Words and gestures threatened, of course, because they raised the specter of real, physical violence. ("Assault" and "insult" derive from a common root word.) Note the very real threat made in the following anonymous, handwritten libel from 1598. Who is being threatened by whom and why? How might anonymity be a weapon? And who (what social group) might use it?

Our most hearty commendation unto you good brethren and apprentices. ... The cause of our writing to you at this time is for to know whether you will put up this injury or no; for to see our brethren whipped and set on the pillory without a cause ... is a grief to us. Desiring you to send answer one way or other, for if you will not put it up we do give consent to gather ourselves together upon [St.] Bartholomew's Day [August 24] in the fields, some with daggers, some with staves, some with one weapon, some with another, such as may be least mistrusted, and to meet in the fields between Islington and London between three and four ... in the afternoon against my lord mayor go[ing] to the wrestling, and there to be revenged of him; but if he go not to the wrestling, then to be revenged of him at his house where he dwells.

5.2 William Fleetwood, London Recorder, to William Cecil, Lord Burghley (July 7, 1585)[3]

By the end of Elizabeth's reign, London's dynamic economy attracted a steady supply of would-be new citizens from around the country; and the freshly imported, often young and always overcrowded population bred threats of disorder, real and imagined. Part of the task facing London's civic authorities (lord mayor, aldermen, etc.) was to keep an eye on these threats and report them to the central government at Westminster. This letter from London Recorder (chief magistrate) William Fleetwood (ca. 1525–94) to Elizabeth's confidant and lord treasurer, Lord Burghley (1520/1–98) suggests

[3] H. Ellis, ed., *Original Letters, Illustrative of English History* (London, 1824; reprinted New York, 1970), 2: 295–9, from BL, MS. Lansdowne 44, art. 38.

that London's sprawl had encouraged organized crime. Why might that be? Was the metropolis more dangerous than the countryside? (What does the use of a secret cant terminology – foister, nipper – suggest?) To what sorts of crimes was the city prey?

Upon Friday last we sat at the Justice Hall at Newgate from 7 in the morning until 7 at night, where were condemned certain horse stealers, cutpurses, and such like, to the number of 10, whereof 9 were executed, and the tenth stayed by a means from the court. These were executed upon Saturday in the morning. There was a shoemaker also condemned for willful murder committed in the Blackfriars, who was executed upon Monday in the morning. The same day my lord mayor being absent ... and also all my lords the justices of the benches ..., we few that were there did spend the same day about the searching out of sundry that were receptors of felons, where we found a great many as well in London, Westminster, Southwark, as in all other places about the same. Amongst our travails this one matter tumbled out by the way, that one Wotton a gentleman born, and sometime a merchant man of good credit, who falling by time into decay, kept an alehouse at Smarts Key near Billingsgate, and after, for some misdemeanor being put down, he reared up a new trade of life, and in the same house he procured all the cutpurses about this city to repair to his said house. There, was a schoolhouse set up to learn young boys to cut purses. There were hung up two devices, the one was a pocket, the other was a purse. The pocket had in it certain counters [counterfeit coins] and was hung about with hawks bells, and over the top did hang a little sacring-bell [rung at the elevation of the host]; and he that could take out a counter without any noise, was allowed to be *a public foister*; and he that could take a piece of silver out of the purse without the noise of any of the bells, he was adjudged *a judicial nipper*. *Nota* that a foister is a pickpocket, and a nipper is termed a pickpurse, or a cutpurse.

the structure of society left many w/o anything and no way to get anything unless by theft.

5.3 Wiltshire Quarter Sessions, deposition of Thomas Mills, cutler, and his wife Agnes (Spring 1618)[4]

Though most crimes prosecuted involved the individual theft of low value items, much of the rest of this chapter focuses on disorderly social or group action that appears to represent communal values. Some historians have discovered two concepts of order in early modern society: that of the elite concerned with keeping the lower orders in line versus that of the commoners concerned with maintaining community consensus. This deposition from a

[4] M. Ingram, "Ridings, Rough Music and the 'Reform of Popular Culture' in Early Modern England," *P & P* 105 (1984): 82, from Wiltshire RO, Trowbridge, Quarter Sessions Great Rolls, Trinity 1618, no. 168.

Plate 5 Scenes of a *charivari*, plaster relief (ca. 1600), Montacute House, Great Hall, Somerset. (Source: National Trust Photo Library.)

The two details from this panel evidently tell a story. What is the cause and what is the effect? Where is private life and where is public life in an early modern village? *Charivaris* could be very disorderly (we often know about them because the recipients of such popular shaming brought the matter to court). Did *charivaris*, then, contribute to local order or local disorder?

Wiltshire court case records a charivari or rough music, a public demonstration in which those who have violated social norms were humiliated and, often, forced out of the community by neighbors. (Compare this document with Plate 5.) What happened during the 1618 affray? What norm might have been violated? Which concept of order does this charivari represent? Did pipes, horns, and cowbells lend the event a festive atmosphere? In what way does it compare to a lynching?

Upon Wednesday [27] May [1618], about eight or nine … in the morning, there came to Quemerford a young fellow of Calne named Croppe, playing upon a drum, accompanied with three or four men and ten or twelve boys; and Ralph Wellsteede of Quemerford, this examinate's landlord, and himself came to them as far as the bridge in Quemerford, and asked them what they meant, and they answered that there was a skimmington dwelling there, and they came for him.… About noon came again from Calne to Quemerford another drummer named William Wiatt, and with him three or four hundred men, some like soldiers armed with pieces and other weapons, and a man riding upon a horse, having a white night cap upon his head, two shoeing horns hanging by his ears, a counterfeit beard upon his chin made of a deer's tail, a smock upon the top of his garments, and he rode upon a red horse with a pair of pots under him, and in them some quantity of brewing grains, which he used to cast upon the press of people, rushing over thick upon him in the way as he passed; and he and all his company made a stand when they came just against this examinant's house, and then the gunners shot off their pieces, pipes and horns were sounded, together with lowbells [cow- or sheep-bell] and other smaller bells which the company had amongst them, and rams' horns and bucks' horns, carried upon forks, were then and there lifted up and shown.… Thomas Mills … locked the street door and locked his wife into his chamber where she lay … and presently the parties abovementioned and diverse others rushed in upon him into his entry, and thence into his hall, and broke open his chamber door upon his wife … and … took her up by the arms and the legs, and had her out through the hall into the entry, where being a wet hole, they threw her down into it and trod upon her and buried her filthily with dirt and did beat her black and blue in many places.

5.4 Petition of the poor of Blackburn Hundred to Lancashire Quarter Sessions (1629)[5]

Rulers and ruled did not always agree as to what constituted orderly behavior. The elite reacted differently to a grain or enclosure riot than they did to

[5] R. C. Richardson and T. B. James, eds., *The Urban Experience, A Sourcebook: English, Scottish and Welsh Towns, 1450–1700* (Manchester, 1983), 52–3, from Lancashire RO, Quarter Sessions, QSB/1/61/36.

a charivari. Ordinary people who complained and, in some cases, took action, about high grain prices (thus, of bread, the mainstay of most meals) and scarcity, often began their search for redress by petitioning officials to enforce laws against forestalling (buying before grain was brought to market), regrating (purchasing grain to sell again at the same or neighboring market at higher price), and engrossing (purchasing grain wholesale at market). The 1629 petition from the poor of Blackburn hundred to their JPs is a good example. Note that their conception of fair play is rooted in collective memory of the past. According to the petitioners, what has gone wrong? Who is in the wrong? What do they expect the government to do about it?

Not many years ago there was usually sold and bought in open market 30, 40, or 50 measures of meal every market day to the help, nourishment, and relief of your petitioners and other poor distressed people within or near the aforesaid town. But now so it is … that there is many licensed badgers [grain middlemen] within this hundred and especially one Lawrence Hargreaves who doth commonly badge, carry and transport much kind of grain either into foreign parts or for his better profit maketh sale thereof in Burnley not frequenting any open market but doth unjustly enrich himself against all equity and good conscience and contrary to the statute in that case provided to the overthrow and impoverishment of your petitioners and many more who cannot buy one half peck [about 1/8 bushel or 1 gallon] of meal or less (if the greatest need required).

5.5   Justice Harvey's opinion on a Star Chamber case (1631)[6]

In 1631, Attorney General William Noy (1577–1634) charged one Mr. Archer of Essex "for keeping in his corn [generic for grain] and consequently for enhancing the price of corn the last year," and at least one justice, Sir Francis Harvey (ca. 1568–1632), justice of Common Pleas, presiding over the Star Chamber case, decided to make an example of the engrosser. What was the idea behind these punishments? To what extent does the metropolitan judge agree with the local poor on the need to police the grain trade? How might the badgers' and Mr. Archer's actions be defended today? Would these modern arguments have carried weight in the sixteenth century?

Justice Harvy delivered his opinion, that whereas it hath pleased God to send a plentiful year, and yet the price of corn continued very high, himself and the rest of the justices of the peace that were in the last Quarter Sessions in Hertfordshire assembled did advise among themselves how they might deal with the country to

[6] S. R. Gardiner, ed., *Reports of Cases in the Courts of Start Chamber and High Commission* (London, Camden Society, new ser. 39, 1886), 43–5, from TNA, STAC 2.

bring down the price.... He was of opinion that this man's [Archer's] punishment and example will do a great deal more good than all their orders which they might have made at the Sessions; and therefore he declared his offence to be very great, and fit to be punished in this Court; and adjudged him to pay 100 marks [£66] fine to the king, and £10 to the poor, and to stand upon the pillory in Newgate Market an hour with a paper, wherein the cause of his standing there was to be written, put upon his hat – For enhancing the price of Corn – and then to be led through Cheapside to Leadenhall Market, and there likewise to stand upon the pillory one hour more with the same paper upon his hat, and after this to be sent to Chelmsford, and there likewise in the market to stand upon the pillory.

5.6   Examination of Anne Carter and others regarding the Maldon Riot (1629)[7]

In times of dearth, when the government either could not or would not act, English townspeople and villagers sometimes took their own action. Grain or bread rioters would halt exports from a particular region, seize the grain and, often, distribute it at what the rioters considered a just price. (Surprisingly, rioters operating under a sense of fair play occasionally even turned over money yielded from the forced sale to the merchants, middlemen, or exporters from whom the grain had been seized.) The women examined below took part in several grain riots in Essex, which had been experiencing a trade depression for clothworkers and high grain prices, in March 1629. (After a further riot in May, one examinant, Anne Carter, and seven others would be hanged.) While men also participated in the Maldon disturbances, why might women be so heavily involved in the grain riots (consider both their status in law and their role in the household economy)? What were the goals of these women? Were any of them achieved?

The examination of Anne wife of John Carter of Maldon butcher taken the 28th day of April *anno* 1629.... The said examinate confesseth touching the late assembling of many women and their taking away of corn out of the ships at Burrow Hills in Totham that before the said assembly, herself heard one Phillip Ewdes a hoyman [a hoy is a small sloop] of Lee complain that the owners of the said vessel were Dunkirks [Dunkirk merchants] and that it was pity they were suffered to lie there, by occasion of which speech and of other men sailors, herself and diverse other women to the number of above a hundred of Maldon, Heybridge, and Witham and from the heath called Totham Heath assembled together to the said Burrow Hills in the parish of Greater Totham where the said vessels did lie in the channel and she and the rest of the women entered into one

[7]   P. Crawford and L. Goring, *Women's Worlds in Seventeenth-Century England: A Sourcebook* (London, 2000), 247–9, from Maldon Court Leet Records, Essex RO, D/B 3/3 208, m. 14, 18.

of the said ships, and the Flemings who were therein filled the rye which was therein into the aprons and coats of many of the women and some children who were in the company which they carried away but that herself took not any whit thereof. And she denieth that she did draw any company of women from Witham to the said Burrow Hills.

Anne the wife of Thomas Speareman of Maldon fisherman examined the fourth day of May before his majesty's bailiffs and justice of the said borough: The said examinate confesseth that she with others (because she could not have corn in the market and certain Flemish ships lying at Borrow Hills in the parish of Little Totham there to receive in corn to carry beyond sea) did go down about the 23rd day of March last past and there being assembled diverse women to the number of about seven score they did enter into one of the said ships and did take away a quantity of corn which was therein but how much she knoweth not, and denieth that any did set her on the said action, and being demanded why she stayed not when she was required and charged by one of the bailiffs of the said town to depart home she saith she saw the rest go and she followed them.

Elizabeth the wife of Samuel Sturgion of Maldon laborer examined the said fourth day of May saith that she being in poverty and wanting victual for her children and being called out of her house by Anne the wife of Thomas Spearman of Maldon and Dorothy the wife of John Berry of the same town about the said 23rd of March she went with them and other women to ... Burrow Hills in Little Totham where the said Flemish ships did lie where there were a great many of women met and they entered into one of the same ships and took out a quantity of corn whereof herself had about half a bushel and she denieth that any did set her on but only the two women aforesaid.

5.7 Sir Roger Wilbraham on enclosure riots in the East Midlands (ca. mid June–December 6, 1607)[8]

A different type of riot was that against enclosure. Enclosure of both open field systems and of common pasturage occurred from the late middle ages through the nineteenth century. Note the enclosure riots described by Sir Roger Wilbraham (1553–1616) below. Do you suppose those participating in the disturbances see themselves as rioters? Are they? What grievances do they have against the "enclosers and depopulators"? Did the government punish the latter? You might compare and contrast the ruling elite's reaction to engrossers of grain (noted earlier in this chapter) and enclosers of land.

Beggars and vagrants in the town of Northampton, angered at the enclosures made near the town, in bands during the night threw down a part thereof. And

---

[8] H. S. Scott, ed., "The Journal of Sir Roger Wilbrahim," *Camden Miscellany* 10 (Camden Society, 3rd ser., 4, 1902): 91–4, original in French.

in as much as they are not put down – their numbers increase, both from this town and diverse towns in the county and in the counties of Warwick, Leicester, etc., and for 20 days their numbers continue to increase, till 300 or more in one place night and day are throwing down the new enclosures; nor do they desist in spite of two proclamations made by the king on different occasions that they should have justice and mercy if they desisted. And yet they continue until Sir A[ntony] Mildmay with some horsemen using force slay some ten in hot blood; and thus they were put down. Afterwards at the assizes of the before mentioned several counties, two or three were hanged as an example. So that, as the king says, the punishment of a few may impress the majority with fear. Moreover the proclamation says that it is not a legal course for subjects to remedy their grievances by force, but that they should petition the king to be relieved according to justice. And the judges of assize in order to satisfy the common people inveigh against enclosers and depopulators; and inquire concerning them and promise reformation at the hands of justice. And this puts courage into the common people, so that with mutterings they threaten to have a more violent revenge if they cannot be relieved. On this the [Privy] Council appoints select commissioners, learned in the law, in the six counties; to inquire concerning the acts of depopulation and conversion of arable into pasture land. And they report to the Council on December 6, 1607, to this effect. That in the counties of Lincoln, Leicester, Northampton, Warwick, Huntingdon, Bedford and Buckingham about 200 or 300 tenements have been depopulated, and a great number of acres have been converted from arable into pasture land. To wit, 9,000 acres in Northamptonshire and a great number in the other counties....

On this directions were given to the learned counsel that the most notorious enclosers in each county should be summoned this Christmas for Hilary Term before the Star Chamber and justice and mercy shown to them, so that they should not despair, nor should the common people insult them or be incited to make rebellion, whereof they are greatly suspected. Also the mayor of Northampton, the sheriff, and the neighboring justices who did not repress the outrages at the beginning should also be brought before the Star Chamber by reason of their remissness. And it is hoped that this public example may stay the fury of the common people. These deliberations I reported to the king at Newmarket on December 8th by order of the Council. And he seems to approve of this course.

5.8 Depositions taken before the mayor and aldermen of Norwich after Kett's Rising (1549–50)[9]

Beyond mere riot lay peasant and popular rebellion, although the line dividing one from the other is not always clear. The Cornish Rebellion (1497), the

---

[9] W. Rye, ed., *Depositions Taken Before the Mayor and Aldermen of Norwich* (Norwich, 1905), 18, 20–2, from Norwich Municipal Archives.

Pilgrimage of Grace (1536, see documents 1.2 and 3.10 above), the Western Rising (1549, see document 3.13 above), Wyatt's Rebellion (1554), and the Rebellion of the Northern Earls (1569, chapter 4) had decidedly political and religious causes, but Kett's Rebellion (1549) and the Rebellion of 1596 had origins closer to those of enclosure or food riots. At the same time, the solutions suggested by some of the poor rebels aimed higher than destroying a hedge or a deer park. We know quite a bit of what motivated Robert Kett (ca. 1492–1549) and his East Anglian followers when they encamped outside Norwich in 1549, for they drew up demands to present to the king. But perhaps even more revealing are the reported mutterings of Kett's followers after the rebellion had been crushed and Kett executed. What did the rebels want and why were local government officials listening so intently? Was this idle talk or a real threat to the Tudor state? From these reports, does it appear as if Kett's followers sought to transform society? (Consider whether or not a mythological "Golden Age" view of the past can be a revolutionary idea.)

Made 21 September [1549]. Edmund Warden and Thomas Dorye churchwardens of the parish of St. Gregory demanded certain ornaments out of the hands of Robert Burnam being our parish clerk ..., and did advise him to turn his heart and become a new man. And he said he had offended no man but that he was able to answer. Then said I unto him that I heard a gentleman say when he was in prison that he was not afraid of his life of no man but of the said Burnam. Then answered the said Burnam and said: "There are too many gentlemen in England by five hundred." Then said I again, if thou speakest such a word again thou shalt go to prison....

The examination of John Redhead before Thomas Cod, mayor of the city of Norwich, and others the 12th day February [1550]. John Redhead of Norwich, of the parish of St. Marten, worsted weaver, sayeth and confesseth: that upon a market day not a month passed ..., being in the market upon his business to buy his victual, walking there he saw two or three persons men of the countryside standing together having conversation betwixt themselves. He heard the one of them speak to the other looking upon Norwich castle toward Kett [his corpse now hanging there in chains] these words, *viz.*: "Oh Kett, God have mercy upon thy soul, and I trust in God that the king's majesty and his Council shall be informed once betwixt this and Midsummer even, that of their own gentleness thou shall be taken down by the grace of God and buried, and not hanged up for Winter store, and set a quietness in the realm, and that the ragged staff [John Dudley's, then earl of Warwick's, badge displayed on prominent houses] shall be taken down also of their own gentleness from the gentlemen's gates in this city, and to have no more King's Arms but one within this city under Christ but King Edward VI, God save his Grace"; which persons he saith he never knew them, nor cannot name them....

[July 2, 1550, before Mayor Robert Rug and other justices.] William Stedde of Norwich, innholder, of the age of 40 years, sworn and examined saith and deposeth upon his oath: that ... he was at Saxlingham at a marriage and there was one

William Cowper of St. Margaret parish in Norwich, cooper, and diverse others; and as they sat at their dinner there amongst other words in communication … Cowper said: "That as sheep or lambs are a prey to the wolves or lions so are the poor men to the rich men or gentlemen." And moreover … Cowper said that there are more merchants now at this present time than there were wont [needed] to be by a hundred thousand, in carrying and conveying of vittles and such other things.

5.9   Robert Crowley, The Way to Wealth (1550)[10]

Who was to blame for riot and rebellion? Usually, the powerful urged stiff penalties for rioters and rebels. Yet, in 1550 author and publisher Robert Crowley (ca. 1517–88) blamed the 1549 risings on "the greedy cormorants," the landlords. What have the landlords done wrong, according to Crowley? Does such a complaint reinforce or contest the Great Chain of Being?

True it is, the poor men (whom ye call peasant knaves) have deserved more [punishment] than you can devise to lay upon them. … But … [i]f you charge them with disobedience, you were first disobedient. For without a law to bear you, yea contrary to the law which forbiddeth all manner of oppression and extortion, and … contrary to conscience, the ground of all good laws, ye enclosed from the poor their due commons, levied greater fines than heretofore have been levied, put them from the liberties (and in a manner inheritance) that they held by custom, and raised their rents. Yea, when there was a law ratified to the contrary, you ceased not to find means either to compel your tenants to consent to your desire in enclosing, or else ye found such mastership that no man durst gainsay your doings for fear of displeasure. And what obedience showed you, when the king's proclamations were sent forth, and commissions directed for the laying open of your enclosures, and yet you left not off to enclose still?

Good Wife, Bad Wife, Poor Wife, Witch

5.10   Phillip Stubbes, "The Godly life of Mistress Stubbes" (1592)[11]

Women held a certain but lowly position on the Great Chain. The attributes of the ideal woman were just as certain, at least in print, but those attributes were

[10]   R. Crowley, *The Way To Wealth, Wherein is Plainly Taught a Most Present Remedy for Sedicion* (London, Feb. 7, 1550), sig. Biii[verso]–Biv.
[11]   P. S[tubbes]., *A Christal Glas for christian women: wherein, they may see a most wonderfull and rare example, of a right vertuous life and Christian death* (n.p., n.d., 1592), sig. A2–3.

often defined by their opposites. Note the qualities (and their opposites) that Philip Stubbes (ca. 1555–ca. 1610) claims were the hallmark of his short-lived wife, Katherine. In what way might one use this "life" to understand late Elizabethan gender relations and family dynamics? What are the drawbacks to using this source?

Calling to remembrance (most Christian reader) the final end of man's creation, which is to glorify God and to edify one another in the way of true godliness, I thought it my duty as well in respect of the one as in regard of the other to publish this rare and wonderful example of the virtuous life and Christian death of Mistress Katherine Stubbes, who whilest she lived was a mirror of womanhood, and now being dead, is a perfect pattern of true Christianity. ...

At fifteen years of age (her father being dead), her mother bestowed her in marriage to one Master Philip Stubbes, with whom she lived four years and almost a half, very honestly and godly, with rare commendations of all that knew her, as well for her singular wisdom as also for her modesty, courtesy, gentleness, affability, and good government. And above all, for her fervent zeal which she bare to the truth ... she seemed to surpass many. ...

She obeyed the commandment of the Apostle who biddeth women to be silent, and to learn of their husbands at home. She would suffer no disorder or abuse in her house to be either unreproved or unreformed. And so gentle was she and courteous of nature that she was never heard to give any the lie in all her life, nor so much as to (thou) any in anger. She was never known to fall out with any of her neighbors, nor with the least child that lived, much less to scold or brawl, as many will now-a-days for every trifle or rather for no cause at all. And so solitary was she given, that she would very seldom or never, and that not without great constraint (and then not neither, except her husband were in company) go abroad with any, either to banquet or feast, to gossip or make merry (as they term it) in so much that she hath been noted to do it in contempt and disdain of others.

When her husband was abroad in London or elsewhere, there was not the dearest friend she had in the world that could get her abroad to dinner or supper, or to any disports, plays, interludes, or pastimes whatsoever. Neither was she given to pamper her body with delicate meats, wines, or strong drinks, but rather refrained [from] them altogether, saying, that we should eat to live, and not live to eat. And as she excelled in the gift of sobriety, so she surpassed in the virtue of humility. For it is well known to diverse yet living that she utterly abhorred all kind of pride both in apparel and otherwise. She could never abide to bear any filthy or unseemly talk of scurrility, bawdry, or uncleanness, neither swearing or blaspheming, cursing, or banning, but would reprove them sharply, shewing them the vengeance of God due for such deserts. And which is more, there was never one filthy, unclean, indecent, or unseemly word heard to come forth of her mouth, nor ever once to curse or ban, to swear, or blaspheme God any manner of way. But always her speeches were such as both might glorify God and minister grace to the hearers, as the Apostle speaketh.

5.11 *"The Confession and repentance of Margaret Ferneseede after her condemnation" (1608)*[12]

If Mistress Stubbes represented the ideal, Margaret Ferneseede, who "kept a most abominable and vile brothel house" and ultimately was executed for murdering her husband, surely represents her opposite. Can we construct a hierarchy of her evil deeds, thoughts, and actions according to contemporaries? Both this and the previous document are from cheap printed pamphlets. Do you think they sold well; why or why not?

According to the testimony of two of her customers, Mr. Ferneseede had lost control of his own house, describing himself and his situation as follows:

"I am," quoth he, "the master of this house if I had my right, but I am barred of the possession and command thereof by a devilish woman who makes a stews [brothel] of it to exercise her sinful practices."... When these bargemen told mistress Ferneseede what they had heard of her husband ..., she replied, "Hang him slave and villain! I will before God be revenged of him (nay ere long) by one means or other, so worked that I will be rid of him"; which making good [that is, she poisoned her husband] in the judgment of the judge together with her life and practices, she as aforesaid was condemned. ...

To prepare the reader for this confession of hers, know that I was credibly satisfied that when the heat of her fury was past (to which she was much subject unto), she [was] a woman well spoken, of fair delivery, and good persuasion. And so to her confession:

"To excuse myself, O Lord, before thee who knows the conspiracies of our thoughts even to the utmost of our actions (however so private or publicly committed) were folly, or to justify myself were sin, since no flesh can appear pure in thy sight. I here therefore with prostrate knees and dejected eyes as unworthy to look up unto thy divine Majesty, with a contrite heart and penitent soul also, here voluntarily confess I am the greatest of sinners which have

---

[12] *The araignement & burning of Margaret Ferne-seede, for the Murther of her late Husband Anthony Ferne-seede, found deade in Peckham Field neere Lambeth, having once before attempted to poyson him with broth, being executed in S. Georges-field the last of Februarie. 1608* (London, 1608), sig. [B2(verso)–B4].

deserved thy wrath and indignation." In this good manner she proceeded and withal satisfied all that came and desired to have private conference with her of the whole course of her life that in her youth, even from the age of aptness, she had been a prostitute whore, but growing into disabled years, to please the loose desires of such customers she after turned bawd, a course of life more hateful in tempting and seducing youth than the other in committing sin. The one makes but spoil and ruin of herself, and the other of a multitude. "For," quoth she, "I myself have had ten several women retaining to my house for that purpose. Some were men's wives, which repaired thither both by appointment and at convenient hours when their husbands might least suspect or have knowledge of their absence, and these women did I first tempt to their fall: some, by persuading them they were not beloved of their husbands, especially if I could at any time have note of any breach or discontent between them; others, that their husbands maintained them not sufficiently to express their beauty and according to their own deserts.... They were as fearful to offend me as their husbands should have knowledge of their offenses; and these allowed me a weekly pension for coming to my house.... To supply my house and make spoil of young maids who were sent out of the country by their friends here with hope to advance themselves, I went weekly to the carriers where, if the maid liked me, I so wrought with the carrier that she seldom left me till I had brought her to be as bad as I purposed; which effected, every one of them I compelled to give me ten shillings a week out of their gettings, having as I said seldom less than ten whose bodies and souls I kept in this bondage. Besides, I confess I was a continual receiver of theft stolen; but in all this, as it was badly got, so was it worse consumed, for nothing of it did prosper with me, whereby (quoth she) I acknowledge I have deserved death and in the highest degree. But for this which I am condemned, Heaven that knoweth best the secrets of our hearts knows I am innocent."

But who knows not that in evil there is a like impudence to deny, as there is a forwardness to act: in which we will leave her whom the law hath found guilty, and having thus truly related her own confession, we proceed to the manner of execution....

On Monday, being the last of February, she had notice given her that in the afternoon she must suffer death and a preacher commended unto her to instruct her for her soul's health, who labored much with her for the confession of the fact which she still obstinately denied but made great show of repentance for her life past. So that about two of the clock in the afternoon she was stripped of her ordinary wearing apparel and upon her own smock put a kirtle [gown] of canvas pitched clean through, over which she did wear a white sheet, and so was by the keeper delivered to the shrive [place of penance], on each hand a woman leading her and the preacher going before her. Being come to the place of execution, both before and after her fastening to the stake with godly exhortations he admonished her that now in that minute she would confess that fact for which she was now ready to suffer, which she denying, the reeds were planted about, unto which fire being given, she was presently dead.

5.12   *Women receiving poor relief, Braintree parish, Essex (1619–21)*[13]

It should be obvious that reputation was just as important for women as for men. Early modern English people drew a distinction between virtuous women and vicious women at all social levels. A bad reputation could be brazened out by an elite woman, but for most the consequences could be severe: social ostracism or the attentions of the law. Courts recorded numerous insults – "whore," "harlot," "witch" – directed towards women at this level, often by other women. When one declared to another on a London street in 1613, "Thou art a quean [hussy] and a wrymouth quean and I will make thee do penance in a white sheet; and I will have thee carted out of the street," she revealed a knowledge that consistory courts could require someone to do penance for moral infractions by standing them in a public place in a white robe with a taper (candle), and that Quarter Sessions could sentence bastard-bearers and others to be tied to the end of a cart and paraded or even whipped around town.[14] Poor women could be denied relief for bad behavior or a reputation for same. But most commentators realized that some of the poor, even bastard-bearers, could be poor through no fault of their own, even though, as the numbers of poor increased before and after 1600, the English rate-paying public became desperate to limit the numbers deserving relief. Consider how the overseers of the poor in Braintree parish, Essex attempted to distinguish deserving from undeserving poor women. How and at what stages in their lives were women particularly prone to poverty? To disorder?

August 2, 1619, Imprimis [Firstly] at this meeting it was agreed that the widow Browne and her son if she do live and recover shall be removed to the almshouse at Braintree bridge, where we the last day did appoint Eliot should be.

September 6, 1619, Imprimis order was taken at this meeting that Anne Gay shall be warned with all speed to provide her a service, or else that she shall be sent to the house of correction....

Item notice is given us by William Stebbing of a wench entertained at John Beckwith's dwelling on Cursing Green, that is supposed to have a great belly [with child]; which the constables have warning to look after, and to take order to remove her if they find the report to be true.

---

[13]   Crawford and Goring, *Women's Worlds*, 110–1, from Braintree Parish Records, Essex RO, D/P 284/8/3, fols. 3(verso)–33 (extracts).

[14]   In L. Gowing, "Language, Power and the Law: Women's Slander Litigation in Early Modern London," in *Women, Crime and the Courts in Early Modern England*, ed. J. Kermode and G. Walker (Chapel Hill, 1994), 33, from Greater London RO, DL/C 221, fol. 1189(verso), Cartwright con Hixwell, 8 June 1613.

February 8, 1620, Imprimis it was agreed that widow Gay be placed in the almshouse with Howell, and the widow Coe shall be put into the house where she is....

February 5, 1621, [On the disposition of five shillings which had been received from the constables for the use of the poor:] It was agreed that Richard Loveday shall have two shillings of this money, in regard of the extraordinary charge he hath been at for the washing of his wife being lame.

It is agreed that the widow Gay shall have 12d. of the said money for pains taken with the widow Eliot and that for the time to come she shall have 6d. a week for attendance given upon the said widow, during the time the overseers shall think fit.

Item it is agreed that Margery Pierson shall be provided of an almshouse at the discretion of the overseers, because she is [a] helpful woman at their request to those that are sick....

March 5, 1621, It is agreed that the widow Coe shall be provided of an almshouse in the Hyde at the discretion of the overseers and that the widow Gay shall be displaced out of the almshouse.

October 8, 1621, Item it is agreed that the widow Boltwood shall have 2s. 6d. allowed her out of the poor man's box and that she shall have an almshouse offered her which if she refuse she shall have no more allowance.

November 5, 1621, Imprimis it was agreed that widow Ingram's boy that should be taken from her and put into the hospital and that she being incorrigible in her idle and vicious course that she shall be sent to the house of correction.

5.13 *"The Examinations of Philippa Flower" (1619)*[15]

It is not much of a leap from the poor woman to the witch, for historians have found that those executed for witchcraft in the early modern period were overwhelmingly female (about 80 per cent) and poor. Successive statutes against witchcraft in 1542, 1563, and 1604 established ever harsher punishments for a wider range of offenses, but also demanded stricter standards of proof until the last witch trial in 1717 and final repeal of the statutes in 1736. Given that the base of a legal charge against a witch was that she or he had made a pact with the Devil, it is surprising to discover that the spells supposedly inflicted – making a person lame, causing milk to spoil – were of such a mundane nature. Moreover those found guilty often confessed to what are to us bizarre scenarios. Note what Philippa Flower confesses to below. What appear to be the charges against her? How does she claim to make her spells effective? Can you place Philippa, her mother, and sister socio-economically? How do you think the social status of the "victims" affected the case?

---

[15] *The Wonderful Discoverie of the Witchcrafts of Margaret and Phillip[a] Flower, daughters of Ioan Flower neere Beuer Castle: Executed at Lincolne, March 11. 1618* (n.p., n.d., 1619?), sig. [F3, F4v].

The examination of Philippa Flower, sister of Margaret Flower and daughter of Joan Flower, before Sir William Pelham and Mr. Butler, justices of the peace, Febr. 4, 1618[/19] which was brought in at the Assizes as evidence against her sister Margaret.

She saith that her mother and her sister maliced [Francis Manners] the earl of Rutland (1578–1632), his countess, and their children, because her sister Margaret was put out of the Lady's service of laundry and exempted from other services about the house; whereupon her said sister, by the commandment of her mother, brought from [Belvoir] Castle the right-hand glove of the Lord Henry Ros [presumably a son who died young, as the earl was granted title of Lord Ros, 1617], which she delivered to her Mother, who presently rubbed it on the back of her spirit Rutterkin and then put it into hot boiling water. Afterward she pricked it often and buried it in the yard, wishing the Lord Ros might never thrive; and so her sister Margaret continued with her mother, where she often saw the cat Rutterkin leap on her shoulder and suck her neck.

She further confessed that she heard her mother often curse the earl and his lady, and thereupon would boil feathers and blood together, using many Devilish speeches and strange gestures. ...

The examination of Philippa Flower, the 25th of February, 1618[/19], before Francis, earl of Rutland; Francis, Lord Willoughby of Eresby; Sir George Manners; and Sir William Pelham

She confesseth and saith that she hath a spirit sucking on her in the form of a white rat, which keepeth her left breast and hath so done for three or four years; and concerning the agreement betwixt her spirit and herself, she confesseth and with that when it came first unto her she gave her soul to it and it promised to do her good and cause Thomas Simpson to love her if she would suffer it to suck her, which she agreed unto; and so the last time it sucked was on Tuesday at night, the 23rd of February.

5.14 *Reginald Scot,* The Discoverie of Witchcraft *(1584)*[16]

Reginald Scot (d. 1599), a talented surveyor, dam builder, and minor local administrator, is most famous for his extensive treatise on witchcraft. Scot's *Discoverie of Witchcraft* was a point-by-point demolition of contemporary witchcraft beliefs. Use his comments along with Flower's confession to compile a list of popular beliefs about witches. How might Scot know about the witchcraft cases he discusses? Why were witches poor women? Why might some poor women actively *cultivate* the reputation of a witch?

Book 1, Chapter 3. One sort of such as are said to be witches, are women which be commonly old, lame, bleary-eyed, pale, foul, and full of wrinkles; poor and

---

[16] R. Scot, *Discoverie*, ed. B. Nicholson (Totowa, N. J., 1973), 5–7, 10.

sullen, superstitious, and papists; or such as know no religion: in whose drowsy minds the Devil hath gotten a fine seat; so as, what mischief, mischance, calamity, or slaughter is brought to pass, they are easily persuaded the same is done by themselves; imprinting in their minds an earnest and constant imagination hereof. They are lean and deformed, showing melancholy in their faces, to the horror of all that see them. They are doting, scolds, mad, devilish; and not much differing from them that are thought to be possessed with spirits.…

These miserable wretches are so odious unto all their neighbors, and so feared, as few dare offend them, or deny them anything they ask: whereby they take upon them; yea, and sometimes think, that they can do such things as are beyond the ability of human nature. These go from house to house, and from door to door for a pot full of milk, yeast, drink, pottage, or some such relief; without the which they could hardly live: neither obtaining for their service and pains, nor by their art, nor yet at the Devil's hands (with whom they are said to make a perfect and visible bargain) either beauty, money, promotion, wealth, worship, pleasure, honor, knowledge, learning, or any other benefit whatsoever.

It falleth out many times, that neither their necessities, nor their expectation is answered or served, in those places where they beg or borrow; but rather their lewdness is by their neighbors reproved. And further, in tract of time the witch waxeth odious and tedious to her neighbors; and they again are despised and despited of her: so as sometimes she curseth one, and sometimes another; and that from the master of the house, his wife, children, cattle, etc., to the little pig that lieth in the sty. Thus in process of time they have all displeased her, and she hath wished evil luck unto them all; perhaps with curses and imprecations made in form. Doubtless (at length) some of her neighbors die, or fall sick; or some of their children are visited with diseases that vex them strangely: as apoplexies, epilepsies, convulsions, hot fevers, worms, etc. Which by ignorant parents are supposed to be the vengeance of witches. Yea and their opinions and conceits are confirmed and maintained by unskillful physicians.… Also some of their cattle perish, either by disease or mischance. Then they, upon whom such adversities fall, weighing the fame that goeth upon this woman (her words, displeasure, and curses meeting so justly with their misfortune) do not only conceive, but also are resolved, that all their mishaps are brought to pass by her only means.

The witch on the other side expecting her neighbors' mischances, and seeing things sometimes come to pass according to her wishes, curses, and incantations … being called before a justice, by due examination of the circumstances is driven to see her imprecations and desires, and her neighbors harms and losses to concur, and as it were to take effect: and so confesseth that she (as a goddess) hath brought such things to pass.…

Another sort of witches there are, which be absolutely cozeners [cheats]. These take upon them, either for glory, fame, or gain, to do anything, which God or the Devil can do: either for foretelling of things to come, betraying of secrets, curing of maladies, or working of miracles.…

Chapter 6. Alas! What an inept instrument is a toothless, old, impotent, and unwieldy woman to fly in the air? Truly, the Devil little needs such instruments to bring his purposes to pass.

Poor Laws and the Reform of Popular Culture

5.15   William Lambarde's "Ephemeris" (1580–8)[17]

Curbing everyday disorder was often the business of overworked justices and bureaucrats. They attempted to stifle miscreants and ensure basic economic justice in order to calm would-be rioters. We have already considered how the government attempted to enforce laws against forestalling, regrating, and engrossing in the grain trade during dearths. At the local level, much of the regulatory action was overseen by the JPs. William Lambarde (1536–1601), author of the earliest county history, *A Perambulation of Kent* (1576), was sworn as a JP for that county in 1580 and kept a diary of his actions in that capacity. What did Lambarde regulate? Seek to prevent? Can one distinguish below between national and local issues? Public and private life? Moral and market economic issues?

October [1580] The 3 of October my father-in-law and I bound Walter Pelsant ... from keeping an alehouse any more; his sureties were Reignold Pelsant and Nicholas Miller of Wrotham, yeomen. ...

The 25 October I delivered to the Lord Chief Baron the said examination of John Sone aforesaid.

My father-in-law and I entreated Nordashe of Kemsing to give over [cease] aleselling because no alehouse had been kept there within the memory of any man. ...

21 May [1583] There was holden at Maidstone a special session of the peace for the rogues, where diverse were bound and whipped.

I have signed a license for Thomas Godfrey to beg till Allhallowtide [1 November] (for his house burnt) within the limits of the Lord Cobham [alehouse?] only. ...

6–7 June [1588] Mr. Leveson and I took order for John Vaughan, a bastard child, begotten at Birling by Thomas Vaughan of Snodland, miller, on Marion Gorby, widow, of Birling also, which Thomas, with John Coveney and William Elfye, all of Birling, were bound, in £30, to save the parish harmless. Mr. Leveson hath the bond.

---

[17]   C. Read, ed., *William Lambarde and Local Government: His "Ephemeris" and Twenty-Nine Charges to Juries and Commissions* (Ithaca, N. Y., 1962), 17–8, 29, 50–1, from Folger Library.

He and I took order also for Agnes Cumber, a bastard begotten on Agnes Cumber of East Malling by John Crowhurst of Aylesford, with the like bond of them and of Thomas Reynes of Burham, yeoman, for discharge of East Malling. And we ordered all the said four offenders to be whipped in the open market of West Malling, 8 June 1588.

5.16   Edward Hext, JP, to Lord Burghley on the increase of rogues and vagabonds (September 25, 1596)[18]

Not everyone was sympathetic to the poor. William Harrison (1535–93), in his *Description of England* (1577), complained of the sort of "thriftless poor, as the rioter that hath consumed all, the vagabond that will abide nowhere but runneth up and down from place to place ..., and finally the rogue and the strumpet."[19] Two interrelated lines of response were to insist on a Reformation of Manners to shape the behavior of ordinary people and to reform statutes regarding the poor, vagabonds, apprentices, and workers. Sir Edward Hext's (d. 1624) somewhat rambling ideas presented to Lord Burghley were born of his own practical experience on Somerset's petty and quarter sessions. Where does he locate the problems facing the poor relief system, and how does he propose to solve them? We might debate the merit of his ideas, then and now. (Were there two distinct cultures: an elite and popular one? See Plate 6 for one view.)

Having long observed the rapines and thefts committed within this county where I serve, and finding they multiply daily to the utter impoverishing of the poor husbandman that beareth the greatest burthen of all services ..., [I] do think it my bounden duty to present unto your honorable and grave consideration these calendars enclosed of the prisoners executed and delivered this year past in this county of Somerset, wherein your Lordship may behold 183 most wicked and desperate persons to be enlarged [that is, to be discharged from prison]. And of these very few come to any good, for none will receive them into service....

I do not see how it is possible for the poor countryman to bear the burdens duly laid upon him, and the rapines of the infinite numbers of the wicked wandering idle people of the land, so as men are driven to watch their sheepfolds, their pastures, their woods, their cornfields, all things growing too too [*sic*] common. Others there be ... that stick not to say boldly, "they must not starve, they will not starve." And this year there assembled 80 in a company and took a whole cart load of cheese from one driving it to a fair and dispersed it amongst them, for which some of them have endured long imprisonment and fine by the judgment of the good Lord Chief Justice at our last Christmas

[18]   R. H. Tawney and E. Power, eds., *Tudor Economic Documents* (London, 1924), 2: 339–46, from BL, MS. Lansdowne 81, art. 6, fols. 161–2.
[19]   W. Harrison, *A Description of Elizabethan England* (New York, 1910), 301.

Plate 6   A morris dance, early seventeenth century. (Source: *The Thames at Richmond, with the Old Royal Palace*, Flemish school, detail, Fitzwilliam Museum, Cambridge.)

The morris dance, with its bells and hobby horse, is considered part of traditional English folk culture. Is it part of popular culture? What is the relation suggested between elite and popular culture in this painting (you might distinguish social status by apparel)? From the documents, who wanted to reform popular culture? Why?

Sessions; which may grow dangerous by the aid of such numbers as are abroad, especially in this time of dearth, who no doubt animate them to all contempt both of noble men and gentlemen, continually buzzing into their ears that the rich men have gotten all into their hands and will starve the poor. And I may justly say that the infinite numbers of the idle wandering people and robbers of the land are the chiefest cause of the dearth, for though they labor not, and yet they spend doubly as much as the laborer doth, for they lie idly in the alehouses days and night eating and drinking excessively. And within these 3 months I took a thief that was executed this last assizes, that confessed unto me that he and two more lay in an alehouse three weeks, in which time they ate 20 fat sheep whereof they stole every night one, besides they breaks many a poor man's plough by stealing an ox or two from him, and [he], not being able to buy more, leaseth a great parts of his tillage that year. ... And such numbers being grown to this idle and thievish life, there are scant sufficient to do the ordinary tillage of the land, for I know that some having had their husbandmen sent for soldiers they have lost a great parts of their tillage that year, and others are not to be gotten by reason so many are abroad practicing all kind of villainy.

And when these lewd people are committed to the jail, the poor country that is robbed by them are enforced there to feed them, which they grieve at. And this year there hath been disbursed to the relief of the prisoners in the jail above £73, and yet they are allowed but 6d. a man weekly. And if they were not delivered at every Quarter Sessions, so much more money would not serve, nor too such jails would not hold them, but if this money might be employed to build some houses adjoining to the jail for them to work in; and every prisoner committed for any cause and not able to relieve himself compelled to work, and as many of them as are delivered upon their trials, either by acquittal of the grand jury or petty jury, burning in the hand, or whipping, presently transferred thence to the houses of correction to be kept in work ..., the 10th felony will not be committed that now is. And if some like course might be taken with the wandering people they would easily be brought to their places of abode. And being abroad they all in general are receivers of all stolen things that are portable, as namely the tinker in his budget, the peddler in his hamper, the glassman in his basket, and the lewd proctors which carry the broad seal and green seals in their bags, covers infinite numbers of felonies, in such sort as the tenth felony cometh not to light, for he hath his receiver at hand in every alehouse in every bush. And these last rabble are very nurseries of rogues. ...

The corn [grain] that is wastefully spent and consumed in alehouses by the lewd wandering people will find the greatest parts of the poor, for it is most certain if they light upon an alehouse that hath strong ale they will not depart until they have drunk him dry. And it falleth out by experience that the alehouses of this land consumeth the greatest parts of the barley. For upon a survey taken of the alehouses only of the towns of Wells, [Somerset,] leaving out the taverns and inns, it appeared by their own confessions that they spent this last year twelve thousand bushels of barley malt, which would have afforded to every market of this shire 10 bushels weekly, and would have satisfied a great parts of the poor, a great part whereof is consumed by these wandering people, who being reduced to conformity, corn no doubt will be much more plentiful.

5.17   *Poor Relief Act (39 Eliz. I, c. 3, 1598)*[20]

Elizabethans turned to a flurry of legislation to restore social order. In 1563, an Act for the Relief of the Poor (5 Eliz. I, c. 3), gave sanction to a system of charitable alms but did nothing to require that parishioners pay them, while a Statute of Artificers (c. 4) kept apprentices and workers in employment for a whole year, but limited wages. In the 1570s, an Act for the Punishment of Vagabonds and Relief of the Poor (14 Eliz. I, c. 5, 1572) required that sturdy beggars avoiding work be whipped and burned through the gristle of the right ear, and that parishes keep a register book of the deserving poor. A further Act for Setting the Poor to Work (18 Eliz. I, c. 3, 1576) required that counties set up a stock of hemp, flax, wool, etc. for the poor to work and earn their own livelihood. But few counties established any such stock before the 1630s, and even then good intentions were evident more than results. Following the disastrous harvests and economic dislocation of the mid-1590s, an onslaught of legislation in the 1597–8 session dwarfed earlier reforms, producing acts: against decaying towns (39 Eliz. I, c. 1, allowing cottages on the commons for the poor), promoting tillage and limiting enclosure (c. 2), and on poor relief (c. 3, below), rogues and vagabonds (c. 4), hospitals for the poor (c. 5), and laborers (c. 12). The 1601 session returned to poor relief and revised 39 Eliz. I, c. 3 (43 Eliz. I, c. 2). Finally James's Parliaments reexamined the 1563 Statute of Artificers (1 James I, c. 6, 1604) and the discouragement of rogues and vagabonds (c. 7, which required the branding of the same with an "R"; and 7 & 8 James I, c. 4, 1610, which required a house of correction in every county); and established laws regarding alehouses (4 James I, c. 4, 1606) and drunkenness (c. 5). How does the 1598 Poor Relief Act define the poor. How are they to be relieved? Who should pay for such relief?

Be it enacted by the authority of this present Parliament that the churchwardens of every parish, and four substantial householders there ... who shall be nominated yearly ..., under the hand and seal of two or more justices of the peace in the same county ... dwelling in or near the same parish, shall be called overseers of the poor.... And they ... shall take order from time to time by and with the consent of two or more such justices of peace for setting to work of the children of all such whose parents shall not by the said persons be thought able to keep and maintain their children; and also all such persons married or unmarried as having no means to maintain them use no ordinary and daily trade of life to get their living by; and also to raise weekly or otherwise (by taxation of every inhabitant and every occupier of lands in the said parish ...) a convenient stock

[20]   *SR*, 4, part 2: 896–9.

of flax, hemp, wool, thread, iron, and other necessary ware and stuff to set the poor on work. And also competent sums of money for and towards the necessary relief of the lame, impotent, old, blind, and such other among them being poor and not able to work, and also for the putting out of such children to be apprentices, to be gathered out of the same parish. ... Which said churchwardens and overseers ..., or such of them as shall not be let by sickness or other just excuse to be allowed by such two justices of peace or more, shall meet together at the least once every month in the church of the said parish, upon the Sunday in the afternoon after divine service, there to consider of some good course to be taken and of some meet order to be set down in the premises ...; upon pain that every one of them absenting themselves without lawful cause as aforesaid from such monthly meeting ..., or being negligent in their office ..., to forfeit for every such default twenty shillings.

2. And be it also enacted, that if the said justices of peace do perceive that the inhabitants of any parish are not able to levy among themselves sufficient sums of money for the purposes aforesaid, that then the said justices shall and may tax, rate, and assess as aforesaid any other of other parishes, or out of any parish within the hundred where the said parish is, to pay such sum and sums of money to the churchwardens and overseers of the said poor parish for the said purpose as the said justices shall think fit. ...

3. And that it shall be lawful for the said churchwardens and overseers ... to levy as well the said sums of money of everyone that shall refuse to contribute according as they shall be assessed by distress and sale of the offenders' goods. ...

4. And be it further enacted that it shall be lawful for the said churchwardens and overseers or the greater part of them, by the assent of any two justices ..., to bind any such children as aforesaid to be apprentices where they shall see convenient, till such man-child shall come to the age of four and twenty years, and such woman-child to the age of one and twenty years. ...

5. And to the intent that necessary places of habitation may more conveniently be provided for such poor impotent people, be it enacted ... that it shall and may be lawful for the said churchwardens and overseers or the greater part of them, by the leave of the lord or lords of the manor whereof any waste or common within their parish is ... to erect, build, and set up in fit and convenient places of habitation in such waste or common, at the general charges of the parish or otherwise of the hundred or county ..., to be taxed, rated, and gathered in manner before expressed, convenient houses of dwelling for the said impotent poor; and also to place inmates or more families than one in one cottage or house. ...

10. And be it further enacted ... that from the first day of November ... no person or persons whatsoever shall go wandering abroad [outside their parish] and beg in any place whatsoever, by licence or without, upon pain to be esteemed, taken, and punished as a rogue. ...

12. And forasmuch as all begging is forbidden by this present act, be it further enacted ... that the justices of peace for every county or place corporate, or the more part of them, in their general Sessions to be holden next ..., shall rate every parish to such a weekly sum of money as they shall think convenient, so as no parish be rated above the sum of 6d. nor under the sum of an half-penny weekly to be paid, and so as the total sum of such taxation of the parishes in every county amount not above the rate of twopence for every parish in the said county; which sums so taxed shall be yearly assessed by the agreement of the parishioners ..., or in default thereof by the churchwardens and constables of the same parish ..., or in default of their agreement by the order of such justice or justices of peace as shall dwell in the same parish or ... in the parts next adjoining. And if any person shall refuse or neglect to pay any such portion of money so taxed, it shall be lawful for the said churchwardens and constables or in their default for the justices of the peace, to levy the same by distress and sale of the goods of the party so refusing or neglecting ..., and in default of such distress it shall be lawful ... to commit such persons to prison. ...

17. Provided always that this act shall endure no longer than to the end of the next session of Parliament. [It was prolonged by numerous acts, revised in 1601, and made permanent in 1640.]

HISTORIANS' DEBATES

Was early modern England violent (variously defined as verbal and/or physical violence)?

L. Stone, "Interpersonal Violence in English Society," *P & P* 101 (1983); A. Macfarlane, "Violence," in *The Culture of Capitalism* (Oxford, 1987); S. D. Amussen, "Punishment, Discipline, and Power: The Social Meanings of Violence in Early Modern England," *JBS* 34, 1 (1995); L. Gowing, "Gender and the Language of Insult in Early Modern London," *HWJ* 35 (1993); P. Rushton, " 'The Matter in Variance': Domestic Conflict in the Pre-Industrial Economy of North-East England," *Journal of Social History* 25, 1 (1991); G. Walker, "Rereading Rape and Sexual Violence in Early Modern England," *Gender and History* 10, 1 (1998); M. Ingram, "Ridings, Rough Music and the 'Reform of Popular Culture' in Early Modern England," *P & P* 105 (1984); J. R. Kent, " 'Folk Justice' and Royal Justice in Early Seventeenth-Century England: A 'Charivari' in the Midlands," *Midland History* 8 (1983); S. Hindle, "Custom, Festival and Protest in Early Modern England: The Little Budworth Wakes, St. Peter's Day, 1596," *Rural History* 6, 2 (1995); "Honour and Reputation in Early-Modern England" (Conference Proceedings), *TRHS* 6th ser., 6 (1996), esp. E. Foyster, "Male Honour, Social Control and Wife Beating in Late Stuart England" and L. Gowing, "Women, Status and the Popular Culture of Dishonour."

Were riots based on poverty or political discontent?

R. Manning, *Village Revolts: Social Protest and Popular Disturbances in England, 1509–1640* (Oxford, 1988), esp. the conclusion; A. Wood, *Riot, Rebellion and Popular Politics in Early Modern England* (Basingstoke, 2002), esp. chs. on rebellion and on riot and popular politics; A. Wall, "Riot," in *Power and Protest in England, 1525–1640* (2000); J. Walter, "Grain Riots and Popular Attitudes to the Law: Maldon and the Crisis of 1629," in *An Ungovernable People: The English and their Law in the Seventeenth and Eighteenth Centuries*, ed. J. Brewer and J. Styles (1980); *idem*, "A 'Rising of the People'?: the Oxfordshire Rising of 1596," *P & P* 107 (1985).

Who acted in riots?

R. Houlbrooke, "Women's Social Life and Common Action in England from the Fifteenth Century to the Eve of the Civil War," *Continuity and Change* 1 (1986); S. Brigden, "Youth and the English Reformation," *P & P* 95 (1982); S. R. Smith, "London Apprentices as Seventeenth-century Adolescents," *P & P* 61 (1973); J. Walter, *Crowds and Popular Politics in Early Modern England* (Manchester, 2006), includes ch. on the geography of food riots; D. Rollison, "The Specter of the Commonalty: Class Struggle and the Commonweal in England before the Atlantic World," *William and Mary Quarterly* 63, 2 (2006).

Were rebellions social? Did they reinforce or undermine order?

Wall, "Rebellion," in *Power and Protest in England*; C. S. L. Davies on popular religion in the Pilgrimage of Grace in *Order and Disorder in Early Modern England*, ed. A. Fletcher and J. Stevenson (Cambridge, 1985); B. L. Beer, *Rebellion and Riot: Popular Disorder in England During the Reign of Edward VI* (Kent, Ohio, 1982, rev. ed. 2005), esp. preface to the rev. ed.; M. E. James on "order" in the Northern Rising of 1569, in his *Society, Politics and Culture: Studies in Early Modern England* (Cambridge, 1986); D. Underdown, *Revel, Riot and Rebellion: Popular Politics and Culture in England, 1603–1660* (Oxford, 1985), esp. chs. on disorder, cultural conflict, and early Stuart popular politics; M. McClain, "The Wentwood Forest Riot: Property Rights and Political Culture in Restoration England," in *Political Culture and Cultural Politics in Early Modern England*, ed. S. D. Amussen and M. A. Kishlansky (Manchester, 1995).

Was there a crisis in gender relations in the early modern period? Alternately, was there a "double standard" for women; or "separate spheres" for gendered activity?

S. D. Amussen, " 'Being Stirred to Much Unquietness': Violence and Domestic Violence in Early Modern England," *Journal of Women's History* 6, 2 (1994); B. Harris, "Women and Politics in Early Tudor England," *HJ* 33 (1990); B. Capp, "The Double Standard Revisited: Plebeian Women and Male Sexual Reputation in Early Modern England," *P & P* 162 (1999); *idem*, "Separate Domains?: Women and Authority in Early Modern England," in *The Experience of Authority in Early Modern England*, ed. P. Griffiths, A. Fox, and S. Hindle (London, 1996); J. Kermode and G. Walker, eds., *Women, Crime and the Courts in Early Modern England* (Chapel Hill, 1994), esp. Gowing, "Language, Power and the Law: Women's Slander Litigation in Early Modern London" and Ingram, " 'Scolding Women Cucked or Washed': A Crisis in Gender Relations in Early Modern England"; S. Hindle, "The Shaming of Margaret Knowsley: Gossip, Gender and the Experience of Authority in Early Modern England," *Continuity and Change* 9 (1994); A. Shepard, "From Anxious Patriarchs to Refined Gentlemen?: Manhood in Britain, circa 1500–1700," *JBS* 44 (2005); L. G. Schwoerer, "Women's Public Political Voice in England: 1640–1740," in *Women Writers and the Early Modern British Political Tradition*, ed. H. L. Smith (Cambridge, 1998).

Is witchcraft a gender-related but not gender-specific issue?

K. Jones and M. Zell, " 'The Divels Speciall Instruments': Women and Witchcraft Before the 'Great Witch Hunt,' " *SocH* 30, 1 (2005); A. Gregory, "Witchcraft, Politics and 'Good Neighbourhood' in Early Seventeenth-Century Rye," *P & P* 130 (1991); C. Holmes, "Women: Witnesses and Witches," *P & P* 140 (1993); J. Sharpe, "Witchcraft and Women in Seventeenth-Century England: Some Northern Evidence," *Continuity and Change* 6 (1991); M. Marwick, ed., *Witchcraft and Sorcery*, 2nd ed. (Harmondsworth, 1986), esp. selections from classic works on witchcraft's social dimension by A. Macfarlane (1970) and K. Thomas (1972); C. Larner, *Witchcraft and Religion: The Politics of Popular Belief* (Oxford, 1984), esp. essays on Scottish witchcraft, on the views of James VI and I, and on English *versus* Scottish witch accusations; L. Jackson, "Witches, Wives and Mothers: Witchcraft Persecution and Women's Confessions in Seventeenth-Century England," *Women's History Review* 4 (1995); S. Parkin, "Witchcraft, Women's Honour and Customary Law in Early Modern Wales," *SocH* 31, 3 (2006).

Was the issue of vagrancy determined more by state or local response or by the agency of vagabonds themselves?

A. L. Beier, *Masterless Men: the Vagrancy Problem in England* (London, 1985), esp. chs. on the rise of subsistence migration and state policy; *idem*, "Vagrants and the Social Order in Elizabethan England," *P & P* 64 (1974), and the debate sparked by Beier, *P & P* 71 (1976); P. Slack, "Vagrants and Vagrancy in England, 1598–1664," *EcHR* 28 (1974); *idem*, "Poverty and Social Regulation," in *The Reign of Elizabeth I*, ed. C. Haigh (London, 1984); *idem*, *From Reformation to Improvement: Public Welfare in Early Modern England* (Oxford, 1999), esp. ch. on the "Common Weal"; M. K. McIntosh, "Local Responses to the Poor in Late Medieval and Tudor England," *Continuity and Change* 3 (1988); D. Woodward, "The Background to the Statute of Artificers: The Genesis of Labour Policy, 1558–63," *EcHR* 33 (1980); A. L. Gillespie, "Negotiating Order in Early Seventeenth-Century Ireland," in *Negotiating Power in Early Modern Society*, ed.

M. J. Braddick and J. Alter (Cambridge, 2001); a special issue of *JBS* 37, 3 (1998) discussing M. K. McIntosh, *Controlling Misbehaviour in England, 1370–1600* (Cambridge, 1998).

Two concepts of order? Were English villages typically the scene of a struggle in the late-Tudor and early-Stuart period between a "godly" minority and a less religious and more traditional "multitude"?

K. Wrightson, "Two Concepts of Order: Justices, Constables and Jurymen in Seventeenth-century England," in Brewer and Styles, *An Ungovernable People*; K. Wrightson and D. Levine, *Poverty and Piety in an English Village: Terling, 1525–1700* (New York, 1979, rev. ed., Oxford, 1995), esp. "The 'Better Sort' and the Labouring Poor," and the postscript "Terling Revisited"; Underdown, "The Taming of the Scold: the Enforcement of Patriarchal Authority in Early Modern England," and M. Spufford, "Puritanism and Social Control?," in Fletcher and Stevenson, *Order and Disorder*; S. Hindle, *The State and Social Change in Early Modern England, 1550–1640* (Basingstoke, 2002), chs. on enforcement of social policy and reformation of manners; M. Ingram, "Reformation of Manners in Early Modern England," in Griffiths, Fox, and Hindle, *The Experience of Authority*; *idem*, "From Reformation to Toleration: Popular Religious Cultures in England, 1540–1690," in *Popular Culture in England, c. 1500–1850*, ed. T. Harris (New York, 1995); Ingram on scolds in Kermode and Walker, *Women, Crime and the Courts*; E. Duffy, "The Godly and the Multitude in Stuart England," *Seventeenth Century* 1 (1986); H. French, "Social Status, Localism and the 'Middle Sort of People' in England 1620–1750," *P & P* 166 (2000).

ADDITIONAL SOURCE COLLECTIONS

K. Aughterson, *The English Renaissance: An Anthology of Sources and Documents* (London, 1998).

B. W. Clapp, H. E. S. Fisher, and A. R. J. Juřica, eds., *Documents in English Economic History* (London, 1977).

B. Coward, *Social Change and Continuity: England, 1550–1750*, rev. ed. (London, 1997).

P. Crawford and L. Goring, *Women's Worlds in Seventeenth-Century England: A Sourcebook* (London, 2000).

H. Haydn, ed., *The Portable Elizabethan Reader* (New York, 1955).

A. Fletcher, and D. MacCulloch, *Tudor Rebellions*, 4th ed. (London, 1997).

K. U. Henderson and B. F. McManus, *Half Humankind: Contexts and Texts of the Controversy about Women in England, 1540–1640* (Urbana, Ill., 1985).

M. L. Kekewich, ed., *Princes and Peoples: France and the British Isles, 1620–1714* (Manchester, 1994).

R. Salter, *Elizabeth I and her Reign* (Basingstoke, 1988).

R. H. Tawney and E. Power, eds., *Tudor Economic Documents* (London, 1924).

CHAPTER SIX

Early Stuart Church and State

It is difficult to read about England during the first four decades of the seventeenth century without focusing on divisions over Church and State. After all, in the 1640s several armies would fight bloody civil wars over just these issues. The victorious Parliament would execute first an archbishop and then a king on the way to abolishing both episcopacy and monarchy. But it is just as true that there was *no* civil war in 1604, nor in 1629, nor in 1640. We should be able to see the time before 1642 in its own terms before determining if the seeds of civil war and revolution lie in that period. Documents from this period suggest two sets of fundamental questions:

- How did religious and constitutional struggles interact?; how were they distinct?
- How were the issues of James's reign and those of Charles's different?; how were they related?

Divine Right of Kings and Ancient Constitutionalism

6.1   *James VI and I,* Trew Law of Free Monarchies *(1598)*[1]

Before James I (d. 1625) ascended the throne of England in 1603, he had already reigned in Scotland as James VI for over 35 years. He drew upon that experience to write the *Trew Law of Free Monarchies*. But monarchy had a divine mystique long before James wrote his manual on kingship: for example, sermons had long used various metaphors to explain the relationship between kings and subjects. James likewise mentions a number of "similitudes" (analogies) for kingly power and rule. What are they? Do all these metaphors work equally well? (For example, don't children grow up? Don't we owe allegiance to both mother and father?) According to James,

---

[1]   *The Workes of the Most High and Mightie Prince, James by the Grace of God, King of Great Britaine, France and Ireland, Defender of the Faith, &c.* (London, 1616), 204–9, 201.

where does royal power, authority, and legitimacy come from? What are the implications of this idea?

If, as James argued, the next person in strict primogeniture succession was God's choice to be the lawful king, then that person, not merely the office of king, was divine and he ruled by "Divine Right." By the same token, regicide – the murder of a king – inverts all order. In fact, where obedience to a monarch was previously conditional on his godliness, James added the idea of indefeasibility – that the people could not reject or resist a lawful king, just because of his bad behavior.

According to James, what options were there for the people to resist a bad, but rightful king, even a tyrant? Why might James have been so fearful of resistance to monarchs? Recall that he was well aware of the various attempts on Elizabeth's life (see chapter 4 above); that his own mother, Mary Queen of Scots, been harried out of her realm; and that several French kings had been assassinated – Henry III in 1589 and Henry IV in 1610. In 1605, at the beginning of James's own English reign Catholic conspirators – Roger Catesby, Guy Fawkes, and others – had stored gunpowder in a room under Westminster Palace for the purpose of blowing up Lords, Commons, and James himself (see Plate 8). Upon what grounds did people resist monarchs in the late sixteenth and early seventeenth centuries? Did God's law (revealed religion) ever justify regicide or did it always forbid it?

The king towards his people is rightly compared to a father of children, and to a head of a body composed of diverse members; for as fathers the good princes and magistrates of the people of God acknowledged themselves to their subjects. And for all other well-ruled commonwealths, the style [title] of *pater patriae* [father of the fatherland] was ever, and is, commonly used to kings. And the proper office of a king towards his subjects agrees very well with the office of the head towards the body and all members thereof; for from the head, being the seat of judgement, proceeds the care and foresight of guiding, and preventing all evil that may come to the body or any part thereof. The head cares for the body: so does the king for his people. ...

So ... if the children may, upon any pretext that can be imagined, lawfully rise up against their father, cut him off, and choose any other whom they please in his room, and if the body for the weal of it may, for any infirmity that can be in the head, strike it off, then I cannot deny that the people may rebel, control, and displace or cut off their king at their own pleasure, and upon respects moving them. (And whether these similitudes represent better the office of a king, or the offices of masters or deacons of crafts, or doctors in physic ..., I leave it also to the reader's discretion. ...)

I grant indeed that a wicked king is sent by God for a curse to his people, and a plague for their sins. But that it is lawful to them to shake off that curse at their own hand, which God has laid on them, that I deny. ...

It is certain ... that patience, earnest prayers to God, and amendment of their lives, are the only lawful means to move God to relieve them of that heavy curse....

And the last objection is grounded upon the mutual paction ... betwixt the king and his people at the time of his coronation ...; although I deny any such contract to be made then ..., yet I confess that a king at his coronation, or at the entry to his kingdom, willingly promises to his people to discharge honorably and truly the office given him by God over them. But, presuming that thereafter he breaks his promise unto them never so inexcusably, the question is, who should be judge of the break ...?

The kings ... in Scotland were before any estates or ranks of men ..., before any Parliaments were holden, or laws made: and by them was the land distributed (which at first was wholly theirs), states erected ..., and forms of government devised and established. And so it follows of necessity that the kings were the authors and makers of the laws, and not the laws of the kings.

6.2   Form of Apology and Satisfaction of the Commons (June 20, 1604)[2]

Some members of Parliament insisted that Divine Right coexisted with Ancient Constitutionalism – the theory that the coronation oath *did* serve as a contract; and that Parliament, especially the Commons, pre-dated the Norman Conquest, and, thus, did not exist solely at the whim of the monarch. They made such an argument, at least in committee, as early as 1604 in the Form of Apology and Satisfaction. What "fundamental privileges" do they assert? What did they offer in return? What claims do they make regarding representation? What do they mean when they assert that "the voice of the people ... is ... the voice of God" (in Latin, *Vox Populi, Vox Dei*)? What would James think of that? Did the Commons' arguments threaten Divine Right? Or could both sets of beliefs be held simultaneously?

The form of apology and satisfaction to be presented to his majesty, penned and agreed by a former select committee, was now reported and delivered into the House....

Now concerning the ancient right of the subjects of this realm, chiefly consisting in the privileges of this house of the Parliament, the misinformation openly delivered to your majesty hath been in three things: first, that we hold not our privileges of right, but of [the king's] grace only, renewed every Parliament by way of donative upon petition, and so to be limited; secondly, that we are no court of record, nor yet a court that can command view of records, but that our proceedings here are only to acts and memorials, and that the attendance with the records is courtesy, not duty; and, lastly, that the examination of the returns

---

[2]   *CJ*, 1: 243 (for the beginning); J. R. Tanner, *Constitutional Documents of the Reign of James I: A.D. 1603–1625* (Cambridge, 1930), 217–30, from TNA, SPD, James I, 8, fol. 60 ff.

of writs [for elections] for knights and burgesses is without our compass, and due to the Chancery. Against which assertion …, tending directly and apparently to the utter overthrow of the very fundamental privileges of our house – and therein of the rights and liberties of the whole commons of your realm of England – we, the knights, citizens, and burgesses in the house of Commons assembled in Parliament …, do expressly protest, as being derogatory in the highest degree to the true dignity, liberty, and authority of your majesty's high courts of Parliament, and consequently to the right of all your majesty's said subjects, and the whole body of this your kingdom; and desire that this our protestation may be recorded to all posterity. And contrariwise … [w]e most truly avouch, first, that our privileges and liberties are our right and due inheritance no less than our very lands and goods. Secondly, that they cannot be withheld from us, denied, or impaired, but with apparent wrong to the whole state of the realm.

From these [aforementioned] misinformed positions … the greatest part of our troubles, distrust, and jealousy have arisen. … For although it may be true that in the latter times of Queen Elizabeth some one privilege now and then were by some particular act attempted against …, yet was not the same ever by so public speech nor by positions in general denounced against our privileges. Besides that in regard to her sex and age which we had great cause to tender, and much more upon care to avoid all trouble, which by wicked practice might have been drawn to impeach the quiet of your majesty's right in the succession, those actions were then passed over, which we hoped, in succeeding times of freer access to your highness' so renowned grace and justice, to redress, restore, and rectify. …

What cause we your poor Commons have to watch over our privileges is manifest in itself to all men. The prerogatives of princes may easily and do daily grow; the privileges of the subject are for the most part at an everlasting stand. …

The right of the liberty of the Commons of England in Parliament consisteth chiefly in these three things: first, that the shires, cities, and boroughs … have free choice of such persons as they shall put in trust to represent them; secondly, that the persons chosen … be free from restraint, arrest, and imprisonment; thirdly, that in Parliament they may speak freely their consciences without check or controlment. …

Let your majesty be pleased to receive public information from your Commons in Parliament as well of the abuses in the church as in the civil estate and government; for private informations pass often by practice. The voice of the people in things of their knowledge is said to be as the voice of God.

6.3   Anthony Weldon on the Character of James I (pub. 1650)[3]

Whatever Divine Right theory implied, the all-too-earthly lives and characters of the Stuarts differed in practice. Minor courtier and future Parliamentarian (see chapter 7 below), Sir Anthony Weldon (ca. 1583–1648) wrote a pen portrait of James's public and personal traits (published after Weldon's

---

[3]   A. W[eldon]., *The Court and Character of King James* (London, 1650), 184, 186–9.

death), in which he noted that the king was sloppy, timid, and showered his young male favorites with gifts and titles. How might the attributes Weldon described add to or detract from the aura of Divine Right kingship? To companionability or respect? Would any of these qualities make James a *more* effective king? Which qualities might play better now than they did in Weldon's time? What do you think was Weldon's overall opinion of James (note the final paragraph of this selection)?

He was very witty, and had as many ready witty jests as any man living, at which he would not smile himself, but deliver them in a grave and serious manner. He was very liberal, of what he had not in his own grip, and would rather part with £100 he never had in his keeping, than one twenty shillings piece within his own custody. He spent much, and had much use of his subjects' purses, which bred some clashings with them in Parliament, yet would always come off, and end with a sweet and plausible close; and truly his bounty was not discommendable, for his raising favorites was the worst. Reward[ing] old servants and relieving his native country-men, was infinitely more to be commended.

He was so crafty and cunning in petty things, as circumventing any great man, the change of a favorite, [etc.,] insomuch as a very wise man was wont to say he believed him the wisest fool in Christendom, meaning him wise in small things, but a fool in weighty affairs. ...

He was infinitely inclined to peace, but more out of fear than conscience, and this [fear] was the greatest blemish this king had through all his reign, otherwise [he] might have been ranked with the very best of our kings.

In a word, take him altogether and not in pieces, such a king I wish this kingdom have never any worse, on the condition, not any better; for he lived in peace, died in peace, and left all his kingdoms in a peaceable condition, with his own motto: *Beati Pacifici* [Blessed are the Peacemakers].

6.4   Robert Filmer, Patriarcha *(ca. 1630, pub. 1680)*[4]

At the end of the 1620s, Sir Robert Filmer (1588?–1653) began to defend at length Divine Right and kingly power, and he appears to have made a manuscript presentation copy of "Patriarcha" for the new king, Charles I (1600–49; reigned 1625–49), before 1632. (After reading the next two sections, consider what about those years provoked such a strident defense of royal prerogative.) Compare the writings of Filmer and James. How is absolutism, or "the absolutest dominion of any monarch," based on God's law? James and others referred to the Bible to defend Divine Right. How does focusing on Adam and his descendants strengthen Filmer's argument?

---

[4]   R. Filmer, *Patriarcha and Other Writings*, ed. J. P. Sommerville (Cambridge, 1991), 6–7, 10, 12, 44.

For as Adam was lord of his children, so his children under him had a command and power over their own children, but still with subordination to the first parent, who is lord-paramount over his children's children to all generations, as being the grandfather of his people.

I see not then how the children of Adam, or of any man else, can be free from subjection to their parents. And this subjection of children being the fountain of all regal authority, by the ordination of God himself. It follows that civil power not only in general is by divine institution, but even the assignment of it specifically to the eldest parent, which quite takes away that new and common distinction which refers only power universal as absolute to God, but power respective in regard of the special form of government to the choice of the people. Nor leaves it any place for such imaginary pactions [contracts] between kings and their people as many dream of.

This lordship which Adam by creation had over the whole world, and by right descending from him the patriarchs did enjoy, was as large and ample as the absolutest dominion of any monarch which hath been since the creation....

It may seem absurd to maintain that kings now are the fathers of their people, since experience shows the contrary. It is true, all kings be not the natural parents of their subjects, yet they all either are, or are to be reputed the next heirs to those progenitors who were at first the natural parents of the whole people, and in their right succeed to the exercise of supreme jurisdiction. And such heirs are not only lords of their own children, but also of their brethren, and all others that were subject to their fathers....

Many will be ready to say it is a slavish and a dangerous condition to be subject to the will of any one man who is not subject to the laws. But such men consider not:

That the prerogative of a king is to be above all laws, for the good only of them that are under the laws, and to defend the people's liberties – as his majesty graciously affirmed in his speech after his last answer to the Petition of Right [see document 6.14].

Puritans and Anti-Puritans

6.5 William Barlow, The Summe and Substance of the Conference ... at Hampton Court *(January 16 and 18, 1604)*[5]

If religion could justify royal power, it could also threaten it, which explains why James and Charles both guarded zealously their status as Supreme Governors of the Church of England. At the very beginning of James's reign, those who wanted reform in the Church bombarded him with advice. They presented the Millenary Petition to him in April 1604, seeking to take away

---

[5] W. Barlow, *The Summe and Substance of the Conference* (London, 1604), 78–9, 82–3, 97–8, 103.

"the cross in baptism ..., the cap and surplice ..., and bow[ing] at the name of Jesus," as well as non-residency and pluralism.[6] The clerical petitioners hoped that James would be amenable to such changes, having been raised under the Scottish Presbyterian Kirk. In fact James had already spoken out against those who would change "the state ecclesiastical" by proclamation and in his advice-book to his son, *Basilikon Doron* (1599): "Take heed ... to such Puritans, very pests in the Church and Commonwealth.... Cherish no man more than a good pastor, hate no man more than a proud Puritan."[7] James nevertheless agreed to a conference between leading Puritans and bishops to be held at Hampton Court, for which we have the somewhat tendentious account of William Barlow (d. 1613), the dean of Chester and later bishop of Rochester and Lincoln. Can you tell from the document how Barlow reacted to John Reynolds' (1549–1607) proposition and James's response? Why did James say "No bishop, no king"?

Second Day [January 16, 1604]): Dr. [John] Reynolds ... desired that ... they of the clergy might have meetings once every three weeks, first in rural deaneries, and therein to have prophesying [meetings to discuss the Scriptures, see documents 4.13 and 4.14 above] ..., [and] that such things as could not be resolved upon there might be referred to the archdeacon's visitation, and so from thence to the episcopal synod, where the bishop with his presbyteri [clergy] should determine all such points as before could not be decided.

At which speech his majesty was somewhat stirred ..., thinking that they aimed at a Scottish presbytery [including laymen in Church government], "which," said he, "as well agreeth with a monarchy, as God and the Devil. Then Jack and Tom, and Will and Dick, shall meet, and at their pleasure censure me and my Council and all our proceedings...."

And then putting his hand to his hat, his majesty said, "My lords the bishops. I may thank you, that these men [Dr. Reynolds, etc.] do thus plead for my supremacy.... But if once you were out, and they in place, I know what would become of my supremacy. No bishop, no king, as before I said...." And rising from his chair, as he was going to his inner chamber, "If this be all," quoth he, "that they have to say, I shall make them conform themselves, or I will harry them out of the land, or else do worse."

Third Day [January 18, 1604]: ... [His] majesty shut up all with a most pithy exhortation to both sides for unity.... To which they all gave their unanimous assent.... Finally, they jointly promised to be quiet and obedient, now they knew it to be the king's mind to have it so.

[6] H. Gee and W. J. Hardy, eds., *Documents Illustrative of English Church History* (New York, 1896), 508–11.
[7] Proclamation in E. Cardwell, *Documentary Annals of the Reformed Church of England* (Oxford, 1844), 2: 65; *Basilikon Doron*, book 2, in *Workes of the Most High and Mightie Prince, James*, 160–1.

6.6–6.7   *Images of Puritans*

How did those who were called Puritan define themselves? By 1621, Puritans had been attacked in the Commons; in response, Sir Robert Harley, MP (1579–1656) penned a positive "Character" of a Puritan (document 6.6). From Puritans' opponents, we have the "Character of a She-Puritan" (document 6.7) by the young John Earle (ca. 1600–65), later bishop of Salisbury. (Why do you suppose Earle made the object of his attack female?) Using these contrasting documents, could you pen a portrait of a Puritan (such "Characters" were a popular pastime in early modern England)?

6.6   Sir Robert Harley's Character of a Puritan (ca. 1621)[8]

A Puritan is he that desires to practice what others profess. Is one that dares do nothing in the worship of God or course of his life but what God's word warrants him and dares not leave undone anything that that word commands him.

His sins are more than other men's because he sees them and greater because he feels them.

He is the best instructor of a prince and the best councillor to a king. The one he will teach first to know God that he may in time be the worthier to bear his great name. The other he will ever persuade that God's word, the perfect rule of good government, is best for him, on whom he hath set his own name, which makes him honored, but his word makes him wise.

He honors and obeys his superiors as children should their parents in the Lord, not for fear but for [con]science sake and as the civil magistrate bears the name of God so he esteems him next to God *ordine et autoritate* [by order and authority].

To things indifferent he thinks himself not born a bondman and wonders why he is styled a man of disorder when he is so willing to obey all law[ful] commands....

He thinks the making of the cross made between the Holy Sacrament of baptism and the humble thanksgiving of the congregation is like the placing of the Apocrypha between the Old and New Testaments, which being a stream without a fountain is unworthy to be joined with the living water of life.

He says a dumb [silent] minister is a dry nurse, one not able to feed God's children, a man not sent by God....

He heartily desires discipline in the Church according to God's word.

[8]   J. Eales, "Sir Robert Harley, K. B., (1579–1656) and the 'Character' of a Puritan," *British Library Journal* 15, 2 (1989): 150–2, from BL, Add. MS. 70, 212 (sections rearranged based on Harley's own marginal numbers).

Join discretion with his zeal, he is a man without compare and most unlike
his description which I have seen in print.

6.7 John Earle, "Character of a She-Puritan" (1628)[9]

She is a Nonconformist in a close stomacher and ruff of Geneva print, and her
purity consists much in her linen. She has heard of the rag of Rome, and thinks
it a very sluttish religion, and rails at the whore of Babylon for a beastly
woman.... She loves preaching better than praying.... She doubts of the Virgin
Mary's salvation, and dares not saint her, but knows her own place in heaven as
perfectly as the pew she has a key to.... She overflows so with the Bible, that she
spills it upon every occasion, and will not cudgel her maids without Scripture....
Nothing angers her so much, as that women cannot preach.... She is more fiery
against the maypole than her husband.

6.8 *Charles I's* Declaration to his Subjects Concerning Lawful Sports to be Used *(1633)*[10]

Earle's comment on maypoles reveals another religious struggle over popular culture. In fact, the "She-Puritan" was not alone in seeking a Reformation of Manners. Justices and observers of all stripes often saw May festivities and church ales, as well as unlicensed alehouses, as sources of disorder and violence. In the 1610s and again in the 1630s, local JPs, often of Puritan sympathies, launched campaigns to curtail or regulate such practices. But adherents of traditional culture defended May games, wakes, and Sunday sports (see Bucholz and Key, chapter 6). In particular, James in 1618 and Charles in 1633 issued proclamations *commending* some of these activities, which became known as the "Book of Sports." What are the arguments in favor of Sunday sport? Are these anti- or irreligious arguments? Why might Puritans oppose dancing, maypoles, Whitsun ales, rushes for decorating the Church? Why did two kings think "sports" so important? Which Sunday activities do James and Charles not approve of?

By the king [Charles]. Our dear father of blessed memory, in his return from
Scotland coming through Lancashire, found that his subjects were debarred
from lawful recreations upon Sundays ... and upon holy days; and he prudently
considered, that if these times were taken from them, the meaner sort who
labor hard all the week should have no recreations at all to refresh their spirits.

[9] J. Earle, *The Autograph Manuscript of Microcosmographie* (London, 1628, facsimile, Leeds, 1966), 115–21.
[10] Cardwell, *Documentary Annals of the Reformed Church*, 2: 188–93.

And ... did therefore in his princely wisdom publish a Declaration to all his loving subjects concerning lawful sports to be used at such times, which was printed and published by his royal commandment in [1618] ... which hereafter followeth:

"*By the king* [James]. ... Whereas we did justly in our progress through Lancashire rebuke some Puritans and precise people, and took order that the like unlawful carriage should not be used by any of them hereafter, in the prohibiting and unlawful punishing of our good people for using their lawful recreations and honest exercises upon Sundays and other holidays after the afternoon sermon or service, we now find that two sorts of people, wherewith that country is much infected (we mean Papists and Puritans) have maliciously traduced and calumniated those our just and honorable proceedings. ...

"The report of this growing amendment amongst them made us the more sorry, when with our own ears we heard the general complaint of our people that they were barred from all lawful recreation and exercise upon the Sunday afternoon, after the ending of all divine service, which cannot but produce two evils: the one the hindering of the conversion of many, whom their priests will take occasion hereby to vex, persuading them that no honest mirth or recreation is lawful on those days, which cannot but breed a great discontent in our people's hearts, especially of such as are peradventure upon the point of turning; the other inconveniency is that this prohibition barreth the common and meaner sort of people from using such exercises as may make their bodies more able for war, whenever we or our successors shall have occasion to use them; and in place thereof, set up filthy tipplings and drunkenness, and breed a number of idle and discontented speeches in their alehouses. For when shall the common people have leave to exercise, if not upon Sundays and holidays ...?

"Our express pleasure therefore is ... that no lawful recreations shall be barred to our good people, which shall not tend to the breach of the ... laws and canons of our Church. ... And ... that after the end of divine service our good people be not disturbed, letted, or discouraged from any lawful recreation, such as dancing, either men or women, archery for men, leaping, vaulting, or any other such harmless recreation, nor from having of May-games, Whitsun ales, and morris dances, and the setting up of maypoles, and other sports ...; and that women shall have leave to carry rushes to church for the decoring of it. ... But withal we do here account still as prohibited all unlawful games to be used on Sundays only as bear and bull baitings, interludes [street theater], and at all times in the meaner sort of people by law prohibited bowling. ..."

Now ..., we [Charles] do ratify and publish this our blessed father's declaration, the rather because of late in some counties of our kingdom we find, that under pretense of taking away abuses there hath been a general forbidding not only of ordinary meetings, but of the feasts of the dedication of the churches, commonly called "wakes." Now our express will and pleasure is, that the feasts with others shall be observed, and that ... all neighborhood and freedom with manlike and lawful exercises be used.

6.9   *Henry Burton,* A Divine Tragedie Lately Acted, or, A Collection of … Gods Judgements upon Sabbath-Breakers *(1636, reprinted 1642)*[11]

The Book of Sports provoked a Puritan outcry about desecrating the Sabbath, and Henry Burton (1578–1647/8) was one who cataloged examples of the evils that befell those profaning that day. Are these stories believable? Can you detect two sides of a cultural and religious war in the localities? Who supported and who opposed Charles? Which is the "popular" side?

These examples of God's judgements hereunder set down, have fallen out within the space of these few years, ever since the Declaration of Sports (tolerated on the Lord's day) was published and read by many ministers in their congregations; for hereupon ill-disposed people … were so encouraged, if not enraged, as taking liberty dispensed, thereby so provoked God, that his wrath in sundry places, hath broken out to the destruction of many.…

Example 3. 1634. A maid at Enfield near London, hearing of the liberty which was given by the Book which was published for sports, would needs go dance with others on the Lord's day, saying she would go dance so long as she could stand on her legs; she danced so long that thereof within two or three days she died.…

Example 5. On January 25, 1634, being the Lord's day, in the time of the last great frost 14 young men presuming to play at football upon the ice on the river Trent, near to Gainsborough, coming all together …, the ice suddenly broke and they were all drowned.…

Example 13. One Wright at Kingston, being a scoffer of religion and rejoicing at the suspending of his minister and others for not reading the Book of Sports in the churches, saying he hoped to see them all so served shortly, was within a day or two after struck with a dead palsy all over the one side and with blindness and dumbness that he could neither go, nor see, nor speak, and so lay in a miserable manner for a fortnight and then died.…

Example 42. At Topudle in Dorset, one John Hooper *alias* Cole, upon the promulgation of the said Book, was let down into a well to cleanse it, for to brew beer for at Whitsun ale by [three] churchwardens …, which John Hooper fell from the rope into the well whereof he died.

Example 43. At Glassenbury in Somersetshire, at the setting up of a maypole, it miscarrying fell upon a child and slew it and it is reported that it was the churchwarden's child, who was the chief stickler in the business. Also when the maypole in the same town was again the second time a setting up, a fire took in

---

[11]   H. Burton, *A Divine Tragedie Lately Acted* (written 1635, pub. 1636, taken from first full ed., London, 1641 [i.e. 1642]), sig. B2, B5[verso], [B6], C[1verso], D3-D3[verso].

the town so as all the people about the maypole were forced to leave it and to run to the quenching of the fire....

Example 45. Also at Battersea near London, the last year a notable example of God's judgement befell a fiddler. The young of the town of both sexes, being assembled solemnly to set up a garland upon their maypole and having got a tabor [drum] and pipe for the purpose, he with the pipe in his mouth fell down dead and never spake [a] word.

The Crisis of Parliaments

6.10 *Debates in the House of Commons (December 3, 1621)*[12]

During Charles's first Parliament in 1625, Sir Benjamin Rudyerd (1572–1658) praised the king as a "prince bred in Parliaments." Yet by 1628, Rudyerd responded to a speech by King Charles by exclaiming: "This is the crisis of Parliaments; by this we shall know whether Parliament will live or die."[13] It could be argued that the entire decade had seen a "crisis of Parliaments." One source of that crisis was religion (as hinted above); another was foreign policy (see Bucholz and Key, chapter 7). James's aspiration to be an international peacemaker collapsed at the outset of the Thirty Years' War (1618–48; see Plate 7) when his son-in-law, the Protestant Frederick, Elector Palatine (lived 1596–1632) was driven, first from the throne of Bohemia, and then even from his own Rhine Palatinate by the Catholic Habsburgs and their allies. Frederick and James's daughter, Elizabeth (1596–1662), were reduced to exile under the sarcastic titles, the Winter King and Queen, because they had only managed to rule Bohemia for one brief season. By the November–December 1621 session, many MPs, fearing threats to Protestantism domestically and abroad, clamored for an expedition to relieve the Palatinate. James, however, worried that such discussion threatened to boil over into a call for war against Habsburg Spain. James, supported by his favorite, George Villiers, duke of Buckingham (1592–1628), still hoped to position himself as peacemaker by arranging the marriage of his son, Charles, into the Spanish royal family to balance that of Elizabeth to Frederick. But such a match promised to be unpopular, as the Spanish royal family was, of course, Catholic. Below, the Commons debates petitioning the king urging a Protestant foreign policy and warning against such a marriage.

[12] W. Notestein, F. H. Relf, and H. Simpson, eds., *The Commons Debates, 1621* (New Haven, 1935), 2: 487 ff.

[13] 1625 speech quoted in C. Russell, *Parliaments and English Politics* (Oxford, 1979), 212; R. C. Johnson and M. J. Cole, eds., *Commons Debates, 1628* (New Haven, 1977), 2: 58 (two versions of Rudyerd's speech, 22 March 1628).

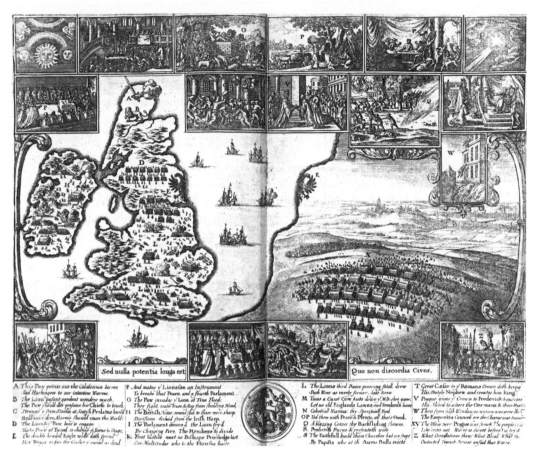

Plate 7 John Rushworth, *Historical Collections.... Remarkable Proceedings in five Parliaments. Beginning the sixteenth year of King James, anno 1618. And ending the fifth year of King Charl[e]s, anno 1629*, 2nd ed. (1659), frontispiece. (Source: © British Library.)

The main picture includes the "double-headed eagle" (E) of the Catholic Habsburgs overlooking both Britain and the battle of White Mountain (1620), while the poem below and insets (V–Y) refer to Frederick and the throne of Bohemia. Overall, the engraving is a history of the British kingdoms and of the continent from the late 1610s to the 1640s. What types of scenes and issues does the engraver emphasize? What link between the continent and the British Isles is suggested? What events of the 1620s or 1630s might also have been included in the insets?

- A. This paw points out the Caledonian jaws,
  Sad harbingers to our intestine wars....
- C. Strange, that from stools at Scottish prelates hurl'd,
  Bellona's dire alarms should rouse the World....
- E. The double-headed eagle wide doth spread
  The wings to fan the coals, that seemed as dead....
- H. The British notes sound flat, to those more sharp
  Divisions, echoed from the Irish harp.
- I. The Parliament convened, the lion tried
  By charging five, the Members to divide....
- V. Prague gives the crown to Frederick and excites
  His sword to assert the Germans and their rights.
- W. Then from high windows unawares were thrown
  The emperor's council, 'ere the charge was known.
- X.Y. The blow near Prague was struck, the people ride,
  Like Jehu out. War's sweet before 'tis tried.
- Z. What decollations then: What blood: What far
  Outacted tragick scenes ensu'd that war.

What arguments for and against the Spanish match are advanced by the MPs? When the learned jurist, Sir Edward Coke (1552–1634) discusses *arcana imperii* (state mysteries) is he agreeing or disagreeing with James's warning to Parliament not to meddle in "princes' prerogatives," like foreign policy?

Sir Edward Sackville took exception to that part of the petition wherein it is desired that the prince might be married to one of his own religion.... We have been careful all this Parliament not to touch the King's prerogative but what greater prerogative is there than to make war, matches, and alliance? By pressing the King hereunto either he must forego his own ways and ends or deny the petition of the commonwealth. What need we to touch this considering we have a prince that anticipates time. He is but young in years but old in judgment. And shall we think that whomsoever he shall marry that he will alter his religion? Or should we not think he will rather convert her than she him? ...

Sir Richard Weston, Chancellor of the Exchequer, said we will not meddle with the marriage for as princes do best when they take counsel of this House so we ought not to speak of what will not be heard.... It's good when the king adviseth with his Parliament of war but for the Parliament to advise the king of war is presumptuous....

Mr. [Thomas] Wentworth.... There is a relation of the Gunpowder Treason [Catholic attempt to blow up Parliament, 1605]; I wish it may be read, for these walls (methinks) do yet shake at it. And I would know whether those 36 barrels of gunpowder under these walls do not require this? ... Methinks it would be suitable to petition God's lieutenant.... The king is never greater than in Parliament, and we can never approach more nearly to our head than there....

Sir George More. The institution of a Parliament is to present grievances to the king. Now the greatest grievance we have is the decay of true religion and here to open the insolencies of popish recusants. And in this if we should not deal plainly, we should not deal faithfully. Moreover, by connivance they will increase and grow in number and arrogancy.

Sir Robert Phelips. If I thought this petition would be offensive to the King I would not have it spoken of. If I thought it would make a breach upon his Majesty's reason, affection or power, I would first bid away with it. But it will not, for his Majesty at a close of his speech at Whitehall bade us speak freely unto him; Wherefore I dare be bold to say that in the match with Spain there is neither honor, profit, nor safety.

Sir Edward Coke.... Marriage and leagues, war and peace, they are *arcana imperii* [state mysteries] and not to be meddled with.... But we desire that we might fight against Spain. We say that the hope of the marriage with Spain is the cause of the insolency of the papists. We advise nothing but what his Majesty liketh, for surely it will avert the hearts of many that he should marry with any but a protestant.... To do this by way of petition is good and hath no hurt in it.

6.11 Tuscan Ambassador Salvetti's report on the influence of the Duke of Buckingham (April 11, 1625)[14]

In 1623, Prince Charles and the duke of Buckingham traveled to Spain, *incognito*, to woo the Spanish *infanta* and secure a marital and diplomatic alliance (see Bucholz and Key, chapter 7). Though the mission failed, the prince and the duke grew closer just as the old king's reign was ending. They returned to London disgusted with the Spanish, but, ironically, hailed as Protestant heroes. (To help understand why Spain loomed so large in popular demonology, see Plate 8.) As a result, the Parliament of 1624 witnessed what is sometimes called a "blessed revolution," or change of heart, as both court and country seemed to unite to prepare for war with Spain. But the war went badly and people immediately blamed Buckingham. To understand why, we need to look to Buckingham's relationship to the new king Charles who succeeded in 1625, and public reaction to both. As you read this and the next selection, note the importance of access to the king. How would you characterize the relationship between Buckingham and Charles? Do contemporary criticisms of Buckingham's influence appear justified by these descriptions of the working relationship between Charles and his favorite? What was it about that relationship that made people feel uncomfortable?

The duke of Buckingham, although deeply grieved by the loss of the late king, his ever liberal master, may feel assured that the countenance and favor of the new king will be extended to him to a greater degree if it be possible. … He is with his majesty all day; he sleeps in a room contiguous to the royal chamber; he has been confirmed in all his offices which are numerous and of the highest importance; and he has also been made Gentleman of the Bedchamber, and has received the golden key, the emblem of his office, so that he can, whenever he pleases, and at any hour, enter that chamber as well as any other part of the palace occupied by his majesty. In fine, nothing is done without him.

6.12 Mr. Mead's letter to Sir Martin Stutevill (May 13, 1626)[15]

If Charles saw Buckingham's strengths and virtues, some MPs saw only his incompetence and corruption. In March 1626, six articles against Buckingham were presented in the Commons preparatory to impeachment

---

[14] HMC, *Eleventh Report, Appendix I, The Manuscripts of Henry Duncan Skrine, Esq. Salvetti Correspondence* (London, 1887), 3.
[15] H. Ellis, ed., *Original Letters, Illustrative of English History* (London, 1824), 3: 225–8, from BL, Harleian MS. 390.

Plate 8 Samuel Ward, *The Double Deliverance: 1588, 1605* (1621), detail. (Source: Bridgeman Art Library.)

Ward (1577–1640) was a Puritan pamphleteer and preacher. Why do you think he chose to portray the Armada on the left, the Gunpowder Plot of November 5, 1605 on the right, and the pope in consultation with the Devil in the center? The Spanish ambassador Gondomar protested the publication of this print and the Privy Council responded by imprisoning Ward. In what way is this print Puritan (see documents 6.5–6.9)?

proceedings in the Lords: chief among which were his failure as admiral (an expedition to Cadiz had ended in disaster), and the offices, money, and land given to him and his relations. How do the rumors related in this letter of May portray the relationship between Charles and Buckingham?

His majesty's affection no whit abates toward him [Buckingham], but seems rather to increase. Lord help us, what will come of these things? ... The duke being in the bedchamber, private with the king, his majesty was overheard ... to use these words. "What can I do more? ... I have in manner lost the love of my subjects. And what wouldst thou have me do?" Whence some think the duke moved the king to dissolve the Parliament, etc.

6.13   Diary of John Rous (1627)[16]

John Rous (1584–1644), minister in a small Suffolk village, recorded local, national, and international events, especially about the Thirty Years' War, for most of his adult life. His diary is a fascinating mix of rumors and reports from unprinted and printed sources (*courantos*, the first newspapers in English, date from the 1620s and reported the war). As we have seen, Charles had followed up the popular refusal of the Spanish Match with war against Spain, but the naval campaign was a disaster, and people blamed Buckingham. Moreover, in 1625 Buckingham had encouraged Charles's marriage to the French Catholic, Henrietta Maria (1609–69), and the English public increasingly viewed this alliance with disfavor as the French began a campaign against their own Protestants (Huguenots) in the South. Partially to restore his Protestant credentials, Buckingham attempted to relieve La Rochelle, attacking the French fort on the Isle of Rhé which effectively blockaded the port. The attack on Rhé, and thus the relief of La Rochelle, was also a disaster; only about 2,900 out of 6,800 English troops who embarked on the expedition came back. The following entries show intense interest in the campaign. In what different ways did Rous learn about the fate of the expedition? Rous's own opinion about Buckingham is ambiguous. Whom does he blame for England's troubles? Where might you place Rous politically? How do you think the Rhé expedition factored in to constitutional debates at home? Is this "public opinion"?

---

[16]   *Diary of John Rous: Incumbent of Santon Downham, Suffolk, from 1625 to 1642*, ed. M. A. E. Green (London, Camden Society, 66, 1856), 11–3.

Nov. 6, 1627. At Brandon, Mr. Paine of Kiddlesworth, Mr. Howlet sitting by, in Grimes Hall, told me that a Frenchman [in margin "or Dutchman"], Sir Thomas Woodhouse's man, told him that one Cornelis, or the like, an engineer that went with the Duke [Buckingham] and yet was now at London, did tell him that the fort was not to be won but by starving; and that it was many times victualed, &c. This said Mr. Paine was *oculatus testis* [eyewitness], &c., and when I went about to tell him of the map I saw of the fort, and what was delivered in it, especially about the ships riding against the fort, and of the provision made by masters for the staying of boats that should victual it, he would not hear it by any means; but fell in general to speak distastefully of the voyage, and then of our war with France, which he would make our King the cause of, for not establishing the queen [Henrietta Maria] in her jointure; to which I answered that I was able, with a little looking, to show statute law requiring such performances of a queen before her crowning, as I thought she had refused. I further said that, as she is, there might be danger, lest, being queen, King Charles should be stabbed, as Henry IV late in France; and then the queen regent might mar all. And the conclusion was, that I thought it foul for any man, not having seen the articles [of the marriage treaty], to lay the blame upon our own king and state. I told them I would always speak the best of that our king and state did, and think the best too, till I had good grounds. They fell upon old discontents, for the Parliament being crossed, expenses, hazard of ships, &c. [in margin "Why did we leave the Palatinate and fall foul with France?"] I answered that … men be disposed to speak the worst of state businesses, and to nourish discontent, as if there were a false carriage in all these things, which if it were so, what would a false heart rather see than an insurrection? A way whereunto these men prepare....

There was some speech of the fort [at Rhé] being taken [in margin, "3 November"]; but the current is so strong against the duke's honor, and the uncertainty of reports such, that few did matter it. The report was [in margin, "17 November"] that the duke had lost most of our men, and that our ships were much hurt, and the duke was returned.

The evil news was so current, that one told me that the French from the fort shot our men, and killed them as they looked out. I replied thus: "Belike our men are fools to put out their heads, and the French very watchful to be so ready."...

About the 16th of November the duke [Buckingham] was come to London, and had relinquished the isle of Rees [Rhé], and lost, at his coming away, many brave captains and … commanders …, some 42 or more, &c....

This news made much muttering, and caused much suspicion....

Nov. 26. The business now on foot betwixt England and France is of great consequence, and the slaughter in Rees will breed but evil blood, &c. The Jesuits, I believe, have made it high time for England to help the Protestants; whom to suppress, the Spanish faction helpeth what they can, and so that is, &c., the king of England might have no friends, and Spain the aid of Catholics in case, &c. – *qui potest capere, capiat* [let him accept it who can; or, if the shoe fits ...] – herein may be double policy; one as before, the other to divert us from helping the Protestants of Germany &c. Well! Be it so! Yet there is no counsel against God.

6.14 Petition of Right (3 Charles I, c. 1, June 2–7, 1628)[17]

As the unpopular war effort expanded against *both* France and Spain, and Parliament proved more interested in impeaching Buckingham than agreeing to more taxes to pay for it, the king began to raise money without parliamentary sanction. When he summoned Parliament again in 1628, the Commons, furious about wartime failures, extra-parliamentary taxation, and arbitrary arrest of loan resisters, began discussions that led to the Petition of Right, which they presented to the Lords as a draft in early May. Consider the Petition as a history of the past decade. How accurate was it? In the Petition, how were the king's actions proved to be illegal? What did the Commons believe their function to be? What was the connection between grievances and supply? After much prevarication on Charles's part, the king agreed to the Petition, although he continued to show his disapproval by ordering it issued without the usual statute number, thus leaving its standing in law questionable. Why do you think he disapproved?

Humbly show unto our sovereign lord the king, the Lords spiritual and temporal and Commons in Parliament assembled, that, whereas it is declared and enacted by a statute made in the time of the reign of King Edward [I], commonly called *Statutum de Tallagio non Concedendo* [not, in fact, a statute but a petition from the parliamentary opposition of 1297] that no tallage or aid should be laid or levied by the king or his heirs in this realm without the goodwill and assent of the archbishops, bishops, earls, barons, knights, burgesses, and other the freemen of the commonalty of this realm; and, by authority of Parliament holden [25] King Edward III [1351], it is declared and enacted that from thenceforth no person should be compelled to make any loans to the king against his will.... And by other laws of this realm it is provided that none should be charged by any charge or imposition, called a benevolence [also abolished by Richard III, 1483], nor by such like charge, by which the statutes before mentioned, and other the good laws and statutes of this realm, your subjects have inherited this freedom, that they should not be compelled to contribute to any tax, tallage, aid, or other like charge not set by common consent in Parliament.

Yet, nevertheless, of late diverse commissions directed to sundry commissioners in several counties with instructions have issued, by means whereof your people have been in diverse places assembled and required to lend

---

[17] *SR*, 5: 23–4.

certain sums of money unto your majesty; and many of them, upon their refusal so to do, have had an oath administered unto them, not warrantable by the laws or statutes of this realm....

And where ... in [28] King Edward III [1354] it was declared and enacted by authority of Parliament that no man, of what estate or condition that he be, should be put out of his land or tenements, nor taken, nor imprisoned, nor disherited, nor put to death, without being brought to answer by due process of law.

Nevertheless, against the tenor of the said statutes and other the good laws and statutes of your realm to that end provided, diverse of your subjects have of late been imprisoned without any cause showed....

And whereas of late great companies of soldiers and mariners have been dispersed into diverse counties of the realm, and the inhabitants against their wills have been compelled to receive them into their houses....

They do therefore humbly pray your most excellent majesty that no man hereafter be compelled to make or yield any gift, loan, benevolence, tax, or such like charge without common consent by act of Parliament; and that none be called to make answer, or take such oath, or to give attendance, or be confined, or otherwise molested or disquieted concerning the same, or for refusal thereof; and that no freeman, in any such manner as is before mentioned, be imprisoned or detained.

6.15   "Upon the Duke's Death" (1628)[18]

With the Petition of Right in hand, Parliament returned to criticizing "the excessive power of the duke of Buckingham, and the abuse of that power."[19] But Buckingham's "excessive power," as well as his plans for a new expedition in defense of La Rochelle, were cut short on August 23 when John Felton sank "a tenpenny knife" into his chest, killing him instantly. Felton was an officer in the last expedition who had been denied a place (and pay) in the new one. Upon his arrest, he said that "it came into his mind" to kill Buckingham after reading both a pamphlet suggesting that the favorite had poisoned James I as well the Commons' Remonstrance against Buckingham (June 1626) and "that in committing the act of killing the duke, he should do his country great good service." Certainly, his drastic action was popular. One report noted that as Felton passed under guard through Kingston-upon-Thames, "an old woman bestowed this salutation upon him: 'Now God bless thee, little David,' quoth she; meaning he had killed Goliath."[20]

[18] F. W. Fairholt, ed., *Poems and Songs Relating to George Villiers, Duke of Buckingham and His Assassination by John Felton, August 23, 1628* (London, 1850), 52–4, from BL, Sloane MS. 603.
[19] J. Rushworth, *Historical Collections* (London, 1721), 1: 625.
[20] Ellis, *Original Letters, Illustrative*, 3: 254–67, esp. 264–5 (Sept. 19, 1628), from BL, Harleian MS. 390.

Dozens of manuscript poems like the one below circulated. What is the value and danger for historians using such verse libels? Does this one have significance beyond reflecting someone's dislike of Buckingham?

The duke is dead, and we are rid of strife,
By Felton's hand, that took away his life.
Whether that fact were lawful or unjust,
In two short arguments may be discussed.
One: though the duke were one whom all did hate,
Being suppos'd a greivance [sic] to the state,
Yet he a subject was; and thence we draw
This argument; he ought to die by law.
Another: were he traitor most apparent,
Yet he that kill'd him had no lawful warrant,
But as a murderer he did it act,
And ought himself to die for such a fact. ...
Now, for an answer, justly is objected,
When law was offer'd, it was then neglected:
For when the Commons did, with just intent,
Pursue his faults in open Parliament,
The highest court of justice, so supreme,
That it hath censur'd monarchs of the realm;
There might his grace have had a legal trial,
Had he not it oppos'd with strong denial.
But he then scorn'd and proudly set at nought
The House, and those that him in question brought.
Therefore when law or justice takes no place,
Some desperate course must serve in such a case.
A rotten member, that can have no cure,
Must be cut off to save the body sure.
So was the duke: for when he did withstand
The ancient course of justice of this land,
Thinking all means too weak to cast him down,
Being held up by him that wears a crown;
Even then, when least he did expect or know,
By Felton's hand God wrought his overthrow
What shall we say? was it God's will or no,
That one sinner should kill another so?
I dare not judge; yet it appears sometime
God makes one sinner [re]venge another's crime. ...
For what the Parliament did fail to do,
God did both purpose and perform it too.
He would no threatnings or affronts receive,
Nor no deep policies could him deceive;
But when his sin was ripe it then must down:
God's sickle spares not either king or crown.

The Personal Rule

6.16   *Sentence and Punishment of Prynne, Burton, and Bastwick (June 30, 1637)*[21]

In 1629, after another agitated session of Parliament, in which the Commons debated religion, foreign policy and the king's prerogative rights, Charles decided to rule without them. The ensuing "Personal Rule" is sometimes called, perhaps unfairly, the "Eleven Years' Tyranny." Charles launched a program of reform in Church and State, known as "Thorough," which attempted to make government more efficient, maximize revenue, and standardize religious practice in ways that many found oppressive. For example, the king launched a campaign against Puritan practice by appointing bishops associated with William Laud (1573–1645), archbishop of Canterbury from 1633. (We have already seen how Charles enraged Puritans by reviving "The Book of Sports," for lawful recreation on the Sabbath, see documents 6.8–6.9.) These Laudians or Arminians (see Bucholz and Key, chapter 7) promoted ceremonial religious practice, the sacred role of clergy and bishops, and the necessity of a well-ordered Church for all in preference to a sermon-based, lay-dominated Church focused on true believers. Laud policed religious expression and punished Puritan clergy through the courts of High Commission and Star Chamber. In 1637, Star Chamber sentenced Henry Burton (document 6.9), William Prynne (1600–69), and John Bastwick (1595?–1654) to a gruesome punishment. Prynne had already been punished in 1634 by having his ears cropped for writing *Histrio-Mastix* (1633), a work denouncing plays and actresses, the latter of which had only appeared so far in court masques, including such luminaries as Queen Henrietta Maria. In 1637, for denouncing Laud and his clerical allies in print, the government trimmed Prynne's ears (along with those of Burton and Bastwick) even further! What do you think was the effect of such punishments as described below?

The said three prisoners were brought to New Palace Yard at Westminster, to suffer according to their sentence.... Dr. Bastwick spake first....

[Secondly,] Mr. Prynne ... showed the disparity between the times of Queen Mary and Queen Elizabeth, and the times [now], and how far more dangerous it was now to write against a bishop or two than against a king or queen: there at the most there was but six months imprisonment in ordinary prisons, and the delinquent might redeem his ears for £200 ...; here they are fined £5,000 a piece, to be perpetually imprisoned in the remotest castles, where no friends

---

[21]   J. Rushworth, *Historical Collections*, abridged ed. (London, 1706), 2: 293–4.

must be permitted to see them, and to lose their ears without redemption. ... He said, if the people but knew into what times they were cast, and what changes of laws, religion, and ceremonies had been made of late by one man [Archbishop Laud], they would look about them. They might see that no degree or profession was exempted from the prelates' malice; here is a divine [Burton] for the soul, a physician [Bastwick] for the body, and a lawyer [Prynne] for the estates, and the next to be censured in Star Chamber is likely to be a bishop. ... The archbishop of Canterbury being informed by his spies what Mr. Prynne said, moved the lords then sitting in the Star Chamber that he might be gagged ..., but that motion did not succeed. ...

[Thirdly,] Mr. Burton ... spake much while in the pillory to the people. The executioner cut off his ears deep and close, in a cruel manner, with much effusion of blood, an artery being cut, as there was likewise of Dr. Bastwick. Then Mr. Prynne's cheeks were seared with an iron made exceeding hot; which done, the executioner cut off one of his ears and a piece of his cheek with it; then hacking the other ear almost off, he left it hanging and went down; but being called up again he cut it quite off.

6.17   The King v. John Hampden in the Case of Ship Money (1638)[22]

As part of the royal attempt to maximize revenue during the Personal Rule, Charles's government searched the law books for old taxes and extended existing ones without parliamentary approval. Ship Money, an old tax on maritime counties to provide protection from pirates was now extended to inland counties in order to pay for the Navy. Although the first writs from 1634 aroused little excitement and brought in full tax returns, by 1636 it was clear that this was to be a permanent tax, and the country divided over the question of the king's prerogative versus Parliament's right to approve or reject taxation. From previous disputes, can you predict which groups would plump for which side of the Ship Money debate and why? When MP John Hampden (1595–1643) refused on principle payment of a mere 20 shillings, he was brought before the Court of the Exchequer and his relatively lengthy trial became a test case. The decision went against Hampden by a vote of seven to five; Sir Robert Berkeley's (1584–1656) explanation for the majority and Sir George Croke's (ca. 1560–1642) explanation for the minority are excerpted below. Upon what bases did they make their decisions? To what extent did these theoretical debates about the constitution affect everyday lives? What problems might a seven to five decision pose for the Crown?

[22]   T. B. Howell, comp., *A Complete Collection of State Trials* (London, 1816), 3: 1089, 1095, 1098, 1144.

Sir Robert Berkeley: … The grand question is shortly this: whether … in this special case … the charges imposed by the king upon his subjects for provision of shipping, without common consent in Parliament, be good in law – yea or no? …

It is to be observed that the principal command in the shipping-writ is not to levy money; it is to provide a ship – which ship being to be provided at the charge of a multitude …, the thing cannot be done any manner of way but by … money.…

as the law was created

Mr. Holbourne [Hampden's counsel] supposed a fundamental policy in the creation of the frame of this kingdom that, in case the monarch of England should be inclined to exact [money] from his subjects at his pleasure, he should be restrained, for that he could have nothing from them but upon a common consent in Parliament. — *not required / muddied because of Personal Rule.*

He is utterly mistaken herein. I agree the Parliament to be a most ancient and supreme court, where the … peers and commons may …, amongst other things, make known their grievances (if there be any) to their sovereign and humbly petition him for redress.

But the former fancied policy I utterly deny. The law knows no such king-yoking policy. The law is of itself an old and trusty servant of the king's; it is his instrument or means which he useth to govern his people by. I never read nor heard that Lex [law] was Rex [king]; but it is common and most true that Rex is Lex, for he is … a living, a speaking, an acting law. …

supreme ruler

Sir George Croke: … Judgment ought to be given for the defendant. My reasons and grounds that I shall insist upon are these: (1) that the command by this writ … for to have ships at the charge of the inhabitants of the county … is illegal and contrary to the common laws, not being by authority of Parliament; (2) that, if at the common laws it had been lawful, yet now this writ is illegal, being expressly contrary to diverse statutes prohibiting a general charge to be laid upon the commons in general without consent in Parliament; (3) that it is not to be maintained by any prerogative or power royal, nor allegation of necessity or danger; (4) admitting it were legal to lay such a charge upon maritime ports, yet to charge any inland county, as the county of Bucks [Hampden was from Buckinghamshire] is, with making ships and furnishing them with masters, mariners, and soldiers at their charge … is illegal and not warranted by any former precedent.

arguing he is just playing on law -to make money given dodgy areas

not near sea or present in naval battle nor construction aka. unnecessary

The Constitution Reformed or Deformed?

6.18 *The Petition accompanying the Grand Remonstrance (December 1, 1641)*[23]

In 1637 Charles attempted to impose an English-style prayer-book on the Presbyterian Scots. The result, the rebellion of the Scots Covenanters,

---

[23] J. Rushworth, *Historical Collections, the Third Part; in Two Volumes* (1692), part 3, 1: 437–8.

in turn, provoked the two Bishops' Wars, which forced the king to call Parliament to raise money for an army (see Bucholz and Key, chapter 7). Between 1640 and 1642 the Short Parliament (April–May 1640) and the Long Parliament (November 1640–April 1653 and May 1659–March 1660) did everything but raise money for an army. Instead, they took up the issues of the 1620s, and added the grievances of the 1630s, as well as the crises of the three British kingdoms (see chapter 7 below). Both houses of parliament united in dismantling the expedients of the Personal Rule, abolishing the courts of Star Chamber and High Commission, fines for distraint of knighthood and the regulation of royal forests, and, as MP Sir Simonds D'Ewes (1602–50) wrote to his wife on December 10, 1640, "on last Monday morning ..., we utterly damned ship monies."[24] But other issues, particularly religion, were more divisive. In December 1641, the leaders of the Commons pulled their various fears and grievances together in the Grand Remonstrance, a grab-bag of no less than 204 numbered complaints about bishops, Catholics, monopolies, and the king's advisors. (How is a remonstrance different from an apology or a petition?) The Petition accompanying the Remonstrance suggested their proposed solution to the faults laid out. It was printed and published in addition to being presented to the king. One can imagine the king's response to this Petition. How do you think the arguments of the Remonstrators appealed to social conservatives like Sir Edward Dering (1598–1644), who during debate on the Remonstrance, objected to its publication by noting, "when I first heard of a Remonstrance, I presently imagined that like faithful councillors, we should hold up a glass unto his majesty.... I did not dream that we should remonstrate downward, tell stories to the people and talk of the king as of a third person"?[25] Why do you think the Commons passed the Remonstrance by only a small margin (159–148)?

Your majesty's most humble and faithful subjects, the Commons in this present Parliament assembled, do with much thankfulness and joy acknowledge the great mercy and favor of God, in giving your majesty a safe and peaceable return out of Scotland into your kingdom of England ..., to give more life and power to the dutiful and loyal counsels and endeavors of your Parliament for the prevention of that eminent ruin and destruction wherein your kingdoms of England and Scotland are threatened. The duty which we owe to your majesty and our country, cannot but make us very sensible and apprehensive, that the multiplicity, sharpness, and malignity of those evils under which we have now many years suffered, are fomented and cherished by a corrupt and ill-affected

---

[24] H. Ellis, ed., *Original Letters of Eminent Literary Men of the Sixteenth, Seventeenth, and Eighteenth Centuries* (London, Camden Society, 23, 1843), 165.
[25] J. Rushworth, *Historical Collections*, part 3, 1: 425, 22 Nov. 1641.

party, who amongst other their mischievous devices for the alteration of religion and government, have sought by many false scandals and imputations, cunningly insinuated and dispersed amongst the people, to blemish and disgrace our proceedings in this Parliament, and to get themselves a party and faction amongst your subjects....

For preventing whereof, and the better information of your majesty, your Peers, and all other your loyal subjects, we have been necessitated to make a declaration of the state of the kingdom, both before and since the assembly of this Parliament, unto this time....

And because we have reason to believe that those malignant parties, whose proceedings evidently appear to be mainly for the advantage and increase of Popery, is composed, set up, and acted by the subtle practice of the Jesuits and other engineers and factors for Rome ..., have so far prevailed as to corrupt diverse of your bishops and others in prime places of the Church, and also to bring diverse of these instruments to be of your Privy Council, and other employments of trust and nearness about your majesty, the prince, and the rest of your royal children.

And by this means have had such an operation in your counsel and the most important affairs and proceedings of your government, that a most dangerous division and chargeable preparation for war betwixt your kingdoms of England and Scotland [see chapter 7], the increase of jealousies betwixt your majesty and your most obedient subjects, the violent distraction and interruption of this Parliament, the insurrection of the Papists in your kingdom of Ireland [from October, see chapter 7], and bloody massacre of your people, have been not only endeavored and attempted, but in a great measure compassed and effected.

For preventing the final accomplishment whereof, your poor subjects are enforced to engage their persons and estates to the maintaining of a very expensive and dangerous war, notwithstanding they have already since the beginning of this Parliament undergone the charge of £150,000 sterling, or thereabouts, for the necessary support and supply of your majesty in these present and perilous designs. And because all our most faithful endeavors and engagements will be ineffectual for the peace, safety, and preservation of your majesty and your people, if some present, real, and effectual course be not taken for suppressing this wicked and malignant party:

We, your most humble and obedient subjects, do with all faithfulness and humility beseech your majesty,

1. That you will be graciously pleased to concur with the humble desires of your people in a parliamentary way, for the preserving the peace and safety of the kingdom from the malicious designs of the popish party:

   For depriving the bishops of their votes in Parliament, and abridging their immoderate power usurped over the clergy, and other your good subjects, which they have perniciously abused to the hazard of religion, and great prejudice and oppression to the laws of the kingdom, and just liberty of your people ...:

For uniting all such your loyal subjects together as join in the same fundamental truths against the Papists, by removing some oppressive and unnecessary ceremonies by which diverse weak consciences have been scrupled, and seem to be divided from the rest, and for the due execution of those good laws which have been made for securing the liberty of your subjects.

2. That your majesty will likewise be pleased to remove from your council all such as persist to favor and promote any of those pressures and corruptions wherewith your people have been grieved; and that for the future your majesty will vouchsafe to employ such persons in your great and public affairs, and to take such to be near you in places of trust, as your Parliament may have cause to confide in; that in your princely goodness to your people you will reject and refuse all mediation and solicitation to the contrary, how powerful and near soever.

6.19–20   The Nineteen Propositions and the King's Answer

By the Spring of 1642, the political nation (the petitioners and others from jurymen, to JPs, to MPs, and Lords) had fractured. Parliamentary leaders and the king each attempted to form a militia under their respective oversight, and scoured the countryside for war *matériel*. But there was one more round of words. Parliament and Charles I made their case towards each other and towards the public in June 1642, when the Nineteen Propositions (document 6.19) and the king's Answer to the Nineteen Propositions (document 6.20) were printed. What does Parliament want? How does the king respond? Are his arguments different from James I's in the first document of this chapter? Which side is defending the English constitution? Which is calling for change? In what ways is either of them compromising or moderate? What is each side's greatest fear? To whom (which social groups) might these arguments appeal? Were these arguments worth fighting over?

6.19   The Nineteen Propositions (June 1, 1642)[26]

Your majesty's most humble and faithful subjects, the Lords and Commons in Parliament, having nothing in their thoughts and desires more precious and of higher esteem (next to the honor and immediate service of God) than the just and faithful performance of their duty to your majesty and this kingdom: and being very sensible of the great distractions and distempers, and of the imminent dangers and calamities which those distractions and distempers are like to bring upon your majesty and your subjects; all which have proceeded from the subtle insinuations, mischievous practices, and evil counsels of men disaffected to

[26]   *LJ*, 5: 97–9 (perhaps not delivered to Charles I until June 3).

God's true religion, your majesty's honor and safety, and the public peace and prosperity of your people, after a serious observation of the causes of those mischiefs, do in all humility and sincerity present to your majesty their most dutiful petition and advice, that ... you will be pleased to grant and accept these their humble desires and propositions, as the most necessary effectual means ... of removing those jealousies and differences which have unhappily fallen betwixt you and your people, and procuring both your majesty and them a constant course of honor, peace, and happiness....

1. That the lords and others of your majesty's Privy Council, and such great officers and ministers of State, either at home or beyond the seas, may be put from your Privy Council, and from those offices and employments, excepting such as shall be approved of by both houses of Parliament....

2. That the great affairs of the kingdom may not be concluded or transacted by the advice of private men, or by any unknown or unsworn councillors, but that such matters as concern the public, and are proper for the high court of Parliament ..., may be debated, resolved and transacted only in Parliament, and not elsewhere ...:

3. That the lord high steward of England, lord high constable ..., lord keeper of the Great Seal, lord treasurer, lord privy seal, earl marshal, lord admiral, warden of the Cinque Ports, chief governor of Ireland, chancellor of the Exchequer, master of the Wards, secretaries of State, two chief justices and chief baron, may always be chosen with the approbation of both houses of Parliament....

4. That he or they unto whom the government and education of the king's children shall be committed shall be approved of by both houses of Parliament ..., in such manner as is before expressed in the choice of councillors....

5. That no marriage shall be concluded or treated for any of the king's children, with any foreign prince, or other person whatsoever, abroad or at home, without the consent of Parliament....

6. That the laws in force against Jesuits, priests, and Popish recusants, be strictly put in execution....

7. That the votes of popish lords in the house of Peers may be taken away....

8. That your majesty will be pleased to consent that such a reformation be made of the Church government and liturgy, as both houses of Parliament shall advise....

9. That your majesty will be pleased to rest satisfied with that course that the Lords and Commons have appointed for ordering of the militia, until the same shall be further settled by a bill....

11. That all Privy Councillors and judges may take an oath, the form whereof to be agreed on and settled by Act of Parliament, for the maintaining of the Petition of Right [document 6.14]....

12 That all the judges, and all the officers placed by approbation of both houses of Parliament, may hold their places *quamdiu bene se gesserint* ["during good behavior," as opposed to "at pleasure" of the king]....

15. That the forts and castles of this kingdom may be put under the command and custody of such persons as your majesty shall appoint, with the approbation of your Parliament....
16. That the extraordinary guards and military forces now attending your majesty, may be removed and discharged....
17. That your majesty will be pleased to enter into a more strict alliance with the States of the United Provinces, and other neighboring princes and states of the Protestant religion, for the defense and maintenance thereof ...; whereby your Majesty will obtain a great access of strength and reputation, and your subjects be much encouraged and enabled, in a parliamentary way, for your aid and assistance, in restoring your royal sister [Elizabeth, the Winter Queen] and her princely issue to those dignities and dominions which belong unto them....
18. That your majesty will be pleased, by Act of Parliament, to clear the Lord Kimbolton and the five members of the house of Commons [whom Charles attempted to seize, January 4, 1642], in such manner that future Parliaments may be secured from the consequence of that evil precedent....

And these our humble desires being granted by your majesty, we shall forthwith apply ourselves to regulate your present revenue in such sort as may be for your best advantage; and likewise to settle such an ordinary and constant increase of it, as shall be sufficient to support your royal dignity in honor and plenty, beyond the proportion of any former grants of the subjects of this kingdom to your majesty's royal predecessors.

6.20 Charles I's Answer to the Nineteen Propositions of Both Houses of Parliament *(1642)*[27]

We call to God to witness that, as for our subjects' sake these rights are vested in us so for their sakes, as well as for our own, we are resolved not to quit them, nor to subvert (though in a parliamentary way) the ancient, equal, happy, well-poised, and never enough commended constitution of the government of this kingdom; nor to make ourself of a king of England, a duke of Venice; and this of a kingdom, a republic.

There being three kinds of government among men (absolute monarchy, aristocracy, and democracy), and all these having their particular conveniences and inconveniences, the experience and wisdom of your ancestors has so molded this out of a mixture of these as to give to this kingdom (as far as human prudence can provide) the conveniences of all three, without the inconveniences of any one, as long as the balance hangs even between the three states.... The ill of absolute monarchy is tyranny; the ill of aristocracy is faction and division; the ills of democracy are tumults, violence, and licentiousness. The good of monarchy is the uniting a nation under one head to resist invasion from abroad

---

[27] J. Rushworth, *Historical Collections*, part 3, 1: 731–2.

and insurrection at home; the good of aristocracy is the conjunction of council in the ablest persons of a state for the public benefit; the good of democracy is liberty, and the courage and industry which liberty begets.

In this kingdom, the laws are jointly made by a king, by a house of Peers, and by a house of Commons chosen by the people, all having free votes and particular privileges. The government, according to these laws, is trusted to the king. Power of treaties, of war and peace; of making peers, of choosing officers and councillors for state, judges for law, commanders for forts and castles; giving commissions for raising men to make war abroad, or to prevent or provide against invasions or insurrections at home; benefit of confiscations, power of pardoning, and some more of the like kind, are placed in the king. And this kind of regulated monarchy, having this power to preserve that authority, without which it would be disabled to preserve the laws in their force, and the subjects in their liberties and properties, is intended to draw to him such a respect and relation from the great ones as may hinder the ills of division and faction; and such a fear and reverence from the people as may hinder tumults, violence, and licentiousness.

Again, that the prince may not make use of this high and perpetual power to the hurt of those for whose good he has it, and make use of the name of *public necessity* for the gain of his private favorites and followers to the detriment of his people, the house of Commons (an excellent conserver of liberty, but never intended for any share in government, or the choosing of them that should govern) is solely entrusted with the first propositions concerning the levies of moneys (which is the sinews as well of peace as of war), and the impeaching of those who, for their own ends, though countenanced by any surreptitiously gotten command of the king, have violated that law which he [the king] is bound (when he knows it) to protect; and to the protection of which they were bound to advise him, at least not to serve him in the contrary. And the Lords, being trusted with a judicatory power, are an excellent screen and bank between the prince and people, to assist each against any encroachments of the other, and by just judgements to preserve that law which ought to be the rule of every one of the three. For the better enabling them in this, beyond the examples of any of our ancestors, we were willingly contented to oblige our self both to call a Parliament every three years, and not to dissolve it in fifty days, and for the present exigency, the better to raise money, and avoid the pressure (no less grievous to us than them) our people must have suffered by a longer continuance of so vast a charge as two great armies, and for their greater certainty of having sufficient time to remedy the inconveniences arisen during so long an absence of Parliaments, and for the punishment of the causers and ministers of them, we yielded up our right of dissolving this Parliament, expecting an extraordinary moderation from it, in gratitude for so unexampled a grace. . . .

Since as great an one [change] in the church must follow this of the kingdom, since the second estate [aristocracy] would in all probability follow the fate of the first [clergy], and by some of the same turbulent spirits jealousies would be soon raised against them, and the like propositions for reconciliation of differences would be then sent to them as they now have joined to send to us, till (all power being vested in the house of Commons, and their number making them incapable of transacting affairs of state with the necessary secrecy and expedition, those being retrusted to some close committee) at last the common people ... discover this *arcanum imperii* [state mystery], that all this was done by them, but not for them, grow weary of journey-work, and set up for themselves, call parity and independence liberty, devour that estate which had devoured the rest; destroy all rights and properties, all distinctions of families and merit; and by this means this splendid and excellently distinguished form of government end in a dark equal chaos of confusion, and the long line of our many noble ancestors in a Jack Cade or a Wat Tyler [peasant rebellion leaders, 1450 and 1381, respectively].

For all these reasons to all these demands our answer is *nolumus leges Angliae mutari* [we do not wish to change the English laws]; but this we promise, that we will be as careful of preserving the laws in what is supposed to concern wholly our subjects, as in what most concerns our self. For, indeed, we profess to believe that the preservation of every law concerns us, those of obedience being not secure when those of protection are violated; and we being most of any injured in the least violation of that by which we enjoy the highest rights and greatest benefits, and are therefore obliged to defend no less by our interest than by our duty, and hope that no jealousies to the contrary shall be any longer nourished in any of our good people by the subtle insinuations and secret practices of men who, for private ends, are disaffected to our honor and safety, and the peace and prosperity of our people.

HISTORIANS' DEBATES

Was there an early Stuart constitutional struggle and a political culture of conflict?

C. Russell's articles in *Unrevolutionary England, 1603–1642* (London, 1990), esp. "Parliamentary History in Perspective, 1604–1629"; K. Sharpe, ed., *Faction and Parliament: Essays on Early Stuart History* (London, 1978), esp. "Parliamentary History, 1603–1629: In or out of Perspective?"; C. Hill, D. Hirst, and T. K. Rabb react to revisionism in *P & P* 92 (1981); R. Cust and A. Hughes, ed., *Conflict in Early Stuart England: Studies in Religion and Politics, 1603–1642* (Harlow, 1989), esp. the introduction "After Revisionism"; T. Cogswell, "A Low Road to Extinction: Parliament and Supply," *HJ* 33, 2 (1990); D. Starkey, ed., *The English Court: From the Wars of the Roses to the Civil War* (London, 1987), articles by N. Cuddy and Sharpe; L. L. Peck, ed., *The Mental World of the Jacobean Court* (Cambridge, 1991), esp. the introduction and M. Smuts on cultural diversity at court; P. Lake and K. Sharpe, ed., *Culture and Politics in Early Stuart England* (London, 1993), esp. J. S. A. Adamson on chivalry and political culture, and A. Bellany on libelous politics in early Stuart England; S. Amussen and

M. Kishlansky, ed., *Political Culture and Cultural Politics in Early Modern England* (London, 1995), esp. articles by Cogswell, Cust, and Kishlansky on early Stuart political culture; J. Kenyon, "Revisionism and Post-Revisionism in Early Stuart History," *Journal of Modern History* 64, 4 (1992); K. Sharpe, ed. *Remapping Early Modern England: the Culture of Seventeenth-century Politics* (Cambridge, 2000), esp. the introduction; T. Cogswell, R. P. Cust, and P. Lake, eds., *Politics, Religion and Popularity in Early Stuart Britain: Essays in Honour of Conrad Russell* (Cambridge, 2002), esp. the introduction "Revisionism and its Legacies"; S. Adams, "Early Stuart Politics: Revisionism and After," in *Theatre and Government under the Early Stuarts*, ed. J. R. Mulryne and M. Shewring (Cambridge, 1993).

Was there an ideological divide behind any constitutional or political struggle?; or was there a general consensus about the nature of rule?

J. P. Sommerville, "The Ancient Constitution Reassessed: The Common Law, the Court and the Languages of Politics in Early Modern England," in *The Stuart Court and Europe,* ed. R. M. Smuts (Cambridge, 1996); *idem,* "James I and the Divine Right of Kings: English Politics and Continental Theory," in Peck, *Mental World; idem,* "Revisionism Revisited: A Retrospect," in his *Royalists & Patriots: Politics and Ideology in England, 1603–1640,* 2nd ed. (London, 1999); G. Burgess, "Becoming English? Becoming British?: The Political Thought of James VI and I Before and after 1603," in *The Struggle for the Succession in Late Elizabethan England: Politics, Polemics and Cultural Representations*, ed. J.-C. Mayer (Montpellier, 2004); G. Burgess, "The Divine Right of Kings Reconsidered," *EHR* 107 (1992); *idem,* "Revisionism, Politics and Political Ideas in Early Stuart England" (review essay), *HJ* 34, 2 (1991); Russell, "Divine Rights in the Early Seventeenth Century," in *Public Duty and Private Conscience in Seventeenth-century England*, ed. J. Morrill, P. Slack, and D. Woolf (Oxford, 1993); A. G. R. Smith, "Constitutional Ideas and Parliamentary Developments in England, 1603–25," in *The Reign of James VI and I*, ed. Smith (London, 1973).

Was there a crisis in the 1620s and, if there was, what were its causes?

The work of Cogswell, Cust, and Russell (above); G. E. Aylmer, "Buckingham as an Administrative Reformer?," *EHR* 105 (1990); R. Cust, "Charles I, the Privy Council and the Parliament of 1628," *TRHS* 6th ser., 2 (1992); *idem,* "Charles I, the Privy Council, and the Forced Loan," *JBS* 24, 2 (1985); J. A. Guy, "The Origins of the Petition of Right Reconsidered," *HJ* 25, 2 (1982); L. J. Reeve, "The Legal Status of the Petition of Right," *HJ* 29, 2 (1986); D. Hirst, "The Privy Council and Problems of Enforcement in the 1620s," *JBS* 18 (1978); K. Sharpe, "Crown, Parliament and Locality: Government and Communication in Early Stuart England," *EHR* 101 (1986); P. Lake, "Puritans, Popularity and Petitions: Local Politics in National Context, Cheshire, 1641," in Cogswell,

Cust, and Lake, *Politics, Religion and Popularity*; Cogswell, "John Felton, Popular Political Culture, and the Assassination of the Duke of Buckingham," *HJ* 49, 2 (2006); A. Bellany, "Railing Rhymes Revisited: Libels, Scandals, and Early Stuart Politics," *HC* 5, 4 (2007); *idem*, "The Embarrassment of Libels: Perceptions and Representations of verse libeling in early Stuart England," in *The Politics of the Public Sphere in Early Modern England*, ed. P. Lake and S. Pincus (Manchester, 2007).

Can one meaningfully distinguish between Calvinists/Puritans and Laudians/ Arminians/"anti-Calvinists" in the Jacobean and Caroline period?; and did either cause a breakdown in the Stuart religious settlement?

P. Lake's introduction to G. F. Nuttall, *The Holy Spirit in Puritan Faith and Experience*, 2nd. ed. (Chicago, 1992); P. Collinson, in *Godly People: Essays on English Protestantism and Puritanism* (London, 1993), esp. opening article on the Godly; *idem*, "A Comment: Concerning the Name Puritan," *JEcclH* 31 (1980); *idem*, "Introduction: Puritanism, Arminianism and Nicholas Tyacke," in *Religious Politics in Post-Reformation England: Essays in Honour of Nicholas Tyacke*, ed. K. Fincham and P. Lake (Woodbridge, 2006); M. Todd, ed., *Reformation to Revolution: Politics and Religion in Early Modern England* (London, 1995), esp. Sharpe on Laud and Tyacke on Puritanism and Arminianism; P. Lake, "The Impact of Early Modern Protestantism" (review essay), *JBS* 28 (1989); J. Eales, "A Road to Revolution: the Continuity of Puritanism, 1559–1642," in *The Culture of English Puritanism, 1560–1700*, ed. C. Durston and J. Eales (Basingstoke, 1996); W. Lamont, *Puritanism and Historical Controversy* (London, 1996); J. Spurr, "Defining Puritans," *English Puritanism, 1603–1689* (New York, 1998); P. White, "The Rise of Arminianism Reconsidered," *P & P* 101 (1983); debate by White, Tyacke, and Lake in *P & P* 115 (1987); K. Fincham, ed., *The Early Stuart Church* (London, 1993), esp. Tyacke's "Archbishop Laud"; P. Lake and D. Como, " 'Orthodoxy' and Its Discontents: Dispute Settlement and the Production of 'Consensus' in the London (Puritan) 'Underground,' " *JBS* 39, 1 (2000); M. Questier, "Arminianism, Catholicism, and Puritanism in England during the 1630s," *HJ* 49, 1 (2006).

Do we need to reassess James I and Charles I?

J. Wormald, "James VI & I," *HT* 52, 6 (2002); *idem*, "James VI and I, Basilikon Doron and The Trew Law of Free Monarchies: the Scottish Context and the English Translation," in Peck, *Mental World*; *idem*, "James VI and I: Two Kings or One?," *History* 68 (1983); A. W. R. E. Okines, "Why Was There So Little Government Reaction to Gunpowder Plot?," *JEcclH* 55, 2 (2004); J. Richards, " 'His nowe Majestie' and the English Monarchy: the Kingship of Charles I before 1640," *P & P* 113 (1986); M. Kishlansky, "Charles I: A Case of Mistaken Identity," *P & P* 189 (2005); R. Cust, "Charles I and Popularity," in Cogswell, Cust, and Lake, *Politics, Religion and Popularity*.

Did radicals and revolutionaries cause the crisis, 1637–42 and the onset of civil war?

C. Russell on 1637 in M. Todd, *Reformation to Revolution*; R. Lockyer, "Postscript: the Causes of the Civil War," in *The Early Stuarts: A Political History of England, 1603–1642*, 2nd ed. (London, 1999); D. Como, "Secret Printing, the Crisis of 1640, and the Origins of Civil War Radicalism," *P & P* 196 (2007); D. Cressy, "Revolutionary England 1640–1642," *P & P* 181 (2003); *idem*, "The Protestation Protested, 1641 and 1642," *HJ* 45, 2 (2002); J. Walter, "Popular Iconoclasm and the Politics of the Parish in Eastern England, 1640–1642," *HJ* 47, 2 (2004).

ADDITIONAL SOURCE COLLECTIONS

M. Bennett, *The English Civil War, 1640–1649* (London, 1995).

I. Carrier, *James VI and I: King of Great Britain* (Cambridge, 1998).

S. Davies, ed., *Renaissance Views of Man* (New York, 1979).

B. D. Henning, A. S. Foord, and B. L. Mathias, eds., *Crises in English History, 1066–1945: Select Problems in Historical Interpretation* (New York, 1949).

S. J. Houston, *James I* (London, 1973).

A. Hughes, ed., *Seventeenth-Century England: A Changing Culture*, 1, *Primary Sources* (Totowa, New Jersey, 1980).

C. Petrie, ed., *The Letters, Speeches and Proclamations of King Charles I* (London, 1935, 1968).

G. W. Prothero, ed., *Select Statutes and other Constitutional Documents Illustrative of the Reigns of Elizabeth and James I*, 4th ed. (Oxford, 1913).

B. Quintrell, *Charles I, 1625–1640* (London, 1993).

L. A. Sasek, ed., *Images of English Puritanism: A Collection of Contemporary Sources, 1589–1646* (Baton Rouge, La., 1989).

G. E. Seel and D. L. Smith, *The Early Stuart Kings, 1603–1642* (London, 2001).

V. Stater, *The Political History of Tudor and Stuart England: A Sourcebook* (London, 2002).

C. Stephenson and F. G. Marcham, eds., *Sources of English Constitutional History: A Selection of Documents*, rev. ed., 2 vols. (New York, 1972).

D. Wootton, *Divine Right and Democracy: An Anthology of Political Writing in Stuart England* (Harmondsworth, 1986).

CHAPTER SEVEN

Civil War and Revolution

It might be argued that the British Civil Wars and Interregnum are the central and most dramatic events of the early modern period. Why? One place to begin is with the lives they cost: according to a recent calculation, while 3 percent of the population of the British Isles died from "war-attributable" causes in World War I, over 11 percent did so during the Civil Wars. Another measure of their significance is their effect on speech and culture: after years of Church-imposed censorship, printing and pamphleteering flourished in the 1640s and 1650s. One collection alone, that of London bookseller George Thomason, contains over 20,000 items from these decades. Finally, there is the Revolution that followed Civil War: at no other time in the history of the British Isles was the monarch tried and executed by his own people; nor were monarchy, the Lords, and the bishops abolished; nor as many new political and religious groups, such as the Levellers and Quakers, formed. As you read the following sources, ask yourself:

- What impact did civil war have on the lives and psyches of the English people?; How did this impact differ between men and women?
- To what extent were the political, religious, and social issues and ideas of the 1640s and 1650s new or unique?; to what extent were they rooted in controversies left over from the late Tudor and early Stuart periods?

War and Reaction in the Three British Kingdoms

7.1   Walter Balcanquhall, A Large Declaration Concerning the Late Tumults in Scotland (1639)[1]

The violence which tore apart Scotland, England, and Ireland began with the Edinburgh "Prayer Book" riots of 1637. These erupted after Charles I

---

[1]   [W. Balcanquhall], *A Large Declaration Concerning the Late Tumults in Scotland, from their First Originals* (London, 1639), 1–2, 23–4.

attempted to impose an Anglican-style Prayer Book on largely Presbyterian Scotland (see Bucholz and Key, chapter 8). Walter Balcanquhall (ca. 1586–1645), dean of Durham, ghost-wrote a narrative of the "late tumults" which was published under the king's name "for the further and full satisfaction of all our true-hearted and loyal subjects in all Our Kingdoms." Where do his sympathies lie? How did Balcanquhall discredit the rioters?

On the twenty third day of July 1637, being Sunday, according to the public warning given the Sunday before, the service book was begun to be read in Edinburgh in St. Giles's church.... No sooner was the book opened by the dean of Edinburgh, but a number of the meaner sort, who used to keep places for the better sort, most of them women, with clapping of their hands, cursings, and outcries, raised such a barbarous hubbub in that sacred place, that not any one could either hear or be heard. The bishop of Edinburgh, who was to preach, stepped into the pulpit ..., intending to appease the tumult, by putting them in mind that the place, in which they were, was holy ground, and by entreating them to desist from that fearful and horrible profanation of it. But ... if a stool, aimed to be thrown at him, had not by the providence of God been diverted by the hand of one present, the life of that reverend bishop, in that holy place, and in the pulpit, had been endangered, if not lost. The archbishop of St. Andrews, lord chancellor, and diverse others offering to appease the multitude, were entertained with such bitter curses and imprecations, as they not being able to prevail with the people, the provost, bailiffs, and diverse others of the council of that city were forced to come down from the gallery ..., and ..., in a very great tumult and confusion, thrust out of the church these disorderly people, making fast the church doors. After all which, the dean devoutly read service.... Yet the outcries, rapping at the church doors, throwing of stones at the church windows by the tumultuous multitude without, was so great as the bailiffs of the city were once more put to ... use their best endeavors for the appeasing of the rage and fury of those who were without.

7.2 The Covenanters and the King at camp before the Pacification of Berwick (June 11, 1639)[2]

In February 1638, Presbyterian Scots nobles responded to the Prayer Book crisis by approving a National Covenant "to defend the foresaid true religion ..., forbearing the practice of all innovations already introduced in the matters

---

[2] P. Y. Hardwicke, *Miscellaneous State Papers: From 1501–1726* (London, 1778), 2: 131–7.

of the worship of God ..., till they be tried and allowed in ... Parliaments."[3] Later that year the Glasgow Assembly abolished the power of the bishops and nullified all royal religious legislation in Scotland since 1606. By January 1639, the Covenanters had raised an army, which fought the king in two successive Bishops' Wars. By the end of the Second Bishops' War in 1640 the Scots Covenanters occupied the northern counties of England (see Bucholz and Key, chapter 7). The settlement of that occupation would force Charles to call first the Short Parliament and then the Long Parliament in 1640. In the following discussion, King Charles surprised the leading covenanting lords – John Leslie, earl of Rothes (ca. 1600–41) and John Campbell, earl of Loudoun (1598–1662) – by entering the army tent in which they were discussing peace terms with his officers, and proceeding to debate with them directly. What do the Covenanters want? What does the king want? According to each, who has the power to make laws for the Scottish Kirk? What is the king's idea of representation? What are possible answers to the king's query: "when I say one thing, and you another, who shall judge?" (This question dominated discussions in all three kingdoms for the next decade.)

The King. My Lords, you cannot but wonder at my unexpected coming hither; which I would myself have spared, were it not to clear myself of that notorious slander laid upon me, that I shut my ears from the just complaints of my people in Scotland; which I never did, nor shall. But on the other side, I shall expect from them, to do as subjects ought....

Loudoun. ... Our purpose is no other but to enjoy the freedom of that religion, which we know your Majesty and your kingdom do profess; and to prevent all such innovations as be contrary to the laws of the kingdom, and all alterations of that religion which we profess. Which finding ourselves likely to be deprived of, we have taken this course, wherein we have not behaved ourselves, nor proceeded, any otherwise than becometh loyal subjects....

The King. Here his Majesty interrupted this long intended declaration, saying, That he would neither answer any proposition which they made, nor receive any, but in writing.

Then they withdrew themselves to a side table, and wrote this following supplication....

> First, It is our humble desire, that his Majesty would be graciously pleased to assure us, that the acts for the late assembly holden at Glasgow, by his Majesty's indiction, shall be ratified by the ensuing Parliament to be holden at Edinburgh, July 23rd....

---

[3]   J. Rushworth, *Historical Collections* (London, 1721), 2: 734–5, 739–70.

Secondly, That his Majesty, from his tender care of the preservation of our religion and laws, will be graciously pleased to declare and assure that it is his will, that all matters ecclesiastical be determined by the assembly of the kirk, and matters civil, by Parliament. ...

Thirdly, That a blessed pacification may be speedily brought about, and his Majesty's subjects may be secured, our humble desire is, that his Majesty's ships, and forces by land, be recalled ..., and we made safe from invasion. ...

The King. This supplication being presented and read, his Majesty said, he could give no sudden answer to it; subjoining, here you have presented your desires; as much as to say, "Give us all we desire"; which, if no other, than settling of your religion and laws established, I never had other intentions than to settle them. His Majesty withal told them, that their propositions were a little too rude at the first.

Loudoun. We desire your Majesty, that our grounds laid down, may receive the most favorable construction.

The King. ... Here his Majesty again protested, that he intended not to alter any thing, either in their laws or religion, that had been settled by sovereign authority. Neither will I, saith he, at all encroach upon your laws by my prerogative; but the question will be at last, Who shall be the judge of the meaning of those laws? His Majesty then farther told them, that their pretenses were fair, but their actions otherwise.

Rothes. We desire to be judged by the written word of the laws. Here he proceeded in justifying the assembly at Glasgow.

The King. You cannot expect the ratification of that assembly, seeing the election of the members of it were not lawful, nor was there any free choice of them.

Rothes. There was nothing done in it, which was not answerable to the constitutions of the church. Adding, that there is no other way for settling differences in religion, but by such an assembly of the kirk.

The King. That assembly was neither free nor lawful, and so consequently the proceedings could not be lawful. But when I say one thing, and you another, who shall judge? ...

Loudon. Here the Lord Loudon began to make a relation of the nature of the assembly, saying, How that in every parish there is a presbyter, and a lay elder who in every assembly is joined with the minister. And this order he affirmed to be so settled by the Reformation, as is to be found in the Book of Discipline [Knox's plan for Church government, 1560, and another in 1578, had been adopted by the Scottish Church but not fully ratified by Scottish parliaments], which is authentic of itself, and ever heretofore received, without needing to be confirmed by act of Parliament, it having been continually observed, as valid enough of itself, though it had not so been ratified.

The King. The book of discipline was never ratified, either by king or Parliament; but ever rejected by them. Besides this, there were never in any assembly, so many lay elders as in this.

Rothes. Lay elders have been in all assemblies, and, in some, more than of the clergy. And in this assembly, every lay elder was so well instructed, as that he could give judgment of any one point, which should be called in question before them.

The King. To affirm thus much of a truth, seems very ridiculous; namely, that every illiterate person should be able to be a judge of faith and religion. Which yet, his Majesty said, was very convenient and agreeable to their disposition; for by that means they might choose their own religion.

7.3 "Heads of the causes which moved the Northern Irish and Catholics of Ireland to take arms" (1641)[4]

In October 1641, as the Long Parliament debated both the Scottish problem and the past policies of Charles's Personal Rule in England, the Gaelic Irish rose against English rule. The rebels' plan to seize Dublin failed, but was more successful in Ulster. According to the following "Heads" (main points), why did they rebel? Why did they think themselves the victims of a plot? Recall that after the Flight of the Earls, the Crown had evicted Catholic–Gaelic landowners from this part of Ireland and redistributed their holdings to Presbyterian Scots colonists (see chapter 4). In fact, thanks to Charles I's religious policies, the rising of Irish Catholics against their Protestant landlords seemed to confirm a widespread English belief that *they* were the intended victims of a royal conspiracy uniting Popery with prelacy (see documents 7.4 and 7.5). It did not help that the rebels brandished forged letters of support from Charles I, thus enabling them to claim to be the loyal faction. How could they claim this? Which points from the following list seem exaggerated? Which seem convincing? Which points are rooted in the Irish context alone?; which reflect a wider, British context?

1. It was plotted and resolved by the Puritans of England, Scotland, and Ireland, to extinguish quite the Catholic religion, and the professors and maintainers thereof, out of all those kingdoms; and to put all Catholics of this realm to the sword, that would not conform themselves to the Protestant religion.
2. The State of Ireland did publicly declare, that they would root out of this realm all the natives, and make a total second conquest of the land, alleging that they were not safe with them. ...
4. That the subjects of Ireland, especially the Irish, were thrust out forcibly from their ancient possessions, against law, without color or right; and could not have propriety or security in their estates, goods or other rights, but were wholly subject to an arbitrary power, and tyrannical government, these forty years past, without hope of relief or redress. ...

---

[4] E. Lodge, *Desiderata Curiosa Hibernica: or, A Select Collection of State Papers* (Dublin, 1772), 2: 78–81.

6. The Catholics of this realm are not admitted to any dignity, place, or office, either military or civil, spiritual or temporal, but the same conferred upon unworthy persons, and men of no quality, who purchase it for money, or favor, and not by merit. ...

12. His majesty's royal power, honor, prerogative, estate, revenue and rights, invaded upon, by the Puritan faction in England. ...

17. All the natives in the English plantations of this realm, were disarmed by proclamation, and the Protestant plantators armed, and tied by the conditions of their plantations, to have arms, and to keep certain numbers of horse and foot continually upon their lands, by which advantage, many thousands of the natives were expelled out of their possessions, and as many hanged by martial law, without cause, and against the laws of this realm; and many of them otherwise destroyed, and made away, by sinister means and practices.

7.4   *Lucy Hutchinson,* Memoirs of the Life of Colonel Hutchinson *(written ca. 1664–71, pub. 1806)*[5]

Lurid reports of the Irish Rebellion claiming 200,000 victims (instead of the more probable 12,000 historians have reckoned) captured the English imagination. Three decades later, Lucy Hutchinson (1620–81) noted how first the Bishops' Wars in Scotland, and second the Catholic Rebellion in Ireland, pushed many English people to oppose their king and to side with Parliament. In fact, her biography of her husband, Col. John Hutchinson (1615–64), reads as a defense of Parliamentarian actions and views. In the following passage, is she impartial in her description of 1639–41? How does Hutchinson relate the Bishops' Wars and Irish Rebellion to divisions within English politics and religion? What is her most serious charge against the king?

About the year 1639, the Scots having the English service-book obtruded upon them violently refused it and took a national covenant against it, and entered England with a great army to bring their complaints to the king, which his unfaithful ministers did much, as they [the Scots] supposed, misreport. The king himself levied an army against them, wherein he was assisted ... most of all by the prelates, insomuch that the war got the name of *Bellum Episcopale* [Bishops' Wars]; but the commonality of the nation, being themselves under grievous bondage, were loath to oppose a people that came only to claim their just liberties. ...

While the king was in Scotland, that cursed rebellion in Ireland broke out [October 23, 1641], wherein about 200,000 were massacred in two months'

[5] L. Hutchinson, *Memoirs of Colonel Hutchinson*, ed. N. H. Keeble (London, 1968, 1995), 71, 73–4.

space, being surprised, and many of them most inhumanely butchered and tormented; and besides the slain, abundance of poor families stripped and sent naked away out of all their possessions; and had not the providence of God miraculously prevented the surprise of Dublin Castle the night it should have been seized, there had not been any remnant of the Protestant name left in that country. As soon as this sad news came to the Parliament, they vigorously set themselves to the work of relieving them; but then the king returned from Scotland, and being sumptuously welcomed home by the city, took courage thereby against the Parliament, and obstructed all their proceedings for the effectual relief of Ireland. Long was he before he could be drawn to proclaim those murderers rebels, and when he did, by special command there were but 40 proclamations printed, and care taken that they should not be much dispersed; which courses afflicted all the good Protestants in England, and confirmed that this rebellion in Ireland received countenance from the king and queen of England.

[handwritten margin note: changed position under the idea of being liked.]

7.5 Richard Baxter on Royalists and Parliamentarians (written ca. 1664, pub. 1696)[6]

After neither King Charles nor the Long Parliament would entrust the other with command of an army to suppress the Scottish and Irish Rebellions, the former declared war on the latter by raising the royal standard at Nottingham on August 22, 1642. How did individuals decide whether to fight with the king or with Parliament? Some knew clearly where their duty lay. For example, Sir Edmund Verney (1590–1642) is supposed to have said "my conscience is only concerned in honor and in gratitude to follow my master. I have eaten his bread and served him near thirty years, and will not do so base a thing as forsake him."[7] Compare Verney's reasoning with that of Richard Baxter (1615–91), a Puritan minister, whose posthumously published autobiography is an insightful narrative of the 1640s–80s. First, note how Baxter distinguishes Royalists from Parliamentarians by class, by religion, and by constitutional viewpoint. How does he link allegiances in 1642 with struggles of the 1620s and 1630s? Are his assessments fair? If so, what were the motivating factors in choosing sides? Then, consider Baxter's own allegiance: what issues loomed largest for him? Finally, consider that Baxter wrote some time *after* the Restoration of monarchy in 1660. How might that affect his reliability as a guide to choices made in 1640–2? (For propaganda published *during* the war in an attempt to influence allegiance, see Plate 9.)

---

[6] *Reliquiae Baxterianae* (London, 1696), 1, part 1: 28–31, 33, 39.
[7] F. P. Verney, *Memoirs of the Verney Family during the Civil War* (London, 1892), 2: 126.

Plate 9 Francis Quarles, *The Shepherds Oracles* (1644), frontispiece. (Source: © British Library.)

Who is watering and defending the tree of religion, and who is lopping off branches or attempting to uproot it? (Hints: who wields a sword against its enemies? Radical religious clergy often preached outside, thus were known as tub-preachers – the equivalent of soap-box speakers today.) What documents or sources might this comment on?

It is of very great moment here to understand the quality of the persons which adhered to the king and to the Parliament, with their reasons.

A great part of the Lords forsook the Parliament, and so did many of the House of Commons, and came to the king; but that was, for the most of them, after Edgehill fight (October 1642, see document 7.6), when the king was at Oxford. A very great part of the knights and gentlemen of England in the several counties (who were not Parliament-men) adhered to the king.... And most of the tenants of these gentlemen, and also most of the poorest of the people, whom the other call the rabble, did follow the gentry and were for the king.

On the Parliament's side were (besides themselves) the smaller part (as some thought) of the gentry in most of the counties, and the greatest part of the tradesmen and freeholders and the middle sort of men, especially in those corporations and countries which depend on clothing and such, manufactures....

But though it must be confessed that the public safety and liberty wrought very much with most, especially with the nobility and gentry who adhered to the Parliament, yet was it principally the differences about religious matter that filled up the Parliament's armies and put the resolution and valor into their soldiers, which carried them on in another manner than mercenary soldiers are carried on.... But the generality of the people through the land ... who were then called Puritans, precisians, religious persons, that used to talk of God, and heaven, and Scripture, and holiness.... I say, the main body of this sort of men, both preachers and people, adhered to the Parliament. And on the other side [the Royalists], the gentry that were not so precise and strict against an oath, or gaming, or plays, or drinking nor troubled themselves so much about the matters of God and the world to come, and the ministers and people that were for the King's Book [of Sports, document 6.8 above], for dancing and recreations on the Lord's days, and those that made not so great a matter of every sin, but went to church and heard Common Prayer, and were glad to hear a sermon which lashed the Puritans, and which ordinarily spoke against the strictness and preciseness in religion ..., these were against the Parliament....

And abundance of the ignorant sort of the country, who were civil, did flock in to the Parliament, and filled up their armies afterward, merely because they heard men *swear* for the Common Prayer and bishops, and heard others *pray* that were against them; and because they heard the king's soldiers with horrid oaths abuse the name of God, and saw them live in debauchery and the Parliament's soldiers flock to sermons and talking of religion, and praying and singing Psalms together on their guards. And all the sober men that I was acquainted with, who were against the Parliament, were wont to say, "The king hath the better cause, but the Parliament hath the better men."

7.6 *Captain Edward Kightley on the battle of Edgehill, October 23, 1642 (November 4, 1642)*[8]

The first major battle of the *English* Civil Wars was fought in October, at Edgehill. The violence of actual civil war came as a shock. In this account by a Parliamentarian officer, what signs can you detect of the commanders' and soldiers' inexperience? Why was discipline such a problem on both sides? Can you see why the battle was a draw? (This account was published; how is it propaganda?)

On Sunday 23 October [1642] about one o'clock in the afternoon the battle did begin and continued until it was very dark; the field was very great and large and the king's forces came down a great and long hill. He had the advantage of the ground and the wind, and they gave a brave charge and did fight very valiantly.... My lord general [Robert Devereux, earl of Essex (1591–1646), commander of the parliamentary forces] did give first charge, presenting them with two pieces of ordinance which killed many of their men, and then the enemy did shoot one to us which fell twenty yards short in ploughed land and did no harm; our soldiers did many of them run away ... and there did run away 600 horse ... and when I was entering the field I think 200 horse came by me with all the speed they could out of the battle, saying that the king hath the victory and that every man cried "God and King Charles." I entreated, prayed, and persuaded them to stay and draw up in a body with our troops, for we saw them fighting and the field was not lost, but no persuasions would serve, and then turning to our three troops, two of them were run away [and] of my troop I had not six and thirty men left.... I stayed with those men I had ... and diverse of the enemy did run that way, both horse and foot. I took away about ten or twelve horse, swords and armor. I could have killed 40 of the enemy [but] I let them pass, disarming them and giving spoil to my troopers. The armies were both in confusion.... The enemy ran away as well as our men....

Let us pray one for another, God I hope will open the King's eyes, and send peace to our kingdom.... (All my run-aways, I stop their pay ..., and give their pay to the rest of the soldiers.)

[8] *A full and true Relation Of the great Battle fought between the Kings Army, and his Excellency, the Earle of Essex, upon the 23. of October last past* (London, Nov. 4, 1642), 3–4, 6–7.

7.7   Oliver Cromwell's letters about the English Civil War (1643–4)[9]

As in all wars, some rose to the occasion. Among the best sources on the Civil Wars and the religious politics of the Parliamentary army are the letters of Oliver Cromwell (1599–1658). Cromwell was an obscure fenland farmer who became, first, an MP in the Short and Long Parliaments; then, from early 1643, a captain in a regional army (the Eastern Association); and from early 1644, a lieutenant-general of horse. What does the letter of September 11, 1643 reveal about the staffing, logistics, and expenses of such an army? Why was the issue of the soldiers' religion so volatile? The letter of July 5, 1644 is a famous letter of condolence informing a father that his son has died in battle. Note the structure and the message(s). Do you think this letter was effective? Why or why not? This letter also describes the important battle of Marston Moor. According to Cromwell, why were the Parliamentarians victorious? Can you suggest other reasons? We will return to Cromwell; in the meantime, what do these letters reveal about his nature?

September 11, 1643, Oliver Cromwell with the Parliamentarian Eastern Association army to Oliver St. John, Esq., at London

Of all men I should not trouble you with money matters, did not the heavy necessities my troops are in, press me beyond measure. I am neglected exceedingly!

I am now ready for my march towards the enemy; who hath entrenched himself over against Hull, my Lord Newcastle having besieged the town. Many of my lord of Manchester's troops are come to me: very bad and mutinous, not to be confided in; they paid to a week almost; mine no ways provided for to support them, except by the poor sequestrations of the county of Huntingdon. My troops increase. I have a lovely company; you would respect them, did you know them. They are no Anabaptists, they are honest sober Christians: they expect to be used as men.

If I took pleasure to write to the House in bitterness, I have occasion. Of the £3,000 allotted me, I cannot get the part of Norfolk nor Hertfordshire: it was gone before I had it. I have minded your service to forgetfulness of my own and soldiers' necessities. I desire not to seek myself, but I have little money of my own to help my soldiers. My estate is little. I tell you, the business of Ireland and England hath had of me, in money, between eleven and twelve hundred pounds; therefore my private can do little to help the public. You have had my money: I hope in God I desire to venture my skin. So do mine. Lay weight upon their patience; but break it not. Think of that which may be a real help. I believe £5,000 is due....

---

[9]   *The Writings and Speeches of Oliver Cromwell*, ed. W. C. Abbott (Oxford, 1937, 1988), 1: 258–9, 277–8, 287–8.

July 5, 1644, Oliver Cromwell, before York to his brother-in-law
Col. Valentine Walton

It's our duty to sympathize in all mercies; that we may praise the Lord together in chastisements or trials, that so we may sorrow together.

Truly England and the Church of God hath had a great favor from the Lord in this great victory given unto us, such as the like never was since this war began. It had all the evidences of an absolute victory obtained by the Lord's blessing upon the godly party principally. We never charged but we routed the enemy. The left wing, which I commanded, being our own horse, saving a few Scots in our rear, beat all the prince's [Rupert's] horse. God made them as stubble to our swords; we charged their regiments of foot with our horse, routed all we charged. The particulars I cannot relate now, but I believe, of twenty thousand the prince hath not four thousand left. Give glory, all the glory, to God.

Sir, God hath taken away your eldest son by a cannon-shot. It brake his leg. We were necessitated to have it cut off, whereof he died.

Sir, you know my trials this way, but the Lord supported me with this: that the Lord took him into the happiness we all pant after and live for. There is your precious child full of glory, to know sin nor sorrow any more. He was a gallant young man, exceeding gracious. God give you His comfort. Before his death he was so full of comfort that to Frank Russell and myself he could not express it, it was so great above his pain. This he said to us. Indeed it was admirable. A little after, he said one thing lay upon his spirit. I asked him what that was. He told me that it was that God had not suffered him to be no more the executioner of His enemies. At his fall, his horse being killed with a bullet, and as I am informed three horses more, I am told he bid them open to the right and left, that he might see the rogues run. Truly, he was exceedingly beloved in the army, of all that knew him. But few knew him, for he was a precious young man, fit for God. You have cause to bless the Lord. He is a glorious saint in Heaven, wherein you ought exceedingly to rejoice. Let this drink up your sorrow; seeing these are not feigned words to comfort you, but the thing is so real and undoubted a truth. You may do all things by the strength of Christ. Seek that, and you shall easily bear your trial. Let this public mercy to the Church of God make you to forget your private sorrow. The Lord be your strength.

7.8   Oliver Cromwell at Dublin to William Lenthall, Esq., Speaker of the Parliament of England (September 17, 1649)[10]

Parliament's war against the Irish could not begin in earnest until the wars against the king were over in England. The first Civil War ended in 1646 and the king surrendered, but negotiations for a settlement were still ongoing

[10]   *Writings and Speeches of Oliver Cromwell*, 2: 125–8.

when a second Civil War broke out in May 1648. It was not until after the trial and execution of the king in January 1649 (see next section) that Cromwell landed with an army in Ireland (August 15), and led his troops in the siege and sack of Drogheda (September 11) and Wexford (October 11). How had the nature of the fighting changed since Edgehill? What was Cromwell's explanation for the Drogheda massacre? Why were priests treated so harshly? Why did it not matter to him that most of the Irish defenders of Drogheda were Old English and not native Irish, the group that had actually risen in October 1641? Should it matter to historians? (Note that, whatever its morality, the violence was effective: towns like Ross soon submitted to terms, and, thus, Ireland submitted to Cromwell and Parliament.)

Your army came before the town [Tredah, Drogheda] upon [September 3], where having pitched, as speedy course was taken as could be to frame our batteries. ... Upon [September 10] ..., the batteries began to play. Whereupon I sent Sir Arthur Ashton, the then governor, a summons to deliver the town to the use of the Parliament of England. To the which I received no satisfactory answer, but proceeded that day to beat down the steeple of the church on the south side of the town, and to beat down a tower not far from the same place. ...

Upon [September 11] ..., about five o'clock in the evening, we began the storm, and after some hot dispute we entered about seven or eight hundred men, the enemy disputing it very stiffly with us. And indeed, through the advantages of the place, and the courage God was pleased to give the defenders, our men were forced to retreat quite out of the breach, not without some considerable loss. ...

Although our men that stormed the breaches were forced to recoil ..., yet, being encouraged to recover their loss, they made a second attempt, wherein God was pleased [so] to animate them that they got ground of the enemy, and by the goodness of God, forced him to quit his entrenchments. And after a very hot dispute ..., they gave ground, and our men became masters both of their retrenchments and the church; which indeed, although they made our entrance the more difficult, yet they proved of excellent use to us, so that the enemy could not now annoy us with their horse. ...

The enemy retreated, diverse of them, into the Mill-Mount: a place very strong and of difficult access, being exceedingly high, having a good graft, and strongly palisadoed. The governor, Sir Arthur Ashton, and diverse considerable officers being there, our men getting up to them, were ordered by me to put them all to the sword. And indeed, being in the heat of action, I forbade them to spare any that were in arms in the town, and, I think, that night they put to the sword about 2,000 men, diverse of the officers and soldiers being fled over the bridge into the other part of the town, where about one hundred of them possessed St. Peter's church-steeple, some the west gate and others a strong round tower next the gate called St. Sunday's. These being summoned to yield to mercy, refused, whereupon I ordered the steeple of St. Peter's Church to be fired, where one of them was heard to say in the midst of the flames: "God damn me, God confound me; I burn, I burn."

The next day, the other two towers were summoned, in one of which was about six or seven score; but they refused to yield themselves, and we knowing that hunger must compel them, set only good guards to secure them from running away until their stomachs were come down. From one of the said towers, notwithstanding their condition, they killed and wounded some of our men. When they submitted, their officers were knocked on the head, and every tenth man of the soldiers killed, and the rest shipped for the Barbados. The soldiers in the other tower were all spared, as to their lives only, and shipped likewise for the Barbados.

I am persuaded that this is a righteous judgment of God upon these barbarous wretches, who have imbrued their hands in so much innocent blood; and that it will tend to prevent the effusion of blood for the future, which are the satisfactory grounds to such actions, which otherwise cannot but work remorse and regret. The officers and soldiers of this garrison were the flower of all their army, and their great expectation was, that our attempting this place would put fair to ruin us....

I believe all their friars were knocked on the head promiscuously but two; the one of which was Father Peter Taaffe (brother to the Lord [Theobold] Taaffe [earl of Carlingford, d. 1677]), whom the soldiers took the next day and made an end of; the other was taken in the round tower, under the repute of lieutenant, and when he understood that the officers in that tower had no quarter, he confessed he was a friar; but that did not save him....

I do not think we lost one hundred men upon the place, though many be wounded.

Constitutional Experiments, Regicide, and Reconfiguration

7.9   *The Heads of the Proposals agreed upon by Sir Thomas Fairfax and the Council of the Army (August 1, 1647)*[11]

The king lost the first English Civil War, but there was a good chance he could win the peace. First the Scots and the English disputed the settlement, and then the English themselves divided between moderate Parliamentary Presbyterians and more radical Parliamentary Independents and their allies in the army. After the war, the Rump sought to curry favor with the landowning

---

[11]   *A Declaration from his Excellency Sr. Thomas Fairfax, And his Councell of Warre* (London, "Aug. 5," 1647), 6–8, 9–10 (mispaginated, B2–2verso). Dates in quotes are when purchased by the original owner (e.g., George Thomason)

classes by disbanding the army in order to lower taxes or by sending them to subdue the Irish Rebellion (as they would do in 1649: see document 7.8). The army responded by airing their grievances in a series of addresses, electing political "agitators" from each regiment, and offering their own proposals for a new constitution. In August 1647, the army leadership proposed the following blueprint for a settlement, drawn up principally by Cromwell's son-in-law Henry Ireton (1611–51). If it represents army officer opinion, what issues in the settlement were most important to them? What is their attitude to the Rump Parliament? What is their principle of representation? Which issues discussed have come up before and which are new? What is their attitude toward the king's role?

I. That the things hereafter proposed, being provided for by this Parliament, a certain period may by act of parliament be set for the ending of this Parliament (such period to be put within a year at most). And in the same Act provision to be made ... as followeth:

1. That Parliaments may biennially be called and meet at a certain day, with such provision for the certainty thereof, as in the late Act was made for triennial Parliaments [1641]. ...
2. Each biennial Parliament to sit 120 days certain (unless adjourned or dissolved sooner by their own consent), afterwards to be adjournable or dissolvable by the king, and no Parliament to sit past 240 days from their first meeting. ...
3. The king, upon advice of the Council of State, in the intervals between biennial Parliaments, to call a Parliament extraordinary, provided it meet above 70 days before the next biennial day, and be dissolved at least 60 days before the same; so as the course of biennial elections may never be interrupted. ...
5. That the elections of the Commons for succeeding Parliaments may be distributed to all counties, or other parts or divisions of the kingdom, according to some rule of equality or proportion, so as all counties may have a number of Parliament members allowed to their choice, proportionable to the respective rates they bear in the common charges and burdens of the kingdom, according to some other rule of equality or proportion, to render the House of Commons (as near as may be) an equal representative of the whole; and in order thereunto, that a present consideration be had to take off the elections of burgesses for poor, decayed, or inconsiderable towns, and to give some present addition to the number of Parliament members for great counties that have now less than their due proportion, to bring all (at present), as near as may be, to such a rule of proportion as aforesaid.

6. That effectual provision be made for future freedom of elections, and certainty of due returns. ...

XI. An Act to be passed to take away all coercive power, authority, and jurisdiction of bishops and all other ecclesiastical officers whatsoever. ...

XII. That there be a repeal of all Acts or clauses in any Act enjoining the use of the Book of Common Prayer, and imposing any penalties for neglect thereof; as also of all Acts or clauses of any Act, imposing any penalty for not coming to church, or for meetings elsewhere for ... religious duties ..., and some other provision to be made for discovering of Papists and popish recusants, and for disabling of them. ...

XIII. That the taking of the Covenant [an English version of the Scottish one, adopted largely in order to win Scottish armed support for the Parliamentary side] be not enforced upon any, nor any penalties imposed on the refusers. ...

XVI. That there may be a general Act of Oblivion to extend unto all (except the persons ... in exception as before), to absolve from all trespasses, misdemeanors, etc. done in prosecution of the war.

7.10   An Agreement of the People *(ca. late October 1647)*[12]

┌ challenged pol.
  soverieqnty

Two months later, the army agitators and the political Levellers, claiming to represent the rank-and-file, drafted their own plan, the *Agreement of the People*. (Although its authorship is unknown, the civilian Levellers Maximilian Petty, 1617–1661?, and John Wildman, 1622/3–93, defended it at Putney, see document 7.11.) While the *Agreement* never had the backing of more than a minority of the army, it had support among the cavalry and from a portion of London's citizens. Compare and contrast the settlement envisioned in the Heads and that in the *Agreement* (especially compare "Head" 5 with article I of the *Agreement*). To what extent did the latter move into new territory? According to the *Agreement*, who is sovereign in England?

Having by our late labors and hazards made it appear to the world at how high a rate we value our just freedoms, and God having so far owned our cause, as to deliver the enemies thereof into our hands: We do now hold ourselves bound in mutual duty to each other, to take the best care we can for the future, to avoid both the danger of returning into a slavish condition, and the chargeable remedy of another war. For as it cannot be imagined that so many of our country-men would have opposed us in this quarrel, if they had understood their own good;

---

[12] *Proposalls from Nine Regiaments of Horse, and Seven Regiaments of Foot, for a Modell of an Agreement of the People for A firme and present Peace, upon grounds of common-right and freedom* (London, Nov. 4, 1647), 2–6.

so may we safely promise to ourselves, that when our common rights and liberties shall be cleared, their endeavors will be disappointed, that seek to make themselves our masters: since therefore our former oppressions, and scarce yet ended troubles have been occasioned, either by want of frequent national meetings in council, or by rendering those meetings ineffectual. We are fully agreed and resolved, to provide that hereafter our representatives be neither left to an uncertainty for the time, nor made useless to the ends for which they are intended. In order whereunto we declare:

I. That the people of England being at this day very unequally distributed by counties, cities, and boroughs, for the election of their deputies in Parliament, ought to be more indifferently proportioned, according to the number of the inhabitants: the circumstances whereof, for number, place, and manner, are to be set down before the end of this present Parliament.
II. That to prevent the many inconveniences apparently arising from the long continuance of the same persons in authority, this present Parliament be dissolved upon the last day of September ... 1648.
III. That the people do of course choose themselves a Parliament once in two years....
IV. That the power of this, and all future representatives of this nation, is inferior only to theirs who choose them, and doth extend ... to the enacting, altering, and repealing of laws; to the erecting and abolishing of offices and courts; to the appointing, removing, and calling to account magistrates, and officers of all degrees; to the making war and peace, to the treating with foreign states: and generally, to whatsoever is not expressly, or impliedly reserved by the represented to themselves.

Which are as followeth,

1. That matters of religion, and the ways of God's worship, are not at all intrusted by us to any humane power, because therein we cannot go remit or exceed a tittle of what our consciences dictate to be the mind of God, without wilful sin: nevertheless the public way of instructing the nation (so it be not compulsive) is referred to their discretion.
2. That the matter of impressing and constraining any of us to serve in the wars, is against our freedom; and therefore we do not allow it in our representatives....
3. That after the dissolution of this present Parliament, no person be at any time questioned for anything said or done, in reference to the late public differences....
4. That in all laws made, or to be made, every person may be bound alike, and that no tenure, estate, charter, degree, birth, or place, do confer any exemption....
5. That as the laws ought to be equal, so they must be good, and not evidently destructive to the safety and well-being of the people.

These things we declare to be our native rights, and therefore are agreed and resolved to maintain them with our utmost possibilities, against all opposition whatsoever, being compelled thereunto … by our own woeful experience, who having long expected, and dearly earned the establishment of these certain rules of government are yet made to depend for the settlement of our peace and freedom, upon him that intended our bondage, and brought a cruel war upon us.

7.11   The Putney Debates of the General Council of the Army (October 29, 1647)[13]

The *Agreement*, particularly the first article on the franchise, became the basis of the first day's discussion when the army met for three days in October 1647 at Putney Church (ominously close to Westminster) for what became known as the Putney Debates. (William Clarke, 1623/4–66, secretary to the Army Council, recorded the Debates in shorthand.) The second day's debate focused both on the franchise and the redistribution of seats in the Commons. There were essentially two types of seats: those for the counties and those for boroughs (town corporations). Traditionally, all freeholders with land worth 40 shillings (£2) per annum could vote for the county representatives (also known as knights of the shire). This was a small amount of land, but requiring it effectively excluded the landless and farmers who only rented land. The borough franchise varied: in some towns it was fairly open, including all freemen or all who did not receive alms. Other towns restricted the vote more severely, sometimes just to the town council (often only 32 voters). And new towns and cities, such as Manchester, did not return any members to Parliament, because they had no medieval charter. One protagonist in the debate on this issue was Ireton, a Nottinghamshire country gentleman, general, MP, and Cromwell's son-in-law. Opposing him was Col. Thomas Rainsborough (d. 1648), also an MP. Rainsborough, an obscure figure before Putney, appears to have been much influenced by Leveller ideas. Over what issue do Ireton and Rainsborough disagree? Where would they stand on older disputes over divine right and the ancient constitution? How does each define "interest" and "property"? If traditional arguments about political authority had been based on the law of God (the Bible) and law of man (the civil constitution), upon what *new* basis does Rainsborough make his claim? That is, how does he justify change? Cromwell took the moderator's chair when General Fairfax refused to participate. Why might Fairfax refuse? From this excerpt, where do you think Cromwell stood on the issues?

---

[13]   C. H. Firth, ed., *The Clarke Papers* (London, Camden Society, 1891), 1: 299–310; compared with A. S. P. Woodhouse, *Puritanism and Liberty* (London, 1938, 1992), 52–60; and G. E. Aylmer, ed., *The Levellers in the English Revolution* (Ithaca, N. Y., 1975), 99–119, from Worcester College, Oxford, Clarke MSS., vol. 67.

The paper called the *Agreement* read. Afterwards the first article read by itself....

Mr. Maximilian Petty [a civilian Leveller]: We judge that all inhabitants that have not lost their birthright should have an equal voice in elections.

Rainborough: I desired that those that had engaged in it [might be included]. For really I think that the poorest he that is in England hath a life to live as the greatest he; and therefore truly, sir, I think it's clear, that every man that is to live under a government ought first by his own consent to put himself under that government. And I do think that the poorest man in England is not at all bound in a strict sense to that government that he hath not had a voice to put himself under. And I am confident that, when I have heard the reasons against it, something will be said to answer those reasons, insomuch that I should doubt whether he was an Englishman or no, that should doubt of these things.

Ireton: That's [the meaning of] this ["according to the number of inhabitants"].

Give me leave to tell you, that if you make this the rule I think you must fly for refuge to an absolute natural right, and you must deny all civil right; and I am sure it will come to that in the consequence.... For my part, I think it is no right at all. I think that no person hath a right to an interest or share in the disposing of the affairs of the kingdom, and in determining or choosing those that shall determine what laws we shall be ruled by here, no person hath a right to this, that hath not a permanent fixed interest in this kingdom, and those persons together are properly the represented of this kingdom, and consequently are also to make up the representers of this kingdom, who taken together do comprehend whatsoever is of real or permanent interest in the kingdom. And I am sure otherwise I cannot tell what any man can say why a foreigner coming in amongst us – or as many as will coming in amongst us, or by force or otherwise settling themselves here, or at least by our permission having a being here – why they should not as well lay claim to it as any other. We talk of birthright. Truly by birthright there is thus much claim. Men may justly have by birthright, by their very being born in England, that we should not seclude them out of England, that we should not refuse to give them air and place and ground, and the freedom of the highways and other things, to live amongst us – not any man that is born here, though by his birth there come nothing at all (that is part of the permanent interest of this kingdom) to him. That I think is due to a man by birth. But that by a man's being born here he shall have a share in that power that shall dispose of the lands here, and of all things here, I do not think it a sufficient ground.... That those that choose the representers for the making of laws by which this state and kingdom are to be governed, are the persons who, taken together, do comprehend the local interest of this kingdom; that is, the persons in whom all land lies, and those in corporations in whom all trading lies. This is the most fundamental constitution of this kingdom and that which if you do not allow, you allow none at all.... It is true, as was said by a gentleman near me, the meanest man in England ought to have a voice in the election of the government he lives under – but only if he has some local interest. I say this: that those that have the meanest local interest – that man that hath but forty shillings a year, he hath as great voice in the election of a knight for the shire as he that hath ten thousand a year, or more if he had never so much; and therefore there is that regard had to it. But this local interest, still the constitution of this government hath had an eye to (and what other government hath not an eye to this?).... And if we shall go to take away this, we shall plainly go to take away all property and interest that any man hath either in land by inheritance, or in estate by possession, or anything else – I say, if you take away this fundamental part of the civil constitution.

Rainsborough: Truly, sir, I am of the same opinion I was, and am resolved to keep it till I know reason why I should not. I confess my memory is bad, and therefore I am fain to make use of my pen. I remember that, in a former speech which this gentleman brought before this meeting, he was saying that in some cases he should not value whether there were a king or no king, whether lords or no lords, whether a property or no property. For my part I differ in that. I do very much care whether there be a king or no king, lords or no lords, property or no property; and I think, if we do not all take care, we shall all have none of these very shortly. But as to this present business. I do hear nothing at all that can convince me, why any man that is born in England ought not to have his voice in election of burgesses.... I do think that the main cause why almighty God gave men reason, it was that they should make use of that reason, and that they should improve it for that end and purpose that God gave it them. And truly, I think that half a loaf is better than none if a man be an-hungry. [This gift of reason without other property may seem a small thing], yet I think there is nothing that God hath given a man that any one else can take from him. And therefore I say, that either it must be the law of God or the law of man that must prohibit the meanest man in the kingdom to have this benefit as well as the greatest. I do not find anything in the law of God, that a lord shall choose twenty burgesses, and a gentleman but two, or a poor man shall choose none. I find no such thing in the law of nature, nor in the law of nations....

And truly I have thought something else: in what a miserable distressed condition would many a man that hath fought for the Parliament in this quarrel, be! I will be bound to say that many a man whose zeal and affection to God and this kingdom hath carried him forth in this cause, hath so spent his estate that, in the way the state and the army are going, he shall not hold up his head, if when his estate is lost, and not worth forty shillings a year, a man shall not have any interest ..., so that a man cannot lose that which he hath for the maintenance of his family but he must also lose that which God and nature hath given him! ...

Ireton: ... I think I agreed to this matter, that all should be equally distributed. But the question is, whether it should be distributed to all persons, or whether the same persons that are the electors now should be the electors still, and it be equally distributed amongst them. I do not see anybody else that makes this objection; and if nobody else be sensible of it I shall soon have done....

All the main thing that I speak for is because I would have an eye to property. I hope we do not come to contend for victory – but let every man consider with himself that he do not go that way to take away all property. For here is the case of the most fundamental part of the constitution of the kingdom, which if you take away, you take away all by that.... Why now I say then, if you, against the most fundamental part of the civil constitution ..., will plead the law of Nature, that a man should ... have a power of choosing those men that shall determine what shall be law in this state, though he himself have no permanent interest in the state, but whatever interest he hath he may carry about with him – if this be allowed, because by the right of nature we are free, we are equal, one man must have as much voice as another, then show me what step or difference there is, why I may not by the same right take your property....

Rainsborough: I shall now be a little more free and open with you than I was before.... For my part, as I think, you forgot something that was in my speech, and you do not only yourselves believe that some men are inclining to anarchy, but you would make all men believe that. And, sir, to say because a man pleads that every man hath a voice by right of nature, that therefore it destroys by the same argument all property – this is to forget the law of God. That there's a property, the law of God says it; else why hath God made that law, "Thou shalt not steal?" I am a poor man, therefore I must be oppressed: if I have no interest in the kingdom, I must suffer by all their laws be they right or wrong. Nay thus: a gentleman lives in a country and hath three or four lordships, as some men have (God knows how they got them); and when a Parliament is called he must be a Parliament-man [MP]; and it may be he sees some poor men, they live near this man, he can crush them.... Therefore I think that to that it is fully answered: God hath set down that thing as to propriety with this law of his, "Thou shalt not steal." And for my part I am against any such thought, and, as for yourselves, I wish you would not make the world believe that we are for anarchy.

Cromwell: I know nothing but this, that they that are the most yielding have the greatest wisdom; but really, sir, this is not right as it should be. No man says that you have a mind to anarchy, but that the consequence of this rule tends to anarchy, must end in anarchy; for where is there any bound or limit set if you take away this limit, that men that have no interest but the interest of breathing shall have no voice in elections? Therefore I am confident on it, we should not be so hot one with another.

Rainsborough: I know that some particular men we debate with believe we are for anarchy.

Ireton: I profess I must clear myself as to that point. I would not desire, I cannot allow myself, to lay the least scandal upon anybody. And truly, for that gentleman that did take so much offence, I do not know why he should take it so. We speak to the paper – not to persons – and to the matter of the paper. And I hope that no man is so much engaged to the matter of the paper – I hope that our persons, and our hearts and judgments, are not so pinned to papers but that we are ready to hear what good or ill consequence will flow from it.

7.12 King Charles's Refusal to Plead at His Trial (January 20, 1649)[14]

[margin handwritten note: Impeached as tyrant?]

Having been forced to defeat King Charles again in the Second Civil War, it was clear to the army leaders by December 1648 that the time for negotiation was over: the only hope for a peaceful settlement in England was to eliminate him. On the morning of the 6th, Col. Thomas Pride (d. 1658) and his men occupied the entrances to Parliament and allowed in only those MPs who had rejected further negotiations with the king. The resulting Rump Parliament set up a High Court of Justice, and, on January 20, the trial of the king began with Lord President Bradshaw's address to the prisoner. This was followed by the reading of a lengthy charge recounting much of the history of the Civil Wars from a parliamentary perspective. It concluded: "that the said Charles Stuart hath been, and is the occasioner, author, and continuer of the said unnatural, cruel and bloody wars; and therein [is] guilty of all the treasons, murders, rapines, burnings, spoils, desolations, damages and mischiefs to this nation, acted and committed in the said wars, or occasioned thereby."

Why did the king refuse to plead to these charges? Why does he distinguish between "authority" and "lawful authority"? How could he claim to "stand more for the liberty of my people than any here that come to be my pretended judges"? How does Bradshaw (1602–54), previously a provincial judge, justify the court's legitimacy? The verdict a foregone conclusion, King Charles was executed on January 30, 1649. On March 17, the Commons abolished "the kingly office in England and Ireland."

Lord president [John Bradshaw]: Sir, you have now heard your charge read, containing such matter as appears in it. You find that in the close of it, it is prayed to the court in the behalf of the Commons of England that you answer to your charge. The court expects your answer.

The king: I would know by what power I am called hither. I was not long ago in the Isle of Wight. How I came there is a longer story than I think is fit at this time for me to speak of. But there I entered into a treaty [at Newport] with both Houses of Parliament with as much public faith as it's possible to be had of any people in the world. I treated there with a number of honorable lords and gentlemen, and treated honestly and uprightly; I cannot say but they did very nobly with me. We were upon a conclusion of the treaty. Now, I would know by what authority – I mean lawful – there are many unlawful authorities in the

---

[14]   D. Iagomarsino and C. T. Wood, ed., *The Trial of Charles I: A Documentary History* (Hanover, N. H., 1989), 64–5; Rushworth, *Historical Collections* (London, 1721), 7: 1396–8 (for the charge).

world – thieves and robbers by the highways – but I would know by what authority I was brought from thence and carried from place to place, and I know not what. And when I know what lawful authority, I shall answer. Remember, I am your king – your lawful king – and what sins you bring upon your heads and the judgment of God upon this land, think well upon it – I say think well upon it – before you go further from one sin to a greater. Therefore let me know by what lawful authority I am seated here and I shall not be unwilling to answer. In the meantime, I shall not betray my trust. I have a trust committed to me by God, by old and lawful descent [by hereditary right]. I will not betray it to answer to a new unlawful authority. Therefore, resolve me that, and you shall hear more of me.

Lord president: If you had been pleased to have observed what was hinted to you by the court at your first coming hither, you would have known by what authority. Which authority requires you – in the name of the people of England, of which you are elected king – to answer them.

The king: No, sir, I deny that.

Lord president: If you acknowledge not the authority of the court, they must proceed.

The king: I do tell them so – England was never an elective kingdom but an hereditary kingdom for near these thousand years. Therefore, let me know by what authority I am called hither. I do stand more for the liberty of my people than any here that come to be my pretended judges. And, therefore let me know by what lawful authority I am seated here, and I will answer it. Otherwise I will not answer it.

Lord president: Sir, how really you have managed your trust is known. Your way of answer is to interrogate the court, which beseems not you in this condition. You have been told of it twice or thrice.

The king: … I do not come here as submitting to the court. I will stand as much for the privilege of the House of Commons, rightly understood, as any man here whatsoever. I see no House of Lords here that may constitute a Parliament, and the king too should have been. Is this the bringing of the king to his Parliament? Is this the bringing an end to the treaty in the public faith of the world?

Radicals, Sectaries, and Revolving New Notions

7.13   *Thomas Edwards*, Grangraena *(1646)*[15]

The execution of the king and dissolution of the monarchy, combined with the earlier elimination of strict controls on religion and the press, opened up a

[15]   T. Edwards, *Gangraena: or a Catalogue and Discovery of Many of the Errours, Heresies, Blasphemies and Pernicious Practices of the Sectaries of this Time, Vented and Acted in England in These Four Last Years* (London, "Feb. 16," 1646, facsimile, Exeter, 1998), 1st part, 16–7, 74–5 [sig. m1verso]; 2nd part, 46; 3rd part, 242–3, 245, 246–7.

brave new world of political, social, and economic possibilities. Historians know of those possibilities because the Civil War also opened the floodgates of pamphleteering; between 1644 and 1653 the press was probably the freest it had ever been. John Milton (1608–74), in his pamphlet *Areopagitica* (1644), celebrated London as "a city of refuge, a mansion house of liberty," and its printers during the 1640s as so many artisans "sitting by their studious lamps, musing, searching, revolving new notions and ideas wherewith to present ... the approaching Reformation."[16] Not everyone appreciated the cacophony of the press, with its competing news and ballad sellers promoting ideas which would lead to a bewildering array of new political groups and religious sects. The Presbyterian Thomas Edwards (ca. 1599–1648), in his popular *Gangraena* (published in three parts), portrayed these radical Protestant religious sects as illnesses of the body politic, spread by print and the parliamentary army. What do the selections in this section tell us about the role of print culture in the mid-1640s? What do they tell us about the role of Scripture? Compare Edwards's views with the varieties of sects categorized in *The Discription* [sic] *of the Severall Sorts of Anabaptists* (1645, Plate 10). Given that our knowledge of these sects comes from the attacks of more conservative Puritans, can we be certain that they were really so radical; or that they even existed?

The army that is so much spoken of upon all occasions in the news books, pulpits, conferences, to be Independent [favoring autonomous congregations] ..., yet of that army, called by the sectaries, Independent ..., I do not think there are 50 pure independents, but [rather it is] ... made up and compounded of Anabaptism, Antinomianism, Enthusiasm, Arminianism, Familism; all these errors and more too sometimes meeting in the same persons, strange monsters, having their heads of Enthusiasm, their bodies of Antinomianism, their thighs of Familism, their legs and feet of Anabaptism, their hands of Arminianism, and Libertinism as the great vein going through the whole; in one word, the great religion of that sort of men in the army, is liberty of conscience, and liberty of preaching....

They upbraid in printed books and speeches many Presbyterians, particularly of the [Westminster] Assembly [which met from 1643, and produced the Presbyterian Confession of Faith], with their former conformity [i.e., many Presbyterians had formerly been Anglican clergy], yea they brand and asperse them, that they have been great time-servers ..., and this they do to make the people believe that what they do now is not out of conscience, but to serve the times, and that such men are not likely to have the truth revealed to them, nor fit to have a hand in the Reformation....

---

[16] *Complete Prose Works of John Milton* (New Haven, 1959), 2: 553–4.

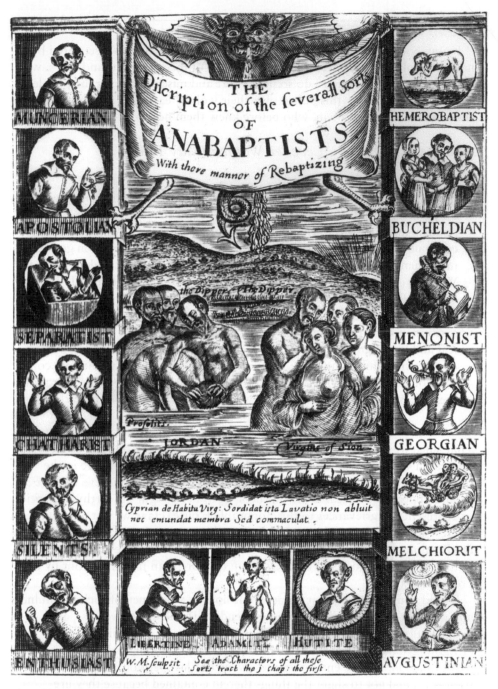

Plate 10 "The Discription of the severall Sorts of Anabaptists with there [*sic*] manner of Rebaptizing." (Source: Daniel Featley, *Katabaptistai kataptüstoi: The dippers dipt, or, The anabaptists duck'd and plung'd over head and eares, at a disputation in Southwark,* 1645, Bridgeman Art Library.)

"Anabaptists" was the contemporary name given to various groups ranging from what are modern-day Mennonites to Calvinist Baptists whose one common trait was a belief in adult baptism. What is wrong with adult baptism according to the central image of this woodcut (the sun appears to be setting)? What appear to be the beliefs of the "Separatist"; the "Silents"; the "Hemerobaptist"; the "Adamite"? Is this a positive or negative image of these groups? Did all these groups exist?

By my books, especially *Gangraena*, many sectaries being so discovered by name and places of abode, laid open in several of their opinions and ways, will not be able for the future to do so much hurt and mischief among the people; their sheepskins are by this pulled over their wolves' ears, and many will now shun, and be afraid of them, who before knew them not.

7.14   Leveller Women (May 1649)[17]

For all those who feared new ideas, there remained a vocal minority pushing for political, social, and religious change. We have already seen basic Leveller political ideas in the *Agreement of the People* (document 7.10). The Levellers continued to advocate reformed elections and a written constitution granting individual civil rights in print. When, in March 1649, Leveller leaders William Walwyn (1600–81), John Lilburne (1615?–57), Thomas Prince (fl. 1630–57), and Richard Overton (fl. 1640–63) were thrown in prison after publication of Lilburne's *Second Part of Englands New Chains Discovered* (1649), a group of Leveller women in London petitioned for their relief. What political and legal rights do the protesting women claim for the prisoners? What do they claim for themselves? How do they play with more traditional concepts of gender order and hierarchy? What do you suppose was the source of their ideas? How radical were the Levellers between 1647 and 1649?

That since we are assured of our creation in the image of God, and of an interest in Christ, equal unto men, as also of a proportionable share in the freedoms of this Commonwealth, we cannot but wonder and grieve that we should appear so despicable in your eyes, as to be thought unworthy to petition or represent our grievances to this honorable House. Have we not an equal interest with the men of this nation in those liberties and securities contained in the Petition of Right and other the good laws of the land? Are any of our lives, limbs, liberties, or goods to be taken from us more than from men, but by due process of law? ...

Would you have us keep at home in our houses, when men of such faithfulness and integrity as the four prisoners our friends in the Tower [Levellers], are fetched out of their beds, and forced out of their houses by soldiers to the affrighting and undoing of themselves, their wives, children, and families? ...

And therefore ... we entreat you to review our last petition in behalf of our friends ..., and not to slight the things therein contained because they are presented unto you by the weak hand of women, it being a usual thing with God, by weak means to work mighty effects.

[17] *To the Supreme Authority of England The Commons Assembled in Parliament. The humble Petition of diverse wel-affected Weomen [sic].... Affecters and Approvers of the Petition of Sept. 11. 1648* (n.p., n.d., "May 5," 1649), broadside.

7.15   Gerrard Winstanley, "To His Excellency Oliver Cromwell, General of the Commonwealth's Army" (1652)[18]

One of the groups from which the Levellers sought to distance themselves was the Diggers, or self-styled "True Levellers," who advocated a primitive communism. In mid-April 1649, the government received report that at St. George's Hill, Surrey, in the Thames Valley not far from London, this group "began to dig on that side the hill … and sowed the ground with parsnips and carrots and beans." While the Diggers there numbered several dozen, "they give out they will be four or five thousand within ten days."[19] The Diggers' leader, Gerrard Winstanley (1609?–76?), was arrested at Kingston at least twice in the summer of 1649. Just what was so alarming about a dozen people digging on a hillside? In *The True Levellers' Standard Advanced* (ca. April 1649) Winstanley outlined the Digger rationale: "the great Creator, Reason, made the Earth to be a common treasury.… But not one word was spoken in the beginning, that one branch of mankind should rule over another."[20] He also accompanied his masterpiece, *The Law of Freedom in a Platform*, with a long prefatory letter – or, rather, lecture – to Oliver Cromwell, already one of the most powerful MPs and army generals and, within a year, to rule as lord protector. Upon what basis does Winstanley argue for socio-economic change? Are his grievances old or new? Is this revolutionary?

God hath made you a successful instrument to cast out that conqueror, and to recover our land and liberties again, by your victories, out of that Norman hand.

That which is yet wanting on your part to be done, is this, to see the oppressor's power to be cast out with his person; and to see that the free possession of the land and liberties be put into the hands of the oppressed commoners of England. …

Now you know sir, that the kingly conqueror was not beaten by you only as you are a single man, nor by the officers of the army joined to you; but by the hand and assistance of the commoners, whereof some came in person, and adventured their lives with you; others stayed at home, and planted the earth, and paid taxes and free-quarter to maintain you that went to war.

So that whatsoever is recovered from the conqueror is recovered by a joint consent of the commoners. Therefore it is all equity, that all the commoners who assisted you should be set free from the conquerors power with you. …

---

[18]   G. Winstanley, *The Law of Freedom in a Platform, or, True Magistracy Restored*, in *Gerrard Winstanley: Selections from His Works*, ed. L. Hamilton (London, 1944), 109, 112–4.

[19]   *The Clarke Papers* (London, Camden Society, n.s. 54, 1894), 2: 210–1.

[20]   *The Works of Gerrard Winstanley*, ed. G. H. Sabine (New York, 1965), 76–95.

I have asked diverse soldiers what they fought for; they answered, they could not tell; and it is very true, they cannot tell indeed, if the monarchial law be established without reformation. ...

If we look into parishes, the burdens there are many.

First, for the power of lords of manors remains still over their brethren, requiring fines and heriots [customary payment upon death of tenant]; beating them off the free use of the common land, unless their brethren will pay them rent; exacting obedience, as much as they did, and more, when the king was in power. ...

Secondly, in parishes where commons lie, the rich Norman freeholders, or the new (more covetous) gentry, over-stock the commons with sheep and cattle; so that inferior tenants and poor laborers can hardly keep a cow, but half starve her; so that the poor are kept poor still, and the common freedom of the earth is kept from them. ...

Thirdly, in many parishes two or three of the great ones bears all the sway, in making assessments, over-awing constables and other officers. ...

Fourthly ..., country people cannot sell any corn or other fruits of the earth in a market town, but they must either pay toll, or be turned out of town. ...

Now saith the whisperings of the people, the inferior tenants and laborers bears all the burdens, in laboring the earth, in paying taxes and free-quarter beyond their strength, and in furnishing the armies with soldiers, who bear the greatest burden of the war; and yet the gentry, who oppress them, and that live idle upon their labors, carry away all the comfortable livelihood of the earth.

For is not this a common speech among the people, we have parted with our estates, we have lost our friends in the wars, which we willingly gave up, because freedom was promised us; and now in the end we have new task-masters, and our old burdens increased? And though all sorts of people have taken an Engagement to cast out kingly power, yet kingly power remains in power still in the hands of those who have no more right to the earth than ourselves.

7.16 Abiezer Coppe, A Fiery Flying Roll: a Word from the Lord to All the Great Ones of the Earth *(January 1650)*[21]

Just as Presbyterians like Edwards warned of new sectarian groups, and just as Levellers attempted to distance themselves from Diggers, so too did *all* groups attempt to distance themselves from Ranters, or "the ranting crew."[22] Who were "the ranting crew"? Unfortunately, most of our evidence for the Ranters comes from anti-Ranter pamphlets. But several writers of the period did develop an extensive theology that could be called Ranter, arguing that, since Gods' goodness dwelt in all things, sin was impossible to those who

[21] A. Coppe, *Fiery Flying Rolle*, 1–2, 5; *A Second Fiery Flying Rolle*, 8–9 (both, London, "January 4," 1649 [i.e. 1650], facsimile, Exeter, 1973).
[22] *Works of Gerrard Winstanley*, 392.

embraced him or it. Abiezer Coppe (1619–72?), a former Oxford undergraduate, wrote a tract which so upset the Rump Parliament that they not only condemned it to be burnt by the common hangman but also passed the Blasphemy Act of August 1650 to outlaw similar tracts and the behavior they inspired. As you read this and the following selection, ask yourself why the authorities found these writings so threatening. Coppe contrasts his own "blood-life-spirit levelling" with "sword levelling" and "digging levelling": how does his argument relate to those of the Levellers and the Diggers described above? How does he apply this to the recent history of England?

Thus saith the Lord, *I inform you, that I overturn, overturn, overturn.* And as the bishops, Charles, and the lords, have had their turn, overturn, so your turn shall be next (ye surviving great ones) by what name or title soever dignified or distinguished) who ever you are, that oppose me, the eternal God, who am universal love, and whose service is perfect freedom, and pure libertinism.

But afore I proceed any further, be it known to you, that although that excellent Majesty, which dwells in the writer of this roll, hath reconciled all things to himself, yet this hand (which now writes) never drew sword, or shed one drop of any man's blood. (I am free from the blood of all men) though (I say) all things are reconciled to me, the eternal God (in Him) yet sword levelling, or digging-levelling, are neither of them his principle. . . .

Though you can as little endure the word Levelling, as could the late slain or dead Charles (your forerunner, who is gone before you) and had as live [rather] hear the Devil named, as hear of the Levellers (Men-Levellers) which is, and who (indeed) are but shadows of most terrible, yet great and glorious good things to come. . . .

Not by sword; we (holy) scorn to fight for anything; we had as live be dead drunk every day of the week, and lie with the whores i'the market place, and account these as good actions as taking the poor abused, enslaved ploughman's money from him.

7.17   *Laurence Clarkson,* The Lost Sheep Found *(1660)*[23]

Laurence Clarkson (1615–67), like many of the radicals during the Civil Wars and Interregnum, drifted from Presbyterianism to Independency, to Baptism, and beyond. His autobiography suggests that his questioning of Scripture changed his life, causing him about 1650 to follow the implications of Ranter theology to their logical – and physical – conclusions. What is a Ranter, according to Clarkson's description? How does he justify it? What was the relation between that Ranterism and Puritanism? Who might Coppe's and Clarkson's ideas most upset? Are they revolutionaries?

[23]   Laur. Claxton [pseud.], *The Lost Sheep Found* (London, 1660), 25–6.

Now observe at this time my judgment was this, that there was no man could be freed from sin, till he had acted that so-called sin as no sin; this a certain time had been burning within me, yet durst not reveal it to any.... I pleaded the words of Paul, That I know and am persuaded by the Lord Jesus, that there was nothing unclean, but as man esteemed it [Romans 14, 14], unfolding that was intended all acts, as well as meats and drinks, and therefore till you can lie with all women as one woman, and not judge it sin, you can do nothing but sin: now in Scripture I found a perfection spoken of; so that I understood no man could attain perfection but this way, at which Mr. Rawlinson was much taken, and Sarah Kullin, being then present, did invite me to make trial of what I had expressed, so as I take it, after we parted she invited me to Mr. Wats in Rood Lane, where was one or two more like herself; and as I take it, lay with me that night.... Now [Abiezer] Coppe was by himself with a company ranting and swearing, which I was seldom addicted to, only proving by Scripture the truth of what I acted; and indeed Solomon's writings was the original of my filthy lust.... Now I being as they said, "Captain of the Rant," I had most of the princip[al] women come to my lodging for knowledge, which then was called The Head-quarters.

7.18–7.19   Quakers

A religious group with greater staying power arose in the 1650s called the Quakers. Today we view Quakers as benign: pacifists of few words, reliable in negotiations, searching within for guidance from the Spirit. But in the 1650s that search took them out into the world and led them to criticize its Great Ones in a manner not unlike Coppe. Quakers also engaged in symbolic demonstrations intended to testify to their faith and the world's hypocrisy, but which, in fact, only brought notoriety and infamy. For example, Quaker women went "naked for a sign," usually wearing sackcloth with hair undone and uncovered rather than actual nakedness, in order to demonstrate humility and purity of spirit (document 7.18). James Nayler (1618–60), a prominent Quaker preacher and apostle reenacted Christ's entry into Jerusalem in Bristol in the autumn of 1656 (document 7.19). How did the authorities react to these displays? Why was Parliament so much more severe towards Naylor than the Bristol city officers towards the Quaker women? (Despite Lord President Lawrence's plea for toleration, most MPs felt that the last decade had been a referendum on the dangers of religious freedom and they resolved to have Nayler whipped, pilloried, his tongue bored through, branded with a B [for blasphemy], and committed to solitary confinement.) What justifications did Nayler give for his actions? How did the MPs interpret what he had done? What were they afraid of?

7.18   Quaker women going "naked" for a sign (May 3, 1655)[24]

On the 3d of the 3d month [May: Quakers did not believe in pagan names for days of the week nor for months], 1655, Sarah Goldsmith, being moved to put on a coat of sackcloth of hair next her, to uncover her head and put earth thereon, with her hair hanging down about her, and without any other clothes upon her, excepting shoes on her feet, and in that manner to go to every gate, and through every street within the walls of the city, and afterward to stand at the High-Cross in the view of the town and market, as a sign against the pride of Bristol, and to abide so in that habit seven days, in obedience thereto, though in great self-denial, and in a cross to her natural inclinations, she cheerfully prepared her garment, being long and reaching to the ground; and on the 5th of the 3rd month early in the morning, two friends accompanying her, passed through the streets to the several gates, some people following them, but doing no harm: then she returned home. And about the ninth hour came to the High-Cross, and one friend with her, a great multitude of people following; there she stood about half an hour, till the tumult, which consisted of many hundred, grew so violent, that some bystanders, in compassion, forced them into a shop, out of which the multitude called to have them thrown, that they might abuse them; but by the intervention of the chamberlain kept out of their hands, and carried to the tolzey [tolbooth, guildhall]. The mayor came thither, and asked her, why she appeared in the city in that habit? She answered, "in obedience to the light in my conscience." "What if you," said the mayor, "in your obedience had been killed by the rude multitude?" She replied, "I am in the hands of Him that ruleth all things. I have harmed none, yet have I been harmed; neither have I broken any law by which I can be brought under just censure; if I had appeared in gay clothing you would [not?] have been troubled." In conclusion, the mayor, at the instigation of Joseph Jackson one of the aldermen sent her to Bridewell [prison], and with her Anne Gunnicliffe and Margaret Wood, for owning and accompanying her.

7.19   Parliament on James Nayler (December 5–8, 1656)[25]

Dec. 5, 1656. Resolved, That Nayler's report be heard....

The articles against him read, and summed thus – That he assumed the gesture, words, names, and attributes of our Savior Christ.

Major-General [Philip] Skippon [d. 1660].... It has been always my opinion, that the growth of these things is more dangerous than the most intestine or foreign enemies. I have often been troubled in my thoughts to think of this

[24]   P. Crawford and L. Goring, *Women's Worlds in Seventeenth-Century England: A Sourcebook* (London, 2000), 256, from Friends House Library, London, The Great Book of Sufferings, 1: 548, and Abstract of the Sufferings, 1: 15.
[25]   J. T. Rutt, ed., *The Diary of Thomas Burton, Esquire* (London, 1828), 1: 24–6, 46–7, 63.

toleration; I think I may call it so. Their great growth and increase is too notorious, both in England and Ireland; their principles strike both at ministry and magistracy.

Many opinions are in this nation, (all contrary to the government), which would join in one to destroy you, if it should please God to deliver the sword into their hands. Should not we be as jealous of God's honor, as we are of our own? Do not the very heathens assert the honor of their Gods, and shall we suffer our Lord Jesus thus to be abused and trampled upon? ...

Major-General [William] Boteler [fl. 1645–70]. ... My ears did tingle, and my heart tremble, to hear the report. I am satisfied that there is too much of the report true. I have heard many of the blasphemies of this sort of people; but the like of this I never heard of. The punishment ought to be adequate to the offence. By the Mosaic law, blasphemers were to be stoned to death. The morality of this remains, and for my part, if this sentence should pass upon him, I could freely consent to it. ...

It is not intended to indulge such grown heresies and blasphemies as these, under the notion of a toleration of tender consciences. He that sets himself up in Christ's place, certainly commits the highest offence that can be. ...

Dec. 6, 1656. James Nayler being brought to the bar, refused to kneel or to put off his hat. The House agreed beforehand that they would not insist upon his kneeling, being informed that he would not do it, and that he might not say that was any part of his crime. They would not give him that advantage; but commanded the serjeant to take off his hat. ...

Question. King of Israel; assumed you thus?

Answer. As I have dominion over the enemies of Christ, I am King of Israel spiritually.

Q. Are you the judge of the world?

A. I cannot deny what I said at the Committee. But the Speaker, desirous to help him, here said, "Mind what you say; are you the judge, have you no fellow-judges." Then he answered "No;" saying again, "I hope you have so much justice and charity as not to wrest my words."

Q. Why did you ride into Bristol in that manner?

A. ... I knew that I should lay down my life for it.

Q. Whose will was it, if not yours?

A. It was the Lord's will, to give it into me to suffer such things to be done in me; and I durst not resist it, though I was sure to lay down my life for it.

Q. How were you sure?

A. It was so revealed to me of my father, and I am willing to obey his will in this thing. ...

Q. Are there any more signs than yours?

A. I know no other sign. There may be other signs in some parts of the nation; but I am set up as a sign to this nation, to bear witness of his coming. You have been a long time under dark forms, neglecting the power of godliness, as bishops. It was the desire, of my soul, all along, and the longing expectation of many godly men engaged with you, that this nation should be redeemed from such forms. God hath done it for you, and hath put his sword in the hands of those from whom it cannot be wrested. That sword cannot be broken, unless you break it yourselves, by disobeying the voice, the call, and rejecting the sign set up amongst you to convince them that Christ is come. ...

Dec. 8, 1656. Lord President [Henry Lawrence (1600–64)]. This gentleman has spoken very zealously, yet they were honest men, too, that called for fire from heaven, and we know how they were reproved. ...

I wonder why any man should be so amazed at this. Is not God in every horse, in every stone, in every creature. ...

If you hang every man that says, Christ is in you the hope of glory, you will hang a good many. You shall hear this in every man's mouth of that sect, and others too, that challenge a great interest in Christ.

I do not believe that James Nayler thinks himself to be the only Christ; but that Christ is in him in the highest measure. This, I confess, is sad. But if, from hence, you go about to adjudge it, or call it blasphemy, I am not satisfied in it. It is hard to define what is blasphemy.

HISTORIANS' DEBATES

A high road (long-term causes, revolt from below) or a low road (short-term events, high politics of the elite) to the Civil Wars?

C. Hill, *Puritanism and Revolution* (London, 1958), esp. essay on interpretations; *idem*, "A Bourgeois Revolution?," in *The Collected Essays of Christopher Hill* (Brighton, 1986, orig. pub. 1980), vol. 3; G. Eley and W. Hunt, eds., *Reviving the English Revolution: Reflections and Elaborations on the Work of Christopher Hill* (London, 1988), esp. essays by D. Underdown and B. Reay; C. Russell, *Unrevolutionary England, 1603–1642* (London, 1990), esp. essays on the British problem and the English Civil War and the Irish Rebellion; *idem*, "Why Did Charles I Fight the Civil War?," *HT* 34, 6 (1984); T. Cogswell, R. Cust, and P. Lake, "Revisionism and Its Legacies: the Work of Conrad Russell," in *Politics, Religion and Popularity in Early Stuart Britain*, ed. Cogswell, Cust, and Lake (Cambridge, 2002); J. S. A. Adamson, "The Baronial Context of the English Civil War," *TRHS* 5th ser., 40 (1990); A. Hughes, *The Causes of the English Civil War*, 2nd ed. (London, 1998), esp. new introduction and ch. 3; C. Holmes, *Why Was Charles I Executed?* (London, 2006), esp. the introduction; M. Kishlansky, "Charles I: A Case of Mistaken Identity," *P & P* 189 (2005); N. Keeble, ed., *The Cambridge Companion to Writing of the English Revolution* (Cambridge, 2001), esp. J. Morrill on the causes and course of the wars, and T. Corns on radical pamphlets; R. Hutton, *Debates in Stuart History* (Basingstoke, 2004), essays on the Civil War and on Cromwell; B. Coward, ed., *A Companion to Stuart Britain* (Oxford, 2003), articles by J. Peacey on causes of the outbreak, D. Scott on the wars, S. Kelsey on the revolution, A. Hughes on religion, and J. C. Davis on political thought; B. Manning, "The English Revolution: The Decline and Fall of Revisionism," *Socialist History* 14 (1999); "Rethinking the English Revolution" (a special section), *HWJ* 61, 1 (2006), articles by Q. Skinner, J. Walter, R. Weil, and A. Hughes.

Did regional identity, national identity, or ethnic difference shape the Civil Wars? Did neutralism and consensual county communities dominate provincial response to the wars or did national/ethnic divisions heighten conflict?

M. Stoyle, "English 'Nationalism,' Celtic Particularism, and the English Civil War" (review essay), *HJ* 43, 4 (2000); S. Barber, "'A Bastard Kind of Militia,' Localism, and Tactics in the Second Civil War," in *Soldiers, Writers and Statesmen of the English Revolution*, ed. I. Gentles, J. Morrill, and B. Worden (Cambridge, 1998); J. Adamson, "The English Context of the British Civil Wars," *HT* 48, 11 (1998); P. Lenihan, ed., *Conquest and Resistance: War in Seventeenth-century Ireland* (Leiden, 2001), esp. J. Young, "Invasions: Scotland and Ireland 1641–1691"; J. Morrill, *Revolt in the Provinces: The People of England and the Tragedies of War, 1630–1648* (London, 1976, 1999), esp. the new introduction and conclusion; A. Fletcher, "National and Local Awareness in County Communities," in *Before the English Civil War*, ed. H. Tomlinson (London, 1983); A. Hughes, "Local History and the Origins of the Civil War," in *Conflict in Early Stuart England: Studies in Religion and Politics, 1603–1642*, ed. A. Hughes and R. Cust (London, 1989); R. C. Richardson, ed., *Town and Countryside in the English Revolution* (Manchester, 1992), esp. B. Sharp, "Rural Discontents and the English Revolution"; R. Cust and A. Hughes, eds., *The English Civil War* (London, 1997), articles reprinted, esp. C. Holmes, "The County Community in Stuart Historiography," and A. Hughes, "The King, the Parliament and the Localities in the English Civil War."

How did the wars in the three British kingdoms influence each other?

J. Ohlmeyer, ed., *Ireland from Independence to Occupation* (Cambridge, 1995), esp. N. Canny, "What Really Happened in Ireland in 1641?," and S. Wheeler, "Four Armies in Ireland"; J. R. Young, ed., *Celtic Dimensions of the British Civil Wars* (Edinburgh, 1997), esp. introduction by J. Morrill; J. Morrill, ed., *The Impact of the English Civil War* (London, 1991), essays by C. Carlton on the fighting, I. Gentles on the army, and J. Walter on the social impact; J. G. A. Pocock, "The Atlantic Archipelago and the War of the Three Kingdoms," in *The British Problem, c. 1534–1707: State Formation in the Atlantic Archipelago*, ed. B. Bradshaw and J. Morrill (Basingstoke, 1996).

What was the role of popular politics in the wars?; can popular allegiance be measured?

D. Underdown, "The Problem of Popular Allegiance," *TRHS* 31 (1981); *idem, Revel Riot, and Rebellion: Popular Politics and Culture in England 1603–1660*

(Oxford, 1985), chs. 6–10; J. Morrill, *The Nature of the English Revolution* (London, 1993), chs. 8–11; D. Underdown, "The Chalk and the Cheese: Contrasts among the English Clubmen," in Cust and Hughes, *English Civil War*; P. Gladwish, "The Herefordshire Clubmen: a Reassessment," *Midland History* 10 (1985); A. Wood, *Riot, Rebellion and Popular Politics in Early Modern England* (Basingstoke, 2002), ch. 4, sections on origins, rural riot, clubmen, Levellers; *idem*, "Beyond Post-Revisionism?: the Civil War Allegiances of the Miners of the Derbyshire 'Peak Country'," *HJ* 40, 1 (1997); J. Adamson, "The Triumph of Oligarchy: the Management of War and the Committee of Both Kingdoms, 1644–1645," in *Parliament at Work: Parliamentary Committees, Political Power, and Public Access in Early Modern England*, ed. C. R. Kyle and J. Peacey (Woodbridge, 2002).

Was Cromwell a religious radical, a social conservative, a Machiavellian, or out of his depth?

D. L. Smith, *Cromwell and the Interregnum* (Oxford, 2003), esp. articles by Morrill and Baker, Worden, Woolrych, Davis; J. Morrill, ed., *Oliver Cromwell and the English Revolution* (London, 1990), esp. essays by the editor and J. C. Davis; I. Roots, ed., *Cromwell: A Profile* (New York, 1973), esp. H. R. Trevor-Roper, "Oliver Cromwell and His Parliaments"; B. Worden, "The English Reputations of Oliver Cromwell, 1660–1900," in *Historical Controversies and Historians*, ed. W. Lamont (London, 1998).

Who was a radical? How should radicals be defined? Did they matter?

C. Hill, *The World Turned Upside Down: Radical Ideas During the English Revolution* (London, 1975); P. Mack, *Visionary Women: Ecstatic Prophecy in Seventeenth-Century England* (Berkeley, 1992), esp. ch. 3 on 1640–55; P. Crawford, "The Challenges to Patriarchalism: How Did the Revolution Affect Women?," in *Revolution and Restoration: England in the 1650s*, ed. J. Morrill (London, 1992); A. M. McEntree, " 'The [Un]Civill-Sisterhood of Oranges and Lemons': Female Petitioners and Demonstrators, 1642–53," in *Pamphlet Wars: Prose in the English Revolution*, ed. J. Holstum (London, 1992); E. Hobby, "Prophecy, Enthusiasm and Female Pamphleteers," in Keeble, *Cambridge Companion*; B. Reay and I. McGregor, eds., *Radical Religion in the English Revolution* (Oxford, 1984), esp. Reay's introduction; B. Reay, "Popular Hostility Towards Quakers in Mid-Seventeenth-Century England," *SocH* 5, 3 (1980); C. Hill, L. Mulligan, J. K. Graham, and J. Richards, debate on "The Religion of Gerrard Winstanley," *P & P* 89 (1980); J. C. Davis, "Religion and the Struggle for Freedom in the English Revolution," *HJ* 35, 3 (1992); Davis and Hill, debate on the Ranters *P & P* 129 (1990) and 140 (1993); M. Kishlansky, in "Ideology and Politics in the Parliamentary Armies, 1645–9," in *Reactions to the English Civil War*, ed. J. Morrill (London, 1982); B. Manning, *The Far Left in the English Revolution 1640 to 1660* (London, 1999), ch. on the "Corporal's Revolt" of 1649; D. Wootton, "From Rebellion to Revolution: the Crisis of the Winter of

1642/3 and the Origins of Civil War Radicalism," in Cust and Hughes, *English Civil War*; G. Burgess and M. Festenstein, eds., *English Radicalism, 1550–1850* (New York. 2007), esp. G. Burgess on radicalism in the English Revolution, and C. Condren on the concept; M. Mendle, ed., *The Putney Debates of 1647: the Army, the Levellers and the English State* (Cambridge, 2001), esp. articles by the editor, A. Woolrych, and I. Gentles.

Was it a revolution?

Hill, "The Word 'Revolution,'" in *A Nation of Change and Novelty*, rev. ed. (London, 1993); J. Peacey, ed., *The Regicides and the Execution of Charles I* (Basingstoke, 2001), esp. D. Scott on motives for king-killing, A. Sharp on the Levellers and the regicide, and J. Morrill on the religious context; J. Morrill, "Christopher Hill's Revolution," in *The Nature of the English Revolution*; "What Was the English Revolution?," a debate by J. Morrill, B. Manning, and D. Underdown in *HT* 34, 3 (1984); A. Woolrych, "Shifting Perspectives on the Great Rebellion,' *HT* 52, 11 (2002); I. Rachum, "The Meaning of 'Revolution' in the English Revolution (1648–1660)," *Journal of the History of Ideas* 56, 2 (1995); S. Kelsey, "The Trial of Charles I," *EHR* 118 (2003).

A Cromwellian dictatorship?

A. Woolrych, "The Cromwellian Protectorate: A Military Dictatorship?," *History* 75 (1990); J. Peacey, "Cromwellian England: A Propaganda State?," *History* 91 (2006); D. Hirst, "Locating the 1650s in England's Seventeenth Century," *History* 81 (1996); *idem*, "The Failure of Godly Rule in the English Republic," *P & P* 132 (1991); C. Durston, "'Settling the Hearts and Quieting the Minds of All Good People': the Major-Generals and the Puritan Minorities of Interregnum England," *History* 85 (2000); J. R. Collins, "The Church Settlement of Oliver Cromwell," *History* 87 (2002); P. Little, ed., *The Cromwellian Protectorate* (Woodbridge, 2007), esp. D. L. Smith, "Oliver Cromwell and the Protectorate Parliaments"; D. L. Smith, "Politics and Military Rule in Cromwellian Britain" (review essay), *HJ* 48, 2 (2005); J. S. Morrill, "Postlude: Between War and Peace, 1651–1662," in *The Civil Wars: a Military History of England, Scotland, and Ireland 1638–1660*, ed. J. Kenyon and J. H. Ohlmeyer (Oxford, 1998); B. Worden, "Providence and Politics in Cromwellian England," *P & P* 109 (1985); E. Porter, "A Cloak for Knavery: Kingship, the Army, and the First Protectorate Parliament 1654–55," *Seventeenth Century* 17, 2 (2002).

ADDITIONAL SOURCE COLLECTIONS

C. Blitzer, ed., *The Commonwealth of England: Documents of the English Civil Wars, the Commonwealth and Protectorate* (New York, 1963).
B. Coward, *The Cromwellian Protectorate* (Harlow, 2002).

P. Crawford and L. Goring, *Women's Worlds in Seventeenth-Century England: A Sourcebook* (London, 2000).

S. R. Gardiner, ed., *The Constitutional Documents of the Puritan Revolution, 1625–1660*, 3rd ed. (Oxford, 1906).

C. Hill and E. Dell, eds., *The Good Old Cause: The English Revolution of 1640–1660*, 2nd ed. (London, 1949, 1969).

A. Hughes, ed., *Seventeenth-Century England: A Changing Culture*, 1, *Primary Sources* (Totowa, New Jersey, 1980).

M. L. Kekewich, ed., *Princes and Peoples: France and the British Isles, 1620–1714* (Manchester, 1994).

W. M. Lamont and S. O. Oldfield, eds., *Politics, Religion, and Literature in the Seventeenth Century* (London, 1975).

K. Lindley, *The English Civil War and Revolution: A Sourcebook* (London, 1998).

A. Stroud, *Stuart England* (London, 1999).

D. Wootton, *Divine Right and Democracy: An Anthology of Political Writing in Stuart England* (Harmondsworth, 1986).

CHAPTER EIGHT

Religion, Restoration, and Revolution

In 1656, Edward Harley (1624–1700), a Presbyterian and Parliamentarian officer in the Civil Wars who had distanced himself from the regicide and the Cromwellian regime, wrote to his mentor, Richard Baxter (see chapter 7), asking for advice "how to move in this ensuing Parliament for the service of the distressed Church." Harley was "sure that only *Fata Ecclesiae* [the fate of the Church] can *auspiciat Fata Imperii* [foretell the fate of the State]."[1] This prediction proved true for more than thirty years. The Restoration religious settlement of the 1660s, Charles II's Declaration of Indulgence in 1672 and the backlash of the Test Act in 1673, the fear of Popery and of Dissent during the Exclusion Crisis, James II's Declarations of Indulgence in 1687 and 1688, and his overthrow in the Glorious Revolution of 1688–9 – all involved struggles over the Church which rocked the English government. As you read the documents from this period, consider the following questions:

- To what degree *did* the fate of the Church foretell the fate of the State? Likewise, how did the State's fortunes determine the destiny of the Church?
- To what degree were the political issues and debates between the Restoration and the Glorious Revolution new; to what degree did they continue older struggles dating back to the early Stuarts or even before?

Dissenters, Catholics, and the Church of England

8.1 Charles II, Declaration of Breda (April 14, 1660)[2]

In 1659, as the Protectorate crumbled and a series of short-lived governments came and went, many began to hope for a restoration of the pre-war
constitution in Church and State. Out of the chaos emerged General George

---

[1] R. Schlatter, *Richard Baxter and Puritan Politics* (New Brunswick, N. J., 1957), 45.
[2] *LJ*, 11: 7 (April 4, n.s., i.e., on the continent).

Monck (1608–70), Cromwell's overseer of Scotland, who marched south in early January 1660, seized London with a well-paid army purged of sectarians and radicals, and called for a new parliament to settle the nation. While Monck and the Convention (that is, a parliament called into existence other than by a king) debated constitutional and religious possibilities, Charles I's eldest son, the exiled Charles II of Scotland, angled for his return to the English throne by issuing a declaration from Breda on the continent. What is the Declaration's tone? To whom was it intended to appeal? Who might have been reassured by it? Who alarmed? What are "tender consciences"? What particular promises does Charles II make? Why? Finally, how can Charles claim to be "king of England," etc., if he has not yet been restored? In his formulation, where does sovereign power come from?

Charles, by the grace of God, king of England, Scotland, France [the old Medieval claim] and Ireland, defender of the Faith, etc., to all our loving subjects, of what degree or quality soever, greeting. If the general distraction and confusion which is spread over the whole kingdom doth not awaken all men to a desire and longing that those wounds which have so many years together been kept bleeding may be bound up, all we can say will be to no purpose. However, after this long silence, we have thought it our duty to declare how much we desire to contribute thereunto; and that as we can never give over the hope, in good time, to obtain the possession of that right which God and nature hath made our due, so we do make it our daily suit to the Divine Providence, that He will, in compassion to us and our subjects, after so long misery and sufferings, remit and put us into a quiet and peaceable possession of that our right, with as little blood and damage to our people as is possible. ...

And to the end that the fear of punishment may not engage any, conscious to themselves of what is past, to a perseverance in guilt for the future, by opposing the quiet and happiness of their country, in the restoration of king, Peers, and people to their just, ancient, and fundamental rights, we do, by these presents, declare, that we do grant a free and general pardon, which we are ready, upon demand, to pass under our Great Seal of England, to all our subjects, of what degree or quality soever, who, within forty days after the publishing hereof, shall lay hold upon this our grace and favor, and shall, by any public act, declare their doing so, and that they return to the loyalty and obedience of good subjects (excepting only such persons as shall hereafter be excepted by Parliament). ...

And because the passion and uncharitableness of the times have produced several opinions in religion, by which men are engaged in parties and animosities against each other ..., we do declare a liberty to tender consciences, and that no man shall be disquieted or called in question for differences of opinion in matter of religion, which do not disturb the peace of the kingdom; and that we shall be ready to consent to such an act of parliament, as, upon mature deliberation, shall be offered to us, for the full granting that indulgence.

And because, in the continued distractions of so many years and so many and great revolutions, many grants and purchases of estates have been made to and by many officers, soldiers, and others, who are now possessed of the same and who may be liable to actions at law upon several titles, we are likewise willing that all such differences ... shall be determined in Parliament, which can best provide for the just satisfaction of all men who are concerned.

8.2   Corporation Act (13 Car. II, St. II, c. 1, 1661)[3]

The Declaration of Breda paved the way for Charles II's Restoration on May 29, 1660. Its promise of "liberty to tender consciences" set in motion talks between Presbyterians and Anglicans about a possible Church settlement based either on toleration for different shades of Protestantism or a single Church of England defined so broadly as to comprehend those different shades. But a new parliament was elected in 1661 containing fewer Presbyterians and more Anglican Royalists than the Convention returned in 1660. This "Cavalier Parliament" (1661–78) ignored Charles II's request for religious toleration or comprehension. Instead, it restored the bishops and passed a series of laws (traditionally labeled the Clarendon Code, or more accurately the Cavalier Code) which forced religious uniformity and punished those who would not conform. The keystone of the Church Settlement passed by the Cavalier Parliament was the Act of Uniformity of 1662 (14 Car. II, c. 4). Among its many provisions was: "that every parson, vicar, or other minister ... declare his unfeigned assent and consent to the use of all things in the ... Book" of Common Prayer.[4] Nearly one thousand clergymen, about one tenth of the total in England and Wales, were removed by the Act for not so assenting by St. Bartholomew's Day (August 24) 1662. Altogether about 1,760 clergy were forced out of their livings between 1660 and 1663. The Conventicle Act of 1664 (16 Charles II c. 4) proscribed Nonconformist meetings (conventicles); and the Five Mile Act of 1665 (17 Car. II, c. 2) restricted the freedom of Nonconformist preachers, decreeing that

all such person and persons ... shall not at any time from and after March [24] ... 1665, unless only in passing upon the road, come or be within five miles of any city or town corporate, or borough that send burgesses to the Parliament, within his majesty's kingdom of England, principality of Wales, or of the town of Berwick-upon-Tweed, or within five miles of any parish, town, or place wherein he or they have, since the Act of Oblivion, been parson, vicar, curate, stipendiary, or lecturer, or taken upon them to preach in any unlawful assembly, conventicle, or meeting, under color or pretense of any exercise of religion, contrary to the laws and statutes of this

---

[3] *SR*, 5: 322.
[4] *SR*, 5: 365.

kingdom; before he or they have taken and subscribed the oath ["that it is not lawful to take arms against the king"] aforesaid ... in open court ... upon forfeiture for every such offence the sum of forty pounds.[5]

Towns and borough corporations especially concerned the government for three reasons: Protestant sects had proliferated among urban artisans and tradesmen; corporations had their own legal jurisdiction outside that of country JPs; and incorporated boroughs often returned two MPs to Parliament. The first salvo of the Cavalier Code was the Corporation Act of 1661. How might these concerns have influenced the framers of the Corporation Act? How does the law connect religious with political loyalty? Why might this law have upset former Parliamentarians?

All persons who, upon the 24th day of December, 1661, shall be mayors, aldermen, recorders, bailiffs, town clerks, common-councilmen, and other persons then bearing any office or offices of magistracy or places or trusts or other employment relating to or concerning the government of the said respective cities, corporations, and boroughs ... shall ... take the oaths of allegiance and supremacy and this oath following: "I, A. B., do declare and believe that it is not lawful upon any pretense whatsoever to take arms against the king, and that I do abhor that traitorous position of taking arms by his authority against his person or against those that are commissioned by him; so help me God."...

Provided also, and be it enacted by the authority aforesaid, that, from and after the expiration of the said commissions, no person or persons shall forever hereafter be placed, elected, or chosen in or to any the offices or places aforesaid that shall not have within one year next before such election or choice taken the sacrament of the Lord's Supper according to the rites of the Church of England.

8.3   *First Test Act (25 Car. II, c. 2, 1673)*[6]

In the early 1670s Charles II tried to solve his constitutional, religious, foreign policy, and financial problems by signing the Treaty of Dover with Louis XIV, the secret articles of which promised that the king would publicly convert to Catholicism in exchange for a French stipend (see Bucholz and Key, chapter 9) and, if necessary, troops. Two years later, as part of this strategy and in the hope of securing the support of Dissenters as well as Catholics, he tried to grant "liberty to tender consciences" by a Declaration of Indulgence (March 15, 1672) suspending much of the Cavalier Code. Charles's Indulgence allowed the right of public worship to "all sorts of

[5]   SR, 5: 375.
[6]   SR, 5: 782–4.

Nonconformists and recusants, except the recusants of the Roman Catholic religion ... whom we shall no ways allow in public places of worship, but only indulge them ... the exercise of their worship in their private houses only."[7] Who might welcome such a declaration? Who might fear it, especially the private practice of Catholicism? When Parliament reassembled in February 1673, they were nonplussed that Charles claimed "a power to suspend penal statutes" and petitioned him to the effect that "we find ourselves bound in duty to inform your majesty that penal statutes in matters ecclesiastical cannot be suspended but by act of Parliament."[8] Instead of making the Declaration into a statute, as the king hoped, they passed the Test Act, below. How might the Test Act change the make-up of the government? What are its implications for the issues of sovereignty and religion? For those of foreign policy and finance?

For preventing dangers which may happen from popish recusants and quieting the minds of his majesty's good subjects, be it enacted ... that all and every person or persons as well peers as commoners that shall bear any office or offices civil or military or shall receive any pay, salary, fee, or wages by reason of any patent or grant from his majesty ..., shall personally appear ... and ... in public and open court ... take the several oaths of supremacy and allegiance. ...

And the said respective officers ... shall also receive the Sacrament of the Lord's Supper according to the usage of the Church of England at or before August [1673] in some public Church upon some ... Sunday immediately after Divine Service and sermon. ...

And be it further enacted ... that at the same time when the persons concerned in this Act shall take the aforesaid oaths of supremacy and allegiance, they shall likewise make and subscribe this declaration following ...:

"I, A.B., do declare that I do believe that there is not any Transubstantiation in the Sacrament of the Lord's Supper, or in the elements of bread and wine, at, or after the consecration thereof by any person whatsoever."

8.4   A Letter From a Person of Quality, To His Friend In the Country *(1675)*[9]

After the abortive experiment with religious toleration under the Indulgence, Charles II entrusted his government to the safely Anglican Thomas Osborne, earl of Danby (1632–1712), who concentrated on balancing the king's

---

[7]   *The Parliamentary History of England, from the Earliest Period to the Year 1803* (London, 1808), 4: 515–6.

[8]   *CJ*, 9: 252.

[9]   [A. Ashley Cooper, earl of Shaftesbury,] *A Letter From a Person of Quality, To His Friend In the Country* (n. p., [London], 1675), 1–3.

finances and placating the Anglican majority by enforcing the penal laws. As this implies, from this point king and minister relied for political support upon those who strongly defended the Anglican Church and Divine Right, the political and religious heirs of those who had supported Charles I. These became known in the 1670s as the Court faction, while their opponents were known as the Country faction. *A Letter from a Person of Quality, to His Friend in the Country* was probably composed by a leader of the country opposition, Anthony Ashley Cooper, earl of Shaftesbury (1621–83). The Lords ordered *A Letter from a Person of Quality* burnt by the common hangman. The pamphlet's foremost crime was publishing parliamentary speeches and votes (which was illegal), but can you suggest other reasons for the Lords to single out the *Letter*? What does the author think of the Test Act? What issues divided the two parliamentary factions? Is his portrayal of Anglicans fair?

This session being ended, and the bill of the Test [document 8.3] near finished at the committee of the whole House; I can now give you a perfect account of this State Masterpiece. It was first hatched (as almost all the mischiefs of the world have hitherto been) amongst the great church men, and is a project of several years standing. ...

First, to make a distinct party from the rest of the nation of the high Episcopal man, and the old Cavalier ...; now they are possessed of the arms, forts, and ammunition of the nation.

Next they design to have the government of the Church sworn to as unalterable, and so tacitly owned to be of divine right. ...

Then in requital to the crown, they declare the government absolute and arbitrary, and allow monarchy as well as episcopacy to be *jure divino* [by divine law], and not to be bounded, or limited by humane laws.

And to secure all this they resolve to take away the power, and opportunity of Parliaments to alter any thing in Church or State, only leave them as an instrument to raise money, and to pass such laws, as the court, and Church shall have a mind to. ...

And as the topstone of the whole fabric, a pretense shall be taken from the jealousies they themselves have raised, and a real necessity from the smallness of their party to increase and keep up a standing army. ...

In order to this, the first step was made in the Act for Regulating Corporations [document 8.2], wisely beginning, that in those lesser governments which they meant afterwards to introduce upon the government of the nation, and making them swear to a declaration, and belief of such propositions ..., so that many of the wealthiest, worthiest, and soberest men, are still kept out of the magistracy of those places.

The next step was in the Act of the Militia [1661], which went for most of the chiefest nobility and gentry, being obliged as lord-lieutenants, deputy-lieutenants, &c. to swear to the same declaration, and belief, with the addition only of these words in persuance of such military commissions …: this act is of a piece, for it establisheth a standing army by a law, and swears us into a military government.

Immediately after this, followeth the Act of Uniformity [see document 8.2], by which all the clergy of England are obliged to subscribe, and declare what the corporations, nobility, and gentry, had before sworn, but with this additional clause of the Militia Act omitted. This the clergy readily complied with …: and yet that Bartholomew day [1662, see document 8.2] was fatal to our Church, and religion, in throwing out a very great number of worthy, learned, pious, and orthodox divines, who could not come up to this, and other things in that Act; and … so great was the zeal in carrying on this church affair, and so blind was the obedience required, that if you compute the time of the passing this Act, with the time allowed for the clergy to subscribe the Book of Common Prayer thereby established; you shall plainly find it could not be printed and distributed so as one man in forty could have seen and read the Book they did so perfectly assent and consent to.

8.5 John Bunyan, The Trial of Christian and Faithful at Vanity Fair, from Pilgrim's Progress (1678)[10]

How did Danby's enforcement of the Cavalier Code and Test Act affect Nonconformists? John Bunyan (1628–88) was a Calvinist Baptist who had been imprisoned soon after the Restoration for preaching outdoors, was freed by the Declaration of Indulgence, and then imprisoned again for about six months after the Indulgence lapsed. Bunyan's *Pilgrim's Progress* is an allegory of the protagonist Christian's difficult journey in this life and his salvation. After considering the selection as an allegory of how a Calvinist believer relates to the secular world (What does Vanity Fair symbolize?), consider it again as a description of the relationship between Nonconformists and the Cavalier Code. Why are Bunyan's pilgrims persecuted, below? Do the persecutors have a point? What was Bunyan's view of contemporary social status distinctions?

Then I saw in my dream, that … [Christian and Faithful] saw a town before them, and the name of that town is Vanity; and at the town there is a fair kept, called Vanity Fair: it is kept all the year long.…

This fair is no new-erected business, but a thing of ancient standing.… At this fair are all such merchandise sold, as houses, lands, trades, places,

---

[10] J. Bunyan, *The Pilgrim's Progress from This World to That which is to come* … (London, 1678), 128–36.

honors, preferments, titles, countries, kingdoms, lusts, pleasures, and delights of all sorts, as whores, bawds, wives, husbands, children, masters, servants, lives, blood, bodies, souls, silver, gold, pearls, precious stones, and what not. ...

As in other fairs, some one commodity is as the chief of all the fair, so the ware of Rome and her merchandise is greatly promoted in this fair; only our English nation, with some others, have taken a dislike thereat. ...

Now these pilgrims ... must needs go through this fair. Well, so they did: but, behold, even as they entered into the fair, all the people in the fair were moved, and the town itself as it were in a hubbub about them ..., insomuch that all order was confounded. Now was word presently brought to the great one of the fair, who quickly came down, and deputed some of his most trusty friends to take these men into examination, about whom the fair was almost overturned. So the men were brought to examination; and they that sat upon them, asked them whence they came, whither they went, and what they did there, in such an unusual garb? The men told them that they were pilgrims and strangers in the world, and that they were going to their own country, which was the heavenly Jerusalem. ... But they that were appointed to examine them did not believe them to be any other than bedlams and mad, or else such as came to put all things into a confusion in the fair. Therefore they took them and beat them, and besmeared them with dirt, and then put them into the cage, that they might be made a spectacle to all the men of the fair. ...

Then a convenient time being appointed, they brought them forth to their trial, in order to their condemnation. When the time was come, they were brought before their enemies and arraigned. The judge's name was Lord Hategood. Their indictment was one and the same in substance, though somewhat varying in form, the contents whereof were this:

"That they were enemies to and disturbers of their trade; that they had made commotions and divisions in the town, and had won a party to their own most dangerous opinions, in contempt of the law of their prince." ...

Then proclamation was made, that they that had aught to say for their lord the king against the prisoner at the bar, should forthwith appear and give in their evidence. So there came in three witnesses, to wit, Envy, Superstition, and Pickthank. ...

Then stood forth Envy, and said to this effect: "My lord, I have known this man [Faithful] a long time, and will attest upon my oath before this honorable bench that he is – "

Judge: "Hold! Give him his oath." So they sware him.

Then [Envy] said, "My lord, this man, notwithstanding his plausible name, is one of the vilest men in our country. He neither regardeth prince nor people, law nor custom, but doth all that he can to possess all men with certain of his disloyal notions, which he in the general calls principles of faith and holiness. And, in particular, I heard him once myself affirm that Christianity and the customs of our town of Vanity were diametrically opposite, and could not be reconciled. ..."

Then was Pickthank sworn, and bid say what he knew, in behalf of their lord the king, against the prisoner at the bar.

Pickthank: "My lord, and you gentlemen all, This fellow I have known of a long time, and have heard him speak things that ought not to be spoke; for he hath railed on our noble Prince Beelzebub, and hath spoken contemptibly of his honorable friends, whose names are the Lord Old Man, the Lord Carnal Delight, the Lord Luxurious, the Lord Desire of Vain Glory, my old Lord Lechery, Sir Having Greedy, with all the rest of our nobility; and he hath said, moreover, that if all men were of his mind …, there is not one of these noblemen should have any longer a being in this town. Besides, he hath not been afraid to rail on you, my lord, who are now appointed to be his judge, calling you an ungodly villain, with many other such like vilifying terms, with which he hath bespattered most of the gentry of our town."

When this Pickthank had told his tale, the judge directed his speech to the prisoner at the bar, saying, "Thou runagate [apostate], heretic, and traitor, hast thou heard what these honest gentlemen have witnessed against thee?"

Faithful: "May I speak a few words in my own defense?"

Judge: "Sirrah, sirrah, thou deservest to live no longer, but to be slain immediately upon the place; yet, that all men may see our gentleness towards thee, let us hear what thou, vile runagate, hast to say."

Faithful: "1. I say, then, in answer to what Mr. Envy hath spoken, I never said aught but this, That what rule, or laws, or customs, or people, were flat against the Word of God, are diametrically opposite to Christianity. …

"3. As to what Mr. Pickthank hath said …, the prince of this town, with all the rabblement, his attendants, by this gentleman named, are more fit for a being in Hell, than in this town and country: and so, the Lord have mercy upon me!"

Then the judge called to the jury …: "Gentlemen of the jury, you see this man about whom so great an uproar hath been made in this town. You have also heard what these worthy gentlemen have witnessed against him. Also you have heard his reply and confession. It lieth now in your breasts to hang him or save his life; but yet I think meet to instruct you into our law. …

For … you see he disputeth against our religion; and for the treason he hath confessed, he deserveth to die the death."

Then went the jury out …, and afterwards unanimously concluded to bring him in guilty before the judge. And first Mr. Blind-man, the foreman, said, "I see clearly that this man is a heretic." Then said Mr. No-good, "Away with such a fellow from the earth." "Ay," said Mr. Malice, "for I hate the very looks of him." Then said Mr. Love-lust, "I could never endure him." "Nor I," said Mr. Live-loose, "for he would always be condemning my way."… "Hanging is too good for him," said Mr. Cruelty. … Then said Mr. Implacable, "Might I have all the world given me, I could not be reconciled to him; therefore, let us forthwith bring him in guilty of death." And so they did; therefore he was presently condemned to be had from the place where he was, to the place from whence he came, and there to be put to the most cruel death that could be invented. …

Thus came Faithful to his end. … But as for Christian, he had some respite, and was remanded back to prison.

8.6   Narcissus Luttrell's "Brief Historical Relation" on the Popish Plot (September–November 1678)[11]

In the 1670s, the intensified persecution of Nonconformists; the king's evident sympathy for France; the Catholicism of his consort, Catherine of Braganza (1638–1705); and the apparent conversion to Rome of the king's brother and heir, James, duke of York (1633–1701) all led the Country opposition (see document 8.4) to allege a Catholic-absolutist conspiracy to overthrow the constitution of England in Church and State. In the late summer of 1678, more specific allegations surfaced about a Popish Plot to murder Charles II, massacre eminent Protestants, and re-establish Catholicism in England through Jesuit manipulation of York as a figurehead ruler. The characters who revealed the Plot – the notorious Titus Oates (1649–1705) or the obsessive Israel Tonge (1621–80), for example – were anything but credible, but for a while they were believed. Narcissus Luttrell (1657–1732) was a young barrister at Gray's Inn at the time he began his journal or compilation of news. His first entry was about the discovery of the body of Sir Edmund Berry Godfrey (1621–78), who had taken the depositions of Oates and Tonge regarding the supposed plot to murder Charles II. How might the manner of Godfrey's death have shaped Luttrell's thinking? What was the result of the hunt for Godfrey's murderers? How did rumor and speculation drive events? (For the later influence of Godfrey's death, see Plate 11.) Amid widespread anti-Catholic hysteria, the House of Commons resolved unanimously on 31 October 1678, "that this House is of opinion that there hath been and still is a damnable and hellish plot contrived and carried on by the popish recusants for the assassinating and murdering of the king, and for subverting the government, and rooting out and destroying the Protestant religion."[12] A Second Test Act (30 Car. II. st. 2, c. 1, 1678) required both MPs and Lords to make this additional declaration in addition to the oaths of allegiance and supremacy and that against transubstantiation previously required of officers. A proviso excepting the duke of York from the Act's provisions passed by only two votes. When, on January 24, 1679, Charles dissolved the Cavalier Parliament after 18 years of existence, the age of party politics was about to begin.

---

[11]   N. Luttrell, *A Brief Historical Relation of State Affairs from September 1678 to April 1714* (Oxford, 1857), 1: 1–3.
[12]   *CJ*, 9: 530.

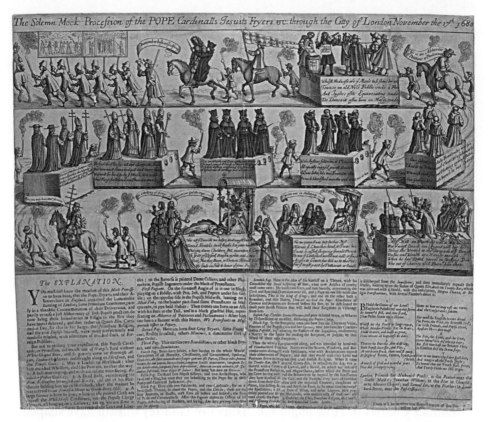

Plate 11 *The Solemn Mock Procession of the Pope Cardinalls Jesuits Fryers &c: through the Citty of London November the 17th 1680* (1680), detail. (Courtesy of the Lewis Walpole Library, Yale University.)

This broadside illustrates a long parade snaking through London with torches, placards, floats (you can see the face-holes of the men pushing them underneath), costumed actors, and effigies, especially that of the pope, which was later burnt. Heading the procession behind a bellman shouting "Remember Justice Godfrey," is a knife-wielding "Jesuit" carrying a dead Godfrey. Later, riding backwards on a horse, is "an Abhorrer of Petitions and Parliaments." How is this a partisan (not simply an anti-papal) procession and broadside? Why is the "Popish Plot" being thus remembered more than two years after its supposed discovery? Why, do you suppose, did large numbers of people join or watch the demonstration?

September 1678. About the latter end of this month was a hellish conspiracy, contrived and carried on by the papists, discovered by one Titus Oates unto Sir Edmondbury Godfrey, justice of peace, who took his examination on oath....

October. On Saturday the 12th of this month was Sir Edmondbury Godfrey, a justice of peace of Middlesex, missing, and so continued till Thursday morning following, when he was found murdered on Primrose Hill, near Hampstead; his stick and gloves set up against the hedge, his money and watch in his pocket, and his sword sticking in his body, but not bloody (which is an argument he was run through when dead), and he had a livid circle round his neck, as if he had been strangled. His death caused variety of talk: but that which is most remarkable are the several reports that run about whilst he was missing; that he was gone into the country; that he was at a relations house in town, and lay secret there whilst he was courting of a lady. Others reported that he had really killed himself; which the posture he was found in confuted.

On the 20th his Majesty, out of his wonted goodness, put forth a proclamation for the discovery of the murderers of the said Sir Edmundbury Godfrey, promising the reward of 500 pounds and pardon to any who shall discover the same....

On the 30th of this month came out a proclamation by the king, commanding all persons being popish recusants, or so reputed, to depart from the cities of London and Westminster, and all other places within ten miles of the same.

November. On the 2nd came out an order of council, promising the reward of £20 to any person who shall discover any officer or soldier in his majesty's guards, that, since the taking of the oaths of allegiance and supremacy and the test, hath or shall be perverted to the Romish religion.

On the 9th the king came into the house of Lords in his robes, and sent for the house of Commons up, and made a most gracious speech, thanking them for the great care they took of his person; and that he was not unmindful of their security, but came to assure them of his readiness to comply with all laws that shall secure the protestant religion, and that not only during his time, but also of any successor, so as they tend not to impeach the right of succession, nor the descent of the crown in the true line. Here it is worth noting, that though this Parliament ... gave those vast sums of money, and [was] therefore called the "Pensioner Parliament"; yet did they all this sessions apply themselves earnestly to the prosecution of the Popish Plot, and went on now very unanimously, and came even to consider about excluding the duke of York from the crown as a papist; which occasioned the preceding speech of the king.

Whig vs. Tory

8.7 *MPs discuss how to secure the kingdom against popery and arbitrary government (December 15, 1680)*[13]

After the dissolution of the Cavalier Parliament, Charles II called three more between 1679 and 1681. The reason for their repeated dissolution was that each seemed bent on a measure which would undermine the foundations of Stuart rule: the exclusion of his brother, the Catholic James, duke of York from the succession to the throne. The resultant Exclusion Crisis and the

[13]   *Parliamentary History of England*, 4: 1234–48.

three elections over which the issue was fought produced England's first two political parties: the Whigs and the Tories. In the first Exclusion Parliament (March 6 to May 27, 1679), the first Exclusion bill, barring York from the succession, passed its second reading by a two-to-one margin in the Commons. To kill the bill, Charles again dissolved Parliament. The elections for the second Exclusion Parliament (autumn 1679) strengthened the exclusionists so the king delayed its first meeting until October 21, 1680. Shaftesbury and other exclusionists petitioned Charles to summon Parliament. These petitioners became known as the "Whigs," whereas those organizing addresses "abhorring" the petitions became the first Tories (see Plates 11 and 12). Whigs argued that Parliament could alter the succession; increasingly most wanted it to do so in favor of the king's Protestant but illegitimate son, James, duke of Monmouth (1649–1685). As this implies, they tended to favor the power of Parliament over that of the king. They also wanted enforcement of the penal laws against Catholics, but toleration for Dissenters and an anti-French foreign policy. Tories believed in the divine appointment of monarchs, saw parliaments as subservient to them, and hated Dissenters and the Dutch more than they did the Catholics and the French. Soon after Parliament finally met in late 1680, the Commons passed the second Exclusion bill, resolving "that … James duke of York shall be and is by authority of this present Parliament excluded and made for ever incapable to inherit, possess, or enjoy the imperial Crown of this realm," and that any attempt for him to claim the throne would be high treason.[14] When the Commons sent their Exclusion bill to the House of Lords, the Lords rejected it by two to one. The Whigs were stymied; the Commons frustrated. In the Commons, MP after MP denounced arbitrary and popish rule, and advanced various bills as remedies to the court's intransigence: banish Catholics, unite all Protestants, and, ominously, create a Protestant paramilitary Association to arm themselves against any Catholic attempting to claim the throne. Can you identify Whig ideas in the discussion below, and/or Tory ones? How do they link the religious issue to those of sovereignty and foreign policy? Why did the Whigs associate arbitrary or absolute rule with Popery? Who, besides the Catholics, did they fear? Indeed, you might make a list of fears on both sides. Charles II next summoned a new parliament to meet at Oxford, distant from London Whig radicals. The third Exclusion Parliament, the Oxford Parliament, met on March 21, 1681 and again considered excluding the duke of York from the throne. But Charles dissolved it a week later.

Sir *George Hungerford* [1637–1712]. Sir, I think you are well advised, that the way to secure ourselves effectually against Popery, is to secure ourselves also against arbitrary government; and that the having of frequent parliaments is the

---

[14] HMC, *Eleventh Report, Appendix II, House of Lords, 1678–1688* (London, 1887), 195–6.

best way to secure both; and therefore I think you may do well to move the house, that a committee be appointed to inspect what old laws there are, for enforcing the sitting of frequent parliaments; that if they should be found deficient, some new laws may be made for that purpose. I do agree, that a bill for banishing out of England the most considerable Papists, may do well; but I hope, sir, that if you banish the men, you will banish some women too; for I do believe, that some of that sex have been great instruments in bringing about our ruin. And if in time you will consider, how to prevent the royal family's marrying popish women, it would be of great security for hereafter. For I am of opinion, that the late queen mother's [Henrietta Maria's] zeal for her religion, was not only a great occasion (amongst many others) of the miseries that befell us in [16]41; but the great cause of all our miseries now, by perverting the duke [of York] from his religion, as is reported.... And no man can doubt, but that the Protestant interest hath been much prejudiced, by his majesty's marrying a princess [Catherine of Braganza] of that religion: for we have plainly seen, since the discovery of the Plot [see document 8.6], how some of the most material Jesuits, and popish instruments, have sheltered themselves under her royal protection; and how they have helped to carry on the Plot, being so impudent, as to pretend they had her patronage, and by abusing her authority; but more especially by the duke's marrying the princess [Mary] of Modena; because of her near relation to the popes and cardinals. All which was plainly foreseen by that parliament which met a little before that marriage in 1673, and therefore they made an address to his majesty, representing the said ill consequences; desiring him not to permit it, because it would tend to the destruction of the Protestant religion.... In the interim, I agree for the Bill of Banishment and [that of] Association too....

Sir Nicholas Carew [1635–88]. Sir, I am not against any of these bills, because they may be all convenient for the present occasion; but if any man think that these bills will do without the Succession [Exclusion] Bill, I believe they will find themselves mistaken, for these bills will signify nothing, unless you can remove your popish successor, and your popish interest. These bills will not reach your Papists in masquerade, who will certainly continue as long as there is a popish successor, and make your Banishing-Bill, and Association-Bill too, as ineffectual as white paper.... As long as the duke hath so many friends at court, (between whose interest and Popery I cannot hear there is any distinction) I think no laws that we can make against Popery will do us any good, because all the laws we have already have done us none.... But if you are resolved to go on with these bills that have been proposed, I will not offer to oppose the sense of the committee, but would move you ... that in the first place you pass a vote, "That it is the opinion of this committee, that as long as the Papists have any hopes of the duke of York's succeeding the king, the king's person, the Protestant religion, and the lives and liberties of the people, are in apparent danger."...

Mr. Ralph Montagu [1638–1709]. Sir, by offering at the Exclusion Bill, we may conclude we have offended the duke; by this Bill for Banishment, all the rest of the considerable Papists in England. As we have made many enemies, so it will be convenient, that we should endeavor to get some law to defend

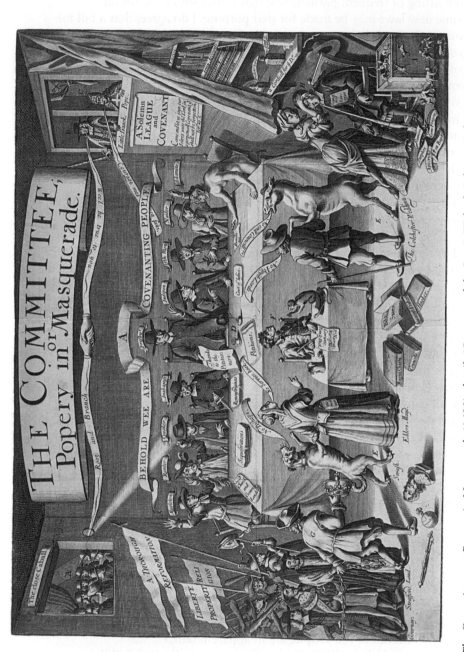

Plate 12 *The Committee; or Popery in Masquerade* (1680), detail. (Courtesy of the Lewis Walpole Library, Yale University.)

Tory Roger L'Estrange (1616–1704) published this complex allegory against the Whigs with a long verse explanation (not included here). With what associations does he try to link the Whig Petitioners (for holding Parliament and excluding "Popish Lords")? Why bring up the bogeymen of Ranters, Quakers, and Adamites (see chapter 7 above) from thirty years ago? Whom does he ultimately suggest is behind the Whigs (look at the upper right)?

ourselves against their implacable designs. For which a Bill for an Association of all his majesty's Protestant subjects may do well; and therefore I pray that we may move the house to have it brought in. ...

Paul Foley [1644/5–99]. I think we cannot but conclude that the duke's [York's] interest, the French interest, and popish interest are all one. ... And will not the divisions they carry on amongst us, as to churchmen and fanatics, Plot or no Plot, be very useful to [the Papists]; but especially their arraignments of Parliaments, and all that speak against Popery, as [16]41 men, and enemies to the government, occasion a great weakness on our side? ... Is it not strange [the Exclusion bill] should be rejected in the house of Lords? I cannot believe that the Fathers of the Church [the bishops] should join in that, which must infallibly give opportunity for the tearing out the bowels of their mother, and destroying her forever. ...

Sir Gilbert Gerrard [d. 1687]. Sir, I am of opinion the Popish Plot goeth on as much as ever, and the Papists are so proud of it, that they cannot forbear bragging of their hopes to see better days speedily. I think, sir, seeing we are not like for one while to have the Exclusion Bill, we shall appear neglectful of our duty, if we do not try what security can be contrived by an Association-Bill: and therefore I humbly pray, that the house may be moved to appoint a committee, to draw up and bring in a Bill for associating all his majesty's Protestant subjects.

8.8   *Selections from newsletters (1675–82)*[15]

Whigs and Tories pioneered many of the techniques of modern political parties: mass rallies, party banquets, print propaganda – and "dirty tricks." Contemporary newsletters and newspapers (document 8.9) provide rich sources for Whig and Tory thought and activism. When the Licensing Act of 1662 lapsed in 1679, a torrent of newspapers and pamphlets flooded England. While newspapers were again effectively censored by the end of 1682, those who could afford it subscribed to a newsletter service, handwritten pages of relatively uncensored news mailed at regular intervals to subscribers. Below, can you follow the progress of the Popish Plot and Exclusion Crisis as a contemporary living in the country might have done? Can you trace the rise of two political parties and their strategies to influence public opinion? Can you distinguish between Whig and Tory activity as reported in the newsletters: Whig versus Tory feasts; street demonstrations; coffee houses? What role did political anniversaries (Gunpowder Treason Day, November 5; or Queen Elizabeth's Accession Day, November 17) play? How would you describe Whig and Tory organizations in the early 1680s? Which side did the Crown favor?

[15] Folger Shakespeare Library, newsletters to Richard Newdigate, Esq., L.C. 700 (Nov. 2, 1678), 1149–50 (Nov. 17, 19, 1681), 1157 (Dec. 6, 1681), 1297 (Nov. 7, 1682), 1299 (Nov. 11, 1682); Huntington Library, HM 30314–30315, Sir Leoline Jenkins's Newsletters, May 15, 1677–Oct. 4, 1678 [J]; University of Texas, Ransome Center, MS.103c, newsletters addressed to Sir Richard Bulstrode and others, Nov. 9, 1675–April 21, 1682 [B].

November 9, 1675 [B]. "The Lords met this day were entertained with a little book called *A Letter to a Friend in the Country* [document 8.4] which is a history of so much of the last sessions ... with sharp reflections and remarks upon several bishops, and some great ministers of state; the book was brought in by a bishop and ordered to be burnt by the common hangman."

May 15, 1677 [J]. "On Friday night was apprehended one Mr. Gosnold a person that had dispersed several scandalous and seditious lampoons against the Government, a collection of which was seized as it was binding in a bookseller's shop. Together with this Gosnold there have been taken one Evans (who went by the name of Clerk) and Acton, who was his copyist."

August 30, 1678 [J]. "Ten days or a fortnight since there was a great election for the knight of the shire in Berkshire, which was highly contested between the Court and Country party as they call them."

October 4, 1678 [J]. "People's heads and hearts are full of reflections upon the late discovery that hath been made of a detestable design against his majesty's person and the peace of the kingdom, and though the Roman Catholics do still say, that all is but a contrivance to ruin them, yet I can assure your excellency that the lords of the Privy Council do all say, that it is as plain as the day, that there has been a most dangerous and pernicious design carrying on for several years past, and therefore the Privy Council hath thought it necessary to send down orders into all the counties for disarming all Roman Catholics and reputed Roman Catholics, and this day they have begun to execute these orders here in towns and in the suburbs."

November 2, 1678. "The corpse of Sir Edmund Berry Godfrey was interred in St. Martins-in-the-Fields, attended thither ... with all due solemnity by about 100 of the clergy and many hundreds of gentry and citizens. The house of Commons ... have unanimously resolved that it appears to them that there has been 'A Most Horrid and Hellish Plot for the Destruction of the King's Person and Government, Religion, etc.'"

March __, 1681 [B]. "The justices of the peace for Middlesex have received orders to issue out their warrants for summoning all such people before them that print publish or spread those pamphlets about town and to proceed against them as spreaders of false news."

July 2, 1681 [B]. "On Thursday last the [ap]prentices of this city presented their petition to his majesty signed by 12,000 hands to give him thanks for his late declaration [explaining why he had dissolved the Oxford Parliament]; it met with a gracious acceptance and those that carried it up were introduced by the lord chamberlain and had the honor to kiss his majesty's hands."

July 30, 1681 [B]. "His majesty hath been graciously pleased to grant a warrant to the keeper of Hyde Park to deliver to the loyal apprentices that made the address two of the fattest bucks ... without fee with which they will make a feast on Wednesday next, several persons of quality being already invited."

October 31, 1681 [B]. "The king was received and entertained in the city on Saturday with all the expressions of duty and affection imaginable; and the king on the other side was very gracious to the [Tory] lord mayor and several of the aldermen but of others and of the two [Whig] sheriffs he took no manner of notice."

November 17, 1681. "[Nathaniel] Thomson the printer [and publisher of a Tory newspaper, document 8.9] was this day assaulted by the rabble in Fleet Street and after being beaten got home."

"This night the [effigy of the] pope was carried through the city attended with [effigies of] Jesuits, etc., then burnt in Smithfield."

November 19, 1681. "At the burning of the pope the people cried 'God bless the king, duke of Monmouth, earl of Shaftesbury, and Capt. [Henry] Wilkinson [an associate of Shaftesbury].'"

December 6, 1681. On Sunday night "the Lord Kingston, Lord Hunsdon, with Capt. Billingsley and about 12 more went from Wills Coffee House to Peters in Covent Garden to affront the Whigs, where they looked about the room and cried 'God Damn all Whigs for rogues and sons of whores,' but nobody speaking to them they took hold of one Peachy a tailor as he was going and asked him whither he was a Whig or a Tory and he crying a Whig they burnt his periwig and Billingsley kicked him downstairs, of which he threatens to complain to the council."

March 27, 1682 [B]. "The addresses declaring their abhorrence of the late designed Association [by Whigs to arm Protestants in defense of the king] come from all the countries [counties], and though there are a sort of people among us that would make light of them, yet I am assured those that are the best friends to my Lord Shaftesbury do not like to see the nation make these declarations against a paper that was sworn to be found in his custody."

April 21, 1682 [B]. "Yesterday the duke [of York] dined at the Artillery feast. His royal highness went thither attended with a great number of nobility and persons of quality, and was met at Merchant Tailors' Hall by the lord mayor, aldermen, etc. In sum all things passed extremely to his royal highness's satisfaction.

The Whigs in opposition to this had designed a mock feast; and for that purpose had given out several hundred of tickets, upon receipt whereof the persons invited gave their [three?] guineas apiece, but his majesty being informed thereof, [forbade] ... the said meeting as you will see by the order of Council which is printed in *The Gazette*."

November 7, 1682. "Last night being kept for the 5th of November many bonfires were enkindled but the rabble began their accustomed rudeness of crying 'No York, but A Monmouth, A Monmouth' and were so outrageous in the Stocks market [Exchange] that they began to burn and pull down a vintner's signs, etc., but the soldiers dissipated the most and seized several who were committed to the Compter and Bridewell [prisons]."

November 11, 1682. "Sunday last several justices of peace at Theobalds coming to disturb a [Dissenting] conventicle found the people gone upon which they pulled down the pulpit and made a bonfire therewith being Gunpowder treason day [November 5].

"Yesterday the lord mayor and aldermen attended his majesty in Council where they gave an account of the late riotous proceeding on Monday last.... Thereupon his majesty was pleased to order that on the 17th being the anniversary of Queen Elizabeth they ordered a strong guard of trained bands and suffer no bonfires to be made and neither pope nor other effigies to be burnt to prevent which that the city gates be kept shut in the evening and all assemblies dispersed."

8.9 Selections from Whig and Tory newspapers (1679–82)[16]

> To judge from the selections below, how reliable and objective were Exclusion-era newspapers? Can you identify which were Whig, which Tory? How do they report the other side's activities? (For a memorable attack on Whig mass petition drives, see Plate 12.)

The Protestant (Domestick) Intelligence: Or, News both from City and Country, by Benjamin Harris

December 26, 1679. There have been several persons in and about this city industriously endeavoring to promote petitions for the sitting of the Parliament, of which some persons in the Strand taking notice, and designing to suppress a petition set on foot in their neighborhood, and to which many hands had been procured, sent to invite the managers thereof to a tavern to take their subscriptions to it, and having by that means got it into their hands; they committed it to the flames.

We may also observe a further project of countermining the said petitions, in the following form of an association, which is published here, *viz.*

The Loyal Protestants Association [that is, an anti-Whig association]. "Whereas several printed forms of petitions have been lately dispersed up and down the kingdom, to procure subscriptions: And whereas the proceedings thereupon have been adjudged ..., to be contrary to law ..., we whose names are hereunder subscribed, out of a sense of our duty both to Church and State, and to witness our detestation of all illegal, and undutiful practices, do hereby unanimously declare ..., that we abhor the thought of any such confederacy."

January 18, 1681. Wapping, London. Two fellows coming into a victualing house, and desiring a private room, were showed up one pair of stairs, where they continued drinking for the space of four or five hours, being often observed to whisper to each other, and to be very private in their discourse.... After they were gone, the boy coming to take away, smelt so strong a scent of brimstone, that mistrusting something more than ordinary, he called up his master, who

---

[16] *The Protestant (Domestick) Intelligence*, no. 50, December 26, 1679; no. 89, January 18, 1681; *Impartial Protestant Mercury*, no. 104, April 18–21, 1682; no. 105, April 21–5, 1682; *Loyal Protestant and True Domestick Intelligence*, no. 1, March 9, 1681; no. 7, March 29, 1681.

searching the room, found it on fire behind the hangings, which, as it is supposed, was done by the dextrous application of Jesuitick fire-balls ..., so that we must conclude they were some of the pope's imps, whom he had employed to make bonfires of the remaining part of our ancient structure.

Impartial Protestant Mercury, *by Richard Janeway*

April 18–21, 1682. There was intended another considerable feast to have been tomorrow in the city. For which purpose Haberdashers Hall and Goldsmiths Hall were taken up, and twas believed there would near a thousand of the nobility, gentry, clergy of the Church of England as established by law, and eminent citizens have there appeared. The occasion and scope of which treat appears in the tickets of invitations; which being maliciously mis-recited by [Nathaniel] Thompson we therefore shall here add a true copy thereof.

"It having pleased Almighty God by his wonderful providence to deliver and protect his majesty's person, the Protestant religion, and English liberties (hitherto) from the Hellish and frequent attempts of their enemies (the Papists): in testimony of thankfulness herein, and for the preserving and improving mutual love and charity among such as are sensible thereof. You are desired to meet many of the loyal Protestant nobility, gentry, clergy, and citizens, on Friday ..., 21 ... April 1682, at ten ..., at St. Michaels...., there to hear a sermon, and from thence to go to Haberdashers Hall to dinner...."

But it seems the intent of this sociable meeting being ... misrepresented ..., it pleased his sacred majesty ..., yesterday to prohibit the same.

April 21–25, 1682. After the Artillery-Dinner yesterday [April 20] was over, the members of that society, according to custom, proceeded to choose eight stewards for the year ensuing ..., [including] the duke of Albemarle, the earl of Oxford ..., [etc.]. His royal highness [the duke of York] was highly caressed amongst them and returned to Whitehall before six.... Amongst the rest of their entertainment, one [Thomas] Durfey a poet sang several Tory-songs and was very much applauded. Though his royal highness was not present at the sermon, yet having an account given him thereof ..., he has desired Dr. [Thomas] Sprat to print the same. In the evening some bonfires were kindled, especially one before the Wonder Tavern in Ludgate Street, and a parcel of blades [young gallants] being planted in the balcony, threw out money to the rabble bidding them cry out "a York!" which they did as long as they got liquor; and some hectors that managed them were very rude and abusive to the coaches and passengers that went by. At last a company of young men came and threw abroad the fire, slinging part of the brands in at the tavern windows and cry'd out "No Papist! no Papist!" and so went their ways.

Loyal Protestant and True Domestick Intelligence, *by Nathaniel Thompson*

March 9, 1681. When a club of factious scribblers do inflame the people against the government, and under the mask of religion, endeavor to run down both

Church and State ...; then I think it high time for all loyal subjects to declare themselves against such pernicious proceedings. ... I have thought fit to renew this my *Intelligence*. ... For it is published for no other end, but to undeceive his majesty's loyal subjects.

March 29, 1681. The inhabitants of [Oxford] conceive no small joy at the favor his majesty has done them in calling his Parliament to sit here; so that whenever his majesty takes coach, or is publicly to be seen, many hundreds flock about him, and express their loyal duty by wishing him a long life, and happy reign; praying that they that seek his hurt, may be taken in their own snares. ...

Whereas in the *Oxford Intelligence* ..., it was inserted that the duke of Monmouth attended with a great retinue was received here ... with many shouts and acclamations of the people; this is to ascertain you, that he came ... with 30 in his attendance, as well servants as gentlemen, some of which company began to make faint essays of humming (or applause), thereby to provoke others to do the like, both in Cat Street ... and at his alighting at his lodging; but they were not in the least seconded by any.

8.10   John Rouse at his execution for his part in the Rye House Plot (July 20, 1683)[17]

The Whigs' strongest suit was their success in parliamentary election campaigns. When Charles II dismissed his last parliament in March 1681, the Whigs became desperate. A few discussed a general insurrection to force the king's hand, or even kidnaping and killing the royal brothers Charles and James. When the government learned of the Rye House Plot, it became the excuse to mop up remaining Whig organization. Tory ideology, which equated Whiggery with fanaticism, was vindicated. The Tories, who had opposed the exclusion of James, duke of York, were in the ascendant. Here, a minor plotter (no relation to the similarly named minister quoted in document 6.13, above) speaks to the crowd assembled to witness his execution. How is this rebellion reminiscent of earlier examples (see chapters 1–5)? How is it different? What influenced him to act? What lessons does he draw? How might you use the documents in this section to portray the role of London tavern and coffee house culture in elite and popular politics?

Since these hurly burlys, concerning parliaments going off, and coming on, did discontent the people upon one account or another, I confess I have been a hearer, and have understood too much of some kind of meetings, which I pray God forgive them for. ... That there have been such kind of designs, and

---

[17]   *The Speeches Of Captain Walcot, Jo. Rouse, and Will. Hone, On Friday the Twentieth of July, 1683* (n.p., n.d., 1683), 7–10.

meetings, and clubs, I have not been ignorant of; God forgive me.... I gave his majesty an account to the best of my knowledge....

I have been in several clubs eating and drinking, where it has been discoursed to accommodate the king's son, the D[uke of] M[onmouth]. That there was a design to set up the D. of M., I will not say while the king reigns, though some extravagant hot-headed men have taken upon them to discourse these things, but not any worthy man. I know those that were worthy to be called by that name, have declared in my hearing, that in opposition to the D[uke] of Y[ork] if the king be seized, they would stand by the D. of M. There are others ... that were for a Commonwealth ..., and some, but very few, not worth naming, were for the D. of Bucks [Buckingham]. But that I think fell at last between these two [Monmouth or a republic]....

He declared further, Mr. Sheriff, that when once the thing came so far that the Tower [of London] and city was taken and so many men gathered together, they would quickly increase; and the method was, to go to Whitehall with swords in their hands, and to demand privileges and liberties, not to take away the king's life, but only let the D. of Y. look to it: for he [Richard Goodenough] was resolved upon it that he [York] should not succeed the king....

Mr. Sheriff, I do freely acknowledge and confess that it is just in God in the first place, and righteous and just in the king, that I die.... I beg a word or two I had almost forgot, as a man and as a Christian, that it is a thing of such evil consequence, I have found it by bitter experience now, for such and such public places to be visited, especially by those that are professors of the Protestant religion, and particularly coffee -houses, where it is very well known too much time is spent, and families, and wives, and children, suffer too much. I pray God the people may take notice of it and lay it to heart that spend their time so, thinking it is but a penny and a penny; and so discourse of state-affairs as if so be they were God's counselors in the government of the world, running from the coffee-house to the tavern and from the tavern to the coffee-house, which hath been the debauchery of this age.

James II, William of Orange, and the Revolution of 1688–9

8.11   *Sir John Bramston on the reign of James II (ca. 1685–8)*[18]

When Charles II died in February 1685 and his brother, James became king, the Tories who had successfully opposed Exclusion dominated local and national politics. The Tory Sir John Bramston (1611–1700) recorded in his autobiography the events of James II's reign, beginning with the king's first

[18]   *The Autobiography of Sir John Bramston, K. B., of Skreens, in the Hundred of Chelmsford*, ed. Lord Braybrooke (London, Camden Society, old ser., 32, 1845), 165–6, 184, 275–6, 308–11, 340–3, 355–7.

speech to his council, which was obviously designed to shore up this loyalist support. Does James simply attempt to reassure his supporters about his religion or does he address other concerns as well? Do you think this speech was successful? Almost immediately James II faced rebellion led by the duke of Monmouth. What did Bramston make of this short-lived revolt? The selections from Bramston also include his discussion of the Trial of the Seven Bishops and the flight of James in 1688. As you read other documents from those events below, refer back to Bramston's "take" on them. How did Bramston's attitude towards the king change as his reign wore on? Is there a clear Tory or Whig version of the events leading to the Glorious Revolution? According to Bramston, was the Revolution justified?

[*The Accession of James II.*] The same day that the King Charles II died his present majesty King James II was proclaimed ... and the next day a Council being called the king spake thus: ...

"My Lords ..., Since it hath pleased almighty God to place me in this station, and I am now to succeed so good and gracious a king, as well as so very kind a brother, I think it fit to declare to you that I will endeavor to follow his example, and most especially in that of his great clemency and tenderness to his people. I have been reported to have been a man for arbitrary power; but that is not the only story has been made of me, and I shall make it my endeavor to preserve this government, both in Church and State, as it is now by law established. I know the principles of the Church of England are for monarchy, and the members of it have showed themselves good and loyal subjects; therefore I shall always take care to defend and support it. I know, too, that the laws of England are sufficient to make the king as great a monarch as I can wish; and as I shall never depart from the just rights and prerogatives of the Crown so I shall never invade any man's property. ...."

[*Monmouth's Rebellion.*] The duke of Monmouth landed at Lyme in Dorsetshire 11 June 1685.... They brought some arms, but not enough for his business. He set out a most malicious, false, and scandalous declaration, wherein he termed the King James "Duke of York," calling him traitor, and laying to his charge the murder of Sir Edmunberry Godfrey [1678], the cutting the throat of the earl of Essex [who committed suicide in the Tower after being seized on discovery of the Rye House Plot, 1683], the firing the city of London [1666], and the poisoning his brother, King Charles II; saying he had taken arms, and would admit of no treaty of peace until he had brought him to condign punishment, etc....

[*The Trial of the Seven Bishops.*] June 15 [1688], the attorney-general moved the court of King's Bench for an *habeas corpus* return immediate for the seven bishops, which was granted, and the seven appeared.... Then ... they pleaded not guilty, and the court demanded and required them to enter into recognizance for their appearance and standing to trial and judgment of the court.... In Hall

Court, Palace Yard, from the water stairs, were infinite numbers of people, lords, gentlemen, and common people. The people on their knees made a lane and begged the bishops' blessing as they passed. In their return, the people seeing them go to their own houses thought they were discharged, and gave great huzzas.

On the day, that is [June] 29th, they [the bishops] came to the bar, and a jury impaneled; they were tried on the information. ... Two of the judges ... spoke largely upon the subject's right of petitioning the king; the other two judges differed in opinion with them, but said not much. The jury went from the bar about 5 of clock; there was a majority for not guilty, but four or five then were for guilty; but by 12 of clock all but Arnold, the brewer, were agreed; about 6 in the morning he also agreed with the rest. ... They resolved to give their verdict in open court; and about ten of clock, when the judges were set, they came and gave their verdict, not guilty. At which some standing within hearing gave a huzza, which others took, and it passed through the hall extreme loud; so into the yards and to the water side, and along the river, as far as the bridge. ... Upon the day that the bishops appeared I was in the hall, and being joined with some of the nobility ... and several gentlemen, I was asked if ever I had seen the hall so full. I said, Yea, and fuller, when the cry was, "No bishops, no magpies, no popish Lords" [that is, in 1641]. But the noise was less now, as the cry was otherwise, save only, "No popish Lords."...

[*The Revolution of 1688–9.*] So soon as it was known that the king was gone, the Lords spiritual and temporal assembled at Guildhall, London, and required the lord mayor to take care of the city; and then and there also sent to the prince of Orange, and invited him to come to London; so also did the lord mayor, aldermen, and common council. The paper left by the king tells what made him go away, and the prince's message was demonstrative what he desired. The prince came to St. James. And tho' King James his reign was short, not full four years; yet was his design very apparent, the Roman religion he resolved to establish, maugre [in spite of] all the laws, and what averseness soever in the nobility, gentry, and the common people also. He closeted particular men, and, tried them by promises and threats. He garbled the corporations, and sent emissaries amongst them to influence them for choice of members for parliament, such as would take away the penal laws and test; gave indulgences, and dispensed by his own authority with all the laws: but this furious hasty driving ruin'd him. ...

I know it will be objected that King James was forced away; that some Lords spiritual and temporal, and some gentlemen had invited the prince of Orange into the kingdom, that he accordingly came with an army, and that the king's army refused to fight, nay, that some were gone over to the prince, so that the king must either fly, or be contented to be a prisoner. I can only say, as to those that invited the prince in, they must answer for themselves; but I hold it was in them perfect rebellion. As to the prince, I think much more may be said for him than for them, tho' they allege religion, property, and liberty were in a dangerous condition, as in truth they were; for, whoever considers well the short reign of King James, he will see what havoc he was making in the Church and universities, the nurseries of our religion, what haste he made to settle Popery, and the means and ways he took to make his power and rule absolute, and the laws dispensable at his will and pleasure, must think all these were in danger; but all were established by laws, and could not be destroyed but by the same power that made them, that is, by a law, and who they are that made our laws, must conclude, as I did, that tho' many particular persons might be destroyed by his power, yet the nation could not, people would not be so mad as to send to Parliament such representatives as would cut their own throats; wherefore I must leave those that called in the prince inexcusable. But as for him [William], if the case be stated (as I think it ought) that he being a free prince, and having a just right in succession in his princess [his wife, Mary], and after her and her sister [Princess Anne], and her issue, in himself also, and that the king, out of fondness for Popery, and enmity to the established religion, and for that cause to his daughters and their issue, and to the prince also, did give way to a Jesuitical contrivance, to impose upon the nation a supposititious son, as born of the body of the queen, and thereby to disinherit the above-mentioned prince and princesses; this, I say, being his belief and opinion, and there being no way for one prince to sue another, nor way to determine their controversies, but the sword, I dare not condemn the prince absolutely for making war on that occasion, tho' against an uncle and father.

8.12   *James II's Declaration of Indulgence (April 4, 1687, reissued April 27, 1688)*[19]

One of the things which upset Bramston and his fellow Tories was that by 1686 James made it clear that he intended to allow fellow Catholics to practice their religion and to serve in the military and government. He did this, first by granting dispensations for specific persons, and, later, by encouraging Parliament to repeal the penal laws and Test Acts (of 1673 and 1678). In preparation for a more malleable Parliament, in April 1687, James II went one step further towards repeal by issuing his Declaration of Indulgence. Compare and contrast it with the extract from Charles II's Declaration of Indulgence (see the introduction to document 8.3). What were James's goals? Did James seek unity of Church and State? What was the reaction? Why might Anglican Tories be especially upset? (This might become clearer as you read the next document.) What reaction would you expect among Whig Dissenters?

[19]   T. B. Howell, comp., *A Complete Collection of State Trials and Proceedings for High Treason and Other Crimes and Misdemeanors ... to the Year 1783* (London, 1816), 12: 234–6.

We ... have thought fit by virtue of our royal prerogative to issue forth this our declaration of indulgence, making no doubt of the concurrence of our two houses of Parliament when we shall think it convenient for them to meet.

In the first place we do declare that we will protect and maintain our archbishops, bishops, and clergy, and all other our subjects of the Church of England in the free exercise of their religion as by law established, and in the quiet and full enjoyment of all their possessions. ...

We do likewise declare ... that from henceforth the execution of all and all manner of penal laws in matters ecclesiastical, for not coming to Church, or not receiving the sacrament, or for any other nonconformity to the religion established, or for or by reason of the exercise of religion in any manner whatsoever, be immediately suspended; and the further execution of the said penal laws and every of them [*sic*] is hereby suspended. ...

We do hereby further declare ... that the oaths commonly called the oaths of supremacy and allegiance, and also the several tests and declarations mentioned in the Acts of Parliament made in the 25th [1673] and 30th years [1678] of the reign of our late royal brother King Charles II, shall not at any time hereafter be required to be taken, declared, or subscribed by any person or persons whatsoever, who is or shall be employed in any office or place of trust, either civil or military, under us or in our government.

8.13   Trial of the Seven Bishops (June 29, 1688)[20]

In 1688 James reissued his Declaration of Indulgence with the added instructions that all Anglican clergy were to read it from their pulpits – in effect, forcing them to abdicate publicly the Church of England's legal monopoly on the religious life of the nation. On May 18, 1688, William Sancroft, archbishop of Canterbury (1617–93) and six other bishops petitioned the king that they not be required to order their clergy to read the Declaration in their dioceses. James, furious, had the bishops arrested. As Bramston noted, the trial of the seven bishops was a *cause célèbre*. What are the key components of the Crown's argument? Of the bishops' defense? How are these issues related to other documents found in this chapter, and to documents found in chapters 6 and 7? Are they related to issues of sovereignty as well as religion? Bramston (document 8.11) was not the only contemporary to note "the great joy and bonfires expressed at the bishops' delivery."[21] What specifically do you think the London populace were celebrating with their bonfires?

[20]   Howell, *State Trials*, 12: 393–4, 397, 412, 416, 425–7.
[21]   HMC, *Fourteenth Report, Appendix II, Portland III* (London, 1894), 414, June 30, and July 3, Edward to his father, Sir Edward Harley.

Serjeant Levinz (for the defense): Now, my lord, this is a petition setting forth a grievance, and praying his majesty to give relief. And what is this grievance? It is that command of his, by that order made upon my lords the bishops, to distribute the declaration and cause it to be read in the churches. And pray, my lord, let us consider what the effects and consequences of that distribution and reading is: it is to tell the people, that they need not submit to the Act of Uniformity [1662], nor to any act of Parliament made about ecclesiastical matters, for they are suspended and dispensed with. This my lords the bishops must do, if they obey this order; but your lordship sees, if they do it, they lie under an anathema by the statute of 1 Eliz. [1559], for there they are under a curse if they do not look to the preservation and observation of that Act. But this command to distribute and read the declaration, whereby all these laws are dispensed with, is to let the people know they will not do what the Act requires of them....

Mr. Somers: My lord, I dare appeal to Mr. Attorney General himself, whether, in the case of Godden and Hales [1686], which was lately in this court.... He admitted it not to be in the king's power to suspend a law, but that he might give a dispensation to a particular person, was all that he took upon to justify him at that time....

The Solicitor-General (for the Crown): I dare say it will not be denied me, that the king may, by his prerogative royal, issue forth his proclamation; it is as essential a prerogative as it is to give his assent to an Act of Parliament to make it a law. And it is another principle, which I think cannot be denied, that the king may make constitutions and orders in matters ecclesiastical; and that these he may make out of Parliament, and without the Parliament. If the king may do so, and these are his prerogatives, then suppose the king do issue forth his royal proclamation (and such in effect is this declaration under the great seal) in a matter ecclesiastical, by virtue of his prerogative royal; and this declaration is read in the council and published to the world, and then the bishops come and tell the king, Sir, you have issued out an illegal proclamation or declaration, being contrary to what has been declared in Parliament, when there is no declaration in Parliament; is not this a diminishing the king's power and prerogative in issuing forth his proclamation or declaration, and making constitutions in matters ecclesiastical? Is not this a questioning his prerogative? Do not my lords the bishops in this case raise a question between the king and the people? Do not they, as much as in them lies, stir up the people to sedition? For who shall be judge between the king and the bishops? ...

Justice Holloway: Pray give me leave, Sir: then the king having made such a declaration of a general toleration and liberty of conscience, and afterwards he comes and requires the bishops to disperse this declaration; this, they say, out of a tenderness of conscience, they cannot do, because they apprehend it is contrary to law, and contrary to their function: What can they do, if they may not petition?

Solicitor-General: I'll tell you what they should have done, Sir. If they were commanded to do anything against their consciences, they should have acquiesced till the meeting of the Parliament. [At which some people in the court hissed.] ...

Lord Chief Justice: Gentlemen, upon the point of the publication, I have summed up all the evidence to you; and if you believe that the petition which these lords presented to the king was this petition, truly, I think, that is a publication sufficient. If you do not believe it was this petition, then my lords the bishops are not guilty of what is laid to their charge in this information, and consequently there needs no inquiry whether they are guilty of a libel. But if you do believe that this was the petition they presented to the king, then we must come to inquire whether this be a libel.

Now, gentlemen, anything that shall disturb the government, or make mischief and a stir among the people, is certainly within the case of "*Libellis Famosis*" [seditious libel, specifically against public persons]; and I must in short give you my opinion, I do take it to be a libel. Now, this being a point of law, if my brothers have anything to say to it, I suppose they will deliver their opinions.

Justice Holloway: Look you, gentlemen, it is not usual for any person to say anything after the chief justice has summed up the evidence ...: but this is a case of an extraordinary nature.... The question is, whether this petition of my lords the bishops be a libel or no. Gentlemen, the end and intention of every action is to be considered; and likewise, in this case, we are to consider the nature of the offence that these noble persons are charged with; it is for delivering a petition, which, according as they have made their defense, was with all the humility and decency that could be. So that if there was no ill intent, and they were not (as it is not, nor can be pretended they were) men of evil lives, or the like, to deliver a petition cannot be a fault, it being the right of every subject to petition....

Lord Chief Justice: Look you, by the way, brother, I did not ask you to sum up the evidence (for that is not usual) but only to deliver your opinion, whether it be a libel or no.

Justice Powell: Truly I cannot see, for my part, anything of sedition or any other crime fixed upon these reverend fathers, my lords the bishops.

For, gentlemen, to make it a libel, it must be false, it must be malicious, and it must tend to sedition. As to the falsehood, I see nothing that is offered by the king's counsel, nor anything as to the malice. It was presented with all the humility and decency that became the king's subjects to approach their prince with....

Justice Allybone: ... Gentlemen, consider what this petition is: this is a petition relating to something that was done and ordered by the government.... The government here has published such a declaration as this that has been read, relating to matters of government; and shall, or ought anybody to come and impeach that as illegal, which the government has done? Truly, in my opinion, I do not think he should, or ought: for by this rule may every act of the government be shaken, when there is not a Parliament *de facto* sitting.

[*Verdict of the jury*: Not Guilty, June 30, 1688.]

8.14   *Letter of the Immortal Seven (June 30, 1688)*[22]

Just a few weeks before the trial of the seven bishops, John Evelyn (1620–1706) had noted in his diary, "A young prince born," adding later, "which will cause dispute."[23] Indeed, Whigs soon charged that the birth of James, prince of Wales (1688–1766) was faked, thus leaving the king's Protestant daughter Mary, her younger sister Anne, and then Mary's husband, William, prince of Orange (1650–1702), *stadholder* of the Netherlands, as the next heirs to the throne What did the birth of the young James portend for the problems of sovereignty and religion (see Bucholz and Key, chapter 9)? How might it relate to the bishops' trial? On the same day as the verdict exonerating the bishops, seven other prominent politicians, including Whigs, Tories, and the bishop of London, wrote to William of Orange in the Netherlands. How would a Whig justify writing this letter? A Tory? Compare their view of the birth of James's son with that of Evelyn and Bramston (document 8.11). What does Bramston mean when he states that this invitation was "perfect rebellion"? Is he correct?

The people are so generally dissatisfied with the present conduct of the government in relation to their religion, liberties, and properties (all which have been greatly invaded), and they are in such expectation of their prospects being daily worse, that your highness may be assured there are nineteen parts of twenty of the people throughout the kingdom who are desirous of a change and who, we believe, would willingly contribute to it, if they had such a protection to countenance their rising as would secure them from being destroyed before they could get to be in a posture to defend themselves. It is no less certain that much the greatest part of the nobility and gentry are as much dissatisfied ...; and there is no doubt but that some of the most considerable of them would venture themselves with your highness at your first landing.... And ... we ... believe that their [James II's] army then would be very much divided among themselves, many of the officers being so discontented that they continue in their service only for a subsistence ..., and very many of the common soldiers do daily show such an aversion to the popish religion that there is the greatest probability imaginable of great numbers of deserters which could come from them should there be such an occasion; and amongst the seamen it is almost certain there is not one in ten who would do them any service in such a war.

But ... we must presume to inform your highness that your compliment upon the birth of the child (which not one in a thousand here believes to be the queen's) hath done you some injury; the false imposing of that upon the princess and the nation being ... an infinite exasperation of the people's minds here.

[22]   J. Dalrymple, *Memoirs of Great Britain and Ireland*, 2nd ed. (London, 1771), 2: 229.
[23]   *The Diary of John Evelyn*, ed. E. S. De Beer (Oxford, 1955), 4: 586.

8.15   *William's Declaration (October 24, 1688, n.s.)*[24]

William of Orange was well known in England as the major adversary of Louis XIV's continental ambitions. He was thus viewed as something of a Protestant champion. The rationale behind William's acceptance of the invitation is complex (see Bucholz and Key, chapter 9). But he realized that he needed to explain it to the English political nation, which was now used to debating such issues. (Indeed, his invasion fleet included a printing press; and this was the second of three versions of the Declaration.) Below, how does William justify his invasion? Was he above "dirty tricks"?

We [William] cannot any longer forbear to declare that, to our great regret, we see that those counselors who have now the chief credit with the king [James II] have overturned the religion, laws, and liberties of those realms and subjected them in all things relating to their consciences, liberties, and properties to arbitrary government. ...

Those evil counselors for the advancing and coloring this with some plausible pretexts did invent and set on foot the king's dispensing power, by virtue of which they pretend that, according to the law, he can suspend and dispense with the execution of the laws that have been enacted by the authority of the king and Parliament for the security and happiness of the subject and so have rendered those laws of no effect. ...

But, to crown all, there are great and violent presumptions inducing us to believe that those evil counselors ..., have published that the queen hath brought forth a son: though there have appeared, both during the queen's pretended bigness, and in the manner in which the birth was managed, so many just and visible grounds of suspicion, that not only we ourselves, but all the good subjects of these kingdoms, do vehemently suspect that the pretended prince of Wales was not born by the queen.

HISTORIANS' DEBATES

Was there a Restoration Crisis? Was it shaped by religion?

T. Harris, P. Seaward, and M. Goldie, eds., *The Politics of Religion in Restoration England* (Oxford, 1990), esp. essay by M. Goldie; M. Goldie, "Restoration Political Thought," and J. Spurr, "Religion in Restoration England," in *The*

---

[24]   *The Declaration Of His Highness William Henry, By the Grace of God Prince of Orange, &c. of the Reasons Inducing Him to Appear in Arms in the Kingdom of England for Preserving of the Protestant Religion, and for Restoring the Laws and Liberties of England, Scotland, and Ireland* (The Hague, [Oct. 24,] 1688, n.s.), 1, 3.

Reigns of Charles II and James VII & II, 1660–1689, ed. L. K. J. Glassey (Basingstoke, 1997); B. Till, "The Worcester House Declaration and the Restoration of the Church of England," *HR* 70 (1997); M. Goldie, "Priestcraft and the Birth of Whiggism," in *Political Discourse in Early Modern Britain*, ed. N. Phillipson and Q. Skinner (Cambridge, 1993); G. S. De Krey, "Reformation in the Restoration Crisis, 1679–1682," in *Religion, Literature, and Politics in Post-Reformation England, 1540–1688*, ed. D. B. Hamilton and R. Strier (Cambridge, 1996); J. A. I. Champion, "Religion after the Restoration" (review essay), *HJ* 36, 2 (1993); M. Goldie and J. Spurr, "Politics and the Restoration Parish: Edward Fowler and the Struggle for St Giles Cripplegate," *EHR* 109 (1994); J. Rose, "Royal Ecclesiastical Supremacy and the Restoration Church," *HR* 80, 209 (2007); W. Gibson, "The Limits of the Confessional State: Electoral Religion in the Reign of Charles II," *HJ* 51, 1 (2008).

Did politics from below or politics from above fuel the Restoration/Exclusion Crisis?

T. Harris, "Perceptions of the Crowd in later Stuart London," in *Imagining Early London: Perceptions and Portrayals of the City from Stow to Strype, 1598–1720*, ed. J. F. Merritt (Cambridge, 2001); *idem*, "The Parties and the People: the Press, the Crowd and Politics 'Out-of-doors' in Restoration England," in Glassey, *Reigns of Charles II and James VII*; *idem*, " 'Venerating the honesty of a tinker': the King's Friends and the Battle for the Allegiance of the Common People in Restoration England," in *The Politics of the Excluded, c. 1500–1850*, ed. Harris (Basingstoke, 2001); R. Hutton, *Debates in Stuart History* (Basingstoke, 2004), ch. on Charles II; J. Miller, "Politics in Restoration Britain," in *A Companion to Stuart Britain*, ed. B. Coward (Oxford, 2003); G. S. De Krey, "Radicals, Reformers and Republicans: Academic Language and Political Discourse in Restoration London," in *A Nation Transformed: England after the Restoration*, ed. A. Houston and S. C. A. Pincus (Cambridge, 2001); B. Worden, "Republicanism and the Restoration, 1660–1683," in *Republicanism, Liberty, and Commercial Society, 1649–1776*, ed. D. Wootton (Stanford, 1994); H. Nenner, ed., *Politics and the Political Imagination in Later Stuart Britain: Essays Presented to Lois Green Schwoerer* (Rochester, N. Y., 1998), esp. M. Goldie on the Hilton Gang; B. Weiser, "Access and Petitioning during the Reign of Charles II," in *The Stuart Courts*, ed. E. Cruickshanks, (Stroud, 2000); N. Key and J. Ward, " 'Divided into Parties': Exclusion Crisis Origins in Monmouth," *EHR* 115 (2000).

Can one locate the "public sphere" in the Popish Plot and Exclusion Crisis?

B. Cowan, "What Was Masculine about the Public Sphere?: Gender and the Coffeehouse Milieu in Post-Restoration England," *HWJ* 51 (2001); *idem*, "Publicity and Privacy in the History of the British Coffeehouse," *HC* 5, 4 (2007); L. E. Klein, "Coffeehouse Civility, 1660–1714: an Aspect of Post-Courtly Culture in England," *Huntington Library Quarterly* 59, 1 (1997); S. C. A. Pincus, " 'Coffee

Politicians Does Create': Coffeehouses and Restoration Political Culture," *JMH* 67 (1995); *idem*, "Shadwell's Dramatic Trimming," in Hamilton and Strier, *Religion, Literature, and Politics*; N. E. Key, " 'High Feeding and Smart Drinking': Associating Hedge-lane Lords in Exclusion Crisis London," in *Fear, Exclusion and Revolution: Roger Morrice and Britain in the 1680s*, ed. J. McElligott (Aldershot, 2006); H. Love, "The Look of News: Popish Plot Narratives 1678–1680," in *The Cambridge History of the Book in Britain*, 4, *1557–1695*, ed. J. Barnard and D. F. McKenzie (Cambridge, 2002); E. R. Clarke, "Re-reading the Exclusion Crisis," *Seventeenth Century* 21, 1 (2006).

Were the first parties ideological or organizational?

J. Scott, "England's Troubles, 1603–1702," in *The Stuart Court and Europe: Essays in Politics and Political Culture*, ed. R. M. Smuts (Cambridge, 1996); R. Weil, "The Family in the Exclusion Crisis: Locke Versus Filmer Revisited," in Houston and Pincus, *A Nation Transformed*; M. Knights, "London's 'Monster' Petition of 1680," *HJ* 36 (1993); *idem*, "London Petitions and Parliamentary Politics in 1679," *PH* 12 (1993); *idem*, "Petitioning and the Political Theorists: John Locke, Algernon Sidney and London's 'Monster' Petition of 1680," *P & P* 138 (1993); G. S. De Krey, "The London Whigs and the Exclusion Crisis," in *The First Modern Society: Essays in English History in Honour of Lawrence Stone*, ed. A. L. Beier and others (Cambridge, 1989); "Restoration Crisis," a special issue of *Albion* 25 (1993), articles and responses by R. Greaves, G. S. De Krey, T. Harris, J. Rosenheim, and J. Scott.

Should we revive the "potential for absolutism" thesis to explain the reign of James II?

J. Miller, "The Potential for 'Absolutism' in Later Stuart England," *History* 69 (1984); G. S. De Krey, "Reformation and 'Arbitrary Government': London Dissenters and James II's Polity of Toleration, 1687–1688," in McElligott, *Fear, Exclusion and Revolution*; D. Dixon, "Godden v Hales Revisited: James II and the Dispensing Power," *Journal of Legal History* 27, 2 (2006); W. Speck, *James II* (London, 2002), ch. on his reign; M. Knights, " 'Meer Religion' and the 'Church-State' of Restoration England: the Impact and Ideology of James II's Declarations of Indulgence," in Houston and Pincus, *A Nation Transformed*; A. R. Walkling, "Court Culture and 'Absolutism' in Restoration England," *Court Historian* 6, 3 (2001).

Was the Glorious Revolution conservative or radical?; Was it European, British, or English?

C. Brooks, "The Revolution of 1688–1689," in Coward, *Companion to Stuart Britain*; S. Pincus, "The Glorious Revolution," *HC* 1, 1 (2003); J. I. Israel, ed., *The Anglo-Dutch Moment: Essays on the Glorious Revolution and its World*

Impact (Cambridge, 1991), esp. essays by Israel, J. R. Jones, and J. Morrill; D. E. Hoak and M. Feingold, eds., *The World of William and Mary: Anglo-Dutch Perspectives on the Revolution of 1688–89* (Stanford, 1996), esp. intro. by Hoak and essay by H. Nenner; R. Beddard, ed., *The Revolutions of 1688* (Oxford, 1991), esp. editor's long essay; E. Cruickshanks, ed., *By Force or by Default?: The Revolution of 1688–1689* (Edinburgh, 1989), esp. T. Harris's "London Crowds and the Revolution of 1688"; L. G. Schwoerer, ed., *The Revolution of 1688–1689: Changing Perspectives* (Cambridge, 1992), esp. the editor's introduction and R. J. Weil on the warming-pan scandal; T. Harris, "Reluctant Revolutionaries?: The Scots and the Revolution of 1688–89," and M. Zook, "Violence, Martyrdom, and Radical Politics: Rethinking the Glorious Revolution," in Nenner, *Politics and the Political Imagination*; M. Knights, " 'Meer Religion' and the 'Church-State' of Restoration England: the Impact and Ideology of James II's Declarations of Indulgence," in Houston and Pincus, *A Nation Transformed*; T. Claydon, "William III's 'Declaration of Reasons' and the Glorious Revolution," *HJ* 39 (1996); O. Stanwood, "The Protestant Moment: Antipopery, the Revolution of 1688–1689, and the Making of an Anglo-American Empire," *JBS* 46, 3 (2007); W. Johnston, "Revelation and the Revolution of 1688–1689," *HJ* 48, 2 (2005); S. Pincus, "Whigs, Political Economy, and the Revolution of 1688–89," in *"Cultures of Whiggism": New Essays on English Literature and Culture in the Long Eighteenth Century*, ed. D. Womersley, P. Bullard, and A. Williams (Newark, N. J., 2005).

ADDITIONAL SOURCE COLLECTIONS

A. Browning, ed., *English Historical Documents, 1660–1714* (New York, 1953).

W. C. Costin and J. S. Watson, eds., *The Law and Working of the Constitution: Documents, 1660–1914, 1, 1660–1783*, 2nd ed. (London, 1961).

H. Gee and W. J. Hardy, eds., *Documents Illustrative of English Church History* (London, 1896).

J. P. Kenyon, *The Stuart Constitution: Documents and Commentary* (Cambridge, 1966).

J. Miller, *Restoration England: The Reign of Charles II*, 2nd ed. (London, 1985, 1997).

S. Pincus, *England's Glorious Revolution, 1688–1689: a Brief History with Documents* (New York, 2006).

S. E. Prall, *The Bloodless Revolution: England, 1688* (Madison, Wisc., 1985).

C. Stephenson and F. G. Marcham, eds., *Sources of English Constitutional History: A Selection of Documents*, rev. ed. (New York, 1972).

A. Stroud, *Stuart England* (London, 1999).

J. Thirsk, *The Restoration* (London, 1976).

J. Wroughton, *Seventeenth-Century Britain* (London, 1980).

CHAPTER NINE

Later Stuart Politics, Thought, and Society

England teetered between anarchy and settlement for nearly fifty years, from the Long Parliament, through the Civil Wars, regicide, Restoration, and Exclusion Crisis, culminating in the regime change of 1688–9. And then what? It depends on your viewpoint. Political, social and religious turmoil continued after the Glorious Revolution as the economy and cultural production witnessed a vast and vibrant expansion and different groups vied with each other to take advantage of it. But England would never again experience a violent revolution and some historians have seen this as the era that laid the foundations for a pluralistic and stable society. Examining the sources in this chapter, you might ask:

- How does the turmoil depicted below compare with that of the previous period? Was this society growing more or less stable?
- What fault lines remained most divisive in Later Stuart society? What ideas, if any, had the potential to lay the foundations for a common English – after the Union of 1707, a British – identity?

Revolution Settlements Debated

9.1 John Evelyn on the Revolution (January 15–29, 1689)[1]

What had happened in 1688 seemed to be clear: the political nation had resisted and overthrown a king who threatened their interpretation of the Constitution in Church and State – and their political and religious hegemony (see chapter 8, and Bucholz and Key, chapter 9). What should happen in 1689 to repair that Constitution was much less clear. A Convention was called for January. John Evelyn witnessed the ensuing drama, and recorded

[1] *The Diary of John Evelyn*, ed. E. S. De Beer (Oxford, 1955), 4: 613–4, 616, 619–20.

it in his *Diary*. A strong Anglican, he belonged to a vast social network which gave him intimate access to the power brokers as they did their work. When he interviewed some of the Convention's clerical and aristocratic members on the 15th he could find no consensus. In the event, the Lords passed the buck to the Commons. There, Hugh Boscawen (1625–1701) urged fellow MPs to issue a declaration of rights to limit the powers of the next ruler. The tough part was deciding who that ruler should be. The Commons opted for a convenient fiction that the old king had abdicated, and a Whig solution that the new one should be William of Orange. But the Tories were stronger in the Lords, where some, still devoted to passive obedience and hereditary monarchy, proposed that James remain king, the kingdom to be administered by a regent. Why might some find a regency attractive with James still on the throne? What were the objections to just giving the crown to William? Why might Mary seem a reasonable compromise in some eyes? Why would the bishops, some of whom had been imprisoned by James, desire his return? How do the positions taken in the Commons debate of February 5 (document 9.2) match those Evelyn notes for the Lords?

Jan. 15., 1689. I went to visit my lord, [William Sancroft] archbishop of Canterbury, where I found [several] bishops [and several secular lords....] Some would have the princess [Mary] made queen without any more dispute, others were for a regency. There was a Tory part (as then called so) who were for inviting his majesty [James II] again upon conditions; and there were republicarians, who would make the prince of Orange [William] like a state-holder [*stadholder*].

Jan. 23, 1689. I went to London. The great Convention being assembled the day before, falling upon the great question about the government, [the Commons] resolved that King James II, having by the advice of Jesuits and other wicked persons, endeavored to subvert the laws of Church and State, and deserting the Kingdom (carrying away the seals, etc.) without taking any care for the management of the government, had by demise, abdicated himself, and wholly vacated his right. And they did therefore desire the Lords' concurrence to their vote, to place the Crown upon the next heirs: the prince of Orange for his life, then to the princess his wife, and if she died without issue to the princess of Denmark [Anne], and she failing to the heirs of the prince, excluding for ever all possibility of admitting any Roman Catholic.

Jan. 29, 1689. I got a station by the prince's lodgings at the door of the lobby to the House, to hear much of the debate which held very long; the Lord Danby being in the chair ... after all had spoken, it coming to the question: it was carried out by 3 voices, against a regency, which 51 of [versus] 54 were for, alleging the danger of dethroning kings, and scrupling many passages and expressions of the Commons' votes.... Some were for sending to his majesty with conditions, others that the king could do no wrong, and that the maladministration was chargeable on his ministers. There were not above 8 or 9 bishops and but two against the regency [two bishops voted against the regency; in fact twelve supported the failed motion]. The archbishop was absent and the clergy now began anew to change their note, both in pulpit and discourse, upon their old passive obedience, so as people began to talk of the bishops being cast out of the House. In short, things tended to dissatisfaction on both sides; add to this the morose temper of the prince of Orange, who showed so little countenance to the noblemen and others, expecting a more gracious and cheerful reception, when they made their court. The English army likewise not so in order and firm to his interest, nor so weakened, but that it might, give interruption. Ireland in a very ill posture, as well as Scotland; nothing yet towards any settlement. God of his infinite mercy, compose these [things], that we may at last be a nation and a Church under some fixt and sober establishment.

9.2   The Commons debates the Lords' Amendments to the Declaration of Rights (February 5, 1689)[2]

On February 6, ironically the anniversary of James II's accession, representatives of the Lords and Commons met to hammer out the wording of the Declaration of Rights and the disposition of the crown. Debate first hinged on the Commons' assertion that James had "abdicated" the throne, which was, therefore, "vacant." Why did the Lords' want to strike these words? What are the implications of abdication and vacancy? Which MPs agreed with the Lords and why? Who disagreed and why? Can you detect Whig and Tory ideas in these positions?

Earl of Nottingham [who managed the Conference]: The Lords have desired this conference with the House of Commons. ... The House of Commons are a wise body, etc.; and I hope they will agree with the Lords in this great conjuncture of affairs.

Mr. Richard Hampden [1631–95, summarizing the Lords' position] ...: The Lords agree not to the word "abdicated"; they do not find it to be a word in our known law of England; therefore they would use such words as are understood according to the law, to avoid doubtful interpretation; the word "abdicate" being a civil law word, instead of "violated," "deserted," etc., which does express the consequence of withdrawing. To the second amendment, "and that the throne is thereby vacant": though the Lords have declared that the king has deserted the government, yet with no other inference, than that the exercise of government ceased; and the Lords would secure the nation against King James's

[2] A. Grey, ed., *Debates of the House of Commons, From the Year 1667 to the Year 1694* (London, 1763), 9: 53–60, 63–5.

return, and no such abdication; though King James II ceased to be king, yet there could be no vacancy in the throne, the monarchy being hereditary, and not elective. No act of the king can destroy the succession of his heirs, and such persons to whom of right the succession of the crown belongs.

Sir Thomas Clarges [ca. 1618–95]: These reasons of the Lords seem to me to be so cogent, that they deserve to be seriously weighed. I take the crown to be hereditary, and that King James has "abdicated" the crown, and the pretended prince of Wales being in the power of the French king, and the throne vacant, the crown ought to proceed to the next Protestant successor.

Serjeant John Maynard [1604–90]: …'Tis a sad thing, that the whole welfare of the nation must depend upon a word of a grammatical construction. …

[Debate] on the first amendment [substituting] "deserted" for "abdicated," etc. …

Sir Joseph Tredenham [ca. 1643–1707]: … I thank God, we have a Protestant heir to the crown. Of the prince of Wales [James II's son] I shall say the less, because much has been said by Clarges; and 'tis the opinion of the House, that there is a legal incapacity, as well as a natural. In the princess of Orange [Mary] there is no incapacity; she is a Protestant; and as for her being a woman, Queen Elizabeth was so, and reigned gloriously. I would be grateful to the prince of Orange, for the great things he has done for the nation; but is this the way, to erect a throne to the ruin of his princess? … If the government [the strict order of succession] be subverted, the whole mob may have some more right than we. … When you eradicate the succession, all the crowns in Christendom will concern themselves. It will make such an earthquake, that all the Protestants in the world will fare the worse for it. … There is no other way to have peace and quiet, but by recognizing the princess, who has no legal nor natural impediment. …

Col. John Birch [1615–91]: … I am glad gentlemen have spoken so plainly of the succession of this noble lady, and to have it there settled. … [You] say, gentlemen, "This is a sacred succession, and must not be altered.". … But I hold, that … the Lords and Commons cannot do an unjust thing. We have taken from one brother to give to another, and it has not been questioned to [until] this hour. The Lords have not agreed the throne to be vacant; and, if so, where is the government? Had you spoken plain English t'other day, that the disposal of the crown was in the Lords and Commons, there had been no room for this debate; and you, by that authority …, might have talked of the succession. … God has brought us from Popery and tyranny; and, at this rate, nothing will content us but to go into it again. You have [Catholic] heirs in Spain, in Savoy, and all up and down, and where more I know not; and poor England, for want of speaking one plain word, will be ruined, you and your posterity. Say but where your power is, and the debate is at an end. There may be claims to the crown, but their claims will signify nothing; for the Lords and Commons have other thoughts. … I will conclude, that the power of disposing of the crown is in the Lords and Commons; and by virtue of that power fill the vacancy. And I would not agree with the Lords in leaving out "The throne is vacant.". …

Mr. Henry Pollexfen [ca. 1632–91]: If this discourse had been made sooner, perhaps we had been much forwarder. ... But lest what has been said should make impression, I shall answer, first, 'tis pretended that this vote does make ours an elective kingdom. All men love their monarchy, and if you make men believe that it is elective, you will catch [offend] a great many. ... I have as much inclination to the princess of Orange as anybody, but you do not really mind the good of your country, and the Protestant religion. If she be now proclaimed queen, can anything be more desirable than that her husband be joined with her in the government? – Now, if you settle the crown on her, and we are to secure a title we cannot make, if any transient issue should arise, she is gone, and he [William] will be in war with her father [James] to defend her title – And does any think the prince of Orange will come in to be a subject to his own wife in England? This is not possible, nor ought to be in nature. ...

Mr. William Williams [ca. 1634–1700]: I take this question to be for the unity of the Lords and Commons in this great conjuncture. Let the power be where it will, I speak for all England. All agree, that the late King James II has departed from the throne, and that his reign over us ceases. If the Lords are of opinion that the reign of King James is ceased, we are all agreed. The Lords say, he shall never return again; they are not for his returning again to his government. I am not for the monarchy of a child; I am not for one to subvert the laws of the government. If this may be done by the Lords and the Commons, I would agree.

(The question being put, That this House do agree with the Lords in the second amendment, it passed in the negative [failed], 282 to 151. A free conference [with the Lords] was desired.)

9.3   The Bill of Rights (presented to William and Mary, February 13, 1689; enacted as statute, 1 Will. and Mary, sess. 2, c. 2, December 16, 1689)[3]

Eventually the Commons and the Lords worked out their differences and presented the Declaration of Rights to William and Mary (who reigned jointly 1689–94; then from Mary's death in 1694 William reigned alone to 1702) at their proclamation ceremony in February. It was later enacted as An Act for Declaring the Rights and Liberties of the Subject and Settling the Succession of the Crown. How does it justify the Revolution? What does it accuse James of doing? Is it an accurate account of James's reign? How does it limit the power of future monarchs? Are the rights articulated below "ancient" or new? How does this compare with the American Bill of Rights of a century later? Is this a contract? Is this constitutional monarchy?

[3]   *SR*, 6: 142–4.

I Whereas the late King James the Second, by the assistance of diverse evil counselors, judges, and ministers employed by him, did endeavor to subvert and extirpate the Protestant religion and the laws and liberties of this kingdom:

1. By assuming and exercising a power of dispensing with and suspending of laws and the execution of laws without consent of Parliament.
2. By committing and prosecuting diverse worthy prelates for humbly petitioning to be excused from concurring to the said assumed power [see document 8.13, above].
3. By issuing and causing to be executed a commission under the great seal for erecting a court called the Court of Commissioners for Ecclesiastical Causes.
4. By levying money for and to the use of the Crown by pretence of prerogative for other time and in other manner than the same was granted by Parliament.
5. By raising and keeping a standing army within this kingdom in time of peace without consent of Parliament, and quartering soldiers contrary to law.
6. By causing several good subjects being Protestants to be disarmed at the same time when Papists were both armed and employed contrary to law.
7. By violating the freedom of election of members to serve in Parliament.
8. By prosecutions in the Court of King's Bench for matters and causes [re] cognizable only in Parliament, and by diverse other arbitrary and illegal courses.
9. And whereas of late years partial corrupt and unqualified persons have been returned and served on juries in trials, and particularly diverse jurors in trials for high treason which were not freeholders.
10. And excessive bail hath been required of persons committed in criminal cases to elude the benefit of the laws made for the liberty of the subjects.
11. And excessive fines have been imposed; and illegal and cruel punishments inflicted.
12. And several grants and promises made of fines and forfeitures before any conviction or judgment against the persons upon whom the same were to be levied.

All which are utterly and directly contrary to the known laws and statutes and freedom of this realm.

And whereas the said late King James the Second having abdicated the government and the throne being thereby vacant, his highness the prince of Orange (whom it hath pleased almighty God to make the glorious instrument of delivering this kingdom from Popery and arbitrary power) did (by the advice of the Lords spiritual and temporal and diverse principal persons of the Commons) cause letters to be written to the Lords spiritual and temporal being Protestants, and other letters to the several counties, cities, universities, boroughs, and cinque ports, for the choosing of such persons to represent them as were of right to be sent to Parliament, to meet and sit at Westminster upon

January 22 [1689], in order to such an establishment as that their religion, laws, and liberties might not again be in danger of being subverted, upon which letters elections having been accordingly made.

And thereupon the said Lords spiritual and temporal and Commons, pursuant to their respective letters and elections, being now assembled in a full and free representative of this nation, taking into their most serious consideration the best means for attaining the ends aforesaid, do in the first place (as their ancestors in like case have usually done) for the vindicating and asserting their ancient rights and liberties declare:

1. That the pretended power of suspending the laws or the execution of laws by regal authority without consent of Parliament is illegal.
2. That the pretended power of dispensing with laws or the execution of laws by regal authority, as it hath been assumed and exercised of late, is illegal.
3. That the commission for erecting the late Court of Commissioners for Ecclesiastical Causes, and all other commissions and courts of like nature, are illegal and pernicious.
4. That levying money for or to the use of the Crown by pretense of preroga-tive, without grant of Parliament, for longer time, or in other manner than the same is or shall be granted, is illegal.
5. That it is the right of the subjects to petition the king, and all commitments and prosecutions for such petitioning are illegal.
6. That the raising or keeping a standing army within the kingdom in time of peace, unless it be with consent of Parliament, is against law.
7. That the subjects which are Protestants may have arms for their defense suitable to their conditions and as allowed by law.
8. That election of members of Parliament ought to be free.
9. That the freedom of speech and debates or proceedings in Parliament ought not to be impeached or questioned in any court or place out of Parliament.
10. That excessive bail ought not to be required, nor excessive fines imposed, nor cruel and unusual punishments inflicted.
11. That jurors ought to be duly impaneled and returned, and jurors which pass upon men in trials for high treason ought to be freeholders.
12. That all grants and promises of fines and forfeitures of particular persons before conviction are illegal and void.
13. And that for redress of all grievances, and for the amending, strengthening and preserving of the laws, Parliaments ought to be held frequently.

And they do claim, demand, and insist upon all and singular the premises as their undoubted rights and liberties ...; to which demand of their rights they are particularly encouraged by the declaration of his highness the prince of Orange [October 10 and 24, 1688, n.s., see document 8.1, above] as being the only means for obtaining a full redress and remedy therein. Having therefore an entire confidence that his said highness the prince of Orange will perfect the deliverance so far advanced by him, and will still preserve them from the

violation of their rights which they have here asserted, and from all other
attempts upon their religion, rights, and liberties.

II. The said Lords spiritual and temporal and Commons assembled at
Westminster do resolve that William and Mary, prince and princess of
Orange, be and be declared king and queen of England, France, and
Ireland and the dominions thereunto belonging, to hold the crown and
royal dignity of the said kingdoms and dominions to them, the said prince
and princess, during their lives and the life of the survivor to them, and
that the sole and full exercise of the regal power be only in and executed
by the said prince of Orange in the names of the said prince and princess
during their joint lives, and after their deceases the said crown and royal
dignity of the same kingdoms and dominions to be to the heirs of the body
of the said princess, and for default of such issue to the Princess Anne of
Denmark and the heirs of her body, and for default of such issue to the
heirs of the body of the said prince of Orange. And the Lords spiritual and
temporal and Commons do pray the said prince and princess to accept the
same accordingly.

III. And that the oaths hereafter mentioned be taken by all persons of
whom the oaths of allegiance and supremacy might be required by law,
instead of them; and that the said oaths of allegiance and supremacy be
abrogated.

"I, A.B., do sincerely promise and swear that I will be faithful and bear true
allegiance to their majesties King William and Queen Mary. So help me God."

"I, A.B., do swear that I do from my heart abhor, detest, and abjure as
impious and heretical this damnable doctrine and position, that princes excommunicated or deprived by the pope ... may be deposed or murdered by their
subjects or any other whatsoever. And I do declare that no foreign prince,
person, prelate, state, or potentate hath or ought to have any jurisdiction, power,
superiority, pre-eminence or authority, ecclesiastical or spiritual, within this
realm. So help me God."

IV. Upon which their said majesties did accept the crown and royal dignity of
the kingdoms of England, France, and Ireland, and the dominions thereunto belonging, according to the resolution and desire of the said Lords and
Commons contained in the said declaration. ...

IX. And whereas it hath been found by experience that it is inconsistent with the
safety and welfare of this Protestant kingdom to be governed by a popish
prince, or by any king or queen marrying a Papist, the said Lords spiritual
and temporal and Commons do further pray that it may be enacted, that all
and every person and persons that is, are or shall be reconciled to or shall
hold communion with the see or Church of Rome, or shall profess the
popish religion, or shall marry a Papist, shall be excluded and be for ever
incapable to inherit, possess or enjoy the crown and government of this
realm and Ireland and the dominions thereunto belonging.

9.4   The Toleration Act (An Act for Exempting their Majesties' Protestant Subjects, Dissenting from the Church of England, from the Penalties of Certain Laws) (1 Will. & Mary, c. 18, 1689)[4]

Like the Restoration Settlement (see chapter 8), the Revolution Settlement included a series of Acts which shaped the country's constitutional, religious, and fiscal arrangements for years to come. While the Bill of Rights was the lynchpin of the Settlement, Parliament, in partial reward to those Dissenters who had not embraced James's Declaration of Indulgence and who (as London goldsmiths) had bankrolled the early part of the Revolution, also passed what has become known as the Toleration Act. What does the original title of the Toleration Act suggest about its intent? Who and what did it tolerate? What did it not tolerate? Parliament followed this with An Act that the Solemn Affirmation and Declaration of the People called Quakers shall be Accepted instead of an Oath in the Usual Form (7 & 8 Will. III, c. 34, 1696). How close was the religious settlement in these Acts to James II's desire to remove the Penal Laws and Test Acts?

I. Forasmuch as some ease to scrupulous consciences in the exercise of religion may be an effectual means to unite their majesties' Protestant subjects in interest and affection:

II. Be it enacted ... that neither the statute ... entitled, "An Act to Retain the Queen's Majesty's Subjects in Their Due Obedience" [1581]; nor the statute ... entitled, "An Act for the More Speedy and Due Execution of Certain Branches of the Statute" [1587] ...; nor that branch or clause of a statute ... entitled, "An Act for the Uniformity of Common Prayer and Service in the Church" [1559] ..., whereby all persons ..., are required to resort to their parish church or chapel, or some usual place where the common prayer shall be used ..., upon pain that every person so offending shall forfeit for every such offence twelve pence; nor ... any other law or statute of this realm, made against Papists or popish recusants, except the statute ... entitled, "An Act for Preventing Dangers Which May Happen from Popish Recusants" [1673]; and except also the statute ... entitled, "An Act for the More Effectual Preserving the King's Person and Government by Disabling Papists from Sitting in Either House of Parliament" [1661]; shall be construed to extend to any person or persons dissenting from the Church of England, that shall take the oaths mentioned in a statute made this present Parliament, entitled "An Act for Removing and Preventing All Questions and Disputes concerning the Assembling and Sitting of this Present Parliament" [1 Will. & Mary, c. 1],

[4]   *SR*, 6: 74–6.

and [that] shall make and subscribe the declaration mentioned in a statute made in [30] King Charles II [1678, Test Act, see chapter 8] ..., which oaths and declaration the justices of peace at the general sessions of the peace ... are hereby required to tender and administer to such persons as shall offer themselves to take. ...

IV. Provided always ... that if any assembly of persons dissenting from the church of England shall be had in any place for religious worship with the doors locked, barred, or bolted during any time of such meeting together, all and every person or persons, that shall come to and be at such meeting, shall not receive any benefit from this law, but be liable to all the pains and penalties of all the aforesaid laws recited. ...

Provided always, that nothing herein contained shall ... exempt any of the persons aforesaid from paying of tithes or other parochial duties. ...

X. And whereas there are certain other persons, dissenters from the Church of England, who scruple the taking of any oath, be it enacted ... that every such person shall make and subscribe the aforesaid declaration, and also this declaration of fidelity following, *viz.*:

"I, A.B., do sincerely promise and solemnly declare before God and the world, that I will be true and faithful to King William and Queen Mary; and I do solemnly profess and declare, that I do from my heart abhor, detest, and renounce, as impious and heretical, that damnable doctrine and position, 'that princes excommunicated or deprived by the pope ..., may be deposed or murdered by their subjects, [etc.]' ... [as that contained in the Bill of Rights, document 9.3]." ...

XIII. Provided always, and it is the true intent and meaning of this Act, that all the laws made and provided for the frequenting of divine service on the Lord's day, commonly called Sunday, shall be still in force. ...

XIV. Provided always ... that neither this Act, nor any clause, article, or thing herein contained, shall extend ... to give any ease, benefit, or advantage to any Papist ..., or any person that shall deny, in his preaching or writing, the doctrine of the blessed Trinity.

9.5   The Act of Settlement (12 & 13 Will., c. 2, 1701)[5]

The Act of Settlement dealt with the very practical problem, evident at the end of William's reign, that neither he nor his successor, Princess Anne (reigned as queen, 1702–14), would produce any children that could inherit the throne. Worse, James II had just died and Louis XIV had recognized his

---

[5]   SR, 7: 636–7.

son as "James III," that is, as the rightful English monarch (James VIII in Scotland). How did the Act "settle" the succession while barring James II's son and other Catholics in line for the throne (those "in Spain, in Savoy ... and where I know not," noted by Col. Birch, document 9.2)? The Act of Settlement revisited the problems of sovereignty debated in 1689. What did it suggest about the constitutional role of Parliament? What were the reasons for clauses II and III? How were they a comment on William's reign so far (see Bucholz and Key, chapter 10)?

It having ... pleased Almighty God to take away our ... sovereign lady [Mary], and also the most hopeful Prince William, duke of Gloucester [1689–1700] (the only surviving issue of her royal highness the Princess Anne of Denmark) to the unspeakable grief and sorrow of your majesty and your said good subjects ...; and it being absolutely necessary for the safety, peace, and quiet of this realm, to obviate all doubts and contentions in the [succession] ...: therefore for a further provision of the succession of the Crown in the Protestant line, we your majesty's most dutiful and loyal subjects, the Lords spiritual and temporal and Commons in this present Parliament assembled, do beseech your majesty that it may be enacted and declared, and be it enacted and declared ..., that the most excellent Princess Sophia, electress and duchess dowager of Hanover, daughter of the most excellent Princess Elizabeth, late queen of Bohemia, daughter of our late sovereign lord King James the First of happy memory, be and is hereby declared to be the next in succession in the Protestant line to the imperial Crown and dignity of the said realms of England, France, and Ireland, with the dominions and territories thereunto belonging, after his majesty, and the Princess Anne of Denmark, and in default of issue of the said Princess Anne, and of his majesty respectively....

II. Provided always, and be it hereby enacted, that all and every person and persons, who shall or may take or inherit the said Crown, by virtue of the limitation of this present Act, and is, are or shall be reconciled to, or shall hold communion with, the See or Church of Rome, or shall profess the popish religion, or shall marry a Papist, shall be subject to such incapacities, as in such case or cases are by the said recited act provided, enacted, and established....

III. And whereas it is requisite and necessary that some further provision be made for securing our religion, laws, and liberties ...; that whosoever shall hereafter come to the possession of this Crown, shall join in communion with the Church of England, as by law established;

That in case the Crown and imperial dignity of this realm shall hereafter come to any person, not being a native of this kingdom of England, this nation be not obliged to engage in any war for the defense of any dominions or territories which do not belong to the Crown of England, without the consent of Parliament;

That no person who shall hereafter come to the possession of this Crown, shall go out of the dominions of England, Scotland, or Ireland, without the consent of Parliament....

That ... no person born out of the kingdoms of England, Scotland, or Ireland or the dominions thereunto belonging (although he be naturalized or made a denizen, except such as are born of English parents), shall be capable to be of the Privy Council, or a member of either house of Parliament, or to enjoy any office or place of trust either civil or military, or to have any grant of lands, tenements, or hereditaments from the Crown....

That no person who has an office or place of profit under the king, or receives a pension from the crown, shall be capable of serving as a member of the House of Commons.

9.6 Earl of Balcarres, "A Brief Account of the State of Scotland, &c." (written ca. 1689, pub. 1714)[6]

Like the Revolution of the 1640s (see chapter 7), the Glorious Revolution had its counterpart in Scotland, Ireland, and even the colonies. The Scottish Revolution of 1688–9 began on Christmas Day 1688 with violence against incumbent Anglican clergy led by covenanting Presbyterians in southwest Scotland. This was revenge for the virtual proscription of Scots Presbyterianism at the Restoration in 1660, and for subsequent persecution (see Bucholz and Key, chapter 10). There followed a Scottish Convention Parliament which settled the Crown as had been done in England. The Jacobite Colin Lindsay, earl of Balcarres (1652–1723) related the proceedings of the Scottish Convention in a letter to the exiled James II. Why would the question of whether James had abdicated be different in Scotland than in England? Why might the Scottish response be more unanimous than that in England? After settling the Crown, the Scottish Convention turned to the religious settlement, confirming previous anti-Catholic legislation, and re-establishing Presbyterianism in 1690, "that is to say, the government of the Church by kirk sessions, presbyteries, provincial synods, and general assemblies."[7] Compare the Scottish and English revolutionary religious settlements. Which was more tolerant?

A few days after the committee prepared all that was intended in the [Scottish] Convention but found great difficulty how to declare the Crown vacant. Some were for abdication, as had been done in England; but that could not pass among the most violent of them, for it could not be imagined that your Majesty [James II, James VII in Scotland] had left [abdicated] Scotland. Others were for

---

[6] *An Account of the Affairs of Scotland, Relating to the Revolution in 1688. As sent to the Late King James II. when in France* (London, 1714), 82–4.
[7] *The Acts of the Parliaments of Scotland* (London, 1822), 9: 133–4.

making use of an old obsolete word, "forefaulting," [a feudal term, often translated as forfeiting, but signaling a more absolute alienation of rights extending to kin] used for a bird's forsaking her nest; but Sir John Dalrymple ended the debate, by [giving] such reasons against both that they agreed to his new proposal, which was that your Majesty, by committing such acts as he named, forfeited your right to the Crown, making this childish distinction, that they intended not to forfeit you as a traitor, but only declare you forfeited, which would make the affair clear and take off any pretensions [remove any right] the prince of Wales might afterwards have.

This immediately was taken and voted the next day by all present except five.... After the crown was declared vacant, the duke of Hamilton proposed filling it again ..., that the humble offer [of the crown] should be made to the prince and princess of Orange.

This [vote] was more unanimously [passed] than the other declaring the throne vacant.... Next they voted ... to carry up [to London] their offer, with their grievances and claim of Right, which were the conditions pretended as giving him [William] the Crown.

9.7   George Holmes at Strabane to William Fleming on the Siege of Londonderry (November 16, 1689)[8]

Following King James's invasion of Ireland in the spring of 1689, Irish Protestants faced not only a Jacobite Parliament in Dublin, but also a Jacobite army. Protestants in the northern towns of Londonderry and Enniskillen held out against James II. Compare the violence and bitterness of their resistance to the relative bloodlessness of England's revolution in 1688 (see chapter 8). Why might Ulster Protestants, who styled themselves Orangemen, remember the siege and its relief by William (of Orange) for hundreds of years after 1689? What did these events mean to them at the time? Why do they frame Irish history to this very day?

I was one of the first (that did wear a red coat [that is, that served in the army]) that revolted from King James and helped to set up a flag of defiance against him and Popery in the city of Londonderry, that now lies in a ruinous condition, yet defies all the king and queen's [William and Mary's] enemies.

After some little routs in the country, on April [12] last the Irish army appeared before our city, but at that distance that one of our cannons had enough to do to reach them; but in short time they approached nearer to our walls. In the first place we burned all our suburbs and hewed down all our brave orchards, making all about us as plain as a bowling-green. About the 18th

---

[8]   HMC, *Twelfth Report, Appendix VII, The Manuscripts of S. H. Le Fleming, Esq., of Rydal Hall* (London, 1890), 264–5.

of April King James came within a mile of our walls, but had no better entertainment than bullets of 14, 16, and 22 pounds weight. He sent us a letter under his own hand, sealed with his own seal, to desire us to surrender, and we should have our own conditions. ... In short, we would not yield.

Then we proceeded and chose captains and completed regiments, made two governors. We had 116 companies in the city. All our officers fled away, so we made officers of those that did deserve to be officers. I was made captain. And then we began to sally out, and the first sally that we made we slew their French general and several of their men, with the loss of nine or ten of our men, which was the greatest loss that ever we lost in the field. Every day afterward we sallied out and daily killed our enemies, which put us in great heart. But it being so soon of the year, and we having no forage for our horses, we was forced to let them out, and the enemy got many. The rest of them died for hunger. ...

But at last our provision grew scant and our allowance small. One pound of oatmeal and one pound of tallow served a man a week; sometimes salt hides. ... I saw 2s. a quarter given for a little dog, horse blood at 4d. per pint; all the starch was eaten, the graves of tallow, horse flesh was a rarity, and still we resolved to hold out. ...

After the ships came in with provision to us our enemies thought it was in vain to stay any longer, so on Lammas day [August 1] they left us the wide fields to walk in. In the siege we had not above 60 men killed, except with the bombs killed. But I believe there died 15,000 men, women, and children, many of which died for meat [solid food]. But we had a great fever amongst us, and all the children died, almost whole families not one left alive.

9.8–9.9   *Defending and attacking the Revolution Settlements*

The Revolution Settlements in Church and State provoked debate high and low. One reason that emotions ran so high was that those settlements precipitated the Nine Years' War with France. In the midst of a French invasion scare, the clergyman William Sherlock (1639/40–1707) defended the Williamite Revolution, and warned about what a French victory would mean (document 9.8). He particularly addresses the case of non-jurors: clergymen who would not take the oaths to William and Mary because they felt themselves bound by their previous, non-resisting, oaths to James. Some took their loyalty to the old king further: lawyer and conspirator Sir William Parkyns (1649–96) explains very simply his Jacobite allegiance, at his execution for engaging in the Assassination Plot of 1696 against William (document 9.9). Compare and contrast these two statements: which appeals to practicality? Which to duty? How can each assert loyalty to the law and constitution of England? Who has the more compelling case? Where would you stand in the 1690s regarding the succession to the crown and why?

9.8   William Sherlock, Letter to a Friend, Concerning a French Invasion,
To Restore the Late King James to his Throne *(1692)*[9]

He [James] wanted [lacked] nothing but power to make himself absolute, and to
make us all Papists, or martyrs, or refugees; and that he will now have. For if a
French power can conquer us, it will make him ..., though not an absolute prince,
yet an absolute viceroy and minister of France. He will administer an absolute
power and government under the influence and direction of French councils: and
then we know what will become of the liberties and religion of England. And
have we so long disdained the thoughts of subjection to France ...? Have we so
detested the French cruelties to Protestants? And shall we now so willingly stoop
to the yoke, and think it a great favor that they will vouchsafe to conquer us ...?
And, whatever some fancy, they will find it a very easy and natural thing for the
late king, if he return by force and power, to make himself absolute by law:
princes always gain new powers by the ineffectual opposition of subjects. If they
lose their crowns and recover them again, they receive them with an addition of
some brighter jewels, and turn disputed prerogatives into legal and undoubted
rights. Thus we know it was when King Charles II returned from a long exile, all
the new acts and declarations were made in favor of the crown, and subjects
bound to their good behavior as fast as laws could bind them. For, in all such
revolutions, those who suffered with or for their prince return with zeal and
resentment, and take care, in the first place, to establish all such prerogatives of
the Crown as were disputed before, and to grant such new powers as they think
are wanting....

Let me then ask them [non-jurors] another question: whether they would
think themselves bound in conscience to fight for him, did they verily believe,
that if he recovered his throne, he would as zealously promote popery and
arbitrary power, as he did before ...? This, I hope, may satisfy the non-swearers
[non-jurors], if they will coolly and seriously consider it, that they are not bound
in conscience to fight for the late king.

9.9   "Sir William Perkins's Paper" delivered at his execution for the
Assassination Plot against William III (March 24, 1696)[10]

I freely acknowledge, and think it for my honor to say, that I was entirely in the
interest of the king [James II], being always firmly persuaded of the justice of his
cause, and looked upon it as my duty, both as a subject and an Englishman, to
assist him in the recovery of his throne, which I believed him to be deprived of,
contrary to all right and justice; taking the laws and constitutions of my country
for my guide.

[9]   [W. Sherlock], *A Letter to a Friend* (London, 1692), 9, 14.
[10]   *An Exact Abridgment Of all the Tryals, Not omitting any Material Passage therein, relating to
High Treasons, Piracies, &c. in the Reigns of the late King William the III ... and of ... Queen Anne*
(London, 1703), 110–1.

As for religion, I die in the communion of the Church of England, in which I was educated.

9.10   Attacks on a Ludlow Dissenter Meeting House (November 1693)[11]

The intersection of religion and politics yielded both debate (above) and action. In theory the Toleration Act (document 9.4) allowed Nonconformists to worship without fear of prosecution, but provincial communities did not always abide by Westminster's dictates. In the assault on a Presbyterian meeting house in Ludlow related below, why did the mob attack not only a meeting house, but also tavern signs, particularly that of "The King's Arms"? Can you characterize the religious and political affiliation of those attacking the meeting house; of the author of the report; of the local authorities? What does their inaction say about the problem of local control? In what way might this attack be seen as a referendum on the recent religious settlement; on the constitutional settlement? Can mobs have ideological agendas?

The house in Ludlow ..., [Shropshire] commonly known by the sign of the Bull was certified [by] Dr. Gilbert Ironside, bishop of Hereford, as a place intended for religious worship....

On Saturday ... November [11] the said license ... was ... shown and delivered to the bailiff of Ludlow ...; and at same time acquainted them [the bailiffs] that according to the liberty granted to their majesties' Protestant subjects by an act of parliament entitled An Act for Exempting Their Majesties' Protestant Subjects Dissenting from the Church of England from the Penalty of Certain Laws [document 9.4], there would be a meeting for religious worship.... They were desired ... that effectual care might be taken for preserving the peace, suppressing any tumult, or insurrection, that might happen.... The high bailiff promised fair but the low bailiff did not.... On the Lords' day ... a meeting for religious worship was held ... by persons of the Presbyterian persuasion; and ... the place was well filled. But then some disturbance arose by breaking of the glass window on the south part from the ... garden of a person of account in the town.... Soon after a solemn signal is made ... by ringing the bells of the parish church backward and crying out "Fire, fire!," which caused a very great uproar in the town. All were directed to The Bull ... by which means vast numbers of idle and ill-affected people were gathered together, whereupon a fierce assault began in showers of stones, bats, etc., for breaking the windows.... The rioters [were] headed ... by ... John Vere an exciseman [a tax collector] ..., [who] for the greater encouragement ... ma[de] use of the power of his office and their majesties' name for the cloaking his rebellion.... By the time they had satiated

---

[11]   Nottingham RO, DD4P 72/115.

their zeal by breaking and destroying all they could come at, the minister had finished.... One of those zealots came into the meeting and cast a stone ... at the minister, but the Lord suffered not his arm to perform his design. The person being suspected and searched was found to have another in his hand for the same purpose which he was persuaded to part with, and so with shame departed.

The meeting being over, the people peaceably repairing home were ... assaulted in the streets.... A gentleman of the neighborhood who hath eminently evidenced his zeal for, and firm adherence to, the present government as well by his early hazardous and chargeable appearance on their majesties' behalf [that is, in 1688] ..., had his coach standing at the door assaulted [with] dirt, etc., thrown at it and into it, and ... his servants and attendants that followed the coach for its preservation were struck, beaten, and abused.... In the beginning of the tumult inquiry was made for the bailiffs but they were found to have withdrawn themselves out of town ... to a small alehouse to pass the Sabbath in....

It was thought fit on Saturday the 18th November that some persons should attend the bailiffs to let them know the meeting was designed to be continued the next day and how that through their absence from the town the last Lords' day a great insurrection had happened.... Accordingly a meeting was had with the high bailiff ..., but after the low bailiff his son-in-law came in ..., he seemed to retract or qualify his former promise; and the low one ... burst forth in a warm, threatening way wishing it ended not in blood, and that what happened to them [the Presbyterians] was their own fault, unhandsomely inveighing against them as the causes of the riot and insurrection, and they might thank themselves if any further mischief befell them.... And it being somewhat warmly urged by a tradesman of the town present that it was his right and liberty confirmed by Parliament ..., he [the under-bailiff] could not bridle himself from saying with a great deal of concern, "Mr. J__s that doctrine won't down in this town," meaning ... Ludlow and that liberty for religious worship allowed by act of parliament ...; that he was not bound to attend and would not be instructed in his duty ...; and all that could be got from them was they intended not to be out of town, whereby those present readily judged the issue would not be peaceable, however having the protection of the laws it was resolved to continue the meeting next day.

Accordingly the place being prepared and beginning to fill with persons drawing thither to hear the Gospel of peace; the minister no sooner got thither but immediately a solemn signal was given by the market bell, and then the alarm was sounded from the parish church as before ..., and the storm began ... led on by the servant of the parson of the parish who appeared as captain general for that day. And the sons of violence and blood gathering together from all parts of the town ... (flushed with drink and money for the work of the day by one who should by virtue of his profession [have] been a promoter of peace and not of tumults insurrections and villains) flocked apace.... It was concluded to adjourn the meeting till there should appear some real authority in the town....

Finding they had missed their prey they became like the ravening wolves of the evening and detaching themselves into several parties ravaged through the whole town where any prey might be found wreaking themselves on any they met, that seemed strangers or supposed to have come to, or had kindness for, the meeting, not sparing women and maidens. ... [One Presbyterian] being alone and peaceably repairing homewards was fiercely set upon by one of the detachments of about a hundred or more and endeavoring to outgo them was followed so closely and furiously, and received so many blows with stones, bats, staves, and clubs and coming so thick on him that he was not likely to support himself anytime resolving rather to die with his face towards them turned upon them and advancing in some rage with an oaken plank in his hand ... that gave him opportunity of withdrawing and securing himself, by which it's seen as the persecuting rabble of Ludlow are cruel so also very cowardly.

After all persons were gone the rage and violence of these dragooners ceased not, but ... broke every window in the house towards the street (the rest being broke before) ..., damaging the rooms and goods therein by the largeness of the stones, bats, etc. ... Having fully perfected that work they fell to further fury ... pulling down the house and ... breaking down the doors ..., and after that, to the destroying the sign post. ... The sign post being down the signs were broken to pieces every one scrambling for a part ..., there being two signs one "The Bull" belonging to the house the other "The King's Arms" at which the people formerly lived, and against which some it's thought had the greatest spite. They yielded many pieces, which were carried away ..., as a trophy of their achievements. ...

Though the bailiffs were ... present this [day] in the town, yet it was observed that the rage and impudence of the dragooning rabble was far greater, and threatened much more bloody work this day than before. ...

The parson of the parish having been absent the former Sabbath day was present this, who always declared himself a most bitter cruel enemy to ... all good people as well as against the present government. 'Tis the same person that upon the __ [6th of?] February 1689 told his congregations from the pulpit he was not come to celebrate the remembrance of an abdicated king, but of King James their rightful legal undeposable prince, and the next day when he should have given thanks for our deliverance from Popery, slavery, and tyranny he appeared not, and forbear to take the oath, till the fear of loss of his place which is the king's gift or the hopes of doing more good to the Jacobite interest thereby obliged him, and it was a longer season ere he prayed for their majesties, and he doth it seldom not and but faintly and for which he was presented by the grand jury at sessions. It's the same person that said he had rather a plague should come to town than a [Dissenter] meeting, nor was he wanting this day to signalize his zeal against the interest of Christ and laws of the land to advance the work he made a sorry sermon on purpose, as all people judge that heard it thereby sounding a trumpet from the pulpit from him and by his directions the alarm was given by ringing the bells by his encouragement. His servant furiously acted as captain general for the great red dragon [the mob].

The Rage of Party

9.11   *Anne to Lord Treasurer Godolphin (August 30, 1706)*[12]

At William III's death in 1702 he was succeeded by his sister-in-law, Anne (reigned to 1714), who would prove to be the last Stuart to rule England, Scotland, and Ireland. Anne has been portrayed as weak and malleable in the hands of favorites like Sarah, duchess of Marlborough (1660–1744), but she has also been shown to have fought hard, like William before her, to maintain her royal prerogative and freedom of maneuver. Such freedom was difficult, however, for both monarchs were dependant upon parliamentary funding to fight the Nine Years War (1688–97) and the War of the Spanish Succession (1702–13), respectively, and Parliament was dominated by whichever party held a majority of seats. While William and Anne wanted to appoint ministries made up of the best men of both parties, Whig and Tory leaders anticipated the modern parliamentary system by demanding a "winner-take-all" arrangement in which the majority party would fill all the offices in government. Thus, a year after the Whig victory in the general election of 1705, that party put pressure on Anne to replace a Tory secretary of state with the Whig earl of Sunderland (1675–1722). Below, Anne writes to her lord treasurer, Sidney, Lord Godolphin (1645–1712) explaining her resistance to this appointment. As you read the letter, does Anne come across as strong or weak? A competent leader? More of a Whig, a Tory, or neither? What was her great fear? What does her letter imply about the strength of party loyalties versus those to the sovereign?

I must own freely to you, I am of the opinion, that making a party man secretary of state, when there are so many of their friends in employment of all kinds already, is throwing myself into the hands of a party, which is a thing I have been desirous to avoid. Maybe some may think I would be willing to be in the hands of the Tories ...; but ... I am not inclined, nor never will be, to employ any of the violent persons, that have behaved themselves so ill towards me. All I desire is, my liberty in encouraging and employing all those that concur faithfully in my service, whether they are called Whigs or Tories, not to be tied to one nor the other. For if I should be so unfortunate as to fall into the hands of either, I shall not imagine myself, though I have the name of queen, to be in reality but their slave, which as it will be my personal ruin, so it will be the destroying all government; for instead of putting an end to faction, it will lay a lasting foundation for it. You press the bringing Lord Sunderland into business, that there may be one of that party in a place of trust, to help carry on the

---

[12]   W. Coxe, *Memoirs of the Duke of Marlborough*, rev. ed. (London, 1893), 2: 2–3.

business this winter; and you think if this is not complied with, they will not be hearty in pursuing my service in Parliament. But is it not very hard that men of sense and honor will not promote the good of their country because everything in the world is not done that they desire! ... Why, for God's sake, must I, who have no interest, no end, no thought, but for the good of my country, be made so miserable, as to be brought into the power of one set of men?

9.12   An assessment of English politics (December 17, 1700)[13]

Anne had her work cut out for her, for the politics of this period are usually referred to as "the Rage of Party." Still, it is important to remember that many MPs, even those nominally Whig or Tory, saw themselves as above partisanship and independent or uncommitted "country" gentlemen (as opposed to a "court" bloc that William and Anne sought to build). The following assessment of English politics was written for Frederick III (1657–1713), elector of Brandenburg. As you consider the various positions of Whigs and Tories, which would appeal to the independent country gentlemen, and why?

Though the English are nearly all divided into Whigs and Tories, there are many country members in Parliament who have never joined with these parties to the extent of closely espousing either. These men speak and vote in the House according to their lights, which rarely reach beyond the shores of their own island. The principles which govern their reasoning are their care for

1. the religion of this country
2. the liberty of the individual
3. the trade which enhances the value of their produce, and
4. the cultivation of their lands.

No matter which is the party in power, and no matter how eloquent its appeal may be, it will never win over these members unless it can convince them that one of these four points is under attack.

9.13   Duchess of Marlborough electioneering at St. Albans (1705)[14]

The demands of the wars increased the importance of Parliament and, so, that of parliamentary elections. In fact, in part because the Triennial Act of

[13] G. Holmes and W. A. Speck, eds., *The Divided Society: Parties and Politics in England, 1694–1716* (New York, 1968), 19, from BL, Add. MS. 30,000D, fol. 363, F. Bonet to Frederick III (trans.).
[14] *CJ*, 15: 37–8.

1694 required a new parliament every three years, more general elections were held between 1690 and 1715 than ever before or since. Because the stakes were so high and the party battle so intense, more individual seats were contested then than in any other period of British history until the first decades of the twentieth century. As a result, popularity and public opinion mattered as never before. Since there was no such thing as a secret ballot, one way to influence elections was for great aristocratic landowners to pressure their tenants and clients to vote as directed (for most constituencies, each voter had two votes). Thus, Sarah Churchill, duchess of Marlborough, a Whig and royal favorite, tried to influence the 1705 election at St. Albans, her family seat. The result was a disputed election return. Such cases were adjudged by the Commons itself, a right asserted in their Apology of 1604 (document 6.2 above). As you examine the Commons' record of this dispute, ask yourself why, if aristocratic and party loyalties were so powerful, it was important for her to claim to represent "the queen's interest and the good of the nation"? How convincing were those claims? Of what does she accuse the Tory candidate? What does this document tell us about the relationship between the ruling elite and those they ruled? How might the duchess's gender matter in the controversy?

Upon the petition of Henry Killigrew, Esq., complaining of an undue election and return of John Gape, Esq., to serve for the borough of St. Albans....

The sitting member's counsel ... insisted on several irregular practices on behalf of the petitioner; and as to that they called several witnesses:

Charles Turner said he was sent for by the duchess of Marlborough; and he went to her, and she desired his vote for both admirals [Killigrew and Churchill, the latter being the duchess's brother-in-law]: that he answered, he was engaged for Mr. Gape; to which the duchess replied, she had no prejudice to Mr. Gape, but it was the queen's desire that no such men should be chosen, for such men would unhinge the government, and the Papists' horses stood saddled day and night, whipping and spurring.

John Miller said that he was asked by one to go to my Lady Marlborough's; and when he came the duchess asked him who he was for, and he answered, for Colonel [*sic*] Churchill and Mr. Gape. Thereupon the duchess asked him if he would be for such men as were against the queen's interest and the good of the nation? That she asked him to oblige her with one vote; and he said, he thought he did by giving her brother [Admiral Churchill] one....

Sam Beech said he was sent for the duchess.... He told her, he had promised Mr. Gape ...; and thereupon the duchess told him, [if] he would not be willing, his goods should be taken out of his shop and torn.

9.14   The trial of Dr. Henry Sacheverell
(February 27 and March 3, 1710)[15]

The survival of the Revolution Settlement in Church and State depended on the outcome of the War of Spanish Succession. During the first half of the reign, victory followed victory, from the duke of Marlborough's brilliant defeat of the French army at Blenheim (1704), Ramillies (1706), and Oudenarde (1708), to the capture of Gibraltar in 1704 and Port Mahon, Minorca in 1708. Following the last, Lieutenant General James Stanhope wrote to Charles, earl of Sunderland upon the strategic significance of this prize: "her majesty being now mistress of the two best ports in the Mediterranean ..., makes me offer it as my humble opinion that England ought never to part with this island, which will give the law to the Mediterranean both in time of war and peace."[16]

But by the end of the decade polemicists like the Tory churchman (and future novelist) Jonathan Swift (1667–1745) began to allege in pamphlets like *The Conduct of the Allies* and periodicals like *The Examiner* that the Whig ministry was perpetuating the war to enrich new men, many of them Dissenters, at the expense of the old landed families. On November 5, 1709, in the wake of a decline in trade, bad harvests, and much war-weariness, Swift's fellow churchman, Henry Sacheverell (1674–1724), went farther, repudiating the Revolution itself. Marking the anniversary of both the Gunpowder Plot of 1605 and William's landing in 1688, Sacheverell preached a sermon, "The Perils of False Brethren, both in Church and State," asserting that "the grand security of our government, and the very pillar upon which it stands, is founded upon the steady belief in the subject's obligation to an absolute and unconditional obedience to the supreme power." What does this say about the Revolution of 1688–9?

If anyone missed the point, Sacheverell portrayed the Marlborough–Godolphin ministry, Whigs, Low Church Anglicans, and occasionally conforming Dissenters as "sworn adversaries to passive obedience, and the royal family ..., [in whom] the old leaven of their forefathers is still working in their present generation, and ... this traditional poison still remains in this brood of vipers to sting us to death.... And what better could have been expected from miscreants, begot in rebellion, born in sedition, and nursed up in faction?"[17]

In December, the Whig ministry launched impeachment proceedings against Sacheverell. Was this wise? How might loyal Anglicans react to prosecution of a Church of England clergyman? The trial began in the House of Lords on February 27: how do the arguments for the prosecution and the defense differ? How different were their views of 1688?

---

[15] *CJ*, 16: 258 (for the articles); and T. B. Howell, comp., *A Complete Collection of State Trials* (London, 1816), 15: 55–6, 202, 205–6.
[16] 30 Sept., *The Byng Papers* (London, 1931), ed. B. Tunstall, 2: 301.
[17] H. Sacheverell, *The Perils of False Brethren, both in Church, and State* (London, 1709), 22, 28, 30.

Articles of Impeachment (January 9, 1710):

I. Henry Sacheverell, in his said sermon preached at St. Paul's, doth suggest
    and maintain that the necessary means used to bring about the said happy
    Revolution were odious and unjustifiable, that his late majesty, in his
    Declaration, disclaimed the least imputation of resistance; and that to
    impute resistance to the said Revolution is to cast black and odious colors
    upon his late majesty and the said Revolution.
II. He ... doth suggest and maintain that the aforesaid Toleration granted by
    law is unreasonable and the allowance of it unwarrantable; and asserts that
    he is a false brother, with relation to God, religion, or the Church, who
    defends Toleration and liberty of conscience....
III. He ... doth falsely and seditiously suggest and assert that the Church of
    England is in a condition of great peril and adversity under her majesty's
    administration; and ... doth suggest the Church to be in danger: and, as a
    parallel, mentions ... that the person of King Charles [I] was voted to be out
    of danger at the same time that his murderers were conspiring his death....
IV. He ... doth falsely and maliciously suggest that her majesty's administration,
    both in ecclesiastical and civil affairs, tends to the destruction of the
    constitution. And that there are men of characters and stations in Church
    and State who are false brethren, and do themselves weaken, undermine,
    and betray, and do encourage, and put it in the power of others, who are
    professed enemies, to overturn and destroy the constitution and
    establishment....

[February 27] *Attorney General Sir John Montague:* ... If what the doctor very
frequently asserts in this sermon be true, that all are false sons of the Church,
who assisted in bringing about the Revolution, or that joined in the opposition
that was made to the encroachments which were begun by evil ministers in the
reign of King James II, against our religion and liberties; let the doctor a little
consider, how far his character of a false brother may be carried!

Everybody knows, that lived in those days, that the body of the clergy of the
Church of England made a noble stand against the encroachments which were
then making, and appeared as active as any of the laity.

And was it not by their writings, preaching, and example, that the nobility and
gentry were animated to maintain and defend their rights, religion, and liberties? ...

[March 3] *Sir Simon Harcourt* (for the defense).... I shall endeavor to satisfy
your lordships, first, that the doctor's assertion of the illegality of resistance to
the supreme power on any pretense whatsoever, in general terms, without
expressing any exception, or that any exception is to be made, is warranted by
the authority of the Church of England. And secondly, that his manner of
expression is agreeable to the law of England....

My lords, is this doctrine of non-resistance taught in the homilies in general
terms, in the same manner as Doctor Sacheverell has asserted it, without

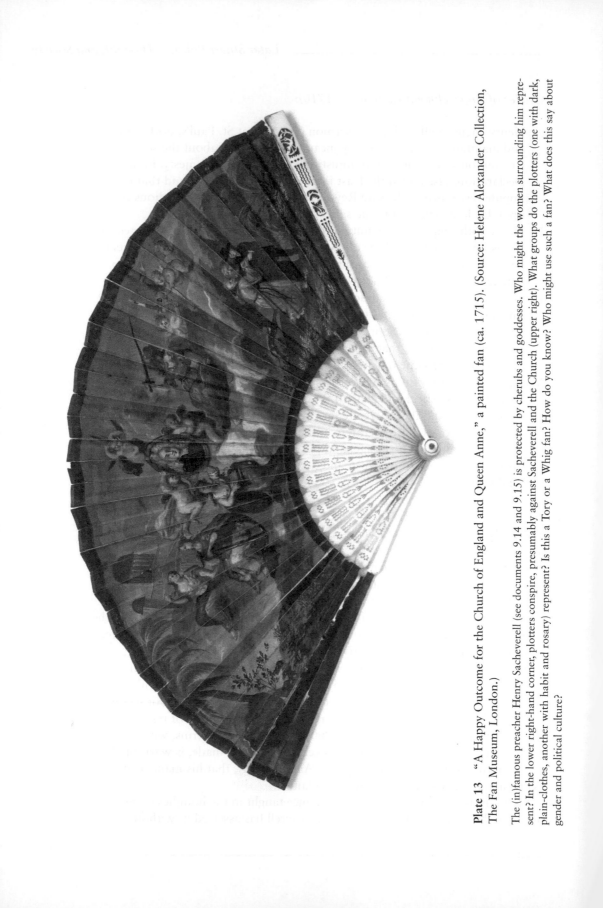

Plate 13 "A Happy Outcome for the Church of England and Queen Anne," a painted fan (ca. 1715). (Source: Helene Alexander Collection, The Fan Museum, London.)

The (in)famous preacher Henry Sacheverell (see documents 9.14 and 9.15) is protected by cherubs and goddesses. Who might the women surrounding him represent? In the lower right-hand corner, plotters conspire, presumably against Sacheverell and the Church (upper right). What groups do the plotters (one with dark, plain-clothes, another with habit and rosary) represent? Is this a Tory or a Whig fan? How do you know? Who might use such a fan? What does this say about gender and political culture?

expressing any exception? Do the articles of our religion declare the doctrine taught in the homilies to be a godly and wholesome doctrine? And will your lordships permit this gentleman to suffer for preaching it? Is it criminal in any man to preach that doctrine, which it is his duty to read? ...

That your lordships may not think this doctrine died at the Revolution, I shall humbly lay before your lordships the opinions of three archbishops, and eleven bishops, made since the Revolution, which will fully shew the doctrine of non-resistance is still the doctrine of our Church. ... I am sure it is impossible to enter into the heart of man to conceive, that what these reverend prelates have asserted, that any general position they have laid down concerning non-resistance, is an affirmance that necessary means used to bring about the Revolution were odious and unjustifiable. Why then is Doctor Sacheverell, by having taught the same doctrine, in the same manner as they did, to be charged for having suggested or maintained any such thing?

9.15   The trial of Daniel Dammarree for his role in the Sacheverell Riots (April 1710)[18]

At the end of March 1710, the Lords found Sacheverell guilty by 69 to 52 votes. They suspended him from preaching for three years and ordered his sermons burnt by the common hangman. While this barely satiated Whig desires, it made him a martyr in the eyes of the Anglican populace (see Plate 13). For example, by November, papers carried advertisements for "Music just published. The True Loyalist's Health to the Church, Queen, Dr. Sacheverell, and the new Loyal Members of Parliament; price 2d."[19] Even the queen had privately urged peers to find Sacheverell guilty, but to moderate his punishment. Damarie was a royal bargeman arrested for his part in the attack on meeting houses after the Sacheverell indictment was announced. Why might he have thought that attacking a Presbyterian meeting house was not inconsistent with his status as a royal servant? That is, why might he have thought that Anne, too, was for "High Church and Sacheverell"? Why did he lose his job? What does this case say about popular politics in the age of Anne? Compare it with the attack on a Ludlow meeting house from 1693 (document 9.10). Were these actions random or well organized? Were they spontaneous or planned – perhaps by members of the ruling elite? In light of these attacks, how convinced are you of the assertion made by some historians that the dawn of the eighteenth century saw a rise of secularism and a decline in religious politics? (Before answering that, you might want to read Locke's *Letter concerning Toleration*, document 9.23.)

---

[18]   A. Knapp and W. Baldwin, eds., *The Newgate Calendar* (London, 1824), 1: 59–60.
[19]   *The Post Boy*, no. 2415, Nov. 2–4, 1710.

Daniel Dammarree ..., waterman [bargeman on the River Thames] to Queen Anne ..., on the 18th of April 1710 was indicted for being concerned with a multitude of men, to the number of five hundred, armed with swords ..., clubs, [etc.], to levy war against the queen.

A gentleman deposed, that, going through the Temple, he saw some thousands of people, who had attended Dr. Sacheverell from Westminster Hall; that some of them said they would pull down Dr. [Daniel] Burgess's [Presbyterian] meeting-house that night; others differed as to the time of doing it; but all agreed on the act, and the meeting-house was demolished on the following night. Here it should be observed that Dr. Burgess and Mr. [Thomas] Bradbury were two dissenting ministers, who had made themselves conspicuous by preaching in opposition to Sacheverell's doctrine.

Captain Orril swore, that, on the 1st of March, hearing that the mob had pulled down Dr. Burgess's meeting-house, he resolved to go among them, to do what service he could to government by making discoveries. This witness, going to Mr. Bradbury's meeting, found the people plundering it, who obliged him to pull off his hat. After this he went to Lincoln's Inn Fields, where he saw a bonfire made of some of the materials of Dr. Burgess's meeting-house, and saw the prisoner [Dammarree], who twirled his hat, and said "Damn it, I will lead you on; we will have all the meeting-houses down. High Church and Sacheverell, huzza!"

It was proved by another evidence, that the prisoner having headed part of the mob, some of them proposed to go to the meeting-house in Wild Street; but this was objected to by others, who recommended going to Drury Lane, saying "that meetinghouse was worth ten of that in Wild Street."

Joseph Collier swore that he saw the prisoner carry a brass sconce from Dr. Burgess's meeting-house, and throw it into the fire in Lincoln's Inn Fields, huzzaing and crying, "High Church and Sacheverell."

[Dammarree was found guilty and sentenced to be hung, drawn, and quartered for high treason. The queen reprieved and subsequently pardoned him and restored him as a royal waterman. He was, however, terminated from this position at Anne's death in 1714.]

Landed Interest versus Monied Interest, and the Reformation of Ideas

9.16   Celia Fiennes journeys to Tunbridge Wells (written 1697–1702, pub. 1888)[20]

As we shall see, late Stuart contemporaries were very concerned with the issue of wealth from cities and trade. But at least 80 percent of the population

---

[20]   C. Morris, ed., *The Journeys of Celia Fiennes* (London, 1949), 132–5.

continued to live in the countryside around 1700. At the apex of the rural social structure still stood the landed interest: the relatively few nobles and the more numerous landed gentry. The gentry's influence (see Bucholz and Key, Conclusion) could be seen in art, dress, the architecture of country estates, and, increasingly, in the culture of country towns and spas. Celia Fiennes (1662–1741) traveled throughout much of England from the 1680s to the early 1700s, and her journal was published in the nineteenth century. About 1697, she visited one of these resorts. Why did the gentry visit Tunbridge Wells? What was most attractive about this tourist spot *vis-à-vis* London or the court? What is the significance of the gentry buying their own dinners? Is this the beginning of a consumer economy? What was the relationship between town and country?

They have made the wells very commodious by the many good buildings all about it and 2 or 3 mile round, which are lodgings for the company that drink the waters, and they have increased their buildings so much that makes them very cheap; all people buy their own provision at the market which is just by the wells and furnished with great plenty of all sorts flesh, fowl, and fish, and in great plenty is brought from Rye and Deal, etc., this being the road to London, so all the season the water is drank they stop here which makes it very cheap, as also the country people come with all their back yard and barn door affords, to supply them with, and their gardens and orchards which makes the markets well stored and provision cheap, which the gentry takes as a diversion while drinking the waters to go and buy their dinners it being every day's market and runs the whole length of the walk, which is between high trees on the market side for shade and secured with a row of buildings on the right side which are shops full of all sorts of toys, silver, china, milliners, and all sorts of curious wooden ware, which this place is noted for, [that is,] the delicate neat and thin ware of wood both white and Lignum vitae wood [inlay work]. Besides which there are two large coffeehouses for tea, chocolate, etc., and two rooms for the lottery and hazard board [gambling game with dice]. These are all built with an arch or pent house beyond the shops some of which are supported by pillars like a peasa [piazza], which is paved with brick and stone for the dry walking of the company in rain.

9.17   Henry St. John on the monied interest (1709)[21]

The great estates in the countryside depended upon careful management of land and marriage, especially as rental values remained depressed for about

---

[21]   G. Holmes, *British Politics in the Age of Anne* (London, 1967, 1987), 177, from Bodl., MS. Eng. misc.e.180, fols. 4–5.

a century after 1640. Land could be consolidated at marriage, especially as the gentry followed a fairly strict pattern of primogeniture. But that meant that younger sons had to find alternate careers, which meant, in turn, that the division between landed and non-landed families was permeable. Daniel Defoe (1660?–1731) commented on the blurred boundary between gentlemen and others through his character Moll Flanders, who, disguising her own humble background, sought to marry a London draper who dressed and acted like a landed squire: that is, "this amphibious creature, this land-water thing called a gentleman-tradesman."[22] While practice made the line between a landed and trade background vague, theory claimed a clear distinction between the landed and the non-landed interest. As one pamphlet from the 1720s recalled, "It was not many years ago, since an unhappy distinction was set on foot, between the landed and the money'd interest."[23] Tory politician, Henry St. John, later Viscount Bolingbroke (1678–1751) developed the distinction at length, with a lament that many landed gentlemen would endorse during Anne's reign. How did the war affect the fate of the landed classes? The monied interest? How was the difference between them political? How was it social?

We have now been twenty years engaged in the two most expensive wars that Europe ever saw. The whole burden of this charge has lain upon the landed interest during the whole time. The men of estates have, generally speaking, neither served in the fleets nor armies, nor meddled in the public funds and management of the treasure.

A new interest has been created out of their fortunes, and a sort of property which was not known twenty years ago is now increased to almost equal to the *terra firma* of our island. The consequence of all this is that the landed men are become poor and dispirited. They either abandon all thoughts of the public, turn arrant farmers and improve their estates they have left; or else they seek to repair their shattered fortunes by [en]listing at Court, or under the head of parties. In the meanwhile those men are become their masters, who formerly with joy would have been their servants.

9.18   Joseph Addison on the Royal Exchange (May 19, 1711)[24]

How the monied interest worked fascinated the English, whether they lauded or decried it. *The Spectator*, an early literary magazine which took

---

[22] D. Defoe, *The Fortunes and Misfortunes of the Famous Moll Flanders* (New York, 1964), 56.
[23] *Considerations on Publick Credit. In a Letter to a Member of Parliament* (London, 1724), 6.
[24] *The Spectator*, ed. D. F. Bond (Oxford, 1965), 1: 292–6.

the form of a "man on the street" column, often lauded it. The framing device of *The Spectator* is that its author, "Mr. Spectator" (most often really Joseph Addison, 1672–1719, or his friend Sir Richard Steele, 1662–1729), was an anonymous but keen (and sometimes satirical) observer of London life. Why does Addison take such satisfaction in the Royal Exchange? What is so good about trade? What is its relationship to land? How did the Royal Exchange reinforce a hierarchical social order? How did it bring that order into question? How might the luxury trades cataloged below have affected the living standards and expectations of contemporary Englishmen?

There is no place in the town which I so much love to frequent as the Royal Exchange. It gives me a secret satisfaction, and in some measure gratifies my vanity, as I am an Englishman, to see so rich an assembly of countrymen and foreigners consulting together upon the private business of mankind, and making this metropolis a kind of *emporium* for the whole earth. I must confess I look upon high-change [time of greatest activity at the Exchange] to be a great council, in which all considerable nations have their representatives. Factors in the trading world are what ambassadors are in the politic world; they negotiate affairs, conclude treaties, and maintain a good correspondence between those wealthy societies of men that are divided from one another by seas and oceans, or live on the different extremities of a continent. I have often been pleased to hear disputes adjusted between an inhabitant of Japan and an alderman of London; or to see a subject of the Great Mogul entering into a league with one of the Czar of Muscovy. I am infinitely delighted in mixing with these several ministers of commerce, as they are distinguished by their different walks and different languages. Sometimes I am jostled among a body of Armenians; sometimes I am lost in a crowd of Jews; and sometimes make one in a group of Dutchmen. ...

   If we consider our own country in its natural prospect, without any of the benefits and advantages of commerce, what a barren, uncomfortable spot of earth falls to our share! Natural historians tell us, that no fruit grows originally among us, besides hips and haws, acorns and pig-nuts, with other delicacies of the like nature. ... Nor has traffic more enriched our vegetable world, than it has improved the whole face of nature among us. Our ships are laden with the harvest of every climate. Our tables are stored with spices, and oils, and wines. Our rooms are filled with pyramids of China, and adorned with the workmanship of Japan. Our morning's draught [drink] comes to us from the remotest corners of the earth. We repair our bodies by the drugs of America, and repose ourselves under Indian canopies. My friend, Sir Andrew [Freeport, a merchant], calls the vineyards of France our gardens; the spice-islands our hot-beds; the Persians our silk-weavers, and the Chinese our potters. Nature, indeed, furnishes us with the bare necessaries of life, but traffic gives us a great variety of what is useful, and at the same time supplies us with every thing that is convenient and ornamental. Nor is it the least part of this our happiness, that whilst we enjoy the remotest products of the north and south, we are free from those extremities of weather which give them birth; that our eyes are refreshed with the green fields of Britain, at the same time that our palates are feasted with fruits that rise between the tropics.

For these reasons there are not more useful members in a commonwealth than merchants. They knit mankind together in a mutual intercourse of good offices, distribute the gifts of nature, find work for the poor, add wealth to the rich, and magnificence to the great. Our English merchant converts the tin of his own country into gold, and exchanges its wool for rubies. The Mahometans [Muslims] are clothed in our British manufacture, and the inhabitants of the frozen zone warmed with the fleeces of our sheep....

Trade, without enlarging the British territories, has given us a kind of additional empire. It has multiplied the number of the rich, made our landed estates infinitely more valuable than they were formerly, and added to them an accession of other estates as valuable as the lands themselves.

9.19 Maximilian Misson's observations on London (pub. in French 1698, trans. 1719)[25]

Late Stuart England provoked as much comment from foreign visitors as did Elizabethan England (see chapter 4, above). French Huguenot Francis Maximilian Misson (ca. 1650–1722) lived most of his life in England and wrote about his new country during the reign of William III, although his work was not published in English until the early Hanoverian period. Misson seemed most fascinated by the huge metropolis, and most of the selections below (his book was arranged alphabetically by subject) refer to aspects of London life. What strikes Misson as noteworthy? Do you think he liked London *circa* 1700? After reading the rest of the documents in this section, would you?

Apprentices. In foreign countries they have a notion, that in England even the greatest lords put their sons 'prentices to merchants and tradesmen. In times past it was much more the practice than now.... It is therefore one thing to say, that a lord has happened to put his younger son to a trade, and another thing to say, it is customary in England for lords to put their children out to trades.

Beaux. England also has a competent share of these animals, and the city of London particularly is thoroughly stocked with 'em. These gentlemen in English are call'd fops and beaux. The play-houses, chocolate-houses, and park in

[25] *M. Misson's Memoirs and Observations in his Travels over England* (London, 1719), 2–3, 16, 39–40, 60, 129, 203–4.

Spring, perfectly swarm with them. Their whole business is to hunt after new fashions. They are creatures compounded of a periwig and a coat laden with powder as white as a miller's, a face besmeared with snuff, and a few affected airs; they are exactly like Moliere's marquesses, and want nothing but that title.... A beau is so much the more remarkable in England, because, generally speaking, the Englishmen dress in a plain uniform manner.

Coffee-houses. These houses, which are very numerous in London, are, extremely convenient. You have all manner of news there; you have a good fire, which you may sit by as long as you please; you have a dish of coffee; you meet your friends for the transaction of business. And all for a penny, if you don't care to spend more.

Courtesans, alias whores. Mr. [Balthasar de] Monconys (1611–65) wrote above 33 or 34 years ago, in his *Little Voyage into England*, that he had been through one of the streets which were wholly inhabited by professed courtesans. At present there's a great alteration in this point, for now those ladies are distributed all the town over.

Horns. I have sometimes met in the streets of London a woman carrying a figure of straw representing a man, crowned with very ample horns, preceded by a drum, and followed by a mob, making a most grating noise with tongs, grid-irons, frying-pans, and saucepans. I asked what was the meaning of all this; they told me, that a woman had given her husband a sound beating, for accusing her of making him a cuckold, and that upon such occasions some kind neighbor of the poor innocent injured creature generally performed this ceremony.

Pamphlets. England is a country abounding in printed papers, which they call pamphlets, wherein every author makes bold to talk very freely upon affairs of state, and to publish all manner of news. I do not say that every one does with impunity speak his own thoughts, but I say, they take great liberties. A friend of mine affirmed to me, that in the reign of the late King Charles, he heard the hawkers cry about the streets a printed sheet, advising that prince to quit the duchess of Portsmouth, or to expect most dreadful consequences. The extreme mildness of the government gives room for this licentiousness.

9.20   Richard Steele's "Discourse upon Wenches" (January 4, 1712)[26]

As Misson hinted, not every form of London commerce was respectable or beneficent, which was also noted by Sir Richard Steele in one issue of *The Spectator*. The piece begins with what may be a veiled reference to the Reformation of Manners movement which, since the 1690s, had been trying

---

[26] *The Spectator*, ed. G. A. Aitken (London, 1898), 4: 73–4, 76.

to eliminate vice from London's streets. What do you suppose Steel thinks of their efforts? The woman he meets was probably one of the 8,000 new immigrants who came to London every year. What were the options for a single woman upon arrival in London? What has happened to this one? Why do you suppose she has opted for this life? *The Spectator* was often viewed, even in its own time, as sexist (later there arose a *Female Spectator* in response). In this case, would you describe Steel's response as sexist or proto-feminist? Was he "wholly unconcerned" with the plight of the young girl? Is there a humanitarian ethos here, and, if so, what should be done?

No vice or wickedness, which people fall into from indulgence to desires which are natural to all, ought to place them below the compassion of the virtuous part of the world; which indeed often makes me a little apt to suspect the sincerity of their virtue, who are too warmly provoked at other people's personal sins. The unlawful commerce of the sexes is of all other the hardest to avoid; and yet there is no one which you shall hear the rigider part of womankind speak of with so little mercy....

The other evening, passing along near Covent Garden, I was jogged on the elbow as I turned into the Piazza, on the right hand coming out of James Street, by a slim young girl of about seventeen, who with a pert air asked me if I was for a pint of wine. I do not know but I should have indulged my curiosity in having some chat with her, but that I am informed the man of the Bumper [Tavern] knows me; and it would have made a story for him not very agreeable to some part of my writings, though I have in others so frequently said that I am wholly unconcerned in any scene I am in, but merely as a spectator. This impediment being in my way, we stood under one of the arches by twilight; and there I could observe as exact features as I had ever seen, the most agreeable shape, the finest neck and bosom, in a word the whole person of a woman exquisitely beautiful. She affected to allure me with a forced wantonness in her look and air, but I saw it checked with hunger and cold; her eyes were wan and eager, her dress thin and tawdry, her mien genteel and childish. This strange figure gave me much anguish of heart, and to avoid being seen with her I went away, but could not forbear giving her a crown [5s.]. The poor thing sighed, curtsied, and with a blessing expressed with the utmost vehemence, turned from me. This creature is what they call "newly come upon the town," but who, I suppose, falling into cruel hands, was left in the first month from her dishonor and exposed to pass through the hands and discipline of one of those hags of hell whom we call bawds....

It must not be thought a digression from my intended speculation to talk of bawds in a discourse upon wenches, for a woman of the town is not thoroughly and properly such without having gone through the education of one of these houses.

9.21   Bernard Mandeville, The Fable of the Bees *(1714)*[27]

The connection between urban capitalism and urban vice was most memorably portrayed by Bernard Mandeville (1670–1733), a Dutch writer who lived in London. He portrayed his adopted city as a corrupt yet prosperous beehive. Does the author approve of London's vices? Does the fact that the subtitle of his "Fable" is "Private Vices, Public Benefits" change your answer? (It should be noted that Mandeville also wrote in favor of public stews, that is regulated brothels, and against charity schools, as educating the poor would only render them unfit for the menial jobs for which they were destined.) How might this be a defense of capitalism?

> Luxury
> Employ'd a Million of the Poor,
> And odious Pride a Million more:
> Envy it self, and Vanity,
> Were Ministers of Industry;
> Their darling Folly, Fickleness,
> In Diet, Furniture and Dress,
> That strange ridic'lous Vice, was made
> The very Wheel that turn'd the Trade.
> Their Laws and Clothes were equally
> Objects of Mutability;
> For, what was well done for a time,
> In half a Year became a Crime....
> Thus Vice nurs'd Ingenuity,
> Which join'd with Time and Industry,
> Had carry'd Life's Conveniences,
> It's [sic] real Pleasures, Comforts, Ease,
> To such a height, the very Poor
> Liv'd better than the Rich before.

9.22   Sir William Petty, "That the Power and Wealth of England Hath Increased this Last Forty Years" (1690)[28]

It is, of course, impossible to determine whether the English were more vicious or virtuous under the late Stuarts than under the early Tudors. Nor is it easy to pin down whether England was more disorderly or orderly in 1700 than in 1500 (compare the documents in this chapter with those in

---

[27]   B. Mandeville, *The Fable of the Bees: Or, Private Vices, Public Benefits*, ed. F. B. Kaye (Oxford, 1924, reprinted Indianapolis, 1988), 25–6.
[28]   W. Petty, *Political Arithmetick* (London, 1690), 96–8.

chapters 1 and 5 above). But many contemporaries had no doubt that England was richer and more populous. Take, for example, Sir William Petty (1623–87). Petty, one of the new theorists of "political arithmetick" and co-founder of the Royal Society for the Improvement of Natural Knowledge (chartered 1662), is a prime exemplar of the increasing use of reason and experiment to understand human nature and society in later Stuart England, itself a reflection of the Scientific Revolution: "I have taken the course ... to express myself in terms of number, weight, or measure; to use only arguments of sense, and to consider only such causes, as have visible foundations in nature."[29] What did Petty think was the basis for a nation's power and wealth? What appears to have been the effect of the Civil Wars and Glorious Revolution on that power and wealth? In explaining them, why does he describe "Negroes [as] ... men of great labor and little expense"? How had the "late tumults in Ireland" affected England's might? What was the human cost of such power and wealth?

It is not much to be doubted but that the territories under the king's dominion have increased: forasmuch as New England, Virginia, Barbados, and Jamaica, Tangier, and Bombay, have, since that time, been either added to his majesty's territories, or improved from a desert condition, to abound with people, buildings, shipping, and the production of many useful commodities. And as for the land of England, Scotland, and Ireland, as it is not less in quantity than it was forty years since [ago], so it is manifest that, by reason of the draining of the fens, watering of dry grounds, improving of forests and commons, making of heathy and barren grounds to bear sainfoin and clover grass, [a]meliorating and multiplying several sorts of fruits and garden-stuff, making some rivers navigable, etc.; I say, it is manifest that the land in its present condition is able to bear more provisions and commodities than it was forty years ago.

Secondly, although the people of England, Scotland, and Ireland, which have extraordinarily perished by the plague and sword, within these last forty years, do amount to about 300,000 above what [would] have died in the ordinary way: yet the ordinary increase by generation of 10,000,000 which doubles in 200 years, as hath been shown by the observators upon the bills of mortality, may, in forty years, which is a fifth part of the same time, have increased one-fifth part of the whole number, or 2,000,000. Where note by the way, that the accession of Negroes to the American plantations, being all men of great labor and little expense, is not inconsiderable. Besides, it is hoped that New England (where few or no women are barren, and most have many children; and where people live long and healthfully) hath produced an increase of as many people as were destroyed in the late tumults in Ireland.

[29] C. H. Hull, ed., *The Economic Writings of Sir William Petty* (Cambridge, 1899), 1: 244.

9.23   *John Locke*, A Letter Concerning Toleration *(1685, pub. 1689)*[30]

More famous and more influential than Petty was John Locke (1632–1704). Locke was physician and secretary to the earl of Shaftesbury (see chapter 8), and it was, perhaps, the Whig leader who inspired him to write his *Two Treatises on Government* in the early 1680s. But their justification of the use of popular resistance to the ruler was too radical for widespread acceptance and Locke only published them anonymously, in the 1690s, to justify the Glorious Revolution. Even then his fame rested on other works which fit the new spirit of rational, calm enquiry adopted by much of the intellectual elite. *Optiks* (1704), by Sir Isaac Newton (1642–1727), which delineated the principles (and the particles) which light obeys, had its philosophical analog in Locke's *Essay concerning Human Understanding* (1690), which used visual metaphor to explain the thought process. How might such a view of the mind, shaped by external stimulus, affect views of government; of education; of religion? "Methinks the understanding is not much unlike a closet wholly shut from light, with only some little opening left, to let in external visible resemblances, or ideas of things without: would the pictures coming into a dark room but stay there, and lie so orderly as to be found upon occasion, it would very much resemble the understanding of a man."[31]

In keeping with this rational spirit, Locke's *The Reasonableness of Christianity* (1695) and Latitudinarian bishops and writers downplayed religious "enthusiasm" such as had gripped England prior to the Restoration, and squared religion with the pursuit of truth, the Scientific Revolution, and the beginnings of the English Enlightenment. As one contemporary noted, "the universal disposition of this age is bent upon a rational religion."[32] How does Locke's *Letter Concerning Toleration* reflect the use of scientific method in questions of religion? How might it have influenced the Revolution Settlement, particularly the Toleration Act (document 9.4)? How are his ideas different from Charles II's and James II's Declarations of Indulgence? What view of the government is shown in the *Letter*? Is he advocating separation of Church and State? One might consider what Sacheverell thought about Locke and *vice versa*. What about the rioters we have met in this chapter? What would they think of Locke's ideas? How is Locke both a conservative and a radical thinker?

[30] J. Locke, *A Letter Concerning Toleration*, in *The Works of John Locke* (London, 1823), 6: 5–6, 9–11.
[31] J. Locke, *Essay concerning Human Understanding*, book 2, ch. 11, para. 17, in *Works of John Locke*, 1: 152.
[32] [P. Pett], *The Happy Future State of England* (London, 1688), 67, quoting T. Sprat, *The History of the Royal Society* (London, 1667), 336.

I esteem that toleration to be the chief characteristic mark of the true church. ... If the Gospel and the apostles may be credited, no man can be a Christian without charity, and without that faith which works, not by force, but by love. Now, I appeal to the consciences of those that persecute, torment, destroy, and kill other men upon pretense of religion, whether they do it out of friendship and kindness towards them or no? And I shall then indeed, and not until then, believe they do so, when I shall see those fiery zealots correcting, in the same manner, their friends and familiar acquaintance for the manifest sins they commit against the precepts of the Gospel. ...

I esteem it above all things necessary to distinguish exactly the business of civil government from that of religion, and to settle the just bounds that lie between the one and the other. If this be not done, there can be no end put to the controversies that will be always arising between those that have, or at least pretend to have, on the one side, a concernment for the interest of men's souls, and, on the other side, a care of the commonwealth.

The commonwealth seems to me to be a society of men constituted only for the procuring, preserving, and advancing of their own civil interests.

Civil interests I call life, liberty, health, and indolency [freedom from pain] of body; and the possession of outward things, such as money, lands, houses, furniture, and the like.

It is the duty of the civil magistrate, by the impartial execution of equal laws, to secure unto all the people in general, and to every one of his subjects in particular, the just possession of these things belonging to this life. ...

Now that the whole jurisdiction of the magistrate reaches only to these civil concernments, and that all civil power, right, and dominion, is bounded and confined to the only care of promoting these things; and that it neither can nor ought in any manner to be extended to the salvation of souls, these following considerations seem unto me abundantly to demonstrate.

First. Because the care of souls is not committed to the civil magistrate, any more than to other men. It is not committed unto him, I say, by God; because it appears not that God has ever given any such authority to one man over another, as to compel any one to his religion. Nor can any such power be vested in the magistrate by the consent of the people, because no man can so far abandon the care of his own salvation as blindly to leave to the choice of any other, whether prince or subject, to prescribe to him what faith or worship he shall embrace. For no man can, if he would, conform his faith to the dictates of another. All the life and power of true religion consist in the inward and full persuasion of the mind; and faith is not faith without believing. ...

In the second place. The care of souls cannot belong to the civil magistrate, because his power consists only in outward force; but true and saving religion consists in the inward persuasion of the mind, without which nothing can be acceptable to God. And such is the nature of the understanding, that it cannot be compelled to the belief of anything by outward force.

9.24   Mary Astell, *Reflections on Marriage* (1706)[33]

Having examined the changing relationships among parties, religions, and interests after the Glorious Revolution, we now turn to that between the genders. Mary Astell (1666–1731) contributed to cultural, philosophical, religious, and political debates, disputing with Gilbert Burnet, Defoe, and Locke (among others). She had been born into a prosperous provincial merchant family and, unusually for a Stuart-era woman, had the equivalent of a university education. But by the late 1680s her father had died penniless and she had moved to London where she lived primarily on the strength of her writing. She was a committed royalist and Anglican and was, successively, a supporter of James II, a Tory, and a friend to non-jurors. She was also deeply involved in the Enlightenment and studied astronomy at the Royal Observatory at Greenwich. Her most successful work, *A Serious Proposal to the Ladies* (1694 and many editions) called for the establishment of a cloistered intellectual community for young women; Princess Anne (as she then was) allowed her to dedicate *A Serious Proposal, Part II* to her in 1697. Writing below about a famous divorce case, Astell asks why marriage should subordinate the wife completely to the husband. At the end, she uses biblical examples, but is this a religious argument? How is this a political argument? How might it relate, for example, to the Glorious Revolution? Is it a feminist argument? Even though Astell is essentially a conservative, does she bring into question any of the models of social order which we have seen earlier in this book and period? How far have we come since the documents in chapter 1?

If absolute sovereignty be not necessary in a state, how comes it to be so in a family? Or if in a family why not in a state ...? If the authority of the husband so far as it extends, is sacred and inalienable, why not of the prince? The domestic sovereign is without dispute elected, and the stipulations and contract are mutual, is it not then partial in men to the last degree, to contend for, and practice that arbitrary dominion in their families, which they abhor and exclaim against in the state? For if arbitrary power is evil in it self, and an improper method of governing rational and free agents, it ought not to be practiced anywhere; nor is it less, but rather more mischievous in families than in kingdoms, by how much 100,000 tyrants are worse than one. What though a husband can't deprive a wife of life without being responsible to the law, he may however do what is much more grievous to a generous mind, render life miserable, for which she has no redress, scarce pity which is

---

[33]   M. Astell, *Reflections on Marriage*, 3rd ed. (London, 1706), preface, unpag.

afforded to every other complainant. It being thought a wife's duty to suffer every thing without complaint. If all men are born free, how is it that all women are born slaves? As they must be if the being subjected to the inconstant, uncertain, unknown, arbitrary will of men, be the perfect condition of slavery? And if the essence of freedom consists, as our masters say it does, in having a standing rule to live by? And why is slavery so much condemned and strove against in one case, and so highly applauded, and held so necessary and so sacred in another?

'Tis true that God told Eve after the fall that her husband should rule over her: and so it is that he told Esau by the mouth of Isaac his father, that he should serve his younger brother, and should in time, and when he was strong enough to do it, break the yoke from off his neck. Now why one text should be a command any more than the other, and not both of them be predictions only; or why the former should prove Adam's natural right to rule, and much less every man's, any more than the latter is a proof of Jacob's right to rule, and of Esau's to rebel, one is yet to learn? The text in both cases foretelling what would be; but neither of them determining what ought to be.

HISTORIANS' DEBATES

The Glorious Revolution – cui bono (who benefits)?

R. Beddard, "The Unexpected Whig Revolution of 1688," and M. Goldie, "The Political Thought of the Anglican Revolution," in *The Revolutions of 1688*, ed. Beddard (Oxford, 1991); W. A. Speck, "William – and Mary?" in *The Revolution of 1688–1689: Changing Perspectives*, ed. L. G. Schwoerer (Cambridge, 1992); "Revolution," in *The World of William and Mary: Anglo-Dutch Perspectives on the Revolution of 1688–89*, ed. D. E. Hoak and M. Feingold (Stanford, 1996); J. C. D. Clark, "1688: Glorious Revolution or Glorious Reaction?," in *Fabrics and Fabrications: the Myth and Making of William and Mary*, ed. C. C. Barfoot and P. Hoftijzer (Amsterdam, 1990); H. T. Dickinson, "The Debate on the 'Glorious Revolution,'" *History* 61 (1976); J. Childs, "1688," *History* 73 (1988); H. Horwitz, "1689 (And All That)," *PH* 6 (1987); J. R. Hertzler, "Who Dubbed it 'the Glorious Revolution'?," *Albion* 19 (1987); T. Harris, "Reluctant Revolutionaries?: The Scots and the Revolution of 1688–89," in *Politics and the Political Imagination in Later Stuart Britain: Essays Presented to Lois Green Schwoerer*, ed. H. Nenner (Rochester, N. Y., 1998).

Was party politics popular?

G. S. Holmes, *Politics, Religion and Society in England, 1672–1742* (London, 1986), esp. "The Electorate and the National Will," and "The Achievement of Stability: The Social Context of Politics from the 1680s to the Age of Walpole"; *idem*, "Revolution, War and Politics, 1689–1714," in *Stuart England*, ed.

B. Worden (Oxford, 1986); Plumb, "The Growth of the Electorate in England from 1600 to 1715," *P & P* 45 (1969); C. Roberts, S. Baxter, and N. Landau reconsider Plumb's thesis of the growth of political stability in *Albion* 25 (1993); W. A. Speck, "The Electorate in the First Age of Party," in *Britain in the First Age of Party*, ed. C. Jones (London, 1987); J. C. D. Clark, "England's Ancien Regime as a Confessional State," *Albion* 21 (1989); P. Jenkins, "Party Conflict and Political Stability in Monmouthshire, 1690–1740," *HJ* 29 (1986); H. Horwitz, "The 1690s Revisited: Recent Work on Politics and Political Ideas in the Reign of William III," *Parliamentary History* 15 (1996); D. Hayton, "The 'Country' Interest and the Party System, c. 1689–1720," in *Party and Party Management in Parliament 1660–1784*, ed. C. Jones (Leicester, 1984); C. R. Roberts, "The Constitutional Significance of the Financial Settlement of 1690," *HJ* 20, 1 (1977); J. P. Kenyon, "The Revolution of 1688: Resistance and Contract," in *Historical Perspectives: Studies in English Thought and Society in Honour of J. H. Plumb*, ed. N. McKendrick (London, 1974); M. Knights, "How Rational Was the Later Stuart Public Sphere?," in *The Politics of the Public Sphere in Early Modern England*, ed. P. Lake and S. Pincus (Manchester, 2007); *idem*, "Read My Lips" (on party politics under Anne), *HT* 54, 11 (2004); *idem*, "Politics after the Glorious Revolution," in *A Companion to Stuart Britain*, ed. B. Coward (Oxford, 2003).

What was the significance of Jacobitism?

J. C. D. Clark, "On Moving the Middle Ground: The Significance of Jacobitism in Historical Studies," in *The Jacobite Challenge*, ed. E. Cruickshanks and J. Black (Edinburgh, 1988); P. Monod, "Jacobitism and Country Principles in the Reign of William III," *HJ* 30 (1987); E. Cruickshanks and E. T. Corp, eds., *The Stuart Court in Exile and the Jacobites* (London, 1995), esp. Cruickshanks, "Attempts to Restore the Stuarts, 1689–96"; D. Szechi, "The Jacobite Revolution Settlement, 1689–1696," *EHR* 108 (1993); E. Cruickshanks, ed., *Ideology and Conspiracy: Aspects of Jacobitism, 1689–1759* (Edinburgh, 1982), esp. P. Hopkins, "Sham Plots and Real Plots in the 1690s"; G. V. Bennett, "English Jacobitism, 1710–1715: Myth and Reality," *TRHS* 5th ser., 32 (1982); C. Jones, "Evidence, Interpretation and Definitions in Jacobite Historiography: a Reply to Eveline Cruickshanks," *EHR* 113 (1998); E. Gregg, "Was Queen Anne a Jacobite?," *History* 57 (1972).

Did the late Stuart court matter?

J. Van den Berg, "Religion and Politics in the Life of William and Mary," in Barfoot and Hoftijzer, *Fabrics and Fabrications*; M. Zook, "History's Mary: the Propagation of Queen Mary II, 1689–1694," in *Women and Sovereignty*, ed. L. O. Fradenburg (Edinburgh, 1992); F. Harris, " 'The Honourable Sisterhood': Queen Anne's Maids of Honor," *British Library Journal* 19 (1993); R. O. Bucholz, " 'Nothing but Ceremony': Queen Anne and the Limitations of Royal Ritual," *JBS* 30, 3 (1991); *idem*, "Queen Anne: Victim of her Virtues?," in *Queenship in Britain 1603–1837: Royal Patronage, Court Culture and Dynastic*

Politics, ed. C. Campbell Orr (London, 2002), and editor's introduction; R. Weil, "Royal Flesh, Gender and the Construction of Monarchy," in *The Body of the Queen: Gender and Rule in the Courtly World, 1500–2000*, ed. R. Schulte (New York, 2006).

Was England in 1700 dominated by an established landed interest or an incipient monied interest?

J. M. Rosenheim, *The Emergence of a Ruling Order: English Landed Society, 1650–1750* (London, 1998), esp. "The Transformation of County Identity," and "The Influence of the Metropolis"; J. Cannon, "The British Nobility, 1660–1800," in *The European Nobilities in the Seventeenth and Eighteenth Centuries*, vol. 1, ed. H. M. Scott (London, 1995); N. Rogers, "Money, Marriage, Mobility: the Big Bourgeoisie of Hanoverian London," *Journal of Family History* 24, 1 (1999); H. Horwitz, " 'The Mess of the Middle Class' Revisited: the Case of the 'Big Bourgeoisie' of Augustan London," *Continuity and Change* 2, 2 (1987); I. Archer, "Social Networks in Restoration London: the Evidence of Samuel Pepys's Diary," in *Communities in Early Modern England: Networks, Place, Rhetoric*, ed. A. Shepard and P. Withington (Manchester, 2000).

What are the relative importance of political, social, and intellectual changes in the creation of the early Enlightenment on the British Isles?

J. Champion, "Political Thinking between Restoration and Hanoverian Succession," in Coward, *Companion to Stuart Britain*; R. Perry, "Mary Astell and Enlightenment," in *Women, Gender, and Enlightenment*, ed. S. Knott, and B. Taylor (Basingstoke, 2005); J. Downie, "Public and Private: the Myth of the Bourgeois Public Sphere," in *A Concise Companion to the Restoration and Eighteenth Century*, ed. C. Wall (Oxford, 2005); P. Borsay, "The Culture of Improvement," in *The Eighteenth Century*, ed. P. Langford (Oxford, 2002); *idem*, "Metropolis and Enlightenment: the British Isles 1660–1800," *Journal for the Study of British Cultures* 10, 2 (2003).

ADDITIONAL SOURCE COLLECTIONS

R. Allen, *The Moving Pageant: A Literary Sourcebook on London Street-Life, 1700–1914* (London, 1998).

A. Browning, ed., *English Historical Documents, 1660–1714* (New York, 1953).

W. C. Costin and J. S. Watson, eds., *The Law and Working of the Constitution: Documents, 1660–1914*, 1, *1660–1783*, 2nd ed. (London, 1961).

G. Holmes and W. A. Speck, eds., *The Divided Society: Parties and Politics in England, 1694–1716* (New York, 1968).

D. L. Jones, *A Parliamentary History of the Glorious Revolution* (London, 1988).

M. L. Kekewich, ed., *Princes and Peoples: France and the British Isles, 1620–1714* (Manchester, 1994).

B. P. Lenman and J. S. Gibson, eds., *The Jacobite Threat–England, Scotland, Ireland, France: A Source Book* (Edinburgh, 1990).

S. Pincus, *England's Glorious Revolution, 1688–1689: a Brief History with Documents* (New York, 2006).

S. E. Prall, *The Bloodless Revolution: England, 1688* (Madison, Wisc., 1985).

R. C. Richardson and T. B. James, eds., *The Urban Experience, a Sourcebook: English, Scottish and Welsh Towns, 1450–1700* (Manchester, 1983).

Bibliography of Online Document Archives

In the "Historians' Debates" section to each chapter we list relevant secondary works, focusing on articles and shorter pieces, as we have indicated in the Preface. For additional works by historians, we recommend consulting the *Royal Historical Society Bibliography: The History of Britain, Ireland, and the British Overseas* (online, http://www.rhs.ac.uk/bibl/). For important monographs and surveys, see the bibliography organized by categories in Robert Bucholz and Newton Key, *Early Modern England, 1485–1714: A Narrative History*, 2nd ed. (Oxford: Blackwell, 2009). For biographical details, consult *The Oxford Dictionary of National Biography* (ODNB online, http://www.oxforddnb.com/, subscription required).

The notes for each chapter list accessible source collections in "Additional Source Collections." Rather than repeating those collections here, we list some of the major document and text sources available online (check http://www.black wellpublishing.com/earlymodernengland/, and http://earlymodernengland.blog spot.com/ for additional documents and materials).

G. B. Adams and H. M. Stephens, eds. *Select Documents of English Constitutional History* (London, 1901). http://home.freeuk.net/don-aitken/ast/astintro. html. Henry VI through George I.

Avalon Project at the Yale Law School: Pre-Eighteenth-Century Documents. http://www.yale.edu/lawweb/avalon/pre18.htm. Colonial Charters, treaties, discourses on trade, Bill of Rights, etc.

Bodleian Library Broadside Ballads. http://www.bodley.ox.ac.uk/ballads/. Searchable images of some 30,000 ballads, a portion of which date from the early modern period.

British History Online. http://www.british-history.ac.uk/. Includes State Papers, Rushworth's *Collections*, contemporary maps.

British Printed Images to 1700. http://www.bpi1700.org.uk/. Annotated broadsides and prints.

Constitution Society, Liberty Library of Constitutional Classics. http://www.con stitution.org/liberlib.htm. Includes works by Francis Bacon, Robert Filmer, and two major print collections: S. R. Gardiner, ed., *The Constitutional Documents of the Puritan Revolution. 1625–1660*, 3rd ed. (Oxford, 1906).

http://www.constitution.org/eng/conpur.htm. And C. Stephenson and F. G. Marcham, eds., *Sources of English Constitutional History: A Selection of Documents from A.D. 600 to the Present* (New York, 1937). http://www. constitution.org/sech/sech_.htm.

Digital Quaker Collection. http://esr.earlham.edu/dqc/. Word-searchable collection, many of which are or are about early modern texts.

Documents Illustrating Jacobite History. http://www.jacobite.ca/documents. Exclusion Crisis, Glorious Revolution, exile.

Early English Books Online (EEBO). http://wwwlib.umi.com/eebo. Massive collection that aims to make all sources in English printed before 1700 available. Available to universities and libraries by subscription only. (Another project, EEBO Text Creation Partnership, http://www.lib.uchicago.edu/efts/EEBO/, makes available a quarter of the EEBO texts in searchable and readable editions. Again, subscription only.)

Early Modern Literary Studies: Electronic Texts. http://www.shu.ac.uk/emls/emlsetxt.html. Linking to mainly literary texts (but including works by Elizabeth, Henry VIII, etc.) online.

Early Stuart Libels. http://www.earlystuartlibels.net/htdocs/. Annotated and searchable early seventeenth-century political poetry from manuscript sources.

Eighteenth Century Collections Online (ECCO). Like EEBO, pdf versions of original 18th century books and pamphlets. Text Creation Partnership has keyed these and made them full-text searchable. Subscription only.

Elizabethan Sumptuary Statutes. http://elizabethan.org/sumptuary/index.html.

English Broadside Ballad Archive (EBBA). http://emc.english.ucsb.edu/ballad_project/. Searchable images of early ballads such as 1,800 ballads in the Samuel Pepys collection, primarily black-letter broadsides of the seventeenth century.

Fire and Ice: Puritan and Reformed Writings. http://www.puritansermons.com/. Richard Baxter, John Calvin, etc.

Internet Archive of Texts and Documents: The Protestant Reformation. http://history.hanover.edu/early/prot.html. Texts from English and Scottish Reformations.

Internet Modern History Sourcebook: The Early Modern West. http://www.fordham.edu/halsall/mod/modsbook1.html. Sources on Reformations, colonial conquests, political theorists and revolutions.

John Foxe's Book of Martyrs. http://www.hrionline.ac.uk/johnfoxe/. Varorium edition.

Philological Museum, Library of Humanistic Texts. http://www.philological.bham.ac.uk/library.html. Sixteenth and seventeenth century texts transcribed.

Proceedings of the Old Bailey, 1674–1913, http://www.oldbaileyonline.org/. Searchable edition of nearly 200,000 criminal trials held at London's central criminal court, a portion of which are from the late-Stuart period.

Renaissance Electronic Texts. http://www.library.utoronto.ca/utel/ret/ret.html. Small collection of coded editions of English Renaissance books and manuscripts, includes George Cavendish's MS. "Life and Death of Cardinal Wolsey."

Renascence Editions. http://www.uoregon.edu/~rbear/ren.htm. Shakespeare and other works, 1477–1799.

Richard III Society, Online Library. http://www.r3.org/bookcase/. Sources on the Wars of the Roses, fifteenth-century society and culture.

Westminster Assembly Project. http://www.westminsterassembly.org/. Sources, transcriptions from the 1640s.

Women Writers Online. http://textbase.wwp.brown.edu/WWO/. Texts by pre-Victorian women (hundreds pre-1714) from the Brown University Women Writers Project. Subscription only.

Index

Printed in the USA/Agawam, MA
November 2, 2021

783827.008